THE PSYCHOLOGICAL IMPACT OF
WAR TRAUMA ON CIVILIANS

Recent Titles in the Psychological Dimensions to War and Peace

Perpetration-Induced Traumatic Stress: The Psychological Consequences of Killing
Rachel M. MacNair

Memory Perceived: Recalling the Holocaust
Robert N. Kraft

The Psychology of Peace: An Introduction
Rachel N. MacNair

THE PSYCHOLOGICAL IMPACT OF WAR TRAUMA ON CIVILIANS
AN INTERNATIONAL PERSPECTIVE

Edited by
**Stanley Krippner and
Teresa M. McIntyre**

Foreword by Stevan E. Hobfoll
Afterword by Jeanne Achterberg

Psychological Dimensions to War and Peace
Harvey Langholtz, Series Editor

Westport, Connecticut
London

Library of Congress Cataloging-in-Publication Data

The psychological impact of war trauma on civilians : an international perspective /
edited by Stanley Krippner and Teresa M. McIntyre ; foreword by Stevan E. Hobfoll ;
afterword by Jeanne Achterberg.
    p. cm.—(Psychological dimensions to war and peace, ISSN 1540–5265)
    Includes bibliographical references and index.
    ISBN 0–275–97202–X (alk. paper)
    1. War victims—Mental health—Cross-cultural studies. 2. Post-traumatic stress
disorder—Cross-cultural studies. 3. War—Psychological aspects—Cross-cultural
studies. I. Krippner, Stanley, 1932–. II. McIntyre, Teresa M. III. Series.
RC550.P76 2003
616.85′21—dc21   2002072549

British Library Cataloguing in Publication Data is available.

Library of Congress Catalog Card Number: 2002072549
ISBN: 0–275–97202–X

ISSN: 1540–5265

First published in 2003

Praeger Publishers, 88 Post Road West, Westport, CT 06881
An imprint of Greenwood Publishing Group, Inc.
www.praeger.com

Printed in the United States of America

The paper used in this book complies with the
Permanent Paper Standard issued by the National
Information Standards Organization (Z39.48–1984).

10 9 8 7 6 5 4 3 2 1

This book is dedicated to the civilian victims of ethnic, political, and religious wars, and to Jerome Frank, Ethel Tobach, Pierre Weil, and the other professional practitioners who have attempted to alleviate the suffering of these victims.

On April 27, 1937, during the Spanish Civil War, the Basque village of Guernica in northern Spain was attacked by air. Chosen for "bombing practice" by the Nazis (who supported the eventual victors of the war), Guernica was pounded with high-explosive and incendiary bombs for over three hours. The airplanes shot down townspeople as they ran from the crumbling buildings. Sixteen hundred civilians were killed or wounded, and the ruins were still burning three days later.

Contents

Foreword
Moving the Borders of Psychology to the Aid of Victims of War

Stevan E. Hobfoll

It is as if the world has gone back in time. Warfare appears to have again become tribal, local, small-scale, widespread, vicious, and personal. As we imagine the horrors of World War I, we envision clear battle lines. Men were slaughtered, certainly, but they were soldiers. And wasn't that the way war was meant to be? The involvement of civilian populations was an aberration, an aside. When was this border recrossed? When did we return to wars of rape, pillage, and massacre as daily events? Perhaps our return was invited by Nazi Germany, with its two wars, one against nations and one against the Jew. Or perhaps we simply idolized war as the meeting of the great gladiators, while all along we had the Armenian massacre, Dresden, Hiroshima, and London.

Most likely it was some of both, as the very idea of "rules of war" seems to have become the exception and the atrocities have become the rule. We have armed men everywhere with the most modern and destructive of weapons. We have a global media that no longer allows us to avoid vivid reality. Indeed, the media is often transmitting events even before governments have access and clear information. Presidents watch CNN to learn about what is happening in real time.

Mental health professionals also had their heads in the sand. Returning from their involvement in World War II, psychologists had a sense of urgency and desire to study real-world events (Stouffer, 1949). Dogmatism (Rokeach, 1960), authoritarianism (Adorno, 1950), and conformity experiments (Asch, 1956) were urgent areas of study for psychologists who needed to digest what the world had experienced. S. Milgram (1964) wanted desperately to know how humans could perpetrate such evil on other humans. But as the decades after the war passed, psychology wanted to become more sterile. The cognitive revolution and, now, a biological revolution are desperate attempts to once again reenter the laboratory and avoid at all costs the real issues facing the world—not because these areas cannot be adopted to the study of the real world, but because they are used as barriers to exclude those who do wish to conduct such studies. The major centers of U.S. learning in psychology want to reinstate an ivory tower psychology and return to the earlier ideology of physics as a model for psychology. From the ivory tower, the real-world problems that a volume such as this faces head-on are too dirty and too removed from the "experimental laboratory," with its clear assignment of cause and effect, even if that cause and effect repeatedly has been shown to be largely artifact.

U.S. psychology as a whole has also been able to avoid the vision of war's impact on civilians because until September 11, 2001, the borders of the "island nation," the United States, were inviolate for nearly 200 years. The leadership in work on the psychological impact of war on civilians has come from Israel, the opposite of an island nation, surrounded by hostile nations since its inception. Work by N. A. Milgram (1982), Hobfoll and Lomranz (Hobfoll et al., 1989; Lomranz, Hobfoll, Johnson, Eyal, & Zemach, 1994), and Solomon (1995) has both paved a path and illuminated a way for other research and model interventions to follow. Indeed, the work from Israel is still the best available on the topic. As an advanced scientific nation with the terrors of war brought to and within its own borders, Israel has been called a living laboratory for the study of stress, and it has lived up to this unfortunate "distinction."

But the current volume goes much further, while building on this firm scientific base. When Perry London and I conducted our studies of the impact of war on civilian populations (Hobfoll & London, 1986; Hobfoll, London, & Orr, 1988), we only needed to go out our back doors in Beersheva and Jerusalem to find our sample. The authors of the chapters of this volume have examined and developed interventions both locally and far from their comfortable universities and homes. They have ventured to Africa, the Balkans, Siberia, the Middle East, and Southeast Asia; they have studied populations who cannot be administered paper-and-pencil questionnaires and asked to respond using number 2 pencils.

This volume also adds to the developing literature (Hobfoll & deVries, 1994; Hobfoll et al., 1991) on the impact of war and extreme stress on civilian populations by opening up the boundaries of questions of culture, gender, and context. As psychology has become more aware of the borders it long placed on itself by ignoring culture, gender, and context, the limitations of gendered, white Eurocentricism have become apparent. Where the West wanted to see its role and the role of religion in foreign lands as benevolent, the realities of colonialization, missionization, and racism are closer to the actuality of what the West imported. Psychology's new openness to gender, culture, and context allows for a rich contextualized study of the impact of war on civilians. Although we must be cautious in translating Western theories to non-Western culture, the growth of psychology worldwide and the new cautiousness in transporting ideas wholesale lead the authors of this volume to thoughtful discussion.

No volume of this type can remain entirely apolitical. Here, there is a need for continued awareness and vigilance because politics can exploit us if we are naive and not circumspect. As a journal editor, I often received work from the Middle East, the former Yugoslavia, and, closer to home, from Detroit and Chicago that was slanted to paint a certain preconceived picture. At times it was clear to me that the authors were conspiring with the study participants to tell a certain story. At other times, the investigators seemed more unwitting accomplices. "Tell me about the atrocities 'they' perpetrated on you" is a political question that ignores verification and a chain of events in which the victim may have been the perpetrator one step earlier in the complex political machinations. Each side has its story to tell, and they do not neatly fit together in a unified, clear picture, even when we think we have all the pieces.

My final fear is of our tendency as scientists to compromise; to be fair, even-handed. It might seem strange to worry about even-handedness, but this is precisely my meaning. We cannot look at Yugoslavian massacres and justify them, even in part, because they are part of an age-old cycle of atrocities. In a poem by the Canadian poet-songwriter Leonard Cohen (1972), he describes Adolf Eichmann by his quite normal physical attributes. He ends the poem with these lines: "What did you expect? Talons? Oversize incisors? Green saliva? Madness?" There is a face of evil in much that has gone and will go on in the world that must not be minimized by our ingrained scientific penchant for qualification. Evil will not appear in the physical form of a monster. Hitler is said to have had a penchant for giving flowers to his close associates. The rape of women as a mechanism of war; the encouragement of conditions that will spread disease; the massacre of unarmed populations; and terrorist attacks in New York, Kashmir, and Jerusalem are evils that we cannot excuse or our work will be ignored or simply used for political purposes. Nor can we allow our liberal tendencies to be abused. It has become commonplace to use children as weapons of war precisely because they invoke pity in the press and among the liberal-viewing public. We must look behind the children who are used to identify the evil that would consider this means to its end, making all means justified.

This is an important volume that will make a key contribution to our understanding of the impact of war on civilian populations. At the same time, it is only a small step toward the study and development of prevention programs and treatments for those ravaged by war. Psychology has entered a global age with volumes such as this, and the authors have taken upon themselves the shared responsibility for the acknowledgment of the ramifications of war. With one hand we must join in the work of peace, while with the other hand we address the victims of war and offer succor to the best of our science.

REFERENCES

Adorno, T. W. (1950). *The authoritarian personality.* New York: Harper.

Asch, S. E. (1956). Studies of independence and conformity: A minority of one against a unanimous majority. *Psychological Monographs, 70.*

Cohen, L. (1972). *Flowers for Hitler.* Toronto: McClelland and Stewart.

Hobfoll, S. E., & de Vries, M. W. (1994). *Extreme stress and communities: Impact and intervention.* Dordrecht, Netherlands: Klewer.

Hobfoll, S. E., Lomranz, J., Bridges, A., Eyal, N., Bridges, A., & Tzemach, M. (1989). Pulse of a nation: Depressive mood reactions of Israelis to the Israel-Lebanon War. *Journal of Personality and Social Psychology, 56,* 1002–1012.

Hobfoll, S. E., & London, P. (1986). The relationship of self-concept and social support to emotional distress among women during war. *Journal of Social and Clinical Psychology, 4,* 189–203.

Hobfoll, S. E., London, P., & Orr, E. (1988). Mastery, intimacy, and stress resistance during war. *Journal of Community Psychology, 16,* 317–331.

Hobfoll, S. E., Spielberger, C. D., Breznitz, S., Figley, C., Folkman, S., Lepper-Green, B., Meichenbaum, D., Milgram, N., Sandler, I., Sarason, I., & van der Kolk, B. (1991). War-related stress: Addressing the stress of war and other traumatic events. *American Psychologist, 46,* 848–855.

Lomranz, J., Hobfoll, S. E., Johnson, R., Eyal, N., & Zemach, M. (1994). A nation's response to attack: Israelis' depressive reactions to the Gulf War. *Journal of Traumatic Stress, 7,* 59–73.

Milgram, N. A. (Ed.). (1982). *Stress and coping in time of war.* New York: Brunner-Mazel.

Milgram, S. (1964). Group pressure and action against a person. *Journal of Abnormal and Social Psychology, 65,* 137–143.

Rokeach, M. (1960). *The open and closed mind.* New York: Basic Books.

Solomon, Z. (1995). *Coping with war-related stress: The Gulf War and the Israeli response.* New York: Plenum.

Stouffer, S. A. (1949). *The American soldier: Adjustment during army life.* Princeton, NJ: Princeton University Press.

Acknowledgments

The editors would like to acknowledge the support of the Saybrook Graduate School and Research Center Chair for the Study of Consciousness. We are grateful to Ron Boyer, Melissa Dubin, Adam Fish, Steve Hart, and Adam Kay for their editorial help, to Mark Sandman for his contact on Pablo Picasso's *Guernica*, to Stephen Brown and Bijan Yashar for tracking down references, and to Milton Schwebbel for his encouragement and initial feedback on the book's prospectus. Special gratitude goes to Debbie Carvalko, our editor at Greenwood Publishing Group, for her enthusiastic comments and meticulous suggestions. We are also grateful to Margarida Ventura for providing the drawings that introduce each part, and for her partnership in research and intervention on this topic in Angola, which inspired this book.

Overview: In the Wake of War

Stanley Krippner and Teresa M. McIntyre

Your naked infants spitted upon spikes,
While the mad mothers with their howls confused
Do break the clouds.

(*Henry V*, act 3, scene iii)

In this passage from *Henry V*, William Shakespeare describes the psychological effects of war on civilians. The suffering inflicted upon the "naked infants" and "mad mothers" has been a horrific part of both history and legend, and the fate of civilian victims has left a relentless blot on humanity's story. If anything, the situation has worsened over the ages. During World War I, combatants represented 95 percent of the people killed. In recent years, it has been estimated that at least 90 percent of people killed in ethnic, political, and religious wars are civilian noncombatants (Kolb-Angelbeck, 2000). Even those who suspect that this estimate is too high admit that civilian victims of armed conflict have increased drastically since the end of the cold war; regional wars have multiplied, competing with one another in terror and atrocity (e.g., Guille-Escuret, 1999; van Geuns, 1987; Winkelman, 1993, p. 2).

For example, on the morning of December 13, 1998, a Colombian woman, her children, and her grandchildren started heating food on their stove in their Santo Domingo home, in the northeastern region of the country. Overhead, government helicopters were shooting it out with guerillas about half a mile from their village, firing machine guns as they swooped low. Suddenly, as the woman walked across the room to put more wood in the fire, everything went black. Seconds later, her children and grandchildren were screaming and bleeding. Two of her daughters and a son were killed, as was a grandson. In all, 19 people, including 7 children, were killed that morning in Santo Domingo, while at least two dozen were seriously injured. Each day of that year, at least one massacre took place in Colombia; a *massacre* being defined as the killing of three or more people at one time in one area. And during the same year, not a single person, from either the government or the guerillas, was brought to trial for any of the deaths (Lydersen, 2000).

On August 28, 1999, just before a United Nations referendum on East Timor's independence, armed soldiers surrounded the Lospalos home of Verissimo Quintas and opened fire. Members of the local militia then rushed inside, hacked Quintas to death with machetes, and burned down the house. At the same time, the home of Ana Lopes was devastated and her family was terrorized. A cab driver's family was forced into Indonesian West Timor just after the independence vote, along with 120,000 other civilians. The United Nations Security Council called upon Indonesia to bring the perpetrators of the violence to justice; instead, Indonesia's parliament passed a constitutional amendment prohibiting prosecution for crimes that did not constitute an offense at the time of their commission, in effect blocking the prosecution of those responsible for the East Timor murders, tortures, and abductions (Jardine, 2000).

In the summer of 2000, a reporter for a local Wisconsin radio program ("Mornings in Madison," WOL) interviewed a Sudanese youngster who had been sold into slavery. He told about being sent to the market by his mother to sell beans that his family had grown on their meager land. While at the market, he witnessed a band of slave raiders, sent down from the north, kill every adult and gather up the children, himself included, stuffing them into baskets for transport north. He told of one boy who could not stop crying after seeing his parents beheaded in front of him. He was shot in the head. When his sister, who had witnessed everything, could not stop crying, the raiders cut off her foot and left her to bleed to death. The surviving boy was beaten nightly until he submitted to slavery. He escaped to provide details of this "ethnic cleansing" committed against southern blacks by the northern Sudanese, who are responsible for an estimated 1.9 million civilian deaths and 4 million refugees since 1983 (Burr, 1998). The Sudan persecution qualifies as political, ethnic, and religious warfare because its victims are black Christians, African traditionalists, and moderate Muslims who refuse to accept the government of Sudan's policies of forced Arabization and radical Islamization.

These are some of the women, men, and children whose plight motivated us to prepare this book. Their suffering falls within what has been named "collective stress" or "social suffering" (Helman, 2000), that is, stress conditions that affect an entire group or population. This collective suffering characterized the 20th century and has affected civilian populations in an unprecedented manner. Furthermore, the fact that many war theaters have been in poorer countries has hampered the access of millions of victims to even minimum medical and psychological care.

Historically, psychology has focused primarily on individuals and combatants in terms of addressing the psychological consequences of war and designing interventions to meet those needs (e.g., Boscarino, 1995, 2000; Rosenbeck & Fontana, 2000; van der Kolk, 1984; Weathers, Litz, & Keane, 1995). The psychological literature on the impact of war stress on civilians is scarce, and there is a lack of theoretical models, assessment tools, and psychologically based models for intervening at a large scale to aid civilian victims. Consequently, psychologists and other aid workers who attempt to address the needs of these populations locally, either directly or in a consultancy role, are faced with a lack of resources in terms of training in this domain.

Yet, in the past 20 years, psychologists have been called upon to collaborate in finding solutions for war-shattered communities in various ways. This call has generated efforts from various areas of psychology in collaboration with other disciplines, in terms of research and experimentation with different models of community intervention with civilian victims of war. We came into contact with this work and, in a few cases, collaborated with these efforts. This prompted us to organize, in 1999, a symposium on the topic at the annual convention of the American Psychological Association (APA), with the aim of disseminating this work at a broader level. The response to our symposium was so positive that we decided to collect the papers that were presented and invite other writers to contribute additional chapters.

We also were inspired by the APA presidential address of Martin P. Seligman (1999), who noted that

with the death of fascism and the winding down of communism, the warfare the world faces in the next century will be ethnic in its roots and hatreds. In contemporary ethnopolitical conflicts . . . , civilian populations are the primary targets of terror. (p. 559)

Seligman teamed with the president of the Canadian Psychological Association (CPA) to create a joint APA/CPA Task Force on Ethnopolitical Warfare, to develop a model curriculum that would blend conflict resolution with trauma intervention, and develop postdoctoral fellowship programs at three universities (in South Africa, Northern Ireland, and the United States) to study ethnopolitical conflict. Seligman's vision was a cadre of trained psychologists

who have the courage and the humanity for such work to better understand, predict, and even prevent such tragedies. When the worst does occur, we can train psychologists to help pick up the pieces by helping people and communities heal and learn to live and trust together again. (p. 559)

The chapter authors of this book have provided information and insights that attempt to implement and foster Seligman's vision.

A BRIEF HISTORICAL PERSPECTIVE

The history of war stress in civilian populations is as old as history itself. However, the scientific study of civilian victims of war is a relatively recent interest in psychology. As noted earlier, most of the early research and clinical work on war trauma until World War II concentrated on combatants, and the studies on civilian populations referred to natural disasters or accidents, such as the disaster of Buffalo Creek and, more recently, the Chowchilla school bus kidnapping (e.g., Erikson, 1976). The exception to this was the Holocaust, which led to extensive research on the experience and chronic sequelae of concentration camp survivors (e.g., Krystal, 1968, 1984; Niederland, 1968; O'Brien, 2000). Van der Kolk (1984) asserts that the victims of Nazi concentration camps were the civilian population most studied, even though the Holocaust experience was singular and perhaps not easily generalizable to other populations.

Since the 1970s, "the troubles" of the civil struggle in Northern Ireland have affected the lives of its entire population. The civilian victims of this violence have been studied by psychiatrists, psychologists, and sociologists since the 1970s (e.g., Bell, Kee, Loughrey, Roddy, & Curran, 1988; Lyons, 1979). Another war scenario that has been studied intensively in terms of civilian impact of war has been the Israeli Yom Kippur War, especially its impact on children, adolescents, and family life (e.g., Milgram & Milgram, 1976; Solomon & Mikulincer, 1988). The work by Hobfoll and his colleagues on the impact of the Israel-Lebanon war on civilians was also pioneer and generated prolific research and intervention (Hobfoll & London, 1986; Hobfoll, London, & Orr, 1988; Hobfoll et al., 1989).

Since the 1990s, the study of the psychological impact of war on civilians has become more widespread, and considerable work has been generated regarding the impact of war stress on civilians in the former Yugoslavia (e.g., Bloch, 1993; Smith & Surgan, 1996), and in such African countries as Angola, Mozambique, and Sierra Leone (e.g., Scheepers, 1995; McIntyre & Ventura, 1998; Save the Children Foundation, 1995; Green & Wessells, 1997). The response of Israeli civilians to the Gulf War has also deserved careful attention (Lomranz, Hobfoll, Johnson, Eyal, & Zemach, 1994; Solomon, 1995; Solomon et al., 1993). The book by Hobfoll & de Vries (1994) has become a reference work on this topic. Several chapters in this book constitute a representation of the major war scenarios in the world in the past three decades, highlight these developments, and provide evidence of greater interest on the part of governmental and nongovernmental organizations in responding to the psychological needs of the civilian populations affected by war. We consider that a shift from a dualistic mind-body perspective toward a more holistic model of care/aid (Bishop, 1994) is essential in providing effective assistance to these populations.

This growing literature about experience in the field also has produced evidence that the psychological sequelae of war have striking similarities across cultures and types of trauma. However, cultural factors play an important role in shaping the response to war stress as well as attempts at subsequent healing (Helman, 2000). Several chapters in this book illustrate how cultural beliefs and practices can be protective or pathogenic in regards to war stress, that is, how beliefs and practices can "kill or heal" (Hahn & Kleinman, 1983).

DEFINITIONS

Even if writers are well intentioned, they cannot transcend their historical situation, temperament, gender, and ethnicity when writing about human experience. Our perspectives are reflected in our definitions, and these definitions set the parameters for the entire book. For example, by *civilian populations* we mean noncombatants. However, some writers would insist that there are no noncombatants in contemporary wars; elderly men can hide soldiers in their homes, children can act as couriers or spies, and women can prepare food for fighters who would otherwise starve or surrender. We acknowledge these limitations in our definition and also admit that in contemporary wars there are children who are fully combatant, such as the thousands of children from northern Uganda abducted from their homes to fight in the rebellious Lord's Resistance Army, and additional thousands of children pressed into service by the rebels in Sierra Leone. One veteran of the latter war admitted that he had killed more than 50 people after being captured at the age of 9 and taught how to use a gun (Vine, 1999).

For us, a *war* is an armed conflict between countries; between groups in the same country; or between ethnic, political, or religious groups regardless of their country of origin. A *civil war* is armed conflict between geographical sections or political factions of the same country attempting to take over the entire country (e.g., North Vietnam vs. South Vietnam) or to gain independence from that particular country (e.g., South Sudan vs. North Sudan). A *country* or *state* is a geopolitical unit that occupies a specified territory and is recognized as being geographically and politically distinct by some (e.g., Taiwan), most (e.g., Macedonia), or all (e.g., China) of its neighbors, even if it is under the control of another country or state (e.g., occupied Belgium during World War II). A *nation* is a historically developed group of people with a distinctive ethnicity, culture, and language; some nations are not states but have a fairly well-identified geographical location (e.g., the "Kurdish nation"), some nations have indistinct boundaries (e.g., the "Cherokee nation"), and some nations have attained the status of country or *nation-state* (e.g., Portugal, arguably the oldest nation-state on the European continent).

The term *political* refers to matters of governmental or administrative power, whether the person or group so identified possesses that power or is vying for that power. The term *religious* refers to institutions characterized by systems of belief, worship, ethics, and conduct, and to the rituals that accompany them. Some wars are basically political (e.g., the border wars between Ecuador and Peru), others are basically religious (e.g., Hindus vs. Muslims on the Indian subcontinent), and some are both (e.g., Roman Catholics vs. Protestants in Northern Ireland). Economic factors can enter into these conflicts, (e.g., the Sendero Luminoso vs. the Peruvian government), as can territorial issues (e.g., Israeli vs. Palestinian) and illegal commodities (e.g., the "drug wars" being waged in such places as Colombia and Mexico).

When we speak of *ethnic* wars, we refer to members of a group distinguished by a distinctive history, culture, and/or language. Many ethnic groups aspire to statehood and enter into armed conflict to establish themselves as nation-states. Admittedly, each of these terms is a hypothetical construct, developed to facilitate discussion and to organize data. The term *race* is another such construct, and one that we will rarely use in this book. Supposedly a biological division of humankind, distinguished by such aspects of physical appearance as body proportions, stature, color and texture of hair, and color of skin and eyes, the term *race* does not stand up to rigorous scrutiny, especially in the wake of human genome data. In 1999, the executive director of the American Anthropological Association commented that the biological basis of race is a "misconception" (Davis, 1999, p. 79). In 2000, the Statistical Assessment Service announced its awards for "the worst science of the century." In first place was "scientific racism," "the most pernicious piece of pseudoscience in history"(p. 1). This construct justified Adolf Hitler's extolling the superiority of the "Nordic race," and its sequelae of concentration camps, gas ovens, and "experiments" on captives' eyes that attempted to turn them into an "Aryan blue." The construct of "race" is supposedly based on genetically determined physical characteristics, but of the tens of thousands of genes that have been catalogued, genetic determinants appear to have a paucity of effect on a person's physical appearance.

Both racial (e.g., "Caucasian," "Negroid") and ethnic (e.g., "Italian-American," "African American," "Hispanic") constructs reflect complex cultural, social, and historical factors (Williams, Spencer, & Jackson, 1999). The criteria used to ascribe "racial identity" are more social and cultural than biological (Davis, 1999; Richards, 1997, p. x), while the term *ethnic* is primarily social, cultural, and/or geographical. However, to use one example, the cultural distinctiveness of second- and third-generation immigrants from the Caribbean to Great Britain may be fairly marginal (p. xi). Nevertheless, "race" remains, in Ashley Montague's (1942) phrase, a "dangerous myth," while ethnic, although imperfect, has not accumulated similar baggage. According to Guille-Escuret (1999), "ethnicity" is

not a superfluous idea, it is an approximative idea. We would be scientifically inept and ethnically perverse to thrust it aside before having managed to replace it by an ordered series of functional concepts representing social collectivities in their different aspects. (p. 2)

This is not to de-emphasize the perfidy of ethnic identity. In the wake of the Rwanda ethnic war, rival Hutu tribespeople slaughtered hundreds of thousands of Tutsis, and later, Tutsi exiles from Burundi fought their war into Rwanda to stop the massacre, killing and wounding numerous Hutu civilians in the process; the total dead approached 1 million (Murphy, 1999). Since 1983, 60,000 people have been killed in Sri Lanka's ethnic war, and since 1984, 37,000 have died in Turkey's ethnic clashes (Epstein, 1999).

We use the term *war stress* to refer to the multiple stressors that people are exposed to when they have experienced war, either directly or indirectly. These stressors can be psychological, chemical, biological, mechanical, social, economical, cultural, and so forth, and are often experienced simultaneously, which demonstrates the intense and complex quality of war stress. Flogel and Lauc

(2000), present an overview of the effects of war stress in the former Yugoslavia in terms of health, mortality, social behavior, and violence, illustrating how pervasive and long-term the effects of war can be. For example, the authors state that despite the preserved quality of the health services, the postwar health of the Croatian population deteriorated significantly, with some 200,000 more people ill due to war-related factors in 1994 than in 1990. Significant decreases in the birthrate and increases in mortality rates and in cases of post-traumatic stress disorder (PTSD) and suicide, as well as in violence, are reported.

The designation *war trauma* is meant to refer to the effects of war as an extreme stressor that threatens human existence, acting upon a human being or a group of people. At an individual level, this may entail physical or psychosocial consequences, such as the inability to talk or relate to other human beings. Such terms as *shell shock, battle fatigue,* and, more recently, *post-traumatic stress disorder* have been used to describe the aftereffects of war trauma. The term *post-traumatic illness* (PTI) (O'Brien, 2000) has been introduced to describe a "recognizable mental disorder other than PTSD which follows a traumatic event and which is postulated to have been caused or precipitated by it" (p. 2). It is a broader category that highlights the variety of psychological responses to traumatic situations other than PTSD. We also assume that not all individuals who are subjected to war stress go on to develop a severe or chronic disease, as the epidemiological data has long demonstrated. In fact, various psychosocial and cultural factors mediate or moderate the impact of war stress on survivors (Joseph, Williams, & Yule, 1998; O'Brien, 2000). The question of whether PTSD or PTI are normal or abnormal reactions to an extreme stressor is still being discussed and deserves our attention. For instance, early surveys of survivors of violence in Northern Ireland showed, to much surprise, no association between PTSD and any premorbid vulnerability factors examined in these studies. More striking was the finding that 75 percent of this population had recovered from their psychological difficulties within 18 months (Bell, 2000b).

Finally, at a collective level, *war trauma* is meant to include all the health, social, economic, cultural, and political consequences of war stress. War stress shatters the individual and his or her network, assaulting the integrity of their world. Irreparable material and kin losses, as well as the loss of everyday routines, values, and important rituals, render collective healing more difficult. And what about peace? We are in accord with Division 48 of the American Psychological Association when it defines *peace* as "both the absence of destructive conflict and the creation of positive social conditions that minimize destructiveness and promote human well-being."

Terrorism is a type of political violence that can assume several forms, constituting a complex array of separate phenomena (Bell, 2000b). It can be more organized or less organized, associated with a state or not, more visible and legitimated (such as in Northern Ireland), or function underground (as with rebels sympathetic to Chechen independence operating inside Russia). It may be fueled by different motives, such as military, political, and/or religious. In this book, we are treating terrorism as a form of war stress that has affected civilians in a preferential manner. As a form of war stress, it has singular features, such as being highly unpredictable, extremely violent, and usually having a well-defined target. These characteristics render this form of war stress particularly devastating for civilians, affecting the victims' lives and those of their families at the core of who they are in relation to their world, often resulting in long-term physical or psychological injuries, such as those Bell (2000a) described in Northern Ireland.

The "terror" element in terrorism is an important ingredient of this violent tactic, shattering the "illusion of invulnerability" of both individuals and states. The September 11, 2001, attacks on the United States showed the world one face of modern terrorism, impacting not only its direct victims but also, through the power of the media, women, men, and children around the world. However, like every adverse situation, it may serve as a "wake-up call," forcing a reflection on the motives behind the attack, attempts to understand these motives, and the creation of opportunities for individual and social growth. As occurred after the discovery of Nazi concentration camps following World War II, humanity is faced with the challenge of its own self-discovery, and its need for coexistence on this diverse and complex planet. We hope that this book makes a modest contribution to this reflection in the service of world peace, as well as promoting compassion for all victims of violence.

A HEALTH PSYCHOLOGY APPROACH

The definitions presented earlier point to the broad foundations that have guided the construction of this book. These include (a) the concern for a culturally sensitive presentation of war and its psychosocial consequences; (b) the need to view the health consequences of war stress holistically, at both an individual and a community level; (c) the importance of considering both the risk and the resilience of traumatic reactions to war stress—both the normal and the abnormal; (d) the social responsibility of psychology to generate and experiment with new models of intervention in situations of war and conflict, which allow for large-scale action; and, most importantly, (e) the imperative of addressing the psychological needs of civilian victims of war along with their other immediate concerns, especially those of the most neglected and underprivileged groups, such as children and women.

There are many perspectives that could guide a book of this nature. We take the position that a focus on health, and psychology's contribution to health as represented in the area of health psychology (Matarazzo, 1980, 1987), is a useful perspective in addressing the psychosocial consequences of war on civilians. Health is understood here in a broad sense, involving a state of well-being, one that implies a delicate balance between the individual and his or her physical and social environment (Thoresen & Eagleston, 1985; World Health Organization, 1948). As such, one can speak of both individual and social health, of health care as well as a *health field*. The latter term implies that all elements of a system can contribute to health, including a healthy environment as well as health-promoting behaviors (Lalonde, 1974, p. 5). Health psychology focuses on a biopsychosocial model (Foss, 2002), a systems approach compatible with the foundations of this book. This systems approach is needed to face contemporary challenges posed by global health, illness prevention, and health promotion. To address these issues, health psychology draws from other areas of psychology in an integrative manner (Belar, 1996). Although demonstrating a strong focus on health consequences, the chapters in this book also draw from social and cognitive psychology, clinical psychology, education, and community psychology (Allen, 1998; Sarafino, 1998). Gender studies need to be included in this list because of the large numbers of women who suffer as a result of these conflicts. For example, Sharratt and Kaschak (2000) have documented the coping strategies of female victims of atrocities committed against them in the former Yugoslavia. Women figure prominently in the millions of people who are now refugees, with additional millions displaced in their own countries by war and disease (Albee, 2000).

Public health services rely on clean water, sanitation, safe food, an intact environment, health education, prophylactic drugs and immunizations, and effective screening for communicable diseases. However, the infrastructure of public health systems has been severely compromised by war, poverty, and the collapse of governments. Laurie Garrett (2000), an investigative journalist, has documented the mishandling of an Ebola outbreak in Africa, the misdiagnosis of pneumonic plague in India, and the breakdown of vaccination and antibiotic distribution in Russia, concluding that health services for major portions of the world's population have deteriorated or are lacking. As a result, the increasing number of civilians exposed to wars and conflicts has not been matched by an increase in the number of health facilities and personnel to deal with the resulting trauma, nor has there been a deeper understanding of the issue by physicians and other health care practitioners. War and conflict present a unique challenge to health psychology and its practitioners because they require new models and tools for large-scale intervention, tools that are flexible, culturally diverse, and adaptable. Some successful pioneer programs are presented in the intervention section of this book.

The first conference of the United Nations' World Health Organization (WHO) on the psychosocial consequences of violence was held in the Netherlands in 1981. The term *violence* was defined there as the human-to-human "infliction of significant and avoidable pain and suffering," echoing Article 5 of the United Nations' Universal Declaration of Human Rights, which reads, in part, "No one shall be subjected to torture or to cruel, inhuman, or degrading treatment or punishment" (van Geuns, 1987, p. 7). In addition to war violence, the definition covered "imprisonment without trial, mock executions, hostage taking," internment in concentration camps, forced migration, and violence inflicted by terrorist groups as an integrated and structural part of their policy and activities. The health hazards of violence were spelled out in a subsequent 1986 WHO conference, again held in the Netherlands. Detailed positions on "health ethics" were spelled out, and various forms of torture were itemized (Svensson, 1987). The abuse of authority and sanctioned torture by the governments of Chile and South Africa were singled out for special mention; a decade later, both regimes had met their demise.

The 1986 WHO conference itemized these health hazards, some of which included weight loss, edema, infections, post-traumatic stress-induced somatic symptoms, organic brain damage, "incomplete recovery after semi-starvation," "mental symptoms" (some of which made up a "neurasthenic syndrome"), "functional or morphological change in the brain in line with the degeneration of other parts of the organism," and "organic damage of the nervous system caused by undernourishment" (Svensson, 1987).

Two conclusions are obvious and confirm one of health psychology's premises, the interconnectedness of mind-body processes: (1) There is no simple way to differentiate the "physical" from the "mental" sequelae of war violence; and (2) the condition of the victims presents a stark contrast to WHO's earlier definition of health as "optimum physical, mental, and social efficiency and well-being" (Thorvaldsen, 1987, p. 38).

The inseparability of physical and mental health issues is acknowledged by those health psychologists who question the adequacy of the biomedical model that has guided health care in the developed nations and also has directed health assistance to war victims, a model that pays short shrift to psychological and social factors. The organization of this book reflects health psychology's demand for a more holistic overview of its field. The book's chapters are organized into four parts. Our first part presents a series of case studies and addresses key issues in assessment of war-related stress reactions. Just as there are case studies of individuals who have experienced severe trauma, there are groups of civilians who have been traumatized by war. The chapters on assessment describe how the effects of war trauma have been measured and diagnosed in various parts of the world. Part II focuses on intervention and reconstruction, presenting innovative models for healing the wounds of war of both individuals and communities ravaged by conflict. Next, part III, on prevention, encompasses regional as well as global peacemaking efforts. The final part comprises a series of chapters that take integrative viewpoints on these issues, ending with an analysis of war itself, one of many psychological approaches that have provided insights into the dynamics of armed conflict (e.g., Chirot & Seligman, 2001; Ehrenreich, 1997; LeShan, 1992).

At first glance, these four parts might seem to cover every aspect of the effects of war trauma on civilian populations. However, there are many blood-spattered conflicts that remain unmentioned and several efforts by courageous people that space precluded us from citing. Nevertheless, we hope that this book will stimulate the realization that "multiculturalism is the future of our society and indeed the entire planet" (Winkelman, 1993, p. 680). Political, religious, and ethnic differences will always be with us. But if people learn to live together, war and violence need not be a permanent ingredient of the human condition.

REFERENCES

Albee, G. W. (2000). Commentary on prevention and counseling psychology. *The Counseling Psychologist, 28*, 845–854.

Allen, F. (1998). *Health psychology: Theory and practice.* St. Leonards, New South Wales, Australia: Allen & Unwin.

Belar, C. (1996). A proposal for an expanded view of health and psychology: The integration of behavior and health. In R. Resnick & R. Rosensky (Eds.), *Health psychology through the life span: Practice and research opportunities* (pp. 77–84). Washington, DC: American Psychological Association.

Bell, P. (2000a). Studies of stress in Northern Ireland. In G. Fink, *Encyclopedia of stress* (Vol. 3, pp. 62–66). San Diego, CA: Academic Press.

Bell, P. (2000b). Terrorism. In G. Fink (Ed.), *Encyclopedia of stress* (Vol. 3, pp. 577–580). San Diego, CA: Academic Press.

Bell, P., Kee, M., Loughrey, G., Roddy, R., & Curran, P. (1988). Post-traumatic stress disorder in Northern Ireland. *Acta Psychiatrica Scandinavia, 77*, 166–179.

Bishop, G. D. (1994). *Health psychology: Integrating mind and body.* Boston: Allyn and Bacon.

Bloch, E. (1993). Psychologists in Croatia work to ease trauma among young war victims. *International Psychology, 4*(3), 1–7.

Boscarino, J. (1995). Post-traumatic stress and associated disorders among Vietnam veterans: The significance of combat and social support. *Journal of Traumatic Stress, 8*, 317–336.

Boscarino, J. (2000). Postwar experiences of Vietnam veterans. In G. Fink (Ed.), *Encyclopedia of stress* (Vol. 3, pp. 656–661). San Diego, CA: Academic Press.

Burr, M. (1998). *Quantifying genocide in southern Sudan and the Nuba Mountains, 1983–1998.* Washington, DC: U.S. Committee for Refugees.

Chirot, D., & Seligman, M. E. P. (2001). *Ethnopolitical warfare: Causes, consequences, and possible solutions.* Washington, DC: American Psychological Association.

Davis, B. (1999). AAA and the challenge of "race." *Anthropology News*, p. 79.

Ehrenreich, B. (1997). *Blood rites: Origins and history of the passions of war.* New York: Henry Holt.

Epstein, R. (1999, November/December). Season of peace. *Psychology Today*, p. 3.

Erikson, K. (1976). *Everything in its path: Destruction of community in the Buffalo Creek flood.* New York: Simon and Schuster.

Flogel, M., & Lauc, G. (2000). War stress in the former Yugoslavia. In G. Fink (Ed.), *Encyclopedia of stress* (Vol. 3, pp. 678–683). San Diego, CA: Academic Press.

Foss, L. (2002). *The end of modern medicine: Biomedical science under a microscope.* Albany, NY: State University of New York Press.

Garrett, L. (2000). *Betrayal of trust: The collapse of global public health.* New York: Hyperion.

Green, E. G., & Wessells, M. G. (1997). *Mid-term evaluation of the province-based war trauma team project: Meeting the psychosocial needs of children in Angola.* Arlington, VA: USAID Displaced Children and Orphans Fund and War Victims Fund.

Guille-Escuret, G. (1999, October). Need anthropology resign? *Anthropology Today*, pp. 1–3.

Hahn, R., & Kleinman, A. (1983). Belief as pathogen, belief as medicine: Voodoo death and the "placebo phenomenon" in anthropological perspective. *Medical Anthropology Quarterly, 14,* 3–10.

Helman, C. (2000). *Culture, health and illness.* Oxford: Butterworth Heinemann.

Hobfoll, S. E., & de Vries, M. W. (1994). *Extreme stress and communities: Impact and intervention.* Dordrecht, Netherlands: Klewer.

Hobfoll, S. E., Lomranz, J., Eyal, N., Bridges, A., & Tzemach, M. (1989). Pulse of a nation: Depressive mood reactions of Israelis to the Israel-Lebanon War. *Journal of Personality and Social Psychology, 56,* 1002–1012.

Hobfoll, S. E., & London, P. (1986). The relationship of self-concept and social support to emotional distress among women during war. *Journal of Social and Clinical Psychology, 4,* 189–203.

Hobfoll, S. E., London, P., & Orr, E. (1988). Mastery, intimacy, and stress resistance during war. *Journal of Community Psychology, 16,* 317–331.

Jardine, M. (2000, October 16). East Timor: Up from ground zero. *In These Times,* pp. 12–14.

Joseph, S., Williams, R., & Yule, W. (1998). *Understanding post-traumatic stress.* New York: Wiley.

Kolb-Angelbeck, K. (2000, October 2). Winona speaks. *In These Times,* pp. 12–13.

Krystal, H. (Ed.). (1968). *Massive psychic trauma.* New York: International Universities Press.

Krystal, H. (1984). Psychoanalytic views on human emotional damages. In B. van der Kolk (Ed.), *Post-traumatic stress disorder: Psychological and biological sequelae* (pp. 1–28). Washington, DC: American Psychiatric Press.

Lalonde, M. (1974). *A new perspective on the health of Canadians: A working document.* Ottawa, ON: Information Canada.

LeShan, L. (1992). *The psychology of war: Comprehending its mystique and its madness.* Chicago: Nobel Press.

Lomranz, J., Hobfoll, S. E., Johnson, R., Eyal, N., & Zemach, M. (1994). A nation's response to attack: Israelis' depressive reactions to the Gulf War. *Journal of Traumatic Stress, 7,* 59–73.

Lydersen, K. (2000, October 10). The truth is out there. *In These Times,* p. 7.

Lyons, H. (1979). Civil violence: The psychological aspects. *Journal of Psychosomatic Research, 23,* 373–381.

Matarazzo, J. D. (1980). Behavioral health and behavioral medicine: Frontiers for a new health psychology. *American Psychologist, 35,* 807–817.

Matarazzo, J. D. (1987). Relationships of health psychology to other segments of psychology. In G. Stone, S. Weiss, J. D. Matarazzo, N. Miller, J. Rodin, C. Belar, J. Follick, & J. Singer (Eds.), *Health psychology: A discipline and a profession* (pp. 41–59). Chicago: University of Chicago Press.

McIntyre, T., & Ventura, M. (1998). Angolan PTSD study re-focuses on adolescent development. *Psychology International, 9(2),* 1, 5.

Milgram, R., & Milgram, N. (1976). The effect of the Yom Kippur War on anxiety level in Israeli children. *Journal of Psychology, 94,* 107–113.

Montague, A. (1942). *Man's most dangerous myth: The fallacy of race.* Oxford, England: Oxford University Press.

Murphy, R. M. (1999, October 18). The law of the battlefield. *The New Leader,* pp. 18–19.

Niederland, W. (1968). Clinical observations on the "survivor syndrome." *International Journal of Psychoanalysis, 4,* 313–315.

O'Brien, L. (2000). *Traumatic events and mental health*. Cambridge, England: Cambridge University Press.

Richards, G. (1997). *"Race," racism and psychology: Toward a reflexive history*. London: Routledge.

Rosenbeck, R., & Fontana, A. (2000). Treatment of war-related post-traumatic stress disorder. In G. Fink (Ed.), *Encyclopedia of stress* (Vol. 3, pp. 672–677). San Diego, CA: Academic Press.

Sarafino, E. P. (1998). *Health psychology: Biopsychological interactions* (3rd ed.). New York: Wiley.

Save the Children Foundation. (1995). *Project on children and war. Despite the odds: A collection of case studies on the Development Project in Mozambique*. New York: UNICEF.

Scheepers, H. (1995). *Projecto piloto Kuito sobre actividades de trauma* [Pilot project Kuito on trauma activities]. Luanda: UNICEF.

Seligman, M. E. P. (1999). The president's address. *American Psychologist, 54,* 559–562.

Sharratt, S., & Kaschak, E. (Eds.). (2000). *Assault on the soul: Women in the former Yugoslavia*. Westport, CT: Haworth.

Smith, B., & Surgan, B. (1996). Model mental health program serves war-weary Sarajevo. *Psychology International, 7*(4), 1, 4.

Solomon, Z. (1995). *Coping with war-related stress: The Gulf War and the Israeli response*. New York: Plenum.

Solomon, Z., Laor, N., Weiler, D., Muller, U., Hadar, O., Waysman, M., Koslowski, M., Mordechai, B., & Bleich, A. (1993). The psychological impact of the Gulf War: A study of acute stress in Israel evacuees. *Archives of General Psychiatry, 50,* 320–321.

Solomon, Z., & Mikulincer, M. (1988). Psychological sequelae of war: A 2-year follow up study of Israeli combat stress reaction casualties. *The Journal of Nervous and Mental Disease, 176*(5), 264–269.

Statistical Assessment Service. (2000, January). The worst science of the century. *VitalSTATS,* pp. 1–3.

Svensson, P.-G. (1987). Health hazards of organized violence: A WHO perspective. In G. M. N. Dukes (Ed.), *Health hazards of organized violence* (pp. 11–17). The Hague, Netherlands: Ministry of Welfare, Health and Cultural Affairs.

Thoresen, C., & Eagleston, J. (1985). Counseling for health. *The Counseling Psychologist, 13,* 15–87.

Thorvaldsen, P. (1987). Organized violence: General outline on the subject. In G. M. N. Dukes (Ed.), *Health hazards of organized violence* (pp. 18–49). The Hague, Netherlands: Ministry of Welfare, Health and Cultural Affairs.

Van der Kolk, B. (1984). *Post-traumatic stress disorder: Psychological and biological sequelae*. Washington, DC: American Psychiatric Press.

van Geuns, H. (1987). The concept of organized violence. In G. M. N. Dukes (Ed.), *Health hazards of organized violence* (pp. 7–9). The Hague, Netherlands: Ministry of Welfare, Health and Cultural Affairs.

Vine, J. (1999, September). Rebels without a cause. *High Life,* pp. 34–36.

Weathers, F., Litz, B., & Keane, T. (1995). Military trauma. In J. Freedy & S. Hobfoll (Eds.), *Traumatic stress: From theory to practice* (pp. 45–65). New York: Plenum.

Williams, D. R., Spencer, M. S., & Jackson, J. S. (1999). Race, stress, and physical health: The role of group identity. In R. J. Contrada & R. D. Ashmore (Eds.), *Self, social identity, and physical health: Interdisciplinary explorations* (pp. 71–100). New York: Oxford University Press.

Winkelman, M. (1993). *Ethnic relations in the U.S.: A sociohistorical cultural systems approach*. St. Paul, MN: West.

World Health Organization. (1948). *Official records of the World Health Organization, No. 2, p.100.* Geneva, Switzerland: Author.

CASE STUDIES AND ASSESSMENT

INTRODUCTION

Ten-year-old Pedro portrays how everyday community life is suddenly disrupted by war. Illustration published with permission of Margarida Ventura.

Part I presents a testimony of the psychological impact of war on civilians by reviewing several types of violence against civilians, such as indigenous colonization in Finland, civil war in Angola and Rwanda, and unification in Germany. These "case studies" provide a personal encounter with the experience of civilian suffering, its personal and cultural meaning. The seven chapters in this part also present evidence of the multifaceted consequences of war stress and point out major tenets for healing, at both individual and communal levels; these will be elaborated further in Part II, Intervention and Reconstruction.

Another important focus of this part is the issues regarding psychological assessment of the impact of war stress on civilian populations, highlighted in the last three chapters. The validation of Western psychological constructs and measurement tools in war-torn countries and the development of assessment strategies that are culturally grounded are essential to carry on sound psychological research and scientifically based interventions directed at war-afflicted civilians. The partnership between Western-trained psychologists and local psychologists or other professionals has proven extremely useful in carrying on this difficult and often lengthy task.

Chapter 1, written by Fish and Popal, is a functional analysis of the effects of the systematic and institutionalized denial of "cognitive liberty" to the women of Afghanistan. It describes how the misuse of Islamic doctrine and the curtailment of education for Aghan women resulted in what could be called "epistemic violence." Chapter 2, by Bastien, Kremer, Kuokkanen, and Vickers, brings to the forefront a more subtle form of violence against civilians, bearing testimony to the colonization of indigenous populations. The authors chose the plights of the Sámi peoples (of Norway, Finland, Sweden, and Russia), the Tsimshian people (of British Columbia), and the Niisitapi peoples (of Canada) to illustrate the pervasive nature of this kind of violence as well as the capacity of indigenous people for survivance. Chapter 4, by Gould, provides a thoughtful reflection upon the psychosocial issues involved in the reunification of Germany in terms of individual and cultural identity. The author argues that a psychological wall persists in the heads of both East and West Germans, and that East Germans have suffered an internal struggle as they have been expected to assimilate into West German society. The legacy of the Holocaust and its associated guilt and shame provides a link between past and current psychological violence and highlights the need to remember as a source of healing and unification.

Chapter 3, by McIntyre and Ventura, asserts the need to consider the psychosocial impact of exposure to war stress among children and adolescents, who are often forgotten victims of war. The authors present the results of a study conducted during the Angolan civil war that focused on determining the impact of prolonged war exposure on adolescents' development. The data indicate a pervasive negative effect of war exposure on affective, cognitive, and behavioral indicators. An important finding is the presence of sociodemographic moderators of the impact of war trauma, such as the endorsement of tribal values, which supports the notion of protective or resilience-building factors in war situations. In Chapter 5, Bolton reports on another African country, Rwanda, addressing important issues regarding measurement of responses to war stress among civilians, especially that of the cross-cultural generalizability of constructs, such as post-traumatic stress disorder (PTSD) or depression. The importance of quantitative assessment in order to allocate resources and evaluate interventions is also stressed. Bolton presents a multistep ethnographic and psychometrically based method of testing and validating the measurement of depression in Rwanda. These two chapters illustrate how a collaborative effort between Western and locally trained professionals can be used in producing culturally valid psychological measures.

In Chapter 6, Carter extends the concept of war by reviewing the spread of infectious disease and HIV/AIDS associated with warfare, from low-intensity to full-fledged wars. The mobility of military and civilians beyond the regions of conflict, such as refugees and sex trafficking, aggravates this situation. Cultural stigma on the part of communities as well as health professionals contributes to the psychological suffering associated with an infectious disease diagnosis. The author points to the pressing need for public health surveillance of civilian populations during civil wars and for early intervention. Finally, in Chapter 7, Foreman presents a different perspective on assessment issues by focusing on the forensic evaluation of a refugee from a war zone, Cambodia. The refugee's historical and cultural background is thoroughly explored as a backdrop for the assessment, and specific guidelines are offered for culturally sensitive psychological assessments of refugee clients.

The Women of Afghanistan and the Freedom of Thought

Adam Fish and Rona Popal

Our concept of government in Afghanistan is very simple: It should be based on democratic values and it should ensure *freedom of thought,* religion and political expression while safeguarding women's rights.
Revolutionary Association of the Women of Afghanistan (2000)

Once the Taliban took power in Afghanistan in 1996, many women were beaten or stoned in public for such infractions as not having the mesh of their *burkas* covering their eyes. One woman was stoned to death for accidentally exposing her arms. Professional women were fired from their jobs as professors, lawyers, artists, and writers (Amnesty International, 2000), even though many international human rights organizations recognize the right to freedom of thought. Cognitive liberty is the right to freedom of thought. This chapter is a functional analysis of the effects of the systematic and institutionalized denial of cognitive liberty on the women of Afghanistan under the Taliban government. In addition to bodily harm, the extreme mental discomforts of the Afghan women are the results of psychological violence, specifically epistemic violence. Mental health is dependent on the presence of cognitive liberty and the absence of epistemic violence.

BACKGROUND

The United States and its allies went to war against the Taliban because its leaders "harbored" the al-Qaeda network of terrorists blamed for the attacks on September 11, 2001, that left nearly 3,000 Americans dead. Between October 2001 and January 2002, air strikes against Afghanistan killed at least that number of Afghan civilians (Milne, 2001); hence, civilians in both countries have been among the fatalities of this conflict.

Afghanistan has been in a state of war for several decades, having long been a theater for the superpower confrontations of the cold war. In the late 1970s, the United States supported the mujahadeen rebels against the Soviet troops sent to support a revolutionary Marxist government. When the communist presence withdrew in the early 1990s, various mujahadeen groups began to fight each other. From 1992 to 1996, the "Northern Alliance" ruled most of the country. When the Taliban took control in 1996, the situation worsened for women; the Taliban's radical rendition of the Qur'an allowed it to perpetuate gender apartheid toward women, accompanied in many instances by physical and psychological abuse. In public, women were forced to wear an all-encompassing *burka* robe and to remain silent. It was illegal to educate young women, and dissent was met with whipping and, sometimes, execution.

This direct, structural violence against the women of Afghanistan was unpardonable and inhuman, but so was the psychological violence. Catherine Hoppers (1999), a Ugandan exile, addressed psychological violence against women when she lamented that "we experience epistemological disjunctures and cognitive dissonances that threaten to render hollow our meanings of the concepts of peace, even justice."

Cultural/epistemic violence was institutionalized by civil war in Afghanistan and the horrors of the Taliban, with an interpretation of the Qur'an as giving men unlimited power over women. However, Hammerle (1999) and other Islamic scholars have argued that the strictures imposed by the Taliban contradict the teachings of the prophet Muhammad because the journey of both women and Islam offers "freedom, equality and unparalleled human rights." According to Farid Younos (personal communication, December 29, 2001), another Islamic scholar, "Islam has been hijacked by the Taliban." The Qur'an does not state the "superiority of man or woman," simply the need for "piety and righteousness." The Taliban's rules are masked as religious necessity, and this epistemic violence robbed the Afghan woman of her thought processes, self-concept, and relationship with Allah and the prophet Muhammad.

ADDRESSING CURRENT PROBLEMS

Years of war have created unfathomable psychological anxiety and depression for Afghan women (Hathout, 1999). Utilizing direct interviews with Afghan citizens, Physicians for Human Rights (1998) found extraordinarily high levels of mental stress and depression. Of those participants in their survey, 81 percent "reported a decline in their mental condition"; 42 percent met the diagnostic criteria for post-traumatic stress disorder (PTSD); 97 percent experienced major depression; 87 percent demonstrated symptoms of anxiety; and 21 percent indicated that they had suicidal thoughts "quite often." By any psychological evaluation standards, these figures are atrociously high. A few years later, Ahmed (2001) filed a similar impression:

Witnessing executions, fleeing religious police with whips who search for women and girls diverging from dress codes; ... having a family member jailed or beaten; such experiences traumatize and retraumatize Afghan women, who have already experienced the horrors of war, rocketing, ever-present landmines ... and the loss of friends and immediate family.

Internationally, freedom of thought (i.e., cognitive liberty) was first proclaimed by the United Nations in the 1948 Universal Declaration of Human Rights and was later reiterated by the International Covenant on Civil and Political Rights (ICCPR). It is Article 18 in both documents that upholds the right to "freedom of thought." The declaration has served as an inspiration for human rights agreements throughout the world, while the ICCPR took effect in 1976 and has been ratified by 140 nations.

The Alchemind Society is an international nonprofit association that works to apply social policies that protect freedom of thought. It is a member of the In Defense of Freedom Coalition (IDOFC, 2001), which consists of some 150 organizations including the Muslim Public Affairs Council, the Arab American Institute, and Amnesty International. IDOFC's primary goal is to ensure that human/civil rights are upheld during the "war against terrorism" initiated by the United States in 2001. One of the authors of this chapter (Fish) is the cultural programs director for the Alchemind Society and has organized IDOFC members to petition the new government of Afghanistan to protect the cognitive liberties of women. In addition, the Revolutionary Association of the Women of Afghanistan (RAWA), an advocacy group for women's rights, has called for the new Afghan government to "ensure freedom of thought" (RAWA, 2000). RAWA has initiated literacy programs and other activities to provide psychosocial support for Afghan women.

The healing process for Afghan women will require patience on the part of those who want to be of assistance. The mind of an Afghani can be described as fiercely independent; unfortunately, these freedom loving people have undergone years of trauma. Inundating Afghans with Western models of psychological "normalcy" may not be efficacious. Yasmine Sherif (2001), who has worked with the United Nations since 1988 on behalf of Afghanistan, recommends that

we [foreign aid workers] put aside our perceptions of being the "helpers," modestly accept the role of a catalyst, and let the Afghans help themselves. If we provide the Afghans with the means, they will show us how to arise from the ashes of human suffering.

Farid Younos (personal communication, December 20, 2001) reminds us that the Afghan people have never been colonized and are rightfully suspicious of foreign powers that attempt to "control their behavior," and that "freedom" for an Afghan "means submission to no other power besides the law of God."

One of the authors of this chapter (Popal) is president of the Afghan Woman's Association International, as well as executive director of the Afghan Coalition. She was one of about 50 invited participants in the Afghan Women's Summit held in Brussels, Belgium, December 4–5, 2001. This summit was the largest global gathering of Afghan women leaders ever held, and its focus was the role of women in a post-Taliban Afghanistan. At the conclusion of the meeting, the summit's Brussels Proclamation addressed "the rebuilding of ... the psychological hospital in Kabul and ... treatments and services, including psychological counseling."

We agree with Sherif (2001) that the Afghan people need to draw upon their own capacities for self-healing. However, Afghanis do not share Western concepts of mental health: There are no strategies for psychological coping with distress, and women are taught that they have to suffer. Traditionally, women would consult with a village elder about psychological issues, but the advice of these male leaders rarely empowered women. Without a concept of mental health, without mental health facilities, without culturally sanctioned coping strategies, and with a legacy opposed to female rights, a woman's sanity is fragile and tenuous. Younos (personal communication, December 29, 2001), who has worked as a psychological counselor with refugees from his native Afghanistan for over 20 years, remarks,

The Afghan women are in a state of confusion, hope, and fear. If the United Nations does not help now, their mental disorders will continue for another generation. The first step in an attempt to heal is to respect women's freedom of choice.

CONCLUSION

RAWA supports the United Nations' Declaration of Human Rights, which asserts that everyone should have "freedom of thought." The Alchemind Society (2001) holds that "any law or cultural commandment that limits the freedom of the individual to form his or her own world view or which restricts his or her freedom to think, perceive, and mentally probe the world" is unjust. Younos (personal communication, December 29, 2001) observes that "in Islam the freedom of thought and mind is taught. It is an obligation to God to use our mind. The freedom of thought and mind is a blessing, a tool that one must exercise in discerning truth from falsehood." Finally, the Brussels Proclamation includes the statement that "education, information and culture empower women" (Afghan Women's Summit for Democracy, 2001).

There is no freedom of thought in a society that stifles self-exploration and forbids education to half its population. By closing schools, suffocating literacy, and manipulating the Qur'an, the Taliban enacted epistemic violence. One would hope that under their burkas the minds of Afghan women retained at least a modicum of autonomy. Unable to direct their social, cultural, educational, and religious ideas into actions, individuals' abilities to generate thought are severely curtailed. New expressions of art, language, fashion, and occupational/educational interests are eliminated, and individuals are left without the ability to explore their own thoughts or creatively participate in society. This liminal state has resulted in high occurrences of anxiety and depression for Afghan women (Ahmed, 2001).

By reducing all issues to polemics, fundamental ideologies reduce choice and attempt to control thought. The Taliban politicized Islam and taught its dogma to the boys in its classes. By reducing options, information is manipulated in a way that negates neutrality and obfuscates the full spectrum of possibilities. The result is epistemic violence.

On the other hand, government recognition of cognitive liberties encourages ethnic, religious, and gender tolerance. By codifying freedom of thought, governments could actively solicit mental health.

There are signs of encouragement in Afghanistan. Following the defeat of the Taliban, many women threw away their burkas. More important, women began to resume their pre-Taliban occupations as teachers, doctors, and merchants. Women's magazines disappeared from Afghanistan in 1992, but in December 2001, *Seerat* ("Attitude") went on sale for 10 cents (U.S.) per copy. One article, written by a teacher who had been dismissed by the Taliban, stated that the Taliban regime "destroyed the rights of orphans and women" ("Women's Attitude," 2001, p. 17). Classes for girls and women, carried on secretly during the years of Taliban oppression, were held openly. A former teacher described how she and two dozen other women had studied literature in secret at the home of a professor of literary theory at Harat University (Waldman, 2001).

The mass media can foster propaganda through "patriotic journalism" and similar procedures (Oberschall, 2001, pp. 136–139). However, the growth of an independent press is only one facet of what is required to rebuild Afghanistan. The Afghanis' emerging freedom of thought needs to be accompanied by freedom from hunger, disease, and fear. Nevertheless, such a freedom is an important component of the human condition.

NOTE

The authors would like to thank Dr. Farid Younos, a truly "pious and righteous" man, for giving freely of his valuable time to assist in this scholarship.

REFERENCES

Afghan Women's Summit for Democracy. (2001, December 4–5). Brussels Proclamation: Equality Now. http://www.equalitynow.org/afghan_womens_summit/brussels_proclamation.html.

Ahmed, N. M. (2001, May 2). Afghanistan, the Taliban and the United States: The role of human rights in Western foreign policy. *Media Monitors Network.* http://www.mediamonitors.net/mosaddeq2.html#_edn6.

Alchemind Society. (2001, July 25). Questions and answers on cognitive liberty. http://www.alchemind.org.

Amnesty International. (2000, Fall). Out of the shadows (an interview with Sajeda Hayat & Sehar Saba). *Amnesty International,* pp. 14–15.

Hammerle, E. E. (1999, August). Women and Islam. *Human Beans/Human Rights.* http://www.humanbeans.com/humanrights/afghanistan-islam/islam.html.

Hathout, H. (1999, August). Perspective on women's plight in Afghanistan. *Human Beans/Human Rights.* http://www.humanbeams.com/humanrights/afghanistan-islam/editorial-0899.html.

Hoppers, C. A. O. (1999, May 12). Founding and launching a global campaign for education towards a culture of peace. Address to the Core Session on Studying Peace,

Human Sciences Research Council, International Civil Society Conference, New York, NY. http://www.hsrc.ac.za/delivered/hoppers1.html.

In Defense of Freedom Coalition. (2001). *In Defense of Freedom*. homepage. http://www.indefenseoffreedom.org/.

Milne, S. (2001, December 20). The innocent dead in a coward's war: Estimates suggest US bombs have killed at least 3,767 civilians. *The Guardian.* http://www.guardian.co.uk/comment/story/0,3604,621931,00.html.

Oberschall, A. (2001). From ethnic cooperation to violence and war in Yugoslavia. In D. Chirot & M. E. P. Seligman (Eds.), *Ethnopolitical warfare: Causes, consequences, and possible solutions* (pp. 119–150). Washington, DC: American Psychological Association.

Physicians for Human Rights. (1998). Afghanistan campaign. The Taliban's war on women: A health and human rights crisis in Afghanistan. Executive Summary. http://www.phrusa.org/research/health_effects/exec.html.

Revolutionary Association of the Women of Afghanistan. (2000). Standpoints. http://rawa.fancymarketing.net/points.html.

Sherif, Y. (2001, October 12). Air strikes on Afghanistan—what comes next? *Reuters AlertNet.* http://www.alertnet.org/thefacts/reliefresources/300506.

Waldman, A. (2001, December 21). Afghan writers emerging from behind closed doors. *San Francisco Chronicle*, p. H2.

Women's attitude hits Afghan shelves. (2001, December 27). *Vietnam News*, p. 17.

2

Healing the Impact of Colonization, Genocide, and Racism on Indigenous Populations

Betty Bastien, Jürgen W. Kremer, Rauna Kuokkanen, and Patricia Vickers

Violence, in an Indigenous context, stems from many sources, including the social sciences that wield "epistemic violence" (Spivak, 1990). Epistemic violence is a continuation of genocide. Genocide is balanced by survivance stories, and "survivance" is "the continuance of native stories, not a mere reaction, or a survivable name. Native survivance stories are renunciations of dominance, tragedy, and victimry" (Vizenor, 1999, p. vii).

The epistemic violence of the social sciences is represented by concepts like the "noble savage" and the "vanishing Native." This chapter attempts to face the genocidal realities of Indigenous peoples, and the politics forced upon them, without succumbing to contemporary expressions of stories of the vanishing native. Stories of survivance contain the greatest healing potential for Indigenous peoples.

WHO ARE THE INDIGENOUS PEOPLES? POLITICAL CONTEXT

In the legal and political contexts, especially within the framework of international organizations such as the United Nations, Indigenous people often use the definition provided by the International Labor Organization, Convention No. 169: The term *Indigenous peoples* refers to

tribal peoples in independent countries whose social, cultural and economic conditions distinguish them from other sections of the national community and whose status is regulated wholly or partially by their own customs or traditions. (International Labor Organization, 1989)

Frustrated in their attempts to work with nation-states, many Indigenous peoples have taken their concerns to the international level. In 1957 the

International Labor Organization (ILO) adopted one of the first international instruments to recognize Indigenous issues, Convention No. 107 on Indigenous Populations. In 1982 the Working Group on Indigenous Populations was established. The working group has provided a Draft Declaration on the Rights of Indigenous Peoples. So far, only a few of the articles have been adopted by the nation-states. As long as the Declaration on the Rights of Indigenous Peoples remains unadopted, Convention No. 169 on Indigenous and Tribal Peoples provides the strongest support for Indigenous rights internationally. The convention states that Indigenous peoples have the right "to control, to the extent possible, their own economic, social and cultural development" (article 8).

This chapter focuses on three examples that are taken from geographical areas where initial colonial violence has given way to other forms of violence:

1. The Sámi people of northern Europe
2. The Tsimshian people of the Canadian Northwest
3. The Niisitapi people of southern Alberta, Canada

GENOCIDE AND VIOLENCE

Defining Genocide

In 1946 the United Nations General Assembly passed a resolution stating that "genocide is the denial of the right of existence to entire human groups" (Stannard, 1992, p. 279). Chrisjohn, Young, and Maraum (1994) discuss "ordinary genocide" as a form of genocide that is relevant for many Indigenous peoples:

"Ordinary genocide" is rarely, if at all, aimed at the total annihilation of the group; the purpose of the violence ... is to destroy the marked category (a nation, a tribe, a religious sect) as a viable community. (p. 30)

Defining Violence

The word *violence* means, in its root, "vital force." In this sense we understand violence as the assertion of one's vital force at the expense of another. This definition is a modification of Galtung (1996, p. 4), who distinguishes three forms of violence: direct, structural, and cultural. *Direct violence* refers to the brutality of murder, slavery, displacement, and expropriation. *Structural violence* refers to the direct, everyday policies that affect the well-being of people. *Cultural violence* refers to racism. *Epistemic violence* (Spivak 1990, pp. 125–126) refers to a process whereby colonial and imperial practices impose certain European codes. *Psychospiritual violence* is another term we use to discuss the impact of genocidal policies.

THE PROCESS OF COLONIZATION

The indirect violence following direct violence can be seen in various dimensions. Economically, it means the destruction of Indigenous self-sustaining economies and the imposition of market or socialist economies. Politically, it means the destruction of traditional forms of governance. Legally, it means that Indigenous oral law and historical rights are invalidated. Socially, it means the destruction of rites of passage. Physically, it means exposure to contagious diseases. Intellectually, it means the invalidation of the Indigenous paradigms and the dominance of an alien language. Spiritually, it means the destruction of ceremonial knowledge. Psychologically, survivors of genocide show symptoms of post-traumatic stress.

Colonial Violence Among the Sámi

The Sámi are the Indigenous people of Sápmi (or Sámiland), which spans central Norway and Sweden through northern Finland to the Kola Peninsula of Russia. A rough estimate of the Sámi population is between 75,000 and 100,000. During the early Middle Ages, the surrounding kingdoms became interested in the land and natural resources of Sámiland.

Due to its location, Sámiland became a war zone during the 12th and 13th centuries. By the end of the 13th century, Denmark and Novgorod had divided the Sámi area by a mutual treaty, and in 1751, in the Treaty of Stroemstad, Norway and Sweden imposed the first foreign boundary on Sámiland. An individual Sámi was no longer able to own land, and grazing and hunting rights on the other side of the border were abolished.

The impact of colonization in Sápmi has various dimensions today. Economically, colonialism has destroyed the local subsistence livelihoods of the Sámi. Mining, forestry, hydroelectric power plants, and tourism have put growing pressure on Sámi lifeways. The first Christian churches in Sápmi were built in the 11th century, and since then Christianity has gradually destroyed the Sámi worldview by banning shamanic ceremonies, executing the *noaidis* (Sámi shamans), burning and destroying the Sámi drums, and even banning the Sámi way of singing and communicating called *yoiking*.

Colonialism also gradually eroded the traditional Sámi system of education by imposing a compulsory school system. However, in many ways, the Sámi are in control of their own education through their education councils. There is a Sámi College, which trains Sámi teachers, and in most places in Sápmi, children are able to study the Sámi language at least a few hours per week.

In 1992 Sámi language legislation in both Norway and Finland gave the Sámi the right to use their mother tongue when dealing with government agencies. In Sweden, the Sámi language is considered one of a number of minority languages. In Russia, there is no special law protecting the Sámi language. Of the four countries where the Sámi live, only Norway had ratified ILO Convention No. 169 on the rights of Indigenous and Tribal Peoples as of 2002. In Finland, a legal study demonstrated that the Sámi had official title to their land as recently as the early 20th century. This discovery has led to a situation in which the state cannot ignore the ownership question any longer.

Considering the material conditions of most of the Sámi, an outsider could come to the conclusion that the Sámi are not colonized. In this sense, the colonial process has found its completion by ideologically cloaking its own violence. Internalized mental colonization has been so exhaustive that even though the Sámi have their own elected bodies, welfare system, and some control over their education, none of these is based on Sámi culture. The Sámi movement of the 1960s and 1970s led to the establishment of Sámi parliaments, first in Finland in 1973, then in Norway in 1989, and in Sweden in 1993. The Sámi parliaments are not based on Sámi models of governance or their spiritual and cultural practices, and they do not have much decision-making power even over issues directly concerning their own culture.

Spivak's (1990) concept of epistemic violence provides probably the best means of understanding this situation. The Sámi *episteme*, their knowledge system, has been replaced by colonial Scandinavian and other European systems to such an extent that it has created Sámi subjects with foreign worldviews. A Sámi person may speak the Sámi language fluently, but use it to express the worldview of the dominant culture. The survival of the Sámi language is not matched by the survival of the Sámi Indigenous worldview.

While the recognition of Sámi political issues improved local conditions, this improvement may have been achieved at the price of the surrender of the Sámi episteme. Epistemic violence is a fact of Sámi reality and makes colonial violence less visible. Structural violence is largely hidden from view as the structure imposed by the dominant societies has been accepted and is used.

Colonial Violence Among the Tsimshian and Niisitapi

Cultural evolution is a concept that has formed the philosophical basis for genocidal policies. Within this framework, Indigenous peoples are commonly seen as in need of development. The ideological rationale of colonization has been the presumed need to alter Indigenous peoples' lifeways to a way of life considered "civilized." Such civilization was to be achieved, first and foremost, through the process of Christianization. Despite the fact that today numerous anthropologists and archaeologists disavow it, cultural evolution continues to have an impact (cf. Kelly, 1995; Kremer, 1998, 1999).

The "Norwegianization" policy of 1879–1940 reflected the nationalism and social Darwinistic thinking of the times and regarded assimilation as the only way to bring "enlightenment" to the Sámi people. The current crisis in Indigenous identity formation has resulted in social science theories evolving that fundamentally continue practices of assimilation. Evolutionary thinking, in Nietzsche's (1967) sense of "truths are illusions of which one has forgotten that they are illusions," has been the foundation of assimilation policies. It is this cognitive framework that created and perpetuates genocide.

The Canadian Indian Act of 1867 (section 24, subsection 91, of the British North American Act) gave the newly formed colonial government of Canada exclusive control over Indigenous territories and declared Indigenous peoples to be wards of the government. The Royal Proclamation of 1873 strengthened the economic base of the dominant culture by establishing procedures for acquiring the lands occupied by Indigenous peoples. Although recognizing Indian title to lands not colonized, it outlined the beginning of an apartheid system. This gave rise to the 1885 policy, enforced as if it were a law even though it was neither an official act nor a proclamation, which forbade Indigenous people to leave the reserve. These acts gave the government exclusive control over economic activities.

Colonialism engenders dependency through legislation, destroys the traditional economic base, and enforces an alien education system. It denies people the capacity to make intelligent decisions based on cultural knowledge. Such knowledge was repressed by the Canadian legislation of the 1920s and 1930s. Legislation in 1920 made school attendance compulsory for Indigenous people's children, and in 1930 noncompliance was legally defined as a criminal offense. These efforts characterized the spiritual and psychological violence that altered the worldviews of Indigenous peoples. Residential schools were introducing the new imperialist culture that defined Indigenous peoples as "savages."

Chief Joe Mathias (Mathias & Yabsley, 1991) defined the Indian Act of 1867 as the conspiracy of suppression of Indian rights in Canada. While Indigenous children and youth were being conditioned by British imperialist values, the government of Canada was imposing a political structure in all Indigenous communities. All communities were redefined as reservations and reduced to smaller territories ignoring tribal history, land use, and understanding of landownership (cf. Wa & Uukw, 1989).

The federally imposed political body of chief and council ignores the traditional systems in Indigenous communities. All federal funding is relegated through this system, creating a fertile environment for internalized oppression to flourish. The Tsimshian live on the northwest coast of British Columbia, where their territory is divided between two areas. Having been banished to reserves, the Tsimshian are now struggling with internalized oppression in the attempt to find balance in a rapidly changing world.

The notion of cultural evolution, the rationalization of necessary progress, perpetuates violence through psychological control. Indigenous peoples have been described as victims. "Victimry" is a pose and dynamic that feeds the game governed by rules of dominance. The social sciences serve this ideology. The notion that the objectified self is the universal nature of humanity describes the process for the desacralization of Indigenous relationships within a universe that is premised on the concrete relationships of a harmonious nature. The detachment from these processes, as enforced by those who design the policies for Indigenous peoples, is the distinguishing mark of ordinary genocide.

Internalized Colonization in Residential Schools

The theoretical frameworks that are used in the perpetuation of psychospiritual violence can be found in the European epistemology. Theories of psychological development are freighted with assumptions that violate the essence of

Indigenous peoples' understanding of human nature. Such assumptions include the following: Each human being has an isolated cognitive self that can best be understood through its components. This assumption underlies all manifestations of European life and constitutes violence to the holistic identity of Indigenous people. In psychospiritual violence, the holistically constructed Indigenous self is forced to become the fragmented Western self.

These assumptions of the nature of humankind have allowed for the genocidal polices of residential schools. The residential school era, which only ended in the 1970s, was the most significant and comprehensive governmental effort, in cooperation with the churches, to alter the reality of Indigenous people. Chrisjohn, Young, and Maraum (1994) point out that "in any intellectually honest appraisal, Indian Residential Schools were genocide" (p. 30). In these institutes the Tsimshian were systematically conditioned to believe that their ancestral ways were inferior to British ways of interpreting the world. When they returned to their communities they found themselves alienated. It is no surprise that addictions and family violence increased.

POST-TRAUMATIC STRESS SYMPTOMS

The consequences of the survival of the direct violence of genocide and of the subsequent structural and cultural violence can be interpreted in terms of what Western psychiatry calls post-traumatic stress disorder (PTSD). The statistics published in the Report of the Royal Commission on Aboriginal Peoples (Chrisjohn, Young, & Maraun, 1994) reveal dramatic figures: The rate for suicide among the total Indigenous population is 25.4 percent, for family violence it is 36.4 percent, for sexual abuse it is 24.5 percent, and for rape it is 15 percent. Beahrs (1990) discusses post-traumatic stress disorders as follows: "PTSD is characterized by intrusive *re-experiencing* of the trauma, persistent *avoiding* of the trauma or *numbing* of responsiveness, and persisting symptoms of *increased arousal*" (p. 15).

In a discussion about Native American genocide, Rivers-Norton has pointed out that genocide is often viewed within the psychological literature as the most devastating and debilitating form of traumatization because it causes enormous physiological and psychic overload, shock, numbing, and grief. It involves the severe devastation caused by cultural destruction, enslavement, relocation, and massive loss of life (Bastien, Kremer, Norton, Rivers-Norton, & Vickers, 1999, p. 18).

CULTURAL AFFIRMATION AND HEALING COLONIAL VIOLENCE

Understanding the Masks of Violence

Within northwest coast art forms, the mask is a representation of a character's or animal's spirit. "Masks give form to thoughts. Masks are images that shine through us from the spirit world" (Steltzer & Davidson, 1994, p. 96). The dancer wearing a mask portrays the characteristics and behavior of the spirit the mask represents, and in doing so becomes familiar with the function of that spirit. We can understand this process as deconstruction or decolonization in Spivak's (1990) sense: "The only things one really deconstructs are things into which one is intimately mired. It speaks you. You speak it" (p. 135). Naming the mask and knowing the song and dance of colonization is the process of deconstructing our present reality.

The Tsimshian have a matrilineal societal structure that is comprised of four clans, or *pteex*. Each clan has a number of houses, or *walp*, with a head chief and chiefs of lesser rank. The hereditary names in each walp hold territories and rights to fishing and hunting within those territories. The Tsimshian societal structure contains methods to address conflicts, disputes, and violations as well as protocols for naming, rites of passage, marriage, and divorce; it also regulates intertribal relationships. Individuals within the clans and families are trained to implement the procedures to resolve and bring restitution to any challenging circumstances within village life. If there is an accidental death through carelessness, the family of the offending party is responsible for recounting the incident in a family meeting at which they are responsible for giving gifts of restitution to the victim's immediate family members. Once the victim's family decides the gifts are sufficient, the incident is forgiven and the offending party is cleansed of their wrongdoings.

Four Critical Aspects in Healing Colonial Violence

There are four critical aspects in healing colonial violence. First, "remembering" acknowledges the destruction that colonization brought; it is identifying the impact of destruction with the willingness to let go of the blame. Each Indigenous nation on the northwest coast of British Columbia has a cleansing ceremony for the purpose of washing away grief and hatred to prepare for healing. The initial step in preparing for the cleansing and washing ceremony is to name the offense. "Research suggests that through a narrative process, through sharing the stories of suffering, individuals begin to organize, structure, and integrate emotionally charged traumatic experiences and events" (Bastien et al., 1999, p. 18).

Second, the reconnection with ancestral healing methods is another critical ingredient. Ancestral teachings have remained in the consciousness and unconsciousness of Indigenous people despite the changes wrought by ongoing colonial and genocidal policies. For example, an individual may approach an elder to ask how to wash away the shame and grief from the past. The individual may be advised to fast and bathe for four days, all the time letting go of hatred and destructive energy that surfaces each day. This is called *si 'satxw* in the Tsimshian language. Through the act of cleansing the individual practices awareness. This awareness is one where individuals observe their behaviors and beliefs, following each to the root of behavior (Levine, 1979). Healing takes patience, requiring cultural support. Indigenous healing programs, such as NECHI (*nechi* is a Cree word meaning "friend") in Canada, use Indigenous approaches combined with Western psychotherapy to deal with issues of alcoholism.

The third crucial ingredient in healing the impact of colonization is reaching out to others. Once one has learned to love and value oneself, it is much easier to love and value one's neighbor. Confronting oppression in communities requires education and a willingness to make relationships that respect the self and others.

A fourth crucial ingredient in healing the results of colonial violence is the reconstruction of Indigenous concepts of community. By reconstructing Indigenous understandings of community we are able to restore our values and spirituality, not as something arbitrary and superficial, limited to occasional prayer or song, but spirituality as our personal and daily relationship with the environment and our community (cf. Brascoupé, 2000, p. 415).

REAFFIRMATIONS OF CULTURAL KNOWLEDGE

The pervasive impact of colonial violence needs to be healed not just on the individual level but also on the cultural level. The self within its Indigenous cosmos is the necessary context for healing. At this point, our chapter turns full circle as we explain one particular Indigenous worldview. This is important in order to avoid psychologizing the ongoing structural and cultural violence to which Indigenous peoples are exposed. It also prepares our discussion of what non-Indigenous people working with Indigenous populations are to do. It gives an opportunity to retract the idealizing or discriminatory projections of the dominant cultures.

The example we give is an attempt to develop a curriculum based in Niisitapi epistemology and ontology. *Niisitapi* can be translated literally as "Real People." The Niisitapi comprise the following tribes: *Aamsskaaippiianii* (South Peigan), *Aapatuxsipiitani* (North Peigan), *Kainah* (Blood/Many Chiefs), and *Siksika* (Blackfoot). Early explorers estimated the population of the Blackfoot-speaking peoples to be 30,000 to 40,000 (McClintock, 1992, p. 5). At present, there are 8,840 members who occupy 535.6 square miles of reserve land. There are 3,072 Kainah between the ages of 5 and 19, but only 20 of them are now fluent speakers (0.65 percent).

Affirmation of the Niisitapi Worldview

The Niisitapi self exists only in relationships. The self is intricately linked with the natural world. The process of knowing is founded upon an intricate web of kinship, the relationships of natural alliances. Knowledge is understood as a source of life, which strengthens the alliances among the cosmic and natural worlds. Knowledge is created and generated through interrelationships with natural alliances. The alliances among the Niisitapi are regenerative and renew the ecological balance of the world.

These alliances can be understood by examining the word *po'nstaan*, "the giving of gifts in ceremony." The cultural meaning provides us with two natural laws: one, that the universe is cyclical and works on the basis of reciprocity; two, that reciprocity is founded upon the principle of "strengthening and supporting life," *niipaitapiiyssin*. Po'nstann refers to what one is willing to give up in exchange for something sought or desired. The common usage refers to giving up aspects/orientations of one's life in exchange for the rebirth of a way of life governed by responsibilities.

The second principle is the nature of truth—*niitsii-issksiniip*, "knowing." Truth is the essential meaning of experience. This principle guides the process of knowing and the knowledge revealed as both are consistent with natural laws. These natural laws support the framework for the interpretation of experiences and are the keys to understanding the meaning of the sacredness of life. Understanding this worldview is crucial for anybody outside the culture attempting to understand the depth of genocide and the requirements for healing.

Niisitapi Ontology

Education and socialization are guided by cultural orientations. In "seeking to understand life," *nipaitapiiyio'pi*, and in "coming to knowing the source of life," *ihtisipaitaoiiyio'pi*, the primary medium is through "transfer," *a'poomo'yiopi*.

The method of inquiry among Niisitapi is entering into relationships and alliances with the spirit of knowledge. The way of coming to know is through participating with and experiencing the knowledge of the natural order. "Knowing," *issksiniip*, is the active participation in relationship with the natural order. Knowing is "experiential," *omohtaanistsihsp*. Knowing and knowledge are living entities, which, through relationships, live in the actions of the participants. In this case, reference can be made to "the way of life of the Niisitapi," *Niipaitapiiyssin*, which encompasses the knowledge and wisdom.

Niisitapi Epistemology

In the traditional context, knowledge is connecting with *ihtisipaitaoiiyio'pi* (spirit). Ihtisipaitaoiiyio'pi manifests through a sacred power, one that is pervasive and manifests through all of creation. This sacred power is gained in the "dream world" and is incorporated into the everyday world of work and play

(Harrod, 1992). Knowledge and wisdom come through the ability to listen and hear the whispers of the wind, the teachings of the rock, the seasonal changes of weather, and by connecting with the animals and plants. Knowing and knowledge are the expression and manifestations of relationships that align with the natural order of the universe.

Knowledge, or knowing (a more accurate Indigenous term because it emphasizes process), is not directly transferable; it is gained through the alliances of interdependent relationships. Knowing is a process of "interpreting experiences with the alliances of the natural world," *isskskataksini/aisskskatakiop'i*. This knowledge and understanding become a basis for effectively participating and functioning in society.

In summary, Niisitapi epistemology manifests in the "transfers," *a'poomo'yiopi*, the theory of knowledge that all knowing comes from the source of life and through kinship alliances. It is through a complex web of relationships that Niisitapi "come to know." Inherent in knowing is the responsibility of living the knowing, a fundamental aspect of identity and the source from which self emerges. These characteristics become the essential elements for interpreting the environment and for experiencing the world.

Niisitapi Pedagogy

"Transfer," *a'poomo'yiopi*, is a process of renewing the alliances of kinship relations. Transfers are found in ceremony. The ceremony takes the form in which a common sense of transformation and transcendence is experienced, and the people (Harrod, 1992, p. 67) share the meanings associated with the transfer. As long as the people retain their connection through their ceremonies, they will retain their transformational and transcendent ways of being through the renewal of their responsibilities as instructed in the original transfer from the sacred spiritual alliances.

Knowing comes with the participation and experience of alliances. Learning is a developmental process that involves an all-inclusive process of living life. *Aatsimoyihskaani* is a concept that addresses the interdependencies that are involved in the processes of coming to knowing. Knowing is through the "active participation with all the alliances of life," *kiipaitapisinnooni*, and, subsequently, knowing is the living knowledge of these relationships.

Niisitapi language education is essential in the process of coming to understanding the alliances essential to participation in a balanced world. Language is spirit. Language is the medium for entering into the relationships forming the Niisitapi culture and society; it allows humans to define their reality and the social order in which they exist. Their language is the expression of the natural alliances of the Niisitapi and embodies the consciousness of the people. Language has the ability to distinguish and define humanity. In other words, language links self to the universe (Bastien, 1998).

DECOLONIZATION FOR PEOPLE OF THE EURO-CENTERED OR "WHITE" MIND

Non-Indigenous persons may wonder how they can be helpful in the healing of colonial genocidal violence. From an Indigenous perspective, the primary need is dialoguing about epistemic violence. Confrontation with the history of genocide and colonization is urgent. Structural violence must be addressed. Persons who are working with Indigenous peoples should reflect critically on the context in which they are working, on whether their work explicitly or implicitly is continuing colonial violence. Persons who are invited to work with Indigenous peoples need to focus particularly on the unconscious forms of epistemic violence their mere presence may perpetrate. Helpers of European descent need to be willing to face the impact of Euro-centered dominance in their personal history and to talk openly about its dynamics with the willingness to work toward positive change.

The importance of awareness of the significant difference in self-construction cannot be stressed enough, as should be obvious from the preceding sections in this chapter. Working with Indigenous peoples in the process of decolonization means that people who are not Indigenous be willing to decolonize themselves and to confront their own historical Indigenous and ancestral origins (Kremer, 2000). This is a difficult task that goes to the core of reality. In this way there can be a gradual interruption of the cycle of genocidal violence.

CONCLUSION

In the process of healing colonial violence the fundamental step is to remember and affirm an Indigenous, culturally specific framework that provides the context for the consideration of educational, psychological, and other interventions. Use of Indigenous culturally available resources is a mandatory ingredient in any healing endeavor. The participation of Indigenous healers and elders, both in education and in psychological interventions, is important. Use of Indigenous languages is invaluable, both as a means of cultural remembrance and affirmation and as a means of expression of the Indigenous self (Allen, 1986). The narration of the experiences of genocidal violence holds tremendous healing potential for both individuals and communities. Witnessing the impact of past and present violence may lead to the release of generative visions that facilitate the remembrance of cultural knowledge; the celebration of relationships and alliances; the impact of Euro-centered knowledge on the basis of Indigenous paradigms; and the expression of Indigenous self and community not as retro-romantic folklore, but as viable, vital, and creative knowledge for future generations—sovereignty, in a sense, that transcends Euro-centered notions and deletes their epistemic and other violence.

NOTE

We dedicate this chapter to the memory of Ingrid Washinawatok, a Menominee woman and the cochair of the Indigenous Women's Network, who in 1999 was kidnapped and killed by Colombian left-wing guerilla forces during her visit to the U'wa people who have been struggling against the intrusion of oil companies, such as Occidental Petroleum and Shell Oil. The purpose of her trip was to support the continuation of U'wa traditional ways of life by assisting them in establishing a cultural education system. (See Washinawatok, 1999, for an example of her work.)

REFERENCES

Allen, P. G. (1986). *The sacred hoop: Recovering the feminine in American Indian traditions*. Boston: Beacon Press.

Bastien, B. (1998). *Blackfoot ways of knowing*. Unpublished doctoral dissertation, California Institute of Integral Studies, San Francisco.

Bastien, B., Kremer, J. W., Norton, J., Rivers-Norton, J., & Vickers, P. (1999). The genocide of Native Americans. *ReVision, 22*(1), 13–20.

Beahrs, J. O. (1990). The evolution of post-traumatic behavior: Three hypotheses. *Dissociation, 3*(1), 15–21.

Brascoupé, S. (2000). Aboriginal peoples' vision of the future: Interweaving traditional knowledge and new technologies. In D. Long & O. P. Dickason (Eds.), *Visions of the heart* (pp. 411–432). Toronto: Harcourt Canada.

Chrisjohn, R. D., Young, S. L., & Maraum, M. (1994). *The circle game: Shadows and substance in residential school experience in Canada*. Unpublished report to the Royal commission on Aboriginal Peoples.

Galtung, J. (1996). *Peace by peaceful means*. London: Sage Press.

Harrod, H. L. (1992). *Renewing the world*. Tucson: University of Arizona Press.

International Labor Organization, Convention #169. (1989). Available at http://www.1.umn.edu/humanarts/instree/r1citp.htm.

Kelly, R. L. (1995). *The foraging spectrum*. Washington: Smithsonian Institution Press.

Kremer, J. W. (1998) The shadow of evolutionary thinking. In D. Rothberg & S. Kelly (Eds.), *Ken Wilber in dialogue* (pp. 237–258). Wheaton, IL: Quest.

Kremer, J. W. (1999). Reconstructing indigenous consciousness: Preliminary considerations. *Ethnopsychologische Mitteilungen, 8*(1), 32–56.

Kremer, J. W. (2000). Shamanic initiations and their loss: Decolonization as initiation and healing. *Ethnopsychologische Mitteilungen, 9*(1/2), 109–148.

Levine, S. (1979). *A gradual awakening*. New York: Anchor Books.

Mathias, J., & Yabsley, G. (1991). Conspiracy of legislation: The suppression of Indian rights in Canada. In D. Jensen & C. Brooks (Eds.), *In celebration of our survival: The First Nations of British Columbia* (pp. 34–45). Vancouver: University of British Columbia Press.

McClintock, W. (1992). *The old north trail: Life, legend and religion of the Blackfeet Indians*. Lincoln: University of Nebraska Press.

Nietzsche, F. (1967). *The will to power*. (W. Kaufmann, Ed. & Trans.; R. Hollingdale, Trans.). New York: Random House. (Original work published 1911)

Spivak, C. G. (1990). *The post-colonial critic: Interviews, strategies, dialogues.* London: Routledge.

Stannard, D. E. (1992). *American holocaust.* Oxford: Oxford University Press.

Steltzer, U., & Davidson, R. (1994). *Eagle transforming: The art of Robert Davidson.* Vancouver, British Columbia: Douglas & McIntyre.

Vizenor, G. (1999). *Manifest manners.* Lincoln: University of Nebraska Press.

Wa, G., & Uukw, D. (1989). *The spirit in the land.* Gabriola, British Columbia: Reflections.

Washinawatok, I. (1999). Sovereignty is more than just power. *Indigenous Woman, 2*(6), 23–24.

3

Children of War: Psychosocial Sequelae of War Trauma in Angolan Adolescents

Teresa M. McIntyre and Margarida Ventura

Come
Abandoned child
Child of circumstances
Of so much and varied sadness
You are child of the storm
Lost mother
Soldier on the run

Angolan poet Tomás Jorge, 1997

In recent conflicts, children and adolescents have been largely the forgotten victims of war. In fact, researchers had neglected the study of the psychological impact of war stress on children and adolescents until the 1990s, thereby hindering the development of psychological intervention programs despite evidence indicating that the younger the victim, the greater the risk of psychological impairment (Pynoos & Eth, 1985). An exception to this are the studies of Freud and Burlingham (1943) on children evacuated from London in World War II, Fraser's book on children in Northern Ireland (1973), and Milgram and Milgram's (1976) study on war-related stress in Israeli children and youth, which are interesting works of description and clinical analysis.

At a political level, the recognition of the psychosocial needs of children in situations of armed conflict also has been slow. Only in 1993, the United Nations Committee on the Rights of the Child prompted the U.N. General Assembly to commission a study investigating the extent of the problem worldwide. The Graça Machel Study (United Nations, 1996) investigates the situation of child soldiers, refugees, and internally displaced children; the extent of sexual exploitation and gender-based violence; landmines; and the impact of war on health, nutrition, and education. This project also addresses the psychosocial impact of armed conflict on children and points out some directives to promote psychosocial recovery and social integration.

Since then, the majority of studies that have examined the impact of war on children have focused on the physical and social consequences of war, such as famine or family separation, but not on children's psychosocial development (Scheepers, 1995). Perhaps the most systematic work on young war victims has been undertaken by Stuvland and Barath since 1992 in Croatia, under the auspices of UNICEF (Bloch, 1993). In a group of 5,835 Croatian children, they found predominantly post-traumatic stress reactions, such as re-experiencing of traumatic events through intrusive memories and "flashbacks," reporting a 40 percent rate of post-traumatic stress disorder. This work has informed several community-oriented intervention programs as described elsewhere in this book. Some studies have also been conducted on psychological symptoms in Israeli children and families who were under SCUD missile attacks during the Gulf War (Laor et al., 1996).

Angola is an African country where civil war has been constant and intense for over 20 years. Some regions of southern Angola experienced the most bloody battles of this war, which forced as much as 88 percent of the civil population to leave their homes and possessions (United Nations Development Program, 1992). It is estimated that this war affected 4.8 million children of Angola, that 1.5 million children were displaced from their homes, and that more than half of the children lost one or both parents. Famine, disease, destruction, death, the massive disorganization of the social and political networks, have characterized the life experience of Angolan youth. The study of the psychological consequences of war in these youth is particularly pertinent due to the pervasive nature of the war trauma in the case of those who have lived through war all their lives. Furthermore, 45 percent of the active Angolan population is less than 15 years old, so the future of the country depends upon the well-being of this generation.

This chapter reports the results of a study conducted in southern Angola since 1993 that aimed at examining the psychological sequelae of war stress in Angolan adolescents. The study compares three groups of Angolan adolescents between the ages of 13 and 16 on the prevalence and characteristics of post-traumatic stress disorder (PTSD) and other psychological measures pertaining to their cognitive, affective, and social development. The study focuses on three questions:

1. What is the prevalence of PTSD and PTSD symptoms in this population, and their variation with degree of war exposure?
2. What are the developmental sequelae associated with war stress in this population, and their variation with PTSD?
3. Which are the sociodemographic moderators of the psychological impact of war stress on these Angolan youth?

METHOD

Subjects

The sample is composed of 231 adolescents divided into three groups differing in severity and length of war exposure. The first is a refugee group of 40 adolescents in refugee camps of Lubango from the areas of southern Angola most affected by war; the second is a nonrefugee group of 150 adolescents from the city of Lubango, one of the least affected by war; the third is a control group of 41 Angolan adolescents residing in Portugal for more than a year, who came from the more protected areas of northern Angola. The participation of all subjects was voluntary, and they were matched on the basis of age, school attendance, and a minimum 4th-grade education.

Instruments

The adolescents were given the *Escala de Avaliação de Resposta ao Acontecimento Traumático (PTSD Scale for Adolescents)*, developed by the authors based on the DSMIV diagnostic criteria for PTSD (American Psychiatric Association, 1994) and validated for the Angolan population (McIntyre & Ventura, 1996). The other measures used were the Angolan versions of the following instruments, which the authors also validated: Piers-Harris Children's Self-concept Scale, Manifest Anxiety Scale, Child Depression Inventory, Teachers' Report Form (TRF), and selected WISC-R scales. A structured sociodemographic questionnaire inquiring about identifying information, migration, family and living situation, and religious as well as tribal values was also developed by the authors.

RESULTS

Prevalence of PTSD

Table 3.1 presents the frequencies for diagnosed PTSD among the three groups of Angolan adolescents by sex, which indicate that the frequency of PTSD diagnosis increases with more exposure to war. The intensity of PTSD symptoms also varies in direct proportion to the degree of war exposure (refugees: $M = 12.70$; nonrefugees [Lubango group]: $M = 10.88$; Portuguese residents: $M = 3.54$).

Further analyses of the three PTSD symptom clusters evidence significant group differences for the Re-experiencing the Event and Avoidance/Numbing clusters but not for Arousal symptoms. Re-experiencing the Event symptoms were also in direct proportion to the degree of war exposure, whereas Avoidance/Numbing symptoms were higher for the refugees than for the other two groups. Regarding the preferred modes of expression of PTSD symptoms, for the refugee and nonrefugee groups, cluster B—Re-experiencing the Event—seems to be the predominant mode of expression of PTSD symptoms, whereas for the Angolans residing in Portugal, this cluster is the least endorsed.

The results show a very high prevalence of PTSD among the adolescents in the refugee and nonrefugee groups in comparison with the Angolans in Portugal. These figures are considerably higher than the ones reported by Barath (Bloch, 1993) in Croatian schoolchildren (40 percent) and by Loughrey, Bell, Kee, Ruddy, & Curran (1988) in adult victims of civil violence in Northern

Table 3.1

Prevalence of PTSD Among Angolan Adolescents by Sex and Degree of War Exposure and Chi-Square Results (N = 231)

Group	Sex	n	PTSD Present	PTSD Absent	% with PTSD
Refugees	Male	19	17	2	89.5
	Female	21	19	2	90.5
	Total	40	36	4	90.0
Nonrefugees	Male	65	49	16	76.0
	Female	85	74	11	87.0
	Total	150	123	27	82.0
Portugal	Male	22	2	20	13.6
	Female	19	7	12	31.6
	Total	41	9	32	22.0

x^2 (2, N = 231) = 65.81, $p < .001$.

Ireland (23.2 percent). Three factors may account for this difference: (a) the younger age of the subjects, which is considered a risk factor in itself for the development of PTSD; (b) the fact that the children in Angola are being evaluated when the threat of war is still present and have been subject to war trauma all their lives; and (c) the greater length of the Angolan war.

The authors conducted two more evaluations of PTSD in random samples of 300 nonrefugees of the city of Lubango (in 1999 and 2000) from 10 to 16 years old, which show a trend toward a decrease in the prevalence of PTSD to 61 percent and 65 percent, respectively, especially in the younger age groups (10–12-year-olds). This decrease may be attributed to the more stable military situation in this region and to decreased war exposure in the younger children. However, these figures are still quite high and affirm the need to intervene with these youth, who may well be the greatest victims of this war.

PSYCHOLOGICAL SEQUELAE

The relationship between war exposure and the adolescents' self-concept, levels of anxiety and depression, cognitive development, and behavioral adjustment were tested in order to ascertain possible psychosocial sequelae and identify specific targets for future intervention.

The results for the Self-concept Scale and subscales are presented in Table 3.2, revealing that for Total Self-concept and the subscales Intellectual Status, Popularity, Physical Attributes, and Satisfaction, the values decrease with increased war exposure. Regarding the Manifest Anxiety Scale, the refugee and Lubango groups reported significantly higher anxiety than the Portuguese residents (see Table 3.3). In contrast, the results for Depression do not reveal significant differences among groups (see Table 3.3). However, when the subjects were divided according to the presence or absence of clinical depression (cut off 19), a higher prevalence of depression appeared in the refugee group (25 percent) followed by the Portuguese (15 percent) and Lubango (7 percent) residents.

The results for the Behavioral Indicators (TRF) showed a significant effect of war exposure for global behavioral adjustment and the dimensions Isolation, Somatic Complaints, Anxiety/Depression, Social Problems, Problem Thinking, Delinquent Behavior, and Internalizing. The results for Attention, Aggressive Behavior, and Externalizing were nonsignificant (see Table 3.4). Overall, the between-group comparisons yielded significant differences between the Portuguese and the Angolan residents but not between the refugee and the Lubango groups.

The results on the WISC-R scales and subscales used in this study showed a similar decrease in performance with the increase in war exposure, affecting verbal skills globally and all the subscales (see Table 3.5).

One question explored additionally was whether a PTSD diagnosis versus the presence of PTSD symptoms alone is related to worse clinical and developmental

Table 3.2
Analysis of Variance Results and Post-hoc Comparisons for the Self-concept Scale and Subscale Scores by Degree of War Exposure (N = 231)

Scale	Group	M	F	p	post-hoc*
Total	Refugees	36.28	7.08	.001	R - P
	Lubango	39.23			L - P
	Portugal	42.46			
Behavior	Refugees	11.15	.159	.853	—
	Lubango	11.36			
	Portugal	11.41			
Anxiety	Refugees	5.48	.288	.743	—
	Lubango	5.17			
	Portugal	5.24			
Intellectual Status	Refugees	6.95	8.18	.000	R - P
	Lubango	8.49			L - P
	Portugal	10.07			R - L
Popularity	Refugees	6.65	6.34	.000	R - P
	Lubango	6.91			L - P
	Portugal	8.22			
Physical Attributes	Refugees	3.70	3.01	.05	R - P
	Lubango	4.38			L - R
	Portugal	4.56			
Satisfaction	Refugees	4.88	4.51	.01	R - P
	Lubango	5.10			L - P
	Portugal	5.73			

*R = Refugees; L = Lubango (Nonrefugees); P = Portuguese residents.

Table 3.3
Analysis of Variance Results for the Anxiety and Depression Scale and Subscale Scores by Degree of War Exposure (N = 231)

Scale	Group	M	F	p	post-hoc*
Total Anxiety	Refugees	23.25	45.63	.000	R - P
	Lubango	21.96			L - P
	Portugal	14.95			
Anxiety	Refugees	17.70	36.31	.000	R - P
	Lubango	17.30			L - P
	Portugal	10.61			
Lie	Refugees	5.55	4.02	.02	R - P
	Lubango	4.66			L - R
	Portugal	4.34			
Depression	Refugees	13.40	2.42	.09	—
	Lubango	13.10			
	Portugal	11.27			

*R = Refugees; L = Lubango (Nonrefugees); P = Portuguese residents.

outcome. The results showed that high-war-exposure adolescents with PTSD faired worse in terms of affective, cognitive, and behavioral adjustment than those without a PTSD diagnosis (see Table 3.6). The results were significant for total self-concept and the Behavior, Anxiety, Intellectual, Popularity, and Satisfaction aspects; for the clinical scales Anxiety and Depression; and for the TRF scales Somatic Complaints, Anxiety/Depression, and Internalizing.

In general, we found that the degree of war exposure is related to several affective, cognitive, and behavioral indicators, suggesting a global negative effect of war trauma on these adolescents' development.

SOCIODEMOGRAPHIC INFLUENCES

The question of whether there are personal or social variables that may moderate the effects of war trauma on Angolan adolescents, including the development of the clinical syndrome PTSD, is very pertinent in a preventive and health promoting perspective. From the previous data, Angolan youth can be considered "at risk" for the development of psychological problems, war being an extreme adversity for these young lives (Rak & Patterson, 1996). However, resiliency theory has led researchers to investigate "the other side of the coin," that is, what are the "protective factors" associated with positive developmental and clinical outcomes despite exposure to adverse situations, such as war trauma (Rutter, 1985; Garmezy, 1991). The identification of risk and protective factors for youth in war situations is an important tool in guiding intervention efforts.

Table 3.4
Analysis of Variance Results and Post-hoc Comparisons for the TRF Scale and Subscale Scores by Degree of War Exposure (N = 231)

Scale	Group	M	F	p	post-hoc*
Total	Refugees	50.23	10.26	.000	R - P
	Lubango	45.21			L - P
	Portugal	31.03			
Isolation	Refugees	5.45	8.21	.001	R - L
	Lubango	3.98			P - R
	Portugal	3.03			
Somatic Complaints	Refugees	5.65	8.68	.000	All
	Lubango	3.67			
	Portugal	2.24			
Anxiety/Depression	Refugees	11.05	10.24	.000	R - P
	Lubango	10.57			L - P
	Portugal	6.21			
Social Problems	Refugees	3.28	8.74	.000	L - P
	Lubango	4.19			
	Portugal	1.73			
Problem Thinking	Refugees	2.48	7.33	.000	All
	Lubango	1.74			
	Portugal	1.06			
Attention	Refugees	10.90	1.58	.21	—
	Lubango	10.20			
	Portugal	7.76			
Delinquent Behavior	Refugees	3.15	5.39	.005	L - P
	Lubango	3.54			
	Portugal	2.15			
Aggression	Refugees	6.33	.13	.88	—
	Lubango	5.99			
	Portugal	6.03			
Internalizing	Refugees	22.00	15.50	.000	All
	Lubango	18.13			
	Portugal	11.48			
Externalizing	Refugees	9.48	.483	.62	—
	Lubango	9.53			
	Portugal	8.18			

*R = Refugees; L = Lubango (Nonrefugees); P = Portuguese residents.

Table 3.5
Analysis of Variance Results and Post-hoc Comparisons for the WISC-R Verbal Scale and Subscale Scores by Degree of War Exposure (N = 231)

Scale	Group	M	F	p	post-hoc*
Total Verbal	Refugees	62.00	146.73	.000	All
	Lubango	92.43			
	Portugal	116.22			
Similarities	Refugees	12.15	35.29	.000	All
	Lubango	18.13			
	Portugal	20.56			
Arithmetic	Refugees	12.20	14.70	.000	R - L
	Lubango	13.54			R - P
	Portugal	14.17			
Vocabulary	Refugees	17.28	134.42	.000	All
	Lubango	30.26			
	Portugal	42.73			
Comprehension	Refugees	12.03	81.87	.000	All
	Lubango	19.56			
	Portugal	24.61			
Digit Span	Refugees	8.40	42.83	.000	All
	Lubango	10.80			
	Portugal	13.90			
Coding	Refugees	35.80	52.59	.000	R - P
	Lubango	39.62			L - P
	Portugal	58.41			
Mazes	Refugees	22.48	8.58	.000	R - P
	Lubango	22.60			L - P
	Portugal	24.63			

*R = Refugees; L = Lubango (Nonrefugees); P = Portuguese residents.

To address this question, the study examined the impact of the sociodemographic variables gender, age, education, motive for relocation, separation from parents, religious and tribal values on the development of PTSD and the developmental indicators. Detailed results are presented below.

Age and Gender Influences

Adolescent girls exhibit a higher prevalence of PTSD than boys and present a higher number of PTSD symptoms ($M1$ = 11.62; $M2$ = 9.91), although age differences are nonsignificant. Girls in the nonrefugee group show more Anxiety than boys ($M1$ = 23.07; $M2$ = 20.51), but not in the refugee or Portugal

Table 3.6
Significant *t* Test Results for the Clinical and Developmental Variables According to the Presence of PTSD (n = 221*)

Scale/Group	With PTSD n = 167		W/out PTSD n = 54			
	M	SD	M	SD	t	p
SELF-CONCEPT						
Total Self-Concept	38.17	7.20	43.04	7.91	−4.01	.000
Behavior	11.14	2.24	11.84	2.37	−2.04	.04
Anxiety	6.63	2.05	7.54	2.85	−2.32	.02
Intellectual	8.20	3.00	9.32	2.79	−2.66	.009
Popularity	6.87	1.75	7.70	1.84	−3.10	.003
Satisfaction	4.96	1.52	5.73	1.27	−3.85	.000
ANXIETY	22.24	4.24	17.17	6.42	5.43	.000
DEPRESSION	13.62	4.97	10.19	4.92	4.44	.000
BEHAVIOR (TRF)						
Somatic Complaints	4.18	3.24	2.81	2.47	3.31	.001
Anxiety/Depression	10.49	4.63	8.61	5.62	2.26	.030
Internalizing	18.84	8.20	15.04	9.26	2.74	.007
COGNITIVE WISC-R						
Verbal Total	86.63	20.20	104.48	21.54	−5.35	.000
Similarities	16.85	5.12	19.17	4.75	−3.22	.002
Arithmetic	13.25	1.52	13.83	1.97	−2.07	.040
Vocabulary	27.96	9.13	36.02	9.82	−5.63	.000
Comprehension	18.11	5.38	21.87	4.96	−4.99	.000
Digit Span	10.39	2.57	12.35	3.28	−4.26	.000
Coding	40.50	11.38	55.00	15.74	−8.01	.000
Mazes	22.7	2.56	24.10	2.18	−4.69	.000

*No test data were available for 10 individuals, making this number smaller than that for the whole sample.

groups. In contrast, the effects of age and gender were nonsignificant for the Child Depression Inventory scores.

The impact of gender and age on global self-concept was nonsignificant. The Anxiety aspect was an exception, with girls in the Lubango and Portugal groups reporting higher anxiety than boys do (Nonrefugee Girls: *M* = 5.65, Nonrefugee Boys: *M* = 4.53; Portuguese-Resident Girls: *M* = 6.32, Portuguese-Resident Boys: *M* = 4.11).

The impact of gender on behavioral adjustment was significant for the TRF scale Internalizing (Isolation, Somatic Complaints, and Anxiety/Depression), with girls showing more problems than boys. Regarding cognitive development, gender seems to play an important role, with girls showing less overall verbal development than boys do (Girls' raw scores: $M = 85.82$; Boys': $M = 92.41$), especially for the more war-exposed groups.

Motive for Relocation

The motive for relocation (War, Other Motives, and Nonrelocated) was a significant factor for the prevalence of PTSD diagnosis, with 86.3 percent of the subjects relocated for war reasons, 78.1 percent of the subjects nonrelocated, and 53.2 percent of the subjects relocated due to other motives presenting a PTSD diagnosis. The motive for relocation was not associated with anxiety or depression, or with any of the self-concept variables.

The motive for relocation seems to be related to global behavioral adjustment and the dimensions Aggressive Behavior and Externalizing, with more behavior problems reported for adolescents relocated due to war than for the other groups. The subjects relocated due to war also showed worse results than the other two groups on the Digit Span scale of the WISC-R.

Parental Status

Contrary to what would be expected, the fact of the adolescents residing with or without their parents did not influence the prevalence of PTSD, the number of symptoms experienced, or anxiety. However, the adolescents in the refugee group who were without their parents presented higher Depression scores than those living with their parents (Without parents: 17.00; With parents: 11.46).

Parental status seems to play an important role in Total Self-Concept and its dimensions. The adolescents who live with their parents have higher scores on self-concept and the dimensions of Behavior and Physical Appearance than those without parents.

Regarding behavioral adjustment, the impact of parental status was limited to the Problem Thinking scale, with those with parents showing a more favorable score in the refugee group. The results for the WISC-R were significant for Digit Span, with the subjects in the Lubango group who live with parents evidencing higher scores.

Religious Values

Among the social consequences of war are the disruption of cultural avenues of social support, such as religious or tribal rituals, and the challenge of personal and shared values. The importance of religious and tribal values in the experience of trauma has been highlighted in other chapters in this book (e.g., Wessells & Monteiro; Bolton) and was investigated in this study as a potential protective factor.

The effect of religious values on the prevalence of PTSD was significant (see Table 3.7), the percentage of PTSD tending to increase with the importance at-

Table 3.7
Means and Standard Deviations for the Self-Concept Subscales by Religious and Tribal Values and War Exposure Group

| Subscales | Group | Religious Values | | | | Tribal Values | | | |
| | | Less Important | | More Important | | Less Important | | More Important | |
		M	SD	M	SD	M	SD	M	SD
Total	Refugees	—	—	36.28	6.23	36.17	6.47	36.41	6.08
	Lubango	38.40	5.46	39.29	7.57	39.44	7.23	37.97	7.83
	Portugal	39.92	10.44	42.56	5.68	39.36	9.65	44.50	8.19
Behavioral	Refugees	—	—	11.15	2.27	11.39	2.17	10.82	2.43
	Lubango	11.55	1.93	11.31	2.11	11.50	1.95	10.80	2.48
	Portugal	10.66	3.34	11.11	2.85	9.82	3.28	12.00	3.56
Physical Ap.	Refugees	4.65	—	3.70	1.30	3.48	1.38	4.00	1.17
	Lubango	4.33	1.27	4.35	1.56	4.54	1.51	3.83	1.51
	Portugal	—	1.92	4.56	.88	4.64	1.63	4.75	.48
Popularity	Refugees	—	—	6.65	1.78	6.96	1.55	6.24	2.02
	Lubango	6.75	1.77	6.87	1.78	6.82	1.82	7.06	1.55
	Portugal	8.08	1.88	8.22	1.30	8.09	1.92	9.00	.82

tributed to religious values (not important: 54.5 percent; less important than others: 66.7 percent; as important as others: 77.8 percent; more important than others: 83.2 percent). However, no significant impact of endorsement of religious values was found for anxiety. In contrast, Depression was affected, with those attributing less importance to religious values showing lower depression scores. The same trend was observed for Total Self-Concept in the Lubango and Portugal groups (see Table 3.7).

Endorsement of religious values seems to be a significant factor for global behavioral adjustment and some of its dimensions (see Table 3.8), with the adolescents who give no or little importance to religious values having more behavioral problems than those who attribute some or much importance to them (less important: 46.38; more important: 45.10). However, a reverse effect was observed for the dimensions Somatic Complaints, Anxiety/Depression, Isolation, and Internalizing, with those endorsing religious values scoring higher on these scales. No significant results were found for cognitive development.

Tribal Values

The endorsement of tribal values had a positive impact on the prevalence of PTSD, the adolescents who attribute no or little importance to tribal values showing a higher rate of PTSD (not important: 58.1 percent; less important than others: 9 percent; as important as others: 15.6 percent; more important than

Table 3.8

Means and Standard Deviations for Significant TRF Subscales by Religious and Tribal Values, and War Exposure Group

| Subscales | Group | Religious Values | | | | Tribal Values | | | |
| | | Less Important | | More Important | | Less Important | | More Important | |
		M	SD	M	SD	M	SD	M	SD
Isolation	Refugee	—	—	5.45	3.46	6.17	3.96	4.47	2.40
	Lubango	4.16	2.27	3.96	2.34	3.85	2.34	4.35	2.20
	Portugal	5.29	4.68	3.00	3.08	4.67	5.24	1.75	2.87
Attention	Refugee	—	—	—	—	10.26	6.86	11.76	6.72
	Lubango	—	—	—	—	10.20	5.38	10.23	5.18
	Portugal	—	—	—	—	9.17	9.60	8.75	7.37
Aggression	Refugee	—	—	—	—	4.83	2.17	8.35	6.00
	Lubango	—	—	—	—	6.09	5.83	5.74	5.70
	Portugal	—	—	—	—	7.00	7.32	5.50	5.45
Somatic	Refugee	—	—	5.65	2.74	3.56	3.02	3.94	3.38
Complaints	Lubango	3.53	2.39	3.71	3.22	5.65	3.05	5.65	2.34
	Portugal	2.57	2.30	3.11	3.69	2.00	2.28	2.00	2.31

others: 12.6 percent). No significant effects were found for anxiety and depression scores.

We found a significant impact of endorsement of tribal values on global self-concept and its dimensions Behavioral Aspects, Physical Appearance, and Popularity, the direction of the differences varying widely according to war exposure (see Table 3.7). Regarding behavioral adjustment, the impact is limited to Isolation, Attention, and Aggressive Behavior, with varying directions as earlier (see Table 3.8). The Verbal WISC-R scores seem to be affected by tribal values for the refugee group, with those attributing more importance to tribal values presenting higher verbal scores (less important: 58.91; more important: 66.18).

In general, these data indicate that several sociodemographic variables interact with war exposure to moderate its impact on the clinical and developmental status of Angolan adolescents, either aggravating or improving their response to war trauma. The sociodemographic variables that appear to have more impact are the endorsement of religious and tribal values, parental status (living with or without the parents), and relocation due to war motives. Gender and age appear to have a more limited impact on the psychological effects of war trauma, indicating that response to war stress is often independent of these variables.

The analyses of sociodemographic moderators of war trauma allow for the determination of which groups are at risk for the development of psychosocial sequelae, a fundamental piece of information for planning intervention strategies, especially in the area of primary and secondary prevention. Our data suggest that these "high risk" groups are those adolescents who have a PTSD diagnosis, are female, are separated from their parents, have been relocated due to war, and have lost a sense of connection to their tribal values.

CONCLUSION

The data presented here indicate a high percentage of PTSD among Angolan adolescents when compared with findings in other war scenarios, such as Croatia, and point to a strong relationship between continued exposure to war stressors and the development of PTSD. Subsequent PTSD random assessments of this population confirmed these findings, although indicating a trend toward a decrease in prevalence. This is consistent with a risk accumulation model (Brown & Fromm, 1987; Pynoos, 1990), which suggests that psychological and behavioral sequelae increase with the number and intensity of the stressors to which the child is exposed.

The developmental data are also consistent with a risk accumulation model, the degree of war exposure being related to several affective and behavioral indicators, suggesting a global negative effect of war trauma on these adolescents' development. The refugee and Lubango groups show lower self-concept and higher levels of anxiety, clinical depression, isolation, somatic complaints, social problems, problem thinking, and delinquent behavior than the Angolans residing in Portugal do. Cognitive development is also related to war exposure and PTSD, affecting both verbal and nonverbal skills. Furthermore, the presence of PTSD diagnosis seems to be related to worse clinical and developmental outcomes, which is in agreement with the literature that highlights the chronic and long-term nature of developmental damage in children who are exposed to continued traumatic stress (Greca, 2000; Pynoos, 1990).

However, the data on the sociodemographic variables show that the response to war trauma in adolescents is not linear and can be buffered by personal and social variables, such as the child's social support system. The separation from parents, typical of a war situation, is clearly a risk factor in terms of clinical and behavioral adjustment. These findings support the directives from several NGOs that make restoring a family or familylike environment a priority in intervention efforts with these youth. Another protective factor is the connection with tribal values. This may function as a source of social support, but also provides a context in which meaning can be attributed to the stressors while offering paths to healing that are culturally appropriate. The sociodemographic data highlights the fact that intervention strategies directed at children in war-torn countries cannot focus on children alone but ought to have a wider social and cultural focus.

Several conclusions can be drawn from these data in terms of intervention strategies. Since PTSD was found to be highly prevalent and is associated with worse clinical and developmental outcomes, PTSD screening, such as through a simple structured interview, may be useful in targeting prevention strategies that can help diminish the long-term effects of PTSD. Model programs such as those used in Croatia, or with the Israeli youth (Milgram & Milgram, 1976), or those prevention programs reviewed by Williams and Berry (1991) offer a starting point for assisting these children and minimizing the effects of PTSD.

The specific developmental and clinical data reported here should encourage further investigation of this question in other war-afflicted countries, preferably with longitudinal designs. The lengthy process of validating Western constructs such as depression or PTSD, adapting instruments, or constructing new ones is a frequent deterrent in this kind of research. However, determining which aspects of development are most affected by war exposure is essential for designing effective, psychologically based intervention programs for these youth.

The global impact of war exposure on affective, cognitive, and social development points to the need for multifaceted prevention and remediation efforts. We found a predominance of internalized responses to war stress, such as depression, somatic complaints, and isolation, signs that are harder to identify than externalized reactions, such as aggressive behavior. Public education of all social agents dealing with these children in terms of war stress reactions in youth, such as health professionals, teachers, family, or family substitutes, would be helpful in increasing early detection of difficulties and quicker response.

The evidence found for sociodemographic moderators of war trauma indicates that interventions should be multifaceted and multidisciplinary, including several community agents in social, educational, cultural, and psychologically based programs. Second, interventions should target "high risk" groups, such as those specified above. Third, the integration of psychologically based interventions in the Angolan community with the cultural and tribal based healing practices is essential for their success.

The Corridor Project in Sarajevo and the Mobile Trauma Teams in Angola are community-based initiatives that offer good models for intervention with these youth. In Angola, the example of CCF and UNICEF in addressing the psychosocial needs of children, not just their physical needs, must be followed by other social agencies. This implies the need to integrate psychological training in the preparation of the volunteers in these organizations, so that they may be able to do basic clinical and developmental screening as well as appropriate referral.

NOTE

A very brief summary of this project was published in the *Psychology International,* 7(1) and 9(2).

REFERENCES

American Psychiatric Association (1994). *Diagnostic and statistical manual of mental disorders* (4th ed.). Washington, DC: Author.

Bloch, E. (1993). Psychologists in Croatia work to ease trauma among young war victims. *Psychology International, 4*(3), 1–7.

Brown, D., & Fromm, E. (1987). *Hypnosis and hypnotherapy.* Hillsdale, NJ: Lawrence Erlbaum.

Fraser, M. (1973). *Children in conflict.* London: Secker & Warburg.

Freud, A., & Burlingham, D. (1943). *War and children.* New York: Medical War Books.

Garmezy, N. (1991). Resilience and vulnerability to adverse developmental outcomes associated with poverty. *American Behavioral Scientist, 34*(4), 416–430.

Greca, A. (2000). Posttraumatic stress disorder in children. In G. Fink (Ed.), *Encyclopedia of stress* (Vol. 3, pp. 181–186). San Diego, CA: Academic Press.

Laor, N., Wolmer, L., Mayes, L., Golomb, A., Silverberg, D., Weizman, R., & Cohen, D. (1996). Israeli pre-schoolers under SCUD missile attacks. *Archives of General Psychiatry, 53,* 416–423.

Loughrey, G., Bell, P., Kee, M., Ruddy, R., & Curran, P. (1988). Post-traumatic stress disorder and civil violence in Northern Ireland. *British Journal of Psychiatry, 153,* 554–560.

McIntyre, T., & Ventura, M. (1996). Escala de Avaliação da Resposta ao Acontecimento Traumático: Versão Adolescente [PTSD Scale for Adolescents]. In L. Almeida et al. (Eds.), *Avaliação psicológica: Formas e contextos* [Psychological assessment: Forms and contexts] (pp. 567–576). Braga, Portugal: APPORT.

Milgram, R., & Milgram, N. (1976). The effect of the Yom Kippur war on anxiety level in Israeli children. *Journal of Psychology, 94,* 107–113.

Pynoos, R. (1990). Post-traumatic stress disorder in children and adolescents. In B. Garfinkel, G. Carlson, & E. Weller (Eds.), *Psychiatric disorders in children and adolescents* (pp. 48–63). Philadelphia: W.B. Saunders.

Pynoos, R., & Eth, S. (1985). Developmental perspective on psychic trauma in childhood. In C. Figley (Ed.), *Trauma and its wake: The study and treatment of post-traumatic stress disorder* (pp. 36–52). New York: Brunner/Mazel.

Rak, C., & Patterson, L. (1996). Promoting resilience in at-risk children. *Journal of Counseling & Development, 74,* 368–373.

Rutter, M. (1985). Resilience in the face of adversity: Protective factors and resistance to psychiatric disorders. *British Journal of Psychiatry, 147,* 598–611.

Scheepers, H. (1995). *Projecto piloto Kuito sobre actividades de trauma* [Pilot project Kuito on trauma activities]. Luanda, Angola: UNICEF.

United Nations (1996). *Impact of armed conflict on children: Report of the expert of the secretary general of the United Nations Ms. Graça Machel.* New York: United Nations Publications.

United Nations Development Program. (1992). *Inquérito socio-económico* [Socio-economic survey] (Gabinete de Planificação Regional). Lubango, Angola: Author.

Williams, C., & Berry, J. (1991). Primary prevention of acculturative stress among refugees. *American Psychologist, 46*(6), 632–641.

4

War on the Internal Self: Memory, Human Rights, and the Unification of Germany

Benina B. Gould

Tomorrow is that which shall be yesterday.

Gunter Grass (1981, p. 3)

It was late afternoon and I sat quietly reading a paper about the propaganda that permeated the German culture during the time of Adolf Hitler (Murray, 1998). The article allowed me to open up to the possibility that had I been an adult in Germany in 1940, I could have been one who joined the Nazi party, or I could have been exterminated. I reflected on the extermination of the Jews. Rather than see the extermination as an exception to our history, my imagination gave way to scenes from the movies about war and violence. I was dealing with the duplicity of war in our imaginations as well as the reality of World War II.

What had become ordinary in my memory finally hit me. The "wall in my head" came down. What had been a form of melancholy, became recognition of the fragility of humanity. I was caught up in the pseudoexcitement that could turn me from being an ordinary person to a willing executioner (Goldhagen, 1996). With a recognition of our potential to be peaceful human beings, as well as malicious ones, I found a renewed strength to invest in finding ways to combat our flaws, to change "modern man's savage treatment of himself ... and the ubiquitous human tendency toward evil" (Treat, 1995, p. 206).

MEMORY AS A CHANGE AGENT

Edmunds says we "resist the work of mourning to the extent that it may require us to acknowledge painful or embarrassing parts of ourselves or those we loved" (1996, p. 83). The "obligation to remember" means imagining oneself to be an active part of Holocaust history, and what Mitscherlich and Mitscherlich

(1980) called the "inability to mourn" resulted from my inability to confront my evil side. At times I dissociated from the process, but when I became an active participant in my imagination, I was able to successfully move to a place of reconciliation. Like Nikita Khrushchev, who exposed Stalin's crimes, I exposed my own hatred. It was in this area of seeing my own obedience to authority, which I detested in others, that I made my most important self-discovery. The extraordinary could become ordinary, and that was the crime of the Holocaust. The war in my self had ended.

It was a sense of humanity, that we are one, that remained. Tears welled up and the words that came to my mouth were ancient ones: *Yitgadal, v'yitkadash, sh'ma* ... "Please God be stronger"[1] (Lew, 1999, p. 180).

During World War II, the importance of each human being was implicitly threatened by a planned program that developed from expressed and historical hatred of Jews in the 1930s and ended with the attempted extermination of all the Jews in the late 1930s and 1940s. For me, a deep process of self-examination and reliving the history of the Holocaust was necessary in order to understand the complexities of a divided and unified Germany.

This chapter is about how healing in Germany, after unification, is taking place on the national and personal level. Both are important, and one without the other is superficial and shallow. While it was necessary to come to a place that expressed my own despair and renewal in order for me to begin to understand what healing from the traumas of the past entailed, it has also been humbling to realize that those still living in Germany face a far greater challenge.

DIVISION OF GERMANY

In 1949 Germany was divided into East Germany, the German Democratic Republic (GDR), and West Germany, the Federal Republic of Germany (FRG). The country was occupied in the East by the Soviets and in the West by the British, French, and Americans. The USSR envisioned East Germany as a stronghold of communism, while the United States and its allies occupied West Germany as an opportunity for capitalism.

In August 1961, the Berlin Wall was erected to stop the flow of East Germans to the West and to further separate the two Germanys. "The shock of The Wall lay in the sudden elimination of the element of choice. . . . People in both East and West felt powerless and helpless" (Heon-Klin, Sieber, Huebner, & Fullilove, 2000, p. 371). Vulnerability and insecurity were increased by the abrupt separation from family on the other side. People in East Germany were deemed "communists" and those in West Germany, "capitalists."

There is an issue paramount to the unification of Germany that we have dealt with only in passing. It concerns the human rights issue pertaining to the building of the Wall and how universal human rights laws and issues prior to 1961 were applied or not applied. It is important to see the human rights of the German people during the 50 years of division into East and West Germany as a separate issue. German history took a distinctive course that set it off from the history of other European nations and that carried within it the seeds of the calamitous events of 1933–1945.

The building of the Wall marked a redefinition of human rights and abuses. Although these issues had been ongoing since the end of World War II in the name of de-Nazification (Neyer, 1998, pp. 67–72), little attention has been paid to crimes inflicted on the German people by the building of the Wall.

Human rights abuses have always interfered with freedom for the German people. In Geneva, Switzerland, in 1962, the International Commission of Jurists, in response to the "closing of the door of freedom" published a report about the Wall. It stated in part that:

The Wall in Berlin is unique because its object was to prevent the men and women behind it from reaching freedom. . . . In building The Wall the GDR regime has publicly given visible and tangible proof of its incapacity to provide for its subjects that minimum degree of freedom, justice and welfare which represents the difference between a State and a concentration camp. (International Commission of Jurists, 1962, p. 11)

The Universal Declaration of Human Rights, which was adopted by the General Assembly of the United Nations in 1948, states this right unequivocally: Everyone has the right to leave any country, including his or her own.

Between 1941 and 1945, several attempts were made by ordinary citizens to rescue thousands of Jewish people during the Holocaust. Studies show that

those who refused to obey the orders of authorities, and came to the aid of persecuted people, were neither saints nor heroes. Rather their goodness was that of ordinary men and women who were responsive to the victim's manifest need for help. The way they acted was part of their everyday life, and they did not perceive it as something extraordinary. (Rochat & Modigilani, 1995, p. 3)

Allen Welsh Dulles's (2000) book *Germany's Underground* tells the story of the group of anti-Nazi Germans who in 1944 tried to assassinate Hitler. In another seminal study, Raul Hilberg (cited by Finkelstein & Birn, 1998) observed that most of the perpetrators of the Nazi Holocaust were "not different in their moral makeup from the rest of the population" (pp. 5–6). His study asks the question, What made the difference in the ordinary people who saved Jews and those who "delighted in their death?" (pp. 5–6).

In 1945 the United States, Great Britain, the USSR, and France appointed judges to the first War Crimes Tribunals in Nuremberg, Germany, to prosecute high-level Nazi officials who had been captured after the war. This process represented an unprecedented effort to punish people accused of war crimes and crimes against humanity. The concepts of collective guilt and conspiracy were used to justify punishment. At the same time, trials were taking place in Tokyo to

prosecute Japanese officials who had overseen that nation's military aggression throughout Asia in World War II. . . . The Nuremberg and Tokyo trials are considered revolutionary because they were the first organized attempt to apply principles of inter-national law. (Facts on File, 1997, pp. 1–2)

The Universal Declaration of Human Rights gave hope to the oppressed and "offered a legislative basis . . . to transform the notion of citizens' rights into pos-itive law" (Lindgren Alves, 2000, p. 478). Since that time a major issue regard-ing the Holocaust is whether a successor government must prosecute the human rights abuses of a prior regime. A German-European Humanist Federation was established in 1993 and joined the worldwide International Humanist and Eth-ical Union, founded in 1952, which "is committed to the view that human beings are responsible for their own self-determination without need of super-natural support" (Kurtz, 1993, p. 4).

Although human rights groups, peace activities, and transcultural laws are often invisible, they are at the apex of war and humanity. Groups such as the German chapter of Amnesty International, founded in 1961, and the German Green Party act as the voice of millions who fight against crimes of humanity and represent universal decency and law. In 1983 Petra Kelly, one of Germany's most prominent activists, tried to bring human rights and peace issues together. She proposed that the Green Party "organize an international hearing on the legality of first-strike weapons of mass destruction" (Parkin, 1994, p. 123).

From 1974 to 1994, various "truth and reconciliation commissions" con-fronted the state crimes of the past in many countries. "To the extent that offi-cial truth is a step towards a full and inclusive national memory which allows the voices of the victims and survivors to be heard, it is a crucial step in transi-tional process" (Hayner, 1998, p. 33). On December 31, 2000, the United States signed an international treaty to create a permanent International Criminal Court to try charges of genocide, war crimes, and other crimes against human-ity (also known as the Rome Statute).

At the same time as these deliberations were taking place, some East Ger-mans were

creating a dynamic civic movement as part of a broader struggle for socialist renewal in the GDR. This civic movement had three main roots: a church supported peace move-ment, a secular human rights movement, and an environmental movement. . . . While these new organizations represented a broad range of political philosophies and strate-gies, most activists shared a similar goal: the creation of a vibrant civil society. (Hart-Landsberg, 1995, pp. 60–61)

UNIFICATION

Economic failure, the escape of thousands of East Germans to West Germany, and Mikhail Gorbachev's lack of support for the GDR were just a few reasons the Berlin Wall came down on November 9, 1989. "Following the mass protests of the GDR 'peaceful revolution' in the last months of 1989, the peaceful revo-lution moved almost seamlessly into the process of German unification, culmi-nating in the Unification Treaty of October 3, 1990" (Hogwood, 2000, p. 45).

German unification meant that two states, with different economic and political systems, were suddenly a single state.

The difficulties imposed by unification, as well as the challenges, have been problematic for the East German people. They have been expected not only to give up all vestiges of communism, but also to embrace West Germany and capitalism. This unique transition has had many political ramifications, but in relation to memory it has also imposed another problem, that of nostalgia for the East Germany of the past, or *Ostalgia*. There has never been a full healing or recovery for the East Germans, and this has resulted in an undefined national identity. There is no doubt "that the social and economic community of the GDR suffered a sudden and traumatic disjuncture with their past lives, one with which many are still struggling to come to terms" (Hogwood, 2000, pp. 45–47).

There was other negative fallout of unification, such as the rise of neo-Nazism in East Germany and unemployment for women, with the loss of state-run daycare and employment opportunities. The East Germans had gained freedom but lost equality.

It is important to not overidealize the utopian alternative West Germany. East Germany is not exempt from its own history of the Holocaust, although its explicitly anti-Fascist regime was thought to take care of this past genocidal act. East Germans were instead besieged by the technology of communism, which included espionage, interrogation, and surveillance at an alarming rate.

Ralph Giordano (1987), a writer of Jewish origin and a survivor of the Nazi era, is concerned about the failure to mourn the past. He worries about the younger generation in Germany and defines this group as suffering from a "second guilt," the suppression and denial of the Nazi era. Psychologists Alexander and Margarete Mitscherlich (1980) define this unmitigated trauma as "the inability to mourn," characterized by defensive attitudes toward the deeds of the Third Reich.

Knowing the history of Germany prior to World War II and after is imperative to understanding the transition for the people during and after unification, as the context of history can never be separated from the fate of the individual. East and West Germans because of their "lack of choice" when the Wall was built are fighting for choice in how the new Federal Republic is defined. The ideal resolution of this issue would be for an acknowledgement of history to contribute to German identity individually and collectively. "For many there is a societal lag in that eastern Germans perceive that they have been left behind and on the margins of directed democratization.... They identify neither with the past nor present cultures and identities" (Yoder, 1999, p. 153).

Understanding the past in terms of social behavior and health requires knowledge of German psychology, philosophy, and political theory as well as contemporary methods of dealing with trauma and post-traumatic syndrome. I maintain that it is necessary for East Germans to recover from the Nazi and Stalinist eras, the "lack of choice" regarding the forced imprisonment by the Berlin Wall, and from the stress of unification.

For West Germans, healing from their Nazi past is also imperative for national identity and individual autonomy. On the macrolevel, as a country, and on the microlevel, as individuals in German society, there is a challenge of finding a new identity during the transition. The nostalgia that has set in for the East Germans has resulted in an oversimplification and overidealization of the past and, in some cases, a xenophobia by youth groups expressed in neo-Nazi terms. These xenophobic youth have nothing to fill the void of the oppressive Communist party that dominated East Germany for 50 years. Although it may be too soon to tell if unification will work, there are signs of insecurity as well as attempts to overcome the past by designing political parties and policies that are nonviolent and open to all people.

To heal the guilt from World War II, some Germans participate in human rights movements, while others oppose nuclear weapons in Germany. Some question the continuous emphasis on the past and consider it a problem that people speak always of the past, rather than speak little of it. For those most traumatized, knowing what to do with this "original societal sin" is of paramount importance. "Virtually everyone ... is struggling with the past; it is the monopoly of neither Gentile nor Jew ... and for everyone this struggle means coming to terms with an inherited past—one created by others." The real dilemma is "in knowing how to handle acceptance of responsibility and living with such an unimaginably grotesque national past" (Freudenheim, 2001, pp. 146–147).

Another issue underlying the unification of Germany is the fear implicitly expressed by the United States, France, and Britain that the unification of Germany could be a threat. A unified Germany would be a major threat to the United States if it entered the arms race. Many believe that the most productive way to assist in the transformation of U.S.-German relations is to encourage Germany's active membership in multinational organizations. Russian-German relations will also be a key factor in determining the new Germany's worldview. Ultimately, "the way Germans view their new world role will depend on how they come to terms with their past" (Gould, 2000).

Working Through Unification Stress

Whereas World War II left a legacy of the necessity to deal with one's memory of the past, as well as with its crimes and brutalities, the building of the Berlin Wall reactivated the importance of human rights for those behind the Wall. German unification has forced the country to deal with unification stress and the psychological as well as political issues of people with different ideologies living together again after 50 years.

National identity and individual autonomy must go hand in hand. In the case of Germans too young to remember the war, renewal will occur when they learn about their family's involvement in war. For some, admitting the guilt of their parents' generation allows them to develop their own relationship to that guilt.

The idea that one can work through the traumas of the past is implicit in trauma psychology. Laub and Auerhahn (1993) propose that different forms of knowing can be organized along a continuum according to their distance from the trauma and level of

integration and ownership of memory. . . . The different forms of remembering trauma range from: not knowing; fugue states (in which events are re-lived in an altered state of consciousness); retention of the experience as compartmentalized, undigested fragments of perceptions that break into consciousness (with no conscious meaning or relation to oneself); transference phenomena (wherein the traumatic legacy is lived out as one's inevitable fate); its partial, hesitant expression as an overpowering narrative; the experience of compelling, identity-defining and pervasive life themes (both conscious and unconscious); its organization as a witnessed narrative; to its use as a metaphor and vehicle for developmental conflict. (p. 289)

An alternative psychology would be for individuals to work through their own trauma at the same time their society is working through its traumatic past. This dual approach to trauma is most appropriate for societies in transition, such as Germany, the former Soviet Union, and the former Yugoslavia.[2]

For the individual to recover internally from the past it is first necessary to go through psychological stages of trauma. It is also necessary for the individual to go through a process of self-reflection and self-discovery.[3] Self-examination can be private, as a part of therapy, in a group situation, or can take the form of testimonial witnessing. Testimonial witnessing is the most frequent form of narrative that survivors of the Holocaust use to tell their story. This "takes place in a belated manner, often after the passage of many years and provides insight into lived experience and its transmission in language and gesture" (La Capra, 1998, p. 11).

The listener becomes a secondary observer and must work out his or her relationship to the witness and the testimony. For many of us who are the children of Jewish families or of Holocaust survivors, this has been our best opportunity for "bearing witness." Without these testimonies, survivors[4] would not finish their grieving and the "task of mourning is passed on to the next generation to be brought closer to completion" (Lawton, 2001, p. 359). In many ways, we are all children of survivors and have been affected by the tragedies of the past and present. No one has been exempt from questions about civilization and war. This is what is meant by "collective memory."[5]

Education is another powerful tool for learning about the past and the lessons it has left for us. A very important example of this is the Berlin Jewish Free School founded in 1978, based on the conviction that education teaches tolerance. The founder of the school, Frau Buhau, the daughter of an SS officer, identified with Jews because of her struggle for religious freedom. The school helps students and teachers ask the questions: "How do the Jews cope with their history, including their history in this century? . . . and how do Germans cope with their history?" (Rodden, 1997, p. 7).

Many Germans have found that reconciliation is harder than reunification and that the work of reunification still demands "conscious effort under God's watchful gaze" (Yoder, 1994, p. 58). A good example of this is the Declaration of Repentance issued by French bishops in 1997 concerning the silence and passivity of the Catholic Church in the face of the Holocaust (Duchesne, 1998, p. 12). Churches also played a significant role in unification because they were the only public places in the GDR not sanctioned by the state where large groups could congregate. Pastors used the pulpit to call for the government to obey basic political and civil rights. Some churches were turned into sanctuaries for conscientious objectors and other political dissidents.

Almost all creative forms of expression have been employed to help people express their emotions about the Holocaust. For many, writing serves as an entry point in their search for national identity. Holocaust survivor Primo Levi was a renowned writer who seemed to have "achieved some permanent artistic control over his experience. Unfortunately, he could not escape through an act of mind, [a mind] that could record the worst of human experience and contain its language" (in Rosenfeld, 1995, pp. 124–126). When he finally expressed his rage, he committed suicide.

For others, taking part in the building of museums or statues has been their route for recovery. Commemorative memorials have been very controversial. The fight over symbols and commemorative events in Germany poses yet another source of confusion about how to represent the past in terms of the postcommunist world. As we fight to provide closure to World War II with our creative efforts, new doors for controversy and disorder are opened.

CONCLUSION

Unification in November 1989 marked the end of the division of the two Germanys. However, for many the "wall in the head" still stands. The psychological division between so-called *Ossis* (East Germans) and *Wessis* (West Germans) did not arise overnight. It was constructed during a mutually antagonistic occupation era (1945–1949) in which the United States and the USSR dominated German affairs. It was solidified across a cold war lasting more than four decades, and the psychological wall continues to be fortified by economic disparities (Rodden, 2000, p. 12).

Nazism has left a complicated legacy because it is a crisis of humanity, one that questions the

annihilator force of modern violence . . . and casts doubt on the very definition of identity, on what it means to know who you are, where you come from, what you are capable or incapable of doing, experiencing or imagining. . . . It is a collective crisis for those of us aware of our responsibility for humanity. (Bartov, 2000, p. 228)

Whether we are survivors, deniers, relativists, or people bearing witness, we all need to sort our past. The end result may be uncertainty, questioning, and disorder. Christa Wolf states, "contradiction must not only be tolerated in the

GDR in the future, but made productive, used as a learning tool to investigate and solve problems which are still denied on a public level" (1993, p. 289).

Hopefully, by looking into a mirror of "decency," whether it be through political action, self-examination, or creative expression, the individual will reflect back the necessity to act with pride in a recovering nation, pride that implicitly demands that "it never happens again." "Since we are incapable of changing the past, we have to use the lessons of the past to improve the future. We have no alternative but to remember" (Edwards, 1994, p. 12). We must talk German again.[6]

NOTES

1. According to Rabbi Allen Lew, one *midrash*, a Jewish legend, explains that whenever anyone dies, God is diminished, so when you say *Yitgadal* you magnify the words working to address this loss and to enhance God.

2. Healing internally is emphasized by psychologists and psychoanalysts in Germany. Other agendas, such as the "leaver's" program in Germany, in which neo-Nazis who want to leave the party are given financial incentives, are hotly debated. Recently, Germany announced a program to compensate foreigners who had been attacked by Nazi youth.

3. An important part of the process I have described is the necessity of finding that part of ourselves in which we can imagine being the perpetrator as well as the victim. The process I am describing comes closest to Laub and Auerhahn's type of knowing called "witnessed narratives." They state that there is a

> seventh form of traumatic memory that involves witnessing, in which the observing ego remains present as a witness. On this level knowing takes the form of true memory. When the individual narrates on this level, there is a distance, a perspective retained by the observing ego. The ego is present and understands itself to be continuous with the remembered subject, but currently at a different stage. The memory is vivid, but not immediate. (p. 297)

In contrast, Primo Levi (1986) sees no way out of the memory of trauma through self-reflection and self-discovery. He states that

> when an offense has been inflicted, there is no healing. It protracts itself endlessly, and the Furies, in whom we cannot help but believe, not only afflict the tormentor ... but perpetuate his work, by denying peace to the tormented. (p. 131)

4. As Norris (2000) stated,

> In some cases, survivors couldn't tolerate more than a few hours of discussion. In other cases, they returned several times.... Some are introspective and revelatory. Others preferred discussing events rather than feelings.... Some didn't want to be found. Others ... didn't mind being found, but didn't want to go public.... A few have written or want to write their own books. Some didn't want to be interviewed because they couldn't tolerate "the stress." (p. 141)

5. Stanley Rosenman (2001), in a review of Vamik Volkan's book *Bloodlines*, states that Volkan employs the term "'chosen trauma' to signify the collective memory of a calamitous shared loss that has not been grieved. Rather it is recalled with mortification and rage as searing as if the misfortune were yesterday, rather than" a long time in the past.

6. The expression "to talk German" is equivalent to the phrase "to speak in plain English" with regard to German racism.

REFERENCES

Bartov, O. (2000). *Mirrors of destruction: War, genocide and modern identity.* New York: Oxford University Press.

Duchesne, J. (1998). Letter from Paris. *First Things: A Monthly Journal of Religion and Public Life, 80,* 12–15.

Dulles, A. W. (2000). *Germany's underground.* New York: De Capo Press.

Edmunds, K. R. (Spring, 1996). Ich bin gebildet genug ... um zu lieben trauern [An attempt to combine the discourse of melancholy and the discourse of mourning]: Wilhelm Meister's apprenticeship in mourning. *Germanic Review, 71,* 83-101.

Edwards, R. (1994). Do mention the war. *New Statesman & Society, 7,* 12–14.

Facts on File. (1997). War crimes tribunals: An in-depth analysis. Available: http://www.facts.com/icof/nazi.htm.

Finkelstein, N., & Birn, R. B. (1998). *A nation on trial: The Goldhagen thesis and historical truth.* New York: Metropolitan Books.

Freudenheim, T. (2001). Confronting memory and museums. In T. Herzog & S. Gilman (Eds.), *A new Germany in a new Europe* (pp. 143–165). New York: Routledge.

Giordano, R. (1987). *Die zweite schuld* [The second blame]. Hamburg: Rasch und Rohring.

Goldhagen, D. J. (1996). *Hitler's willing executioners: Ordinary Germans and the Holocaust.* New York: Alfred A. Knopf.

Gould, B. (2000). Living in the question: The Berlin nuclear crisis critical oral history project. Manuscript submitted for publication.

Grass, G. (1981). *The meeting at Telgate* (R. Manheim, Trans.). San Diego, CA: Harvest/Harcourt.

Hart-Landsberg, M. (1995). Korean unification: Learning from the German experience. *Journal of Contemporary Asia, 26,* 59–80.

Hayner, P. (1998). Truth commissions: Exhuming the past. *NACLA Report on the Americas, 21,* 30–33.

Heon-Klin, V., Sieber, E., Huebner, J., & Fullilove, M. (2000). The influence of geopolitical change on the well-being of a population: The Berlin Wall. *American Journal of Public Health, 91,* 369–374.

Hogwood, P. (2000). After the GDR: Reconstructing identity in post-communist Germany. *The Journal of Communist Studies and Transition Politics, 6,* 45–67.

International Commission of Jurists. (1962). *The Berlin Wall: A defiance of human rights* (pp. 1–54). Geneva, Switzerland: Author.

Kurtz, P. (1993, Fall). Letter from Berlin. *Free Inquiry, 13,* 4–5.

La Capra, D. (1998). *History and memory after Auschwitz.* Ithaca, NY: Cornell University Press.

Laub, D., & Auerhahn, N. C. (1993). Knowing and not knowing. Massive psychic trauma: Forms of traumatic memory. *Journal of Psychoanalysis, 74,* 287–302.

Lawton, H. (2001). [Review of the book *Witnessing psychoanalysis: From Vienna back to Vienna via Buchenwald and the USA*]. *Journal of Psychohistory, 28,* 359–361.

Levi, P. (1986). The memory of offense. In G. Hartman (Ed.), *Bitburg in moral and political perspective* (pp. 131–137). Bloomington: Indiana University Press.

Lew, A. (1999). *One God clapping: The spiritual path of a Zen rabbi.* New York: Kodansha International.

Lindgren Alves, J. A. (2000). The declaration of human rights in postmodernity. *Human Rights Quarterly, 22,* 478–500.

Mitscherlich, A., & Mitscherlich, M. (1980). *Die unfahigkeit zu trauern* [The inability to mourn]. Munich: R. Piper.

Murray, J. W. (1998). Constructing the ordinary. The dialectical development of Nazi ideology. *Communication Quarterly, 46,* 41–60.

Neyer, A. (1998). *War crimes: Brutality, genocide terror, and the struggle for justice.* New York: Random House.

Norris, M. (2000). *Writing war in the twenty-first century.* Charlottesville: University Press of Virginia.

Parkin, S. (1994). *The life and death of Petra Kelly.* New York: Pandora.

Rochat, F., & Modigilani, A. (1995). The ordinary quality of resistance: From Milgram's laboratory to the village of Le Chambon. *Journal of Social Issues, 51,* 195–211.

Rodden, J. (2000, September 22). The Berlin Wall lives. *Commonweal, 127,* 11–12.

Rodden, J. G. (1997). Bridge over broken glass? Crisscrossing history in Germany's sole Jewish high school. *Midwest Quarterly* [On-line series], *1*(39). Available: http://128.48.120.7/mwcgi?sesid = 300520.

Rosenfeld, A. H. (1995). Primo Levi: The survivor as victim. In J. S. Pacy & A. P. Wertheimer (Eds.), *Perspectives on the Holocaust: Essays in honor of Raul Hilberg* (pp. 125–141). San Francisco: Westview Press.

Rosenman, S. (2001). [Review of the book *Bloodlines: From ethnic pride to ethnic terrorism*]. *Journal of Psychohistory, 28,* 354.

Treat, J. W. (1995). *Writing degree zero.* Chicago: University of Chicago Press.

Wolf, C. (1993). *The author's dimension: Selected essays.* Chicago: University of Chicago Press.

Yoder, B. (1994, August 15). One-way street? Germans find reconciliation is harder than reunification. *Christianity Today, 38,* 58.

Yoder, J. A. (1999). *From East Germans to Germans? The new post-communist elites.* Durham, NC: Duke University Press.

5

Assessing Depression Among Survivors of the Rwanda Genocide

Paul Bolton

Progress in improving mental health among trauma-affected populations depends on accurate measurement of the problems being addressed. Without quantitative measurement of mental health indicators there is little basis for allocating resources, for determining whether an intervention has been successful, or for choosing among multiple competing interventions. Most methods of measuring the burden of mental health problems were developed in Western countries. They are based on concepts of mental illness developed among Western populations and defined in the widely used *Diagnostic and Statistical Manual of Mental Disorders (DSM-IV)* of the American Psychiatric Association (1994). There is evidence that at least some of these concepts, such as depression and post-traumatic stress disorder (PTSD), are valid across many cultures; instruments based on them have been adapted for use among many different groups (Abas & Broadhead, 1997; Abdel-Khalek & Soliman, 1999; Carlson & Rosser-Hogan, 1994; Cheung & Bagley, 1998; Howard et al., 1999; Mollica et al., 1992; Pretorius, 1991; Sack, Seeley, & Clarke, 1997). Nevertheless, in each new culture the validity and reliability of these concepts and their associated instruments must be tested anew: Validity in some cultures does not prove validity in every culture.

The major validity issue is criterion validity. Existing criterion validation methods require highly trained health workers very familiar with the local culture and language. These workers assess persons using alternative methods (usually examination), and validation consists of comparing these findings with those made using the instrument. They are also key to adapting and translating the instrument, using their knowledge of the local language and local perceptions of mental illness. However, highly trained health workers are expensive and in many areas, simply unavailable.

This leaves most criterion validation to field workers incapable of accurate quantitative assessment of the mental health needs of those they assist, and unable to measure the impact of their programs. Faculty at Johns Hopkins University (JHU) developed an alternative method to adapt and validate existing instruments that would not require these highly trained workers. Our aim was to produce a method that can be used among any population and that is appropriate for use by nonresearch organizations working in the field. Following theoretical development, JHU faculty approached World Vision (WV), a large nongovernmental organization, to test and further develop this method by field trial. WV agreed to collaborate, and fieldwork was conducted in October–December 1999 among a Rwandan population. This chapter briefly describes the assessment method we developed and the resulting data on mental illness in Rwanda. The aim is to demonstrate to readers that accurate quantitative assessments are possible with few resources, and to suggest an approach that readers can use to achieve them.

BACKGROUND

In 1994, Rwanda endured 100 days of genocide during which extremist ethnic majority Hutus—urged on and organized by the Hutu-dominated government—sought out and killed members of the Tutsi minority and Hutu moderates. By the time the government was overthrown by an invading Tutsi-dominated army and the killing had ceased, between 800,000 and 1 million people had been murdered.

In 1996 WV set up the Psychosocial Support Program (PSSP) to address the perceived psychological aftermath of the genocide. The PSSP employed community-based interventions to improve the capacity of people in the Kigali Rural Prefecture to deal with mental health problems resulting from trauma. This was done by training teachers, community health workers, and special community trauma monitors and counselors to recognize, assist, and refer persons with these problems. Although reactions to this program have been positive, WV staff recognized that they lacked a means of scientifically assessing the program's impact. In both progress reports and the formal evaluation, staff and evaluators were limited to assessing outputs and relying on anecdotal reports. WV staff was therefore interested in the suggestion by JHU faculty to develop methods of objective measurement of need and impact.

METHOD

The method we tested in Rwanda is designed for use with various mental health indicators. For this first trial we chose to study depression as just one indicator of the effects of mental trauma, and to study only adults. We assessed depression using a version of the well-known Hopkins Symptom Checklist (HSCL; Derogatis, Lipman, Rickels, Uhlenhuth, & Covi, 1974), which has been used among many populations (see Appendix 5.1). We chose depression because there is agreement on its basic form, it (along with PTSD) represents those most severely affected by trauma, and it has been studied in a variety of situations and cultures. We chose it over PTSD because PTSD has been studied in relation to trauma in other populations, but depression rarely has. Also, depression occurs in situations other than trauma, so the findings have implications beyond trauma-affected populations.

Controversy exists about the use of these and other Western clinical mental health indicators in non-Western cultures (Summerfield, 1997, 1998). This is partly due to the failure of workers using these indicators to adequately validate them prior to use, thereby leaving the question of their appropriateness unanswered. Therefore, a vital component of this method is preliminary investigation of the local validity of these indicators.

The assessment method has the following six main stages:

1. Collecting ethnographic data on local perceptions of mental health.
2. Analyzing these data for evidence that Western indicators of mental problems are appropriate.
3. If so, using these data to adapt and translate existing questionnaires that measure these indicators.
4. Testing the validity of these questionnaires and indicators.
5. Using the resulting validated instrument in a community-based survey.
6. Analyzing the survey data to assess the local prevalence and characteristics of the selected mental health indicators and further test the validity and reliability of the instruments and indicators.

Ethnographic Study (Stages 1, 2, and 3)

The purpose of the ethnographic study was to determine if local people experienced depression as a result of trauma, and to learn the names and symptoms of comparable depression-like illnesses. If local people experience all or most of the symptoms of depression, this would be evidence that depression occurs among this population. Knowledge about how local people perceive depression would enable staff to work with them to adapt and validate existing depression instruments (in this case the HSCL) for local use. JHU faculty trained PSSP staff in three ethnographic methods—free listing, key informant interviewing, and pile sorts—that they then used to conduct the study (Bernard, 1988; Spradley, 1979).

As a first step, interviewers generated free lists by asking 40 local people to name all the problems that had resulted from the genocide and to briefly describe each one. The words used by respondents were then recorded as a list of problems with descriptions. Whenever informants described a problem that could be related to mental health, interviewers also asked them who in the community was knowledgeable about the problem. Combining all the lists produced a single list of the names and descriptions of the important local mental health problems as perceived by local people, and their relative importance (in terms of frequency mentioned) compared with other problems. This composite list is given in Table 5.1. From this list we identified depression-like symptoms for detailed investigation using key informant interviews, the next step in the ethnographic study.

Key informant interviews are more in-depth than free lists. The emphasis is on obtaining as much information as possible about selected topics. Key informants are those known to be particularly knowledgeable about the topic in question. In Rwanda, the key informants were seven local persons identified by the free list respondents and other local people as being knowledgeable about mental health issues. They were traditional healers and local leaders. Interviewers began the first interview by describing a hypothetical person with many of the depression symptoms that had emerged in the free lists. The respondent was then asked to describe all the illnesses or problems that this person could have. As in the free lists, the respondent's comments were recorded. Key informants were interviewed twice on successive days, in case they recalled im-

Table 5.1
Results of Free Lists on Major Problems Resulting from the Genocide in 1994*

Problem	Ranking	# of responses that include this problem
Poverty	1	41
Lack of food	2	40
Lack of people (from any cause)	3	25
Suspicion/mistrust with breakdown of neighborly relations	4	23
Too many widows and orphans	5	20
Lack of possessions—land, housing, shelter	5	20
Illness (physical)	7	15
Mental trauma (*Guhahamuka*)	8	14
Lack of motivation/hope	8	14
Lack of justice	8	14
Too many people in prison causing a shortage and those outside must care for them	11	13
Lack of schools	12	11
Physical disability	13	7
Grief (*Agahinda*)	13	7
Ignorance	13	7
Government program to resettle villagers	16	5
Drunkenness	16	5
Unwillingness to change	18	4

*Problems stated by a single person only are not included.

portant information after the first interview. The data from these interviews and the free lists were then reviewed to identify mental health symptoms and how local people organize them into syndromes. A summary of the major illnesses and symptoms is given in Figure 5.1. All these syndromes were said by key informants to commonly occur in the same person.

Review of the data in Figure 5.1 reveals that virtually all of the major DSM criteria for both depression and PTSD are recognized to be part of local mental syndromes. These syndromes are not identical to depression and PTSD (both depression and PTSD symptoms are included under *guhahamuka*), but this is not surprising given their high comorbidity. We considered this to be sufficient evidence that these illnesses occur locally as a result of trauma.

Review of Figure 5.1 also reveals local symptoms not part of the DSM criteria. We used pile sorts to determine if these symptoms might comprise important local symptoms of depression-like illness, or were merely unrepresentative opinions. We created a set of 14 cards for each interviewer. On 11 of the cards was a picture and name of one of the local symptoms not part of the DSM criteria; 2 other cards each referred to one of the local syndromes and 1 other card referred to the depression symptom of "not being pleased by anything." (The symptoms and syndromes used in the pile sorts are marked by an asterisk in Figure 5.1). Interviewers asked 40 local people to sort the cards into as many piles as they liked on whatever basis they liked, as long as they did not produce 1 pile or 14 piles. Interviewers then counted how many times each card was in the same pile as every other card. These numbers were then collapsed into a composite list of the number of times each possible pair of cards was put together by all respondents. This list confirmed that three local symptoms were often paired with the local syndromes and the depression symptom and were therefore likely to be important local features of depression. These three symptoms were "lack of trust in others," "loss of intelligence," and "mental instability." Questions on these symptoms were added to the HSCL to produce a questionnaire better adapted to the local situation (see Appendix 5.1).

After adaptation of the HSCL we added questions on basic demographic data and on whether the respondent felt they had *agahinda* (more properly, *agahinda gakabije*). The instrument was then translated from English to Kinyarwanda using a combination of group and translation-backtranslation methods. During the translation we constantly cross-checked the results against the ethnographic data to ensure that the translators used terms that were truly part of the local vocabulary, as word usage frequently varies across regions and socioeconomic groups.

Validity Study (Stage 4)

This was a ministudy conducted prior to the main survey to test the criterion validity of the instrument. The first step was to identify the local syndrome most similar to depression. We chose *agahinda* because *akababaro* was too limited

Figure 5.1
Local Depression-like Syndromes and Their Symptoms

Term: *Guhahamuka*
    Symptoms:
        failure to sleep
        despair, hopelessness
        anger
        failure to eat
        failure to talk
        loss of intelligence*
        attempting suicide
        confusion about issues/different things*
        acting like a crazy person*
        mixed feelings and thoughts in your head at the same time
        feeling extremely weak
        increased startle reaction
        absentmindedness
        too many thoughts
        worthlessness
        feeling as if you would be better off dead
        lack of concentration
        feel like you have a "cloud" within yourself (a vague painful
            constant presence internally)*
        feeling disconnected from others and the world
        falling sick every now and then
        to keep dreaming of the events you went through
        fleeing away from people and hiding*
        lack of trust*
        feeling like fighting*
        making a lot of noise
        being quarrelsome
        being rebellious
        excessive crying (by women and children)
        talking to anybody who comes your way about your pain*
        being violent
        occasional chaos in the mind (can be a flashback)
        mental instability*
        feeling like you are having an epileptic episode (collapse)
        acting without thinking*
        having a nightmare about being in a fight
        deep sadness that can result in death
Term: *Akababaro**
    Symptoms:
        to be extremely quiet
        not pleased by anything*
        feeling very weak
        dying with (not from) sadness

(Cont'd)

Figure 5.1 (*continued*)
Local Depression-like Syndromes and Their Symptoms

Term: *Agahinda**
    Symptoms:
           isolation
           lack of self-care
           loss of mind
           being very talkative*
           not working
           drunkenness
           feeling life is meaningless
           feeling shattered
           committing suicide
           don't feel like talking
           excessive alcohol drinking causing crazy behavior
           being displeased with your living conditions/situation
           not pleased by anything*
           inability to withstand whatever happens to you
           burying your cheek in your palm
           difficulty in interacting with others (poor relationships)
           sadness

*Symptom included in the subsequent pile sort exercise

and *guhahamuka* also contained many of the symptoms of PTSD and so was not very specific. Although *agahinda* was the most similar of the three local syndromes, it was described by local people in terms more akin to grief than depression. We reasoned that because grief and depression are closely related in Western countries, *agahinda* and depression should share a similar relationship if the following were true:

• *Agahinda* is really similar to grief and is accurately diagnosed by local people.

• Depression occurs in this population and is accurately diagnosed by the instrument.

Key informants were asked to identify local people who had severe *agahinda* and those who did not have *agahinda*. The severe form was requested to increase the likelihood of identifying true cases. Interviewers were then assigned to these persons without knowing their reported illness status. They questioned the respondents using the adapted and translated HSCL and, at the end of the interview, asked if the respondents felt they had *agahinda gakabije*. We threw out interviews in which the respondent and the key informant disagreed on the presence of *agahinda gakabije*, to increase the likelihood that the remaining interviews were accurate diagnoses of this problem. We then looked at the relationship between local diagnosis of *agahinda gakabije* and diagnosis of depression according to the instrument.

Of the 93 interviewees, 70 were said to have *agahinda gakabije* by both the respondent and the key informant. This group included 30 of the 31 respondents diagnosed as depressed by the instrument. On the other hand, only a proportion of those with *agahinda gakabije* developed depression. Hence, the depressed were clearly a subgroup of those with *agahinda*. The relationship between *agahinda* and depression was the same as that between grief and depression in Western countries whereby grief can result in depression, but only in a proportion of cases (Craig, 1996). This supported the contention that depression occurred in the local population and was accurately diagnosed by the instrument.

Survey and Analysis (Stages 5 and 6)

The instrument was then used in a typical random survey of the adult population of Kanzenze commune, an administrative region near Rwanda's capital, Kigali. This was one of the areas of operations for PSSP. It has long been a predominantly Tutsi area and was the site of much killing during the genocide. We selected five subdistricts for the survey, based on geographical spread. Within these subdistricts, simple random samples were drawn to select homes for interview. Interviewers then selected an adult at random from each of these homes.

The interviewers came from Kigali because local people with a high school education who could read and write were not available. PSSP staff who had already received training and data-gathering experience in the ethnographic study acted as supervisors. As well as assisting the interviewers, they checked on all refusals and reinterviewed 10 percent of respondents. This provided a quality control measure as well as data to test the instrument's interrater reliability.

To facilitate comparison between first and repeat interviews, we created a single score of depression severity. The HSCL uses a 4-category Likert scale of increasing severity of symptoms. The numbers 1–4 were assigned to each successive category. For each respondent, the numbers corresponding to each response to a depression question were added to give a single summary score of depression severity. On this scale, higher scores represent worsening overall depression symptoms. We then measured the correlation between scores on the first and the repeat interviews.

The survey data were also used to conduct further testing on the instrument. This included assessing internal consistency reliability by means of Cronbach's alpha and Item Analysis. Construct validity was explored by means of a factor analysis using a principal component matrix and varimax rotation.

RESULTS

We interviewed 368 adults. Of these, 17.9 percent met the DSM criteria for depression and 41.8 percent described themselves as having *agahinda gakabije* (severe grief). Studies in other parts of Africa and the world have found prevalences of depression between 0.8 and 5.8 percent (Weissman et al., 1996; Bhagwanjee, Parekh, Paruk, Petersen, & Subedar, 1998). It is likely that the higher rate found in this study is due to the events of 1994.

Cronbach's alpha was .87 for all the depression questions, including the local symptoms. It did not increase significantly with the removal of any question. This suggests that both the original HSCL questions and the local symptoms are indeed part of the local expression of depression illness.

For the 37 respondents who were reinterviewed, the overall correlation between their depression scores on the first and repeat interview was .67, which is adequate for this type of survey. A single factor emerged from the factor analysis that accounted for 32 percent of the total variance (the next most significant factor accounted for only 7 percent). All the depression questions loaded on this factor (correlation of .30 or greater) except for "loss of interest in things" (.27). The questions that loaded most highly were (in decreasing order) "feeling blue," "feeling lonely," "feeling fidgety," "tasks require more effort," "feeling of worthlessness," and the local symptom of "mental instability."

DISCUSSION

In this chapter I have tried to demonstrate that scientifically valid quantitative assessment of mental health issues is possible in the absence of highly trained research and clinical personnel. Since the Rwanda field trial was completed, this assessment approach has been repeated successfully in Uganda and further assessments are planned for West Africa. The resources required to do this type of study are within the scope of most field programs. The only outside resources required are brief training (approximately 1 week total), supervision, and assistance with data analysis and interpretation. These are readily available via short-term consultants. Further advice is available from the author on request.

The major limitation with this approach is that it only provides limited criterion validity, due to the absence of a "gold standard" such as clinical diagnosis or an instrument of known validity. Lacking both of these, we used comparison with diagnoses of a similar local illness by local persons. But we have no data confirming the accuracy of these diagnoses. Therefore, where gold standards are available, these should always be used in preference to this approach.

A second limitation is that the ability to directly compare a diagnosis of local illness with that of a psychiatric illness (such as depression) is dependent on the level of similarity between them. In cultures where there is no easily comparable local syndrome, this type of comparison will be more difficult. In Uganda we identified local syndromes more similar to depression than in Rwanda. The analysis and validity testing were correspondingly much more straightforward. We need to conduct further field trials in other sites to determine how important an issue this is across cultures.

We also need to expand this approach to do the following:

1. To develop and validate instruments that assess other illnesses and aspects of mental health
2. To use these instruments to assess the impact of mental health interventions

At the time of writing, WV is forming plans to use the instruments developed so far to assess program impact in Rwanda and Uganda. Until this type of valid quantitative assessment becomes more commonplace, it is difficult to estimate the real impact of mental health programs. Improving program impact, or choosing between competing and apparently effective programs, is also not possible. Academia has been slow to make these types of assessments or to develop methods that can be used in the field. It is, therefore, up to field workers themselves to assess needs and program impact using whatever resources and methods are available.

Appendix 5.1
Rwanda Mental Health Survey Questionnaire
Depression in Adults (adapted from the Hopkins Symptom Checklist)
I am going to read you a list of problems that people sometimes have. For each one I am going to ask you how much you have experienced each one DURING THE LAST WEEK, including today.

Say each symptom, and after each one ask how much it has bothered the respondent. Repeat the categories after each symptom and let the respondent choose one. Record the response by ticking the appropriate box next to the symptom.

Depression Symptoms	Not at all	A little	Quite a bit	Extremely
B1. Feeling low in energy, slowed down	1	2	3	4
B2. Blaming yourself for things	1	2	3	4
B3. Crying easily	1	2	3	4
B4. Feeling fidgety	1	2	3	4
B5. Poor appetite	1	2	3	4
B6. Difficulty falling asleep or staying asleep	1	2	3	4
B7. Feeling hopeless about the future	1	2	3	4
B8. Feeling blue	1	2	3	4
B9. Feeling lonely	1	2	3	4
B10. Thought of ending your life	1	2	3	4
B11. Feeling of being trapped or caught	1	2	3	4
B12. Worrying too much about things	1	2	3	4
B13. Feeling no interest in things	1	2	3	4
B14. Feeling tasks require more effort	1	2	3	4
B15. Feeling of worthlessness	1	2	3	4
B16. Lack of trust (in others)*	1	2	3	4
B17. Loss of intelligence*	1	2	3	4
B18. Instability of mind*	1	2	3	4
B19. Loss of sexual interest or pleasure	1	2	3	4

*Local symptoms added to original HSCL.

REFERENCES

Abas, M. A., & Broadhead, J. C. (1997). Depression and anxiety among women in an urban setting in Zimbabwe. *Psychological Medicine, 27,* 59–71.

Abdel-Khalek, A. M., & Soliman, H. H. (1999). A cross-cultural evaluation of depression in children in Egypt, Kuwait, and the United States. *Psychological Reports, 85,* 973–980.

American Psychiatric Association (1994). *Diagnostic and statistical manual of mental disorders* (4th ed.). Washington, DC: Author.

Bernard, H. R. (1988). *Research methods in cultural anthropology.* Newbury Park, CA: Sage.

Bhagwanjee, A., Parekh, A., Paruk, Z., Petersen, I., & Subedar, H. (1998). Prevalence of minor psychiatric disorders in an adult African rural community in South Africa. *Psychological Medicine, 28,* 1137–1147.

Carlson, E. B., & Rosser-Hogan, R. (1994). Cross-cultural response to trauma: A study of traumatic experiences and posttraumatic symptoms in Cambodian refugees. *Journal of Traumatic Stress, 7,* 43–58.

Cheung, C. K., & Bagley, C. (1998). Validating an American scale in Hong Kong: The Center for Epidemiological Studies Depression Scale (CES-D). *Journal of Psychology, 132,* 169–186.

Craig, T. K. J. (1996). Adversity and depression. *International Review of Psychiatry, 8,* 341–353.

Derogatis, L. R., Lipman, R. S., Rickels, K., Uhlenhuth, E. H., & Covi, L. (1974). The Hopkins Symptom Checklist (HSCL): A self-report symptom inventory. *Behavioral Science, 19,* 1–15.

Howard, W. T., Loberiza, F. R., Pfohl, B. M., Thorne, P. S., Magpantay, R. L., & Woolson, R. F. (1999). Initial results, reliability, and validity of a mental health survey of Mount Pinatubo disaster victims. *Journal of Nervous & Mental Disease, 187,* 661–672.

Mollica, R. F., Caspi-Yavin, Y., Bollini, P., Truong, T., Tor, S., & Lavelle, J. (1992). The Harvard Trauma Questionnaire. Validating a cross-cultural instrument for measuring torture, trauma, and posttraumatic stress disorder in Indochinese refugees. *Journal of Nervous & Mental Disease, 180,* 111–116.

Pretorius, T. B. (1991). Cross-cultural application of the Center for Epidemiological Studies Depression Scale: A study of black South African students. *Psychological Reports, 69,* 1179–1185.

Sack, W. H., Seeley, J. R., & Clarke, G. N. (1997). Does PTSD transcend cultural barriers? A study from the Khmer Adolescent Refugee Project. *Journal of the American Academy of Child & Adolescent Psychiatry, 36,* 49–54.

Spradley, J. P. (1979). *The ethnographic interview.* Fort Worth, TX: Harcourt Brace Jovanovich College Publishers.

Summerfield, D. A. (1997). Legacy of war: Beyond "trauma" to the social fabric. *Lancet, 349,* 1568.

Summerfield, D. A. (1998). "Trauma" and the experience of war: A reply. *Lancet, 351,* 1580–1581.

Weissman, M. M., Bland, R. C., Canino, G. J., Faravelli, C., Greenwald, S., & Hwu, H. (1996). Cross-national epidemiology of major depression and bipolar disorder. *Journal of the American Medical Association, 276,* 293–299.

6

Infectious Disease, HIV/AIDS, and War: Impact on Civilian Psychological Health

George M. Carter

Throughout human history, the penchant for waging war has carried with it enormous suffering and death for soldiers and civilians alike. Recently, war has become more lethal. "In four major wars of the twentieth century, a minority of all casualties became fatalities. In contrast, among Nicaraguan casualties since 1982, close to half were fatalities" (Garfield & Frieden, 1987, p. 615). Civilians, specifically, are increasingly at risk. In the wars of the 20th century, the rate of civilian death has climbed from an average of 44 percent to 85 percent of deaths, the higher percentages arising primarily from "low intensity" wars waged in the 1980s (Goldson, 1996).

Various noncombat-related events, including infectious diseases, drought, weather (e.g., cyclones), economic deterioration, and so forth, add to the toll of suffering and death (see, among others, Aronson, 1998). To make things worse, humans have harnessed hitherto natural disasters to wage biological warfare. Historically, diseased animals were lobbed into encampments and, later, blankets used by sufferers of smallpox were given to Native Americans to spread disease. This grisly tradition carries forward to the modern day with the threat of the use of agents such as anthrax, smallpox, or botulism to infect and kill both civilian and military populations.

Certainly, human intervention is unnecessary for infectious diseases to constitute a significant proportion of morbidity and mortality, particularly in regions of conflict. Diseases affect both physical and psychological health. Psychological damage may arise from the direct neurological/psychological effects of infectious diseases as well as the social stigmatization of infected individuals. Rape may spread disease while adding yet another layer of psychological damage (afflicting the person raped while underscoring the psychologically diseased state of the rapist as well). Very often, the bigotry of homophobia adds to the stigma and suffering of the gay, lesbian, bisexual, and transgendered community in the face of sexually transmitted diseases, a population vulnerable even in peacetime.

Many infectious diseases have a direct impact on mental health by their interactions with the central nervous system (CNS). Human immunodeficiency virus (HIV) infection, leading to the development of the acquired immune deficiency syndrome (AIDS), as well as diseases such as cryptococcal meningitis, toxoplasmosis, malaria, and syphilis all can directly affect cognitive functioning. Thus, primary medical care to diagnose and treat infectious disease is a critical facet of mental health care.

These diseases are rendered all the more debilitating by the fact that medicines to treat or manage such infections are very often in extremely short supply, if available at all. Only 40 percent of Africans have access to any type of health services (Nur, 1999). Without access to diagnosis and treatment, there is no hope; people die faster.

This situation is further horribly exacerbated by the artificially inflated prices foisted on patented drugs by avaricious pharmaceutical companies that in modern times act as a first and insurmountable barrier to access to care, even in nations not undergoing civil conflict (Bond, 1999). Attempts to obtain cheaper, generic forms of drugs used to treat HIV or opportunistic infections from countries such as India, Brazil, New Zealand, or Thailand are often thwarted by drug companies (e.g., see Rosenberg, 2001; Schoofs, 2000). There is a widespread recognition that the use of patent law to justify artificially inflated pricing has a deleterious effect on human life, particularly in the developing world: "Recently, there has been increasing mobilization around the idea of a right to essential and new drugs and growing resistance to the notion that intellectual property rights should trump other policy considerations" (Reich, 2000, p. 1979). "Other policy considerations" must include human lives.

At the dawn of the 21st century, the meaning of warfare is changing. The world wars dramatically extended the scope of international conflict in terms of the degree of destruction and death on a global scale. Further, low-intensity conflicts such as insurgencies, uprisings, violent coups, terrorism, civil wars, and chronic border disputes have enormously deleterious effects on civilian populations (Goldson, 1996). Terrorists intentionally target civilian populations. War or acts of terrorism destroy infrastructure, highways to transport injured and ill individuals, hospitals and clinics, and, in some cases, there is specific targeting of physicians and nurses in regions of conflict (Beyrer, 1998). Many of these conflicts are rooted in and funded by transnational corporate interests that too often value the bottom line well above human life.

Globally, the numbers of refugees fleeing conflict are increasing, from around 200,000 in the 1960s to over 1 million refugees entering the United States in the 1980s (Aday, 1994). Refugee camps, whether within a country or for those escaping it, are often rife with malnutrition and infectious diseases such as HIV, tuberculosis (TB), cholera, Ebola, malaria, and streptococcus-related "flesh eating" bacteria (Kalipeni & Oppong, 1998; Zacarias et al., 1994). In addition to their not having had routine childhood vaccinations, suffering from gastrointestinal disorders and parasitic infections, and having other serious health problems, "the prevalence of depression and posttraumatic stress syndrome is widespread among refugee populations, and particularly refugee women and children" (Aday, 1994, p. 506). Refugees who remain within their country ("internally displaced persons") often suffer a higher chronic death rate than nondisplaced citizens (Toole & Waldman, 1993).

The notion of the HIV/AIDS pandemic as a war in its own right, one waged at the microbial level but extending to the political and global levels, extends the concept of war. Richard Holbrooke, a United States ambassador to the United Nations, was instrumental in convening the first UN Security Council on a global health issue, specifically to address AIDS. At that meeting, the issue of the increasing spread of HIV among peacekeeping troops was also discussed (Holbrooke, 2000). This meeting was prompted in part by the release of a report by the Central Intelligence Agency (CIA) on the geopolitical threat that AIDS represents (CIA, 2000). President Bill Clinton ultimately signed an executive order recognizing AIDS as a threat to national security (Clinton, 2000; Gellman, 2000).

SCOPE OF INFECTIOUS DISEASES WITH NEUROLOGICAL AND PSYCHOLOGICAL SEQUELAE

A variety of diseases disproportionately afflict many nations in the developing world, many of which are associated with neurological and CNS involvement. Tetanus, measles, meningitis, and meningococcemia (particularly devastating in central Africa); *hemophilus* influenza; and the pork tapeworm (*Taenia solium*) inducing epilepsy can each have direct effects on the brain (Bergen, 1998). Viral hepatitis infections (hepatitis B and C) can result in encephalopathy in their later stages and have been found to be a relatively common contaminant in blood supplies, for example, as found in Somalia (Nur, Groen, Elmi, Ott, & Osterhaus, 2000) and Croatia (Vuk et al., 1998). Gains made in developing an adequate blood supply in Afghanistan have undoubtedly been disrupted since the war there after the September 11, 2001, destruction of the World Trade Center in New York City (Dupire et al., 1999).

The outcome of such diseases is likely to be rendered more dismal by the depression and profound despair associated with wartime conditions, refugee status, malnutrition, and other concomitants of warfare. This sets up a vicious, reverberating cycle of increasing despair, greater susceptibility to disease, worsened outcome, and little hope of treatment for any of the conditions (short of the heroic efforts of groups such as Médecins sans frontières/Doctors Without Borders; see http://www.msf.org for more information).

Malaria kills approximately 1.2 to 2 million people every year. The disease often involves the CNS and, like TB, it is becoming increasingly resistant to treatment (Olliaro, Cattani, & Wirth, 1996). Predominantly, it kills children under the age of 5 (Hotez & Oberhleman, 2000).

Neurosyphilis is a frequent cause of neurodegeneration among individuals infected with this spirochete. In later stages, if untreated (or unsuccessfully treated), dementia and other neurological involvement is common. Sexually transmitted diseases (STDs) often increase dramatically in prevalence during wartime (Hunt, 1996).

Measles also is widespread in urban areas and is associated rather commonly with subacute sclerosing panencephalitis (SSP). This disease also may be prevented in areas where vaccines are available. In the United States, only 21 cases of SSP were reported in the early 1980s. However, this condition remains a serious problem in developing nations (Bergen, 1998).

HIV carries both intense stigmatization as well as a variety of neurological sequelae, including depression and dementia as direct effects of HIV itself, as well as the increased risk of cognitive dysfunction arising from CNS-involving opportunistic pathogens such as cryptococcal meningitis, toxoplasmosis, progress multifocal leukoencephalopathy, untreated syphilis, and other infectious diseases (see Chaisson et al., 1993).

HIV disease has spread throughout the world, with approximately 40 million people estimated by the World Health Organization (WHO and UNAIDS, 2001) to be infected, while 22 million men, women, and children have already died of AIDS (WHO and UNAIDS, 2000). Sub-Saharan Africa has borne the brunt of the disease, with over 28 million individuals estimated to be HIV-infected (WHO and UNAIDS, 2001). This exceeds death rate projections for the year 2000 made in the mid-1990s, indicating that the disease may have only just begun its global conflagration of death (CIA, 2000). While other diseases still kill more people annually, geopolitical instability may be one dangerous sequela as AIDS typically kills those in the prime of their lives (including physicians, nurses, farmers, truckers, miners, and other professionals).

Indeed, education and cognitive development are being severely impacted by the loss of significant numbers of teachers to AIDS (Onishi, 2000). Where war has reared its ugly head, the pattern of HIV disease spread has been patchwork. But the consequences of the disease remain compelling; baseline estimates of the global causes of death show a shift in ranking of HIV from its being the overall 30th leading cause of disease in 1990 to the 9th leading cause of death by the year 2020 (Murray & Lopez, 1997). As with many diseases, infected soldiers returning home and the unfortunate need of many women to resort to sex work further spread it (Holbrooke, 2000). Rape, common in times of civil conflict, constitutes a violent vector for the dissemination of sexually transmitted infections.

Please note that the reference made to HIV specifically relates to HIV-1. HIV-2 is a distinct virus found in western Africa. Infection by this retrovirus tends to cause AIDS at a slower rate. Some researchers have found a likely role for the Guinea-Bissau war for independence of 1963–1974 in explaining the higher incidence of HIV-2 in adults over age 50 in that country. Associations with HIV-

2 infection were found among sex workers, those having sex with a white man, women receiving blood transfusions, and men having served in the colonial army, as well as among other more sexually active individuals (Poulsen, 2000).

A Review of the HIV Pandemic and the Effects of War: Selected Regions

Over the past few decades there have been many conflicts that undoubtedly have fueled the spread of HIV and other diseases. The following represents only a sampling of these. Civil strife is not the only vector for the spread of disease but this brief review serves to illustrate the role it can play. To the extent that war arises, surveillance, prevention, and treatment of infectious diseases remain critical for civilian physical and psychological health.

A chronic state of civil unrest has afflicted many African nations. These wars have resulted in a massive increase in HIV and other diseases (Smallman-Raynor, 1991). In countries like Somalia, the documentation of the first cases of AIDS "coincided with the collapse of the health infrastructure due to civil war" (Nur et al., 2000, p. 140). Fortunately, the Somali people have an opportunity to prevent the epidemic from expanding because the incidence of new HIV infections appears to be low.

The 1994 genocides in Rwanda and Burundi were associated with a massive local increase in refugee camps of shigella, malaria, and pneumonia as well as measles. Cholera was a serious concern among many children in refugee camps. HIV disease prevalence also was high, as much as 30 percent before the ethnic wars but reaching as high as 60 percent in a survey of hospital inpatients (Pearn, 1996; Ramsey, Brdigord, Lusby, & Pearn, 1995). Prevalence rates may often be underestimates. Even in the United States, where screening is commonly available, a shocking number of individuals donating blood after the September 11 attack were found to be HIV- or Hepatitis C–infected (Kinzie, 2001).

The pattern of the HIV-1 and HIV-2 epidemics in Angola and the Democratic Republic of the Congo indicate a rapid dissemination of these viruses in the mid- to late 1980s. "Displacements of people, mainly as a consequence of the war, certainly played an important role in spreading HIV infection from the northern frontier areas of the country [Angola] to the central and southern regions" (Torres-Anjel, 1992, p. 268).

In the southern part of the Sudan, civil war has afflicted the region for nearly 30 years. Not surprisingly, HIV and other diseases harmful to cognitive functions exist in this region as well. The pattern of HIV spread in the southern town of Juba showed a higher incidence among female sex workers, males with sexually transmitted diseases, those who sought the services of sex workers, and people suffering from tuberculosis. The movement of military personnel between southern and northern Sudan may result in a spread of HIV disease into the northern regions (McCarthy, Khalid, & El Tigani, 1995). More recent warnings raise concerns that HIV disease prevalence in the Sudan may soon match that of neighboring African countries, adding to the burden of more than 1 million killed in the civil conflicts and an additional 4 million displaced (Lyon, 2000).

Many other countries, including Botswana, Zambia, Zimbabwe, Uganda, South Africa, Tanzania, Kenya, and Malawi, as well as the KwaZulu Natal nation, have had civil strife, governmental denial, and widespread violence with which to contend, which have further fueled the spread of infectious diseases. These struggles have often been exacerbated by those inherent in overcoming colonial influences. But the scope of the pandemic goes well beyond Africa.

In the case of Haiti, AIDS, a leading cause of death, spread from urban to rural areas in an all-too-familiar pattern that undoubtedly was hastened by the internal civil conflict that further damaged an already infrastructure-weak society. The HIV epidemic in Haiti is fueled by the rapid spread of a variety of other STDs, including syphilis, chancroid, and condylomas, that, by the development of sores, facilitate transmission of HIV (Pierre & Fournier, 1999). As elsewhere, TB is a fundamental killer.

The war in Nicaragua may have actually protected people against the incursion of HIV only because of the international isolation imposed as a result of that conflict. Nicaraguans relied on their own blood supply, and the HIV pandemic had not yet established a foothold by the time the war commenced (Low et al., 1993). However, once the war ended, displaced individuals and refugees returning from regions where the disease was more prevalent, such as the United States and Honduras, resulted in a nascent, local HIV epidemic.

As elsewhere, the chronic warfare in Nicaragua resulted in epidemics of malaria, diarrheal diseases, measles, leishmaniasis, meningitis, and tuberculosis, many of which can contribute to deterioration in cognitive functioning as well as increasing susceptibility to HIV disease (Garfield, 1989). Other countries in Central America, such as Guatemala, Honduras, and El Salvador, as well as many Caribbean countries have suffered enormously from the twin afflictions of HIV disease and, in many areas, profound poverty. Further, there is evidence for the increase of HIV disease in military and civilian populations due to increased sexual risk behavior during the civil war in El Salvador (Wollants et al., 1995).

Severe economic crisis along with the war in Serbia increased mortality related to infectious diseases:

Restrictions imposed on trade through the economic embargo [during the war] caused extreme hardship to medical services as well. These were disrupted due to lack of medical equipment and proper maintenance of the existing equipment, lack of vaccines, drugs and other medical inputs, as well as by lack of funding. (Vlajinac et al., 1997, p. 174)

Similar increases in the incidence of infectious diseases were reported during the conflict in Bosnia and Herzegovina (Puvacic & Weinberg, 1994).

Many countries have underground sex-slave trafficking practices, which often increase during times of war or civil unrest. This situation, for example, has become common among Eastern European women in Kosovo. Many are forced to have unprotected sex against their will, and the rate of sexually transmitted diseases is reportedly high (Finn, 2000). Other regions, too, have had to confront the sex slave trade. Many young women and girls are taken against their will from Nepal and sent to brothels in India (for an excellent review of the complexities of the situation, see Pike, 1999).

In Burma (Myanmar) and Cambodia, protracted civil war over years—even decades—has resulted in a significant deterioration of the medical infrastructure. Indeed, physicians, nurses, and hospitals are often the direct target of violence, and many healthcare providers have either fled or been murdered (Beyrer, 1998).

SPREAD OF DISEASE BEYOND THE REGION OF CONFLICT

The spread of disease is not limited to the region of conflict. Peacekeeping soldiers, foreign combatants, mercenary soldiers, foreign nationals caught in the web of conflict, refugees, and others involved in the conflict may be fortunate to escape with their lives. However, they may bring undiagnosed or untreated diseases with them. For example, the U.S. ambassador to the United Nations Richard Holbrooke noted in a speech to that body that many Finnish peacekeeping soldiers returned home with HIV disease (Pisik, 2000). Five soldiers from Uruguay on a peacekeeping mission returned home from Cambodia with a Southeast Asian strain of HIV (Kelley, 1999). Some have observed new patterns of the spread of HIV by the different subspecies of HIV-1 ("clades") as they appear in different communities around the world (e.g., Carr et al., 1998). Moreover, the various clades of HIV found throughout Africa are mixing up, forming hitherto unseen recombinants (Garrett, 2000). The frightening possibility that these new variants will be resistant to treatment or a vaccine is a serious concern.

Others have studied the extensive travel of workers (e.g., from Haiti to Cuba) and soldiers (e.g., from Cuba to Angola and the Democratic Republic of the Congo) (Torres-Anjel, 1992). Such movement of people is often accompanied by an increase in sex work in areas of regional conflict.

Thus, the impact of war may extend far beyond the confines of the actual fighting, and the tentacles of infection consequently impact the mental health of civilians at a significant remove in space and/or time. For example, the highest rates of HIV-1 and HIV-2 infection in northern Angola were observed in refugees and army personnel (Santos-Ferreira et al., 1990). HIV infections spread more rapidly in Mozambique as a result of the efforts of South Africa's apartheid regime to foster civil war there (Cliff & Noormahomed, 1988). Such spread of infectious disease may include TB and other STDs as well, although these may be treatable in places where medications are more readily available. There is a strong correlation between increased STD rates and the spread of HIV. Clearly, policies designed to treat diseases in developing nations are ethically mandatory and economically wise, as well as serving as a critical component of mental health services.

Effect of HIV/AIDS on Victims of Conflict

Of all the infectious diseases discussed, HIV disease carries a two-pronged effect. First is the direct effect of the disease on the CNS and brain function. Second is the stigmatization of individuals infected with HIV, which not only causes humiliation but may place people at risk from others in the community—the harsh consequences of ignorance and/or misinformation.

Women are more frequently the target of violence related to stigmatization, particularly if the cultural context carries patriarchal or dogmatic religious attitudes or is imbued with a sense of "machismo" that perceives women as inferior beings, or even little more than chattel. Such attitudes may result in a man forcing his wife out of the house if her serostatus is discovered, regardless of whether there has been any infidelity on her part. Further, men often refuse to wear condoms, viewing them as a challenge to their masculinity. Thus, male dominated cultures where men are uneducated to the risk, or view women as property or somehow inferior, increase risks and dangers to women and the family's offspring on a variety of levels, including loss of home, family, and an increased risk of sexually transmitted diseases.

This situation can be worsened by ignorance or frank bigotry on the part of healthcare workers (including physicians, nurses, and other attendants) toward people living with HIV. They may isolate or simply fail to treat patients based on stereotypical notions of "moral degeneracy" that too often stigmatize HIV-infected individuals (Liebschutz, Feinman, Sullivan, Stein, & Samet, 2000). Government leadership is essential both to stem the tide of HIV infections and to overcome dangerous ignorance. This is exemplified by the stark contrast between the effects of the concerted public policy campaign against HIV in Uganda (where incidence of the disease is dropping) and the situation in South Africa, where President Thabo Mbeki flirted with "denialists" who claim HIV either does not exist or does not cause AIDS. These serve as striking illustrations of the need for leadership and the consequences of its failure when it is absent (e.g., see, WHO and UNAIDS, 2000 and 2001).

Further, the very fact of discovering one's serostatus can be immensely demoralizing. Social stigma and its attendant depression may worsen the outcome (Aday, 1994). Depression related to illness is not uncommon and is rendered all the greater in terms of despair when coupled with the loss of family members, friends, one's home, livelihood, and so forth, as a result of warfare.

Indeed, this social stigma can be life threatening. In South Africa, Mpho Motloung and her family were murdered by her husband, who subsequently committed suicide, after he discovered HIV infection among family members. Gugu Dhlamini was open about her HIV+ status and was consequently stoned to death by her neighbors (Cameron, 2000; Treatment Action Campaign [TAC], 2000.)

In the context of war, a frequent cause of infection among women is rape.

Women raped by military personnel suffer not just immediate physical injury and the risk of pregnancy but are also exposed to a far higher risk of HIV and other sexually transmitted infections than they would be through other unprotected sex, not just because rape can result in torn tissue and hence create an easy entry-point for HIV, but because their rapist has a higher risk of being infected. (UNAIDS, 2000)

This may also be true of men and boys who are raped, although statistics on this crime are hard to come by.

Rape, already a serious problem in many regions, may be spurred by the adoption of myths such as "sex with a virgin can cure AIDS" (Altman, 2000). Rape was common in Mozambique during the conflict there in the early 1990s, resulting in an increase in both syphilis and, to a lesser degree, HIV (Cossa et al., 1994). Both the war in the Democratic Republic of the Congo (Garrett, 2000) and the war in the former Yugoslavia reported widespread rape and subsequent increases in HIV and sexually transmitted diseases (Division for the Advancement of Women [DAW], n.d.). Some 1,100 rapes were reported in Bosnia and Herzegovina (DAW, undated). This layers additional burdens upon the damaged psyche of people already devastated by war.

Effect of Nutrient Deficiencies

Starvation increases host susceptibility to infection. Having poor physical health, such as a debilitating chronic illness, may make one more vulnerable to depression and reduced social health arising from a lack of supportive social contacts. "The risk of harm or neglect would be multiplied for those who are in poor health and have few material (economic) and nonmaterial (psychological or social) resources to assist in coping with illness" (Aday, 1994, p. 489). Moreover, poor nutrition is widespread; in Africa, 175 million of a total of 744 million people suffer from chronic hunger, a 50 percent increase from 25 years ago (Nur, 1999). In addition, recent evidence suggests that nutrient-depleted individuals may host pathogens that may actually become more harmful in a starved individual (Levander, 1996).

Malnutrition, particularly in childhood, can reduce intellectual development (Bergen, 1998). HIV disease can result in a wasting syndrome and requires an increased caloric intake (Hogg et al., 1995). Intestinal parasites can accelerate HIV disease progression and exacerbate malnutrition in the context of inadequate caloric intake (Fontanet et al., 2000). A profound lack of available food and the absence of clean water are, of course, common features of regions in conflict. Malnutrition, a common occurrence in war-ravaged areas, thus can increase susceptibility to disease, worsening disease outcome and psychological functioning. These pernicious influences may have, in the aggregate, a serious impact not only on emotional health but on cognitive functioning as well.

Solutions are straightforward conceptually, but sometimes difficult to realize practically. Feeding people is clearly part of the answer, but distribution networks may either be poorly planned or implemented inadequately due to local corruption. However, successful programs may have significant results. Simply supplying children in Papua, New Guinea, with vitamin A helped to lower the morbidity due to malaria caused by *P. falciparum* and also helped to minimize clinical episodes, spleen enlargement, and parasite density in treated children (Shankar et al., 1999).

DISCUSSION

The effect of disease spread in the modern world has dramatic ramifications. Understanding the scope of the problem and the specific issues that must be addressed is the first daunting task, rendered all the more problematic by rapidly changing conditions. While it may seem impossible, public health surveillance of civilian populations during civil conflict is not only possible but very useful (Weinberg & Simmonds, 1995).

Once the local problems have been delineated, basic needs must be met. In general, this means an adequate supply of food, shelter, and clean water. In addition, treatment for injuries—physical *and* psychological—must be available, as must the means to control the spread of infectious diseases (e.g., providing sanitation, supplying condoms) and the tools (syringes, vaccines, etc.) and medicines to treat them. Treating infectious disease can serve in itself as primary care for psychological health and recovery from the multifaceted wounds of war.

Rebuilding the infrastructure can take years, during which time civilian physical and psychological health needs are severely compromised. It is in the global interest that, as even remote areas become accessible, infrastructure and health care be developed concurrently. As civil conflict destroys infrastructure, medical facilities, and the availability of food and clean water, and as war reduces the numbers of health care workers, the spread of disease goes unchecked. The flames of violent conflict can cause widespread reverberations in time and space, disrupting times of peace with the pernicious effects of infectious disease.

Implementation of such procedures can be carried out by and for the benefit of peacekeeping troops as well. It is clear that misdiagnosis may result in a failure to treat infectious diseases appropriately (Kelley, 1999; Ognibene, 1987). Among other interventions, addressing the reality of sexual activity among soldiers and providing condoms may help to slow the spread of HIV and other STDs both in the afflicted region and beyond.

Indeed, as war ravages local environments, many of the natural animal hosts of microbial pathogens will be reduced in numbers. These pathogens come in closer contact with humans, and the very real possibility exists and has been demonstrated for their transfer from animal hosts to humans, with potentially devastating consequences (Gao et al., 1999). In reference to the HIV pandemic that shocked the globe out of its complacent feeling that infectious diseases, at least in the developed world, were under control, Henderson (1993) notes that "the question had to be asked whether this was an exceptional, aberrant phenomenon or whether we might anticipate other microbial challenges of catastrophic proportion" (p. 154).

Perhaps the most important and often overlooked aspect of creating these changes is through the empowerment of the local communities. The lesson that even well-intentioned organizations have frequently failed to learn is the need to listen to individuals in the local community. Others have noted that rather than directing the aid effort, it is important to assure that the aid is available while allowing local populations to manage it (MacFarlane, Racelis, & Muli-Muslime, 2000).

On a broader scale, international support for violent regimes or civil conflicts perpetuates and amplifies the deleterious psychological effects of infectious diseases. Most especially, these solutions must be informed with an abiding recognition of fundamental human rights.

The international community should intervene earlier in the evolution of complex disasters involving civil war, human rights abuses, food shortages, and mass displacement. Relief programs need to be based on sound health and nutrition information and should focus on the provision of adequate shelter, food, water, sanitation, and public health programs that prevent mortality from diarrhea, measles, and other communicable diseases, especially among young children and women. (Toole & Waldman, 1993, p. 600)

The mental and emotional health of parents who lose their children as a result of wartime activities must also be recognized.

For the human species to survive in the face of these enormous challenges will require an evolution not of our bodies so much as our hearts and spirits. Part of that journey will be the global recognition of the need to diagnose and treat infectious disease, assuring access to inexpensive medications, which clearly serves as a basis for primary mental health care. Ultimately, finding and embracing nonviolent solutions to political dilemmas will be the hallmark of a maturing, wiser species that can overcome its own destructive tendencies. As the world shrinks, it becomes clearer that failure to do so may well result in our premature extinction.

REFERENCES

Aday, L. A. (1994). Health status of vulnerable populations. *Annual Review of Public Health, 15,* 487–509.

Altman, L. K. (2000, July 16). Another approach to AIDS in Africa. *New York Times* As reported in Health-L Zambia electronic mailing list health-l@hivnet.ch.

Aronson, S. M. (1998). Conflict and contagion. *Medicine and Health, 81,* 2–3.

Bergen, D.C. (1998). Preventable neurological diseases worldwide. *Neuroepidemiology, 17,* 67–73.

Beyrer, C. (1998). Burma and Cambodia: Human rights, social disruption, and the spread of HIV/AIDS. *Health and Human Rights, 2,* 84–97.

Bond, P. (1999). Globalization, pharmaceutical pricing, and South African health policy: Managing confrontation with U.S. firms and politicians. *International Journal of Health Services, 29,* 765–792.

Cameron, E. (2000, July 10). *The deafening silence of AIDS.* Jonathan Mann Memorial Lecture delivered at the 13th International Conference on AIDS, Durban, South Africa. Available: http://www.woza.co.za/news00/jul/cameron10b.htm.

Carr, J. K., Salminen M. O., Albert, J., Sanders-Buell, E., Gotte, D., Birx, D. L., & Mc-Cutchan, F. E. (1998). Full genome sequences of human immunodeficiency virus type 1 subtypes G and A/G intersubtype recombinants. *Virology, 247,* 22–31.

Central Intelligence Agency. (2000, January). The global infectious disease threat and its implications for the United States. (NIE No. 99–17D)

Chaisson, R. E., Stanton, D. L., Gallant, J. E., Rucker, S., Bartlett, J. G., & Moore, R. D. (1993). Impact of the 1993 revision of the AIDS case definition on the prevalence of AIDS in the clinical setting. *AIDS, 7,* 857–862.

Cliff, J., & Noormahomed, R. (1988). Health as a target: South Africa's destabilization of Mozambique. *Social Science and Medicine, 27,* 717–722.

Clinton, W. J. (2000, May 10). Access to HIV/AIDS Pharmaceuticals and Medical Technologies. Retrieved from http://www.hivnet.ch:8000/asia/bangladesh/viewR?338.

Cossa, H. A., Gloyd, S., Vaz, R. G., Folgosa, E., Simbine, E., Diniz, M., & Kreiss, J. K. (1994, March–April). Syphilis and HIV infection among displaced pregnant women in rural Mozambique. *International Journal of Sexually Transmitted Diseases and AIDS, 5,* 117–123.

Division for the Advancement of Women. (n.d.). Facts and figures on violence against women. Available: http://www.undp.org/unifem/campaign/violence/unkit/daw-facts.htm.

Dupire, B., Abawi, A. K., Ganteaume, C., Lam, T., Truze, P., Martet, G. (1999, January–February). Establishment of a blood transfusion center at Kabul (Afghanistan). *Santé, 9*(1), 18–22.

Finn, P. (2000, April 24). Sex slavery flourishes in Kosovo. *Washington Post,* p. A1.

Fontanet, A. L., Sahlu, T., Rinke de Wit, T., Messele, T., Masho, W., Woldemichael, T., Yeneneh, H., & Coutinho, R. A. (2000). Epidemiology of infections with intestinal parasites and human immunodeficiency virus (HIV) among sugar-estate residents in Ethiopia. *Annals of Tropical Medicine and Parasitology, 94,* 269–278.

Gao, F., Bailes, E., Robertson, D. L., Chen, Y., Rodenburg, C. M., Michael, S. F., Cummins, L. B., Arthur, L. O., Peeters, M., Shaw, G. M., Sharp, P.M., & Hahn, B. H. (1999, February 4). Origin of HIV-1 in the chimpanzee Pan troglodytes. *Nature, 397,* 436–441.

Garfield, R. M. (1989). War-related changes in health and health services in Nicaragua. *Social Science and Medicine, 28,* 669–676.

Garfield, R. M., & Frieden, T. (1987). Health-related outcomes of war in Nicaragua. *American Journal of Public Health, 77,* 615–618.

Garrett, L. (2000, July 9). Allies of AIDS: Among warring factions in Congo, disease is mutating. *New York Newsday.* Available: http://www.newsday.com/special/aids/woaids3.htm.

Gellman, B. (2000, April 30). AIDS is declared threat to security. *Washington Post,* p. A01.

Goldson, E. (1996). The effect of war on children. *Child Abuse and Neglect, 20,* 809–819.

Henderson, D. A. (1993). New challenges for tropical medicine. *American Journal of Tropical Medicine and Hygiene, 49,* 153–157.

Hogg, R. S., Zadra, J. N., Chan-Yan, C., Voigt, R., Craib, K. J., Korosi-Ronco, J., Montaner, J. S., & Schechter, M. T. (1995). Analysis of nutritional intake in a cohort of homosexual men. *Journal of the Acquired Immune Deficiency Syndrome and Human Retrovirology, 9,* 162–167.

Holbrooke, R. C. (2000, March 8). Statement for the record submitted to the House Committee on Banking and Financial Services, Washington, DC. Retrieved from http://www.the body.com/state_dept/holbrooke2.html

Hotez, P., & Oberhleman, R. A. (2000, September). Parasites from around the world I: Clinical update. *Abstracts of the 40th Interscience Conference on Antimicrobial Agents and Chemotherapy*, 521.

Hunt, C. W. (1996). Social vs. biological: Theories on the transmission of AIDS in Africa. *Social Science and Medicine, 42*, 1283–1296.

Kalipeni, E., & Oppong, J. (1998). The refugee crisis in Africa and implications for health and disease: A political ecology approach. *Social Science and Medicine, 46*, 1637–1653.

Kelley, P. W. (1999). Emerging infections as a threat to international peacekeeping forces. *Médecine Tropicale, 59*, 137–138.

Kinzie, S. (2001, September 27). Blood donations yield shock for some. *Scripps Howard News Service* [As reported in Raleigh, NC, News & Observer]. Retrieved from http://archives11.newsbank.com/ar-search/we/archives?p_action+list&p_topdoc = RLEC&PAGE = 3.

Levander, O. A. (1996). Viral evolution as driven by host nutritional selective factors: Influence of dietary oxidative stress. *Food Chemistry, 57*, 47–49.

Liebschutz, J. M., Feinman, M. S., Sullivan, L., Stein, M., & Samet, J. (2000). Physical and sexual abuse in women infected with the human immunodeficiency virus: Increased illness and health care utilization. *Archives of Internal Medicine, 160*, 1659–1664.

Low, N., Egger, M., Gorter, A., Sandiford, P., Gonzalez, A., Pauw, J., Ferrie, J., & Smith, G. D. (1993). AIDS in Nicaragua: Epidemiological, political, and sociocultural perspectives. *International Journal Health Service, 23*, 685–702.

Lyon, A. (2000, May 14). Sudan staring at potential AIDS catastrophe. *Reuters*. Available: http://www.reuters.com.

MacFarlane, S., Racelis, M., & Muli-Muslime, F. (2000, September 2). Public health in developing countries. *The Lancet, 356*, 841–846.

McCarthy, M. C., Khalid, I. O., & El Tigani, A. (1995). HIV-1 infection in Juba, southern Sudan. *Journal of Medical Virology, 46*, 18–20.

Murray, C. J., & Lopez, A. D. (1997). Alternative projections of mortality and disability by cause 1990–2020: Global Burden of Disease Study. *The Lancet, 349*, 1498–1504.

Nur, Y. A. (1999). Current extent of disasters in Africa. *Prehospital and Disaster Medicine, 14*, 66–74.

Nur, Y. A., Groen, J., Elmi, A. M., Ott, A., & Osterhaus, A. D. M. E. (2000). Prevalence of serum antibodies against blood borne and sexually transmitted agents in selected groups in Somalia. *Epidemiology and Infections, 124*, 137–141.

Ognibene, A. J. (1987, January). Medical and infectious diseases in the theater of operations. *Military Medicine, 152*, 14–18.

Olliaro, P., Cattani, J., & Wirth, D. (1996). Malaria: The submerged disease. *Journal of the American Medical Association, 275*, 230–233.

Onishi, N. (2000, August 14). AIDS cuts swath through Africa's teachers. *New York Times*, p. A1.

Pearn, J. (1996). War zone paediatrics in Rwanda. *Journal Paediatric Child Health, 32*, 290–295.

Pierre, J. A., & Fournier, A.M. (1999). Human immunodeficiency virus infection in Haiti. *Journal of the National Medical Association, 91,* 165–170.

Pike, L. (1999, April). Innocence, danger and desire: Representations of sex workers in Nepal. Available: http://www.hsph.harvard.edu/Organizations/healthnet/SAsia/repro2/!LINNETedited.html.

Pisik, B. (2000, July 7). UN: AIDS being spread by its peacekeepers. *The Washington Times.* Available: http://www.washtimes.com/world/default-200077224158.htm.

Poulsen, A. G., Aaby, P., Jensen, H., & Dias, F. (2000). Risk factors for HIV-2 seropositivity among older people in Guinea-Bissau: A search for the early history of HIV-2 infection. *Scandinavian Journal of Infectious Disease, 32,* 169–175.

Puvacic, Z., & Weinberg, J. (1994). Impact of war on infectious disease in Bosnia-Hercegovina. *British Medical Journal, 309,* 1207–1208.

Ramsey, W., Brdigord, L. R., Lusby, R. J., & Pearn, J. H. (1995). The Australian Medical Support Force in Rwanda. *Medical Journal of Australia, 163,* 646–651.

Reich, M. R. (2000). The global drug gap. *Science, 287,* 1979–1981.

Rosenberg, T. (2001, January 28). Patent laws are malleable. Patients are educable. Drug companies are vincible. The world's AIDS crisis is solvable. *New York Times Magazine,* p. 2663.

Santos-Ferreira, M. O., Cohen, T., Lourenco, M. H., Matos Almeida, M. J., Chamaret, S., & Montagnier, L. (1990). A study of seroprevalence of HIV-1 and HIV-2 in six provinces of People's Republic of Angola: Clues to the spread of HIV infection. *Journal of the Acquired Immune Deficiency Syndrome, 3,* 780–786.

Schoofs, M. (2000, December 1). Glaxo enters fight in Ghana on AIDS drug. *Wall Street Journal,* p. A3.

Shankar, A. H., Genton, B., Semba, R. D., Baisor, M., Paino, J., Tamja, S., Adiguma, T., Wu, L., Rare, L., Tielsch, J. M., Alpers, M. P., & West, K. P., Jr. (1999). Effect of vitamin A supplementation on morbidity due to *Plasmodium falciparum* in young children in Papua New Guinea: A randomised trial. *The Lancet, 354,* 203–209.

Smallman-Raynor, M. R., & Cliff, A.D. (1991). Civil war and the spread of AIDS in Central Africa. *Epidemiology and Infection, 107,* 69–80.

Toole, M. J., & Waldman, R. J. (1993). Refugees and displaced persons: War, hunger, and public health. *Journal of the American Medical Association, 270,* 600–605.

Torres-Anjel, M. J. (1992). Macroepidemiology of the HIVs-AIDS (HAIDS) pandemic: Insufficiently considered zoological and geopolitical aspects. *Annals of the New York Academy of Sciences, 653,* 257–273.

Treatment Action Campaign (TAC). (2000, August 23). Mourn Mpho Motloung! Change HIV/AIDS messages to show hope now! False messages increase violence against women! [Press release]. Retrieved from www.tac.org.za/Documents/Statements/pr000823.txt.

UNAIDS. (2000, June). Report on the Global HIV/AIDS Epidemic: What makes people vulnerable? Available: http://hivinsite.ucsf.edu/social/un/2098.478e.html.

Vlajinac, H. D., Marinkovic, J. M., Kocev, N. I., Adanja, B. J., Pekmezovic, T. D., Sipetic, S. B., & Jovanovic, D. J. (1997). Infectious diseases mortality in central Serbia. *Journal of Epidemiology and Community Health, 51,* 172–174.

Vuk, T., Putarek, K., Rojnic, N., Margan, I. G., Balija, M., & Grgiceviĉ, D. (1998). Croatian blood transfusion service in prevention of HIV spread during the war. *Acta Medica Croatica, 52,* 221–222.

Weinberg, J., & Simmonds, S. (1995). Public health, epidemiology and war. *Social Science and Medicine, 40,* 1663–1669.

WHO and UNAIDS. (2000, December). AIDS epidemic update: December, 2000. Available: http://www.unaids.org.

WHO and UNAIDS. (2001, December). AIDS epidemic update: December, 2001. Available: http://www.unaids.org.

Wollants, E., Schoenberg, M., Figueroa, C., Shor-Posner, G., Klaskala, W., & Baum, M. K. (1995). Risk factors and patterns of HIV-1 transmission in the El Salvador military during war time, *AIDS, 9,* 1291–1292.

Zacarias, F., González, R. S., Cuchi, P., Yanez, A., Peruga, A., Mazin, R., Betts, C., & Weisenbacher, M. (1994). HIV/AIDS and its interaction with tuberculosis in Latin America and the Caribbean. *Bulletin of the Pan-American Health Organization, 28,* 312–323.

7

An Asian Youth as Offender: The Legacy
of the Khmer Rouge

Clay Foreman

Near the end of the guilt phase in a capital punishment trial, the defense coun-
sel referred a young Cambodian defendant to me for a forensic evaluation. This
evaluation concerned the effect of the defendant's history of childhood trauma
on his participation in a murder. The defendant had stood trial for multiple murders of parents and their children during a home invasion robbery that was part
of a 2-month crime spree. The jury found him guilty of these murders and sentenced him to death. Although based on a forensic evaluation, the concern of
this chapter is the enduring and dynamic effects of trauma that can perpetuate
tragedy beyond the originating context.

The defendant was a refugee from a war zone, and, as such, his case provides
an understanding of the need to fully assess and treat psychological and physical trauma among refugees. Perhaps proper psychosocial assessment will avoid
further tragedy. It is important to note that no single factor led to the crimes;
rather, several factors interacted dynamically with one another in the defendant
from the age of 2 to 22. This chapter outlines the process of forensic assessment
and diagnosis of this client, who will be referred to by the pseudonym "Rabbit"
because he was born in the Year of the Rabbit.

To develop the psychosocial history, I probed for traumatic events that would
not have surfaced in conversations with the client or family members. This
probing elicited specific traumatic events and detailed accounts needed to
assess the defendant's psychological profile. Rather than merely noting sufficient symptoms for a diagnosis of post-traumatic stress disorder (PTSD; American Psychiatric Association, 1994), a thorough workup uncovered the array
of traumatic events pertinent to proper diagnosis and treatment of trauma survivors. The first step in understanding a psychosocial history is to situate

one's personal development within the historical and social context. In this case, we start with the civil war in Cambodia.

HISTORICAL BACKGROUND

Rabbit, the youngest son of four children born to peasant Cambodian parents, was born during the brutal Cambodian civil war. When Rabbit was 28 months of age, Pol Pot (Saloth Sar) unified the communist factions into the Khmer Rouge and emptied the capital city of Cambodia, exterminating an estimated 1.5 million Cambodians. When Rabbit was 6, the Vietnamese fought the Khmer Rouge forces, at which time Rabbit's family fled into Thailand. A year later the family immigrated to Alabama, and then to California. Throughout Rabbit's childhood he experienced neither a peaceful nor a stable society and was exposed to acts of violence in the midst of continuous warfare.

During his early adolescence, Rabbit joined a gang, began committing crimes, and dropped out of high school. Whenever arrested and sentenced to county juvenile facilities, he would escape. On three occasions he was sent to highly secure state facilities run by the California Youth Authority (CYA). In his early twenties, Rabbit fell in love and married. The couple moved out of state so he could work cooking donuts for his in-laws. The marriage was unstable, but the couple managed to work on their problems. His wife denied any physical violence, saying that Rabbit would leave whenever he became angry. She became pregnant, which distressed Rabbit, as he mistakenly believed he was sterile; eventually he came to accept that he was a prospective father. His son was born after his arrest and incarceration for the murders.

ASSESSMENT

On our first meeting, I was struck by Rabbit's flat affect and general lack of emotional expression. He seemed cold, detached, and altogether unlikable. He described his situation in simple and matter-of-fact terms. Exhibiting little feeling toward the fate of his victims, he expressed the view that if adults fail to protect themselves, they are responsible for their deaths.

He believed the responsibility for self-protection begins around 11 or 12 years of age, the age of many Khmer Rouge soldiers. When asked about the children who died, he said that parents and other adults should protect children. However, although he said he was very remorseful about the deaths of the children, he showed no emotion as he described his thoughts about their death. I explored this disparity with him and with his family to better understand his attitude toward children. He genuinely cared for children and was appropriately empathetic when watching even strangers parenting their children. An emotionally cold killer cares only to advance his or her own interests and does not care when other people die. Rabbit's lack of emotional expression would fit with that of a cold-blooded killer, and such a depiction of him would have fit with the criminal case against him. Yet this impression was contradictory to the empathy he expressed for the interaction of parents and their children. Thus clarification of his seemingly contradictory attitudes and emotions toward interpersonal relations presaged understanding his personality structure.

The diagnostic task was for this understanding to reach a point of coherence with Rabbit's life events and his criminal behavior. Toward this end, a psychosocial history was developed from interviews with Rabbit, his two older brothers, his parents, other Cambodians, and a Buddhist monk. The next section summarizes this psychosocial history.

PERSONAL EXPERIENCES OF KHMER ROUGE CAPTIVITY

Executions

Generally, the Khmer Rouge clubbed people to death. Those executions were based on statements from malicious informants or innocent statements from other people, including children. Two attempted executions failed to kill Rabbit's father, who remains physically disabled from a collapsed chest. The brothers witnessed a number of executions, including that of a man crucified in their village. They commonly saw dead bodies that had been discarded in the jungle.

Beatings

Rabbit was repeatedly beaten on his head, leaving him with chronic headaches. As a child, these headaches caused him to scream, become frantic, and to bang his head against walls. His parents and his older brother received many beatings as well.

Abductions

Soon after the Khmer Rouge gained control of Rabbit's village, they abducted his mother's parents and his two oldest sisters. These family members never returned to the village. Twice the Khmer Rouge abducted his father, Rabbit, and the older brother. All managed to escape their captors and return to the village. While in captivity, the boys were held in a youth work camp where they received Khmer Rouge indoctrination. At this camp, they survived several months on rice water and spent long hours working in the fields.

Starvation

None of the family members received adequate food. Rabbit's mother described him as severely malnourished. His skeleton was visible beneath his skin and his abdomen was distended. They survived by scavenging in the jungle for insects, rodents, and vegetation, risking execution for such scavenging.

Near Drowning

At around age 5, Rabbit fell into a pond and nearly drowned. His mother described him as "so blue he was almost black." Although resuscitated, he could not walk or talk for several days, and he remained unsteady for weeks. Believing he was feigning these neurological symptoms, the Khmer Rouge threatened to kill his parents unless he left his mother's care.

Family Relations

The forced change in all aspects of life shifted relationships throughout the village. This was the mother's ancestral village, so most villagers were related to one another and formed a supportive extended family. This support network ceased to exist, as the parents no longer trusted other villagers. Indeed, someone had informed the Khmer Rouge that Rabbit's father had been part of the village defense force, which led to his abductions.

Fear that their children might repeat what they said caused parents to voice no dissent about the living conditions. Children were not allowed to live with their parents. Insisting that the villagers communally raise the children, the Khmer Rouge executed parents who cared for their own children. Therefore, Rabbit lost not only his grandparents and older sisters as caretakers, but also the care of his parents.

Escape

The invasion by the Vietnamese Army disrupted the Khmer Rouge forces, and during this chaos the family escaped to Thailand. The escape took 2 weeks, as the family dodged Khmer Rouge soldiers, opportunistic bandits, landmines, and artillery bombardment. Rabbit's only traumatic memories were from this escape. He remembered rapes, robberies, and murders as well as people being blown apart by explosions. However, he was uncertain if these images were actual memories from the trip or the recollections of his parents, saying, "It seems like a dream and I don't know if it's real." His parents confirmed that these were actual events.

In Thailand they settled in "New Camp," which was a makeshift settlement for refugees next to the official United Nations camp. New Camp received minimal international support because the UN did not provide supplies and personnel outside its official camp. Although in and around New Camp, robberies, beatings, and rapes continued, the family's diet improved and they gained strength. Rabbit's parents reestablished the family and began to discuss their ordeal of the past 5 years. Rabbit remained detached from his parents, fought viciously with his brother, and scavenged in both refugee camps and the adjacent Thai military base.

IMMIGRATION TO ALABAMA

Rabbit's relocation to the United States occurred by happenstance, when a worker gave his father an immigration petition to complete. Ignorant about the

United States, Rabbit's parents worried about providing for their family. Indeed, the family foraged for berries, fruit, turtles, and rabbits in the local environment, so local people referred to them as "leaf eaters." At school, a teacher made fun of Rabbit because he brought a dirty onion for lunch, calling him "Onion Breath." On arrival in Mobile, Alabama, the boys entered classes according to their ages, irrespective of their lack of English language skills. Eventually the school district evaluated the boys, terming them "educatably retarded," which meant they had low intellectual capabilities but could learn some skills. School records for Rabbit indicated no conduct or attendance problems.

Outside of school, Rabbit continued scavenging by digging in garbage Dumpsters and hunting small animals, long after the rest of the family adopted local customs for obtaining food and clothing. He preferred being alone, even at night. For many years Rabbit suffered from night terrors, night sweats, heightened startle reactions, disrupted sleep, and a dread of some impending doom. Rabbit stated, "I dream about wars" and, "I wish I was older so I could go back and fight that war." In his dreams, "the war never ends."

DISCUSSION

In answering the referral question, I considered a diagnosis of both post-traumatic stress disorder (PTSD) and antisocial personality disorder (ASPD). Both disorders share some common behaviors and often both are considered in a differential diagnosis. They are distinct in that PTSD may occur in either children or adults, while ASPD is a diagnosis for adults who evidenced conduct disorder (CD) in early adolescence. Therefore, the ASPD diagnosis implies a developmental basis.

Due to courtroom restraints, standardized personality tests were not administered and were not included as part of Rabbit's overall assessment. Any psychometric testing for Asian immigrants, however, must carefully consider population norms and language deficits (Hathaway & McKinley, 1967; Sandoval & Durán, 1998).

The *Diagnostic and Statistical Manual of Mental Disorders* (1994) cautions that the clinician should consider alternative explanations for apparently antisocial behavior. These explanations may include a history of trauma, cultural and social differences, stage of development, and neurological defects. A primary distinction between PTSD and ASPD involves determining whether the aggressive or criminal behavior correlates better with the personal trauma history or with the person's character.

Rabbit did not show pervasive sociopathic patterns, although his attitude toward others was certainly brutal. A lack of emotional expression is a sociopathic trait, but Rabbit's allegiance to his gang and his alleged love for children is not consistent with a sociopathic orientation. He would have met the criteria for ASPD only if he evidenced CD as a child. The CD diagnosis is met by criteria from these four areas of behavior: aggression toward people and animals, destruction of property, deceit or theft, and serious violation of rules. Through midadolescence, the only behaviors that fulfilled the CD criteria were continuous with his earlier survival behavior, or resulted from cultural misunderstanding. Certainly, CD should be based on neither nonacculturation nor lack of socialization.

Still, an explanation was needed for the lack of socialization within the family, which led me to consider reactive attachment disorder (RAD). This condition occurs in childhood, with the child either not bonding with caretakers or indiscriminately bonding with anyone. The cause appears to be improper or unresponsive parenting of a child who otherwise would have properly bonded with a caretaker. Rabbit evidenced solid object relations and indicated healthy attachment and nurturing inclination toward young children, a result of healthy parenting during the first few years of life. Just as clearly, he detached later from the family and never successfully reattached, but viewed his parents as mere resources. The severely traumatic conditions under the Khmer Rouge combined with the injunction against parental nurturing may have encouraged the development of RAD. Since his parents lived in the same village, Rabbit may have interpreted this situation as rejection by inadequate and helpless parents, and reacted by rejecting them.

Clearly, RAD best explained his early behavior, such as running away, that otherwise would fulfill a criterion for CD. Similarly, cultural misunderstandings accounted for other CD criteria. For example, private property was not part of the worldview for people raised in a communal village. Both his aggressive and his scavenging behaviors related to his survival behavior and evidenced continuing PTSD.

The one problem with the PTSD diagnosis was that Rabbit did not appear to reexperience the trauma. Clearly, his nightmares when sleeping under a poster of the Buddha in his room seemed related to hiding in a tunnel under the village statue of the Buddha, but he had no imagery or sense of the original trauma. Rather, he experienced pure fright with dissociative features. This dissociative reaction is consistent with Spiegel's (1997) finding that memories from the original trauma maintain the same dissociative quality as when they were stored. Thus, even when Rabbit did reexperience images of the escape to Thailand, he was uncertain if they were actual memories.

As far as the cultural appropriateness of the PTSD diagnosis, other studies (e.g., Sack, Clarke, & Seeley, 1996) have found this condition among Cambodian populations. Additionally, the older brother was diagnosed with PTSD and the parents exhibited both PTSD and major depression, as have been found among other Cambodian refugees (Hubbard & Realmuto, 1996). Therefore, I diagnosed Rabbit with both RAD and PTSD. Furthermore, these diagnoses preceded and best explained the behavioral problems that otherwise indicated either CD or ASPD.

Cognitive Assessment

Still, RAD and PTSD explained only some of Rabbit's cognitive and emotional deficits. During a third and final interview with Rabbit I examined his cognitive abilities. Rabbit was asked to evoke mental imagery, was given a seventh-grade reading assignment in an area of his interest, and was asked to mentally manipulate a familiar object. Generally speaking, his responses showed no appreciation for planning and implied that he did not relate to the world from a logical understanding of cause and effect. From these simple exercises, I determined that Rabbit showed cognitive deficits dissimilar to the perceptions and cognitions of my Southeast Asian students, so cultural differences did not explain his deficiency.

Since the specific processes supporting writing and speaking are located in different parts of the brain, these exercises indicated generalized problems in cognition. In addition, these exercises indicated Rabbit was incapable of accurately completing pen-and-paper psychological testing. The informal results of this testing also indicated deficits in his ability to organize perceptual sets, to identify usually perceived geometric figures in ambiguous stimuli, and to recognize perceptual miscues in sequences of stimuli. In addition, a vivid story about a personally interesting activity did not elicit imagery, nor did he recognize the story's central pattern of activity. Even his few mental images of Cambodia were unclear and uncertain when he reexperienced the original trauma. These observations were consistent with neurological symptoms of diffuse rather than focal brain damage.

Organic Assessment

As a result of this evaluation, I recommended that Rabbit undergo a Positron Emission Tomography (PET) brain scan at a local hospital. The neurologist reported a 60 percent reduction in frontal lobe activity and heightened occipital lobe activity as compared to the expected norms. The findings, consistent with PTSD (van der Kolk, 1996), included diminished activity in Broca's area and heightened metabolism in the amygdala, striatum, dorsal cerebellum, and posterior orbitofrontal. The primary finding, inconsistent with PTSD, was diminished activity in the right hemisphere, which usually shows significantly more activity than expected. Van der Kolk (1996) found that the pattern of a highly active amygdala and right hemisphere indicated, respectively, an experiencing of both trauma-related emotions and imagery, while the decreased activity in Broca's area indicated the inability to generate words to describe the experience.

While finding the PET scan consistent with PTSD, the examining neurologist attributed the extensive and diffuse shifts in brain activity to Rabbit's history of malnutrition, head injuries, and anoxia. In opposing this interpretation, the prosecution psychologist testified that such insults to a child's brain would not have lasting effects and that the PET scan did not necessarily show brain damage. Indeed, the literature contains few studies having to do with neuropsychological dysfunction due to malnutrition. The research on malnutrition consists largely of animal studies of nutritional deprivation under laboratory conditions, and some assessments of adults who were prisoners of war.

Only one study projected possible neurological effects of malnutrition in children by extrapolating from animal studies in a cross-species comparison of brain development (Morgane, Austin-LaFrance, Bronzino, Tonkiss, & Galler, 1992). Some confusion about the effect of starvation on brain function exists (Morgane et al., 1992) because malnutrition does not affect existing neuronal pathways. Thus, starvation does not have lasting impact on brain functions attained before the malnutrition. Instead, severe malnutrition interferes with the growth of glial cells and thus affects later organization and development of neurons. The predicted results would include retardation of future brain development, reduction in neural connections, and poorly insulated and nourished neural processes. One effect of this pattern of restricted growth would be a brain highly vulnerable to insult and with poor resiliency.

The timing of the malnutrition and injury is crucial to understanding the specific impact on Rabbit's neurological development. He had achieved rudimentary object relations and basic trust in his caretakers, and he was beginning to develop autonomy and self-confidence when he experienced abandonment. Thus, his interpersonal relations were stunted at the point where his caretakers were merely resources for needs he could not meet himself.

During this developmental stage, children develop sophisticated language skills; at that point, Rabbit was beginning to learn his native grammar, which is the vehicle for learning the structures and intersubjective meaning imbedded in the culture. Note that the learning of language is typically associated with heightened right hemisphere activity in a toddler's brain (Fischer & Rose, 1998). Since the near drowning occurred around age 5, the neurons in Rabbit's right hemisphere were especially vulnerable to anoxia due to the effects of starvation. Supporting this interpretation is the family's view of Rabbit as "clumsy."

In normal development, fine motor skills and smooth coordination of motor activities follow language acquisition during the toddler years. Clearly, Rabbit had not acquired English language skills to the degree of sophistication found among other members of his Cambodian immigrant cohort who also survived similar conditions (Clarke, Sack, Ben, Lanham, & Him, 1993). The population studied by Clarke et al. (1993) was high school students, which distinguishes them from Rabbit, who did not finish ninth grade in a public school.

Therefore, multiple sources of evidence supported the interpretations of cognitive dysfunction and PTSD in addition to the clinical finding of RAD. Rabbit had multiple cognitive deficits with perception, executive functions, imagery, and language generation. Next, these findings are considered within the overall scope of the clinical evaluation, especially concerning his emotionality.

Implications of the Diagnoses

The early onset of these multiple disorders means that they operate as part of the intrapsychic and interpersonal dynamics. As with other adults suffering from childhood trauma (Pynoos, Steinberg, & Goenjian, 1996), Rabbit's symptoms of PTSD were difficult to separate from features of his personality. However, the in-depth clinical interviews and the neurological findings shed light on his mental processes.

Specific to PTSD, when Rabbit had a startle reaction to an environmental trigger, he experienced the intense helplessness and anger of the original trauma, but his brain dysfunction confined his awareness to the immediate moment. This state of ultimate dissociation was intractable because his damaged right hemisphere provided no imagery or other memory by which to situate the PTSD in its original context. Compounding his dissociation was the inactive Broca's area, which limited his ability to describe this internal state. Furthermore, the greatly reduced cortical activity in his frontal lobe inhibited his ability to monitor and modify his reactions. Lastly, the decreased functioning of the hippocampus reduced his ability to learn new behaviors (van der Kolk, 1996). Therefore, without words to describe his internal state and unable to develop adaptive behavior, Rabbit operated entirely from a survival mode, without regard to other possibilities in the immediate context.

This condition may not have been hopeless; perhaps a remedial parenting and a supportive social milieu could have assisted him to learn adequate coping behavior. Imbedded in most cultural systems are interpersonal structures that support an individual's coping skills and psychic defenses. Conversely, a lack of such external support and protection results in "distorted survival behavior" (DeVries, 1996, p. 408), as exhibited by Rabbit. As his older brother said, "I guess he never left Cambodia." Although cultural systems can aid recovery by reinstituting interpersonal structures and assisting with learning new behavior, there was insufficient social support for Rabbit in either Cambodia or Alabama.

Still, during his childhood, some intervening agent might have helped Rabbit socialize to life away from the jungle. In a CYA facility for delinquent adolescents, he attached to staff and behaved well in response to their praise. In that setting, he did not align himself with peers of his gang, and the CYA report indicated excellent adherence to the institutional rules. It is a sad commentary that staying in the CYA until age 25 might have provided the best chance for Rabbit to acculturate and learn socially acceptable behavior.

Spouses provide another source of social support for adaptation. Both brothers mentioned the important influence of their spouses on directing them away from gang activities. The older brother was married, worked full-time, and no longer associated with criminals. While marriage was a settling influence for Rabbit, he battled with his desire for attachment and fear of attachment. His employment was unstable, as any perceived slight from a supervisor resulted in his leaving the job to avoid becoming violent. He appeared to move onto the socially acceptable path of marriage and gainful employment. Then his wife mistakenly thought he had been arrested for committing a crime and told him the marriage was finished. Although actual violence was atypical for him, the rejection apparently triggered the violent crime spree for which he stood trial.

CONCLUSION

Throughout this chapter, I have accepted that psychological trauma and parental neglect affect children across cultures; my acceptance of psychological trauma is implicit. Aside from arguing the universality of psychological trauma or of any other psychological disorder, clinicians must recognize that the manifestation of psychological distress emerges through a person's personal, ethnic, cultural, and linguistic history. Therefore, the client's expression of psychological reactions is embedded in a historical context distinct from the clinician's own context.

These contextual differences force multiple interpretations in order to derive an accurate clinical assessment. In this forensic case, I sought information from a Buddhist monk and other Khmer people, and this information adjusted my understanding of psychological trauma. From that basis, I assessed psychological trauma in the family to further frame my understanding of the continuing impact on Rabbit. Clinicians working with immigrant clients can follow similar development of understanding for culturally aware assessment. I hope this case presentation has provided specific examples that give life to the detached population statistics and theoretical concepts that usually drive discussions of cross-cultural psychology.

NOTE

I wish to thank Stanley Krippner and Stephen Levin for their kind reviews and comments.

REFERENCES

American Psychiatric Association. (1994). *Diagnostic and statistical manual of mental disorders* (4th ed.). Washington, DC: Author.

Clarke, G. N., Sack, W. H., Ben, R., Lanham, K., & Him, C. (1993). English language skills in a group of previously traumatized Khmer adolescent refugees. *Journal of Nervous and Mental Disease, 181,* 454–456.

DeVries, M. W. (1996). Trauma in cultural perspective. In B. A. van der Kolk, A. C. McFarlane, & L. Weisaeth (Eds.), *Traumatic stress: The effects of overwhelming experience on mind, body, and society* (pp. 398–413). New York: Guilford.

Fischer, K. W., & Rose, S. P. (1998). Growth cycles of brain and mind. *Educational Leadership, 56,* 56–60.

Hathaway, S. R., & McKinley, J. C. (1967). *Minnesota Multiphasic Personality Inventory: Manual for administration and scoring.* New York: Psychological Corporation.

Hubbard, J., & Realmuto, G. M. (1996). Comorbidity of psychiatric diagnoses with post-traumatic stress disorder in survivors of childhood trauma. *Journal of the American Academy of Child and Adolescent Psychiatry, 34,* 1167–1173.

Morgane, P. J., Austin-LaFrance, R. J., Bronzino, J. D., Tonkiss, J., & Galler, J. R. (1992). Malnutrition and the developing central nervous system. In R. L. Isaacson & K. F.

Jensen (Eds.), *The vulnerable brain and environmental risks: Vol. 2. Toxins in food* (pp. 3–44). New York: Plenum Press.

Pynoos, R. S., Steinberg, A.M., & Goenjian, A. (1996). Traumatic stress in childhood and adolescence: Recent development and current controversies. In B. A. van der Kolk, A. C. McFarlane, & L. Weisaeth (Eds.), *Traumatic stress: The effects of overwhelming experience on mind, body, and society* (pp. 331–358). New York: Guilford.

Sack, W.H., Clarke, G.N., & Seeley, J. (1996). Post traumatic stress disorder across two generations of Cambodian refugees. *Journal of the American Academy of Child and Adolescent Psychiatry, 34,* 1160–1166.

Sandoval, J., & Durán, R. P. (1998). Language. In J. Sandoval, C. L. Frisby, K. F. Geisinger, J. D. Scheuneman, & J. R. Grenier (Eds.), *Test interpretation and diversity: Achieving equity in assessment* (pp. 181–211). Washington, DC: American Psychological Association.

Spiegel, D. (1997). Trauma, dissociation, and memory. *Annals of the New York Academy of Sciences, 821,* 225–237.

van der Kolk, B. A. (1996). The body keeps the score: Approaches to the psychobiology of posttraumatic stress disorder. In B. A. van der Kolk, A. C. McFarlane, & L. Weisaeth (Eds.), *Traumatic stress: The effects of overwhelming experience on mind, body, and society* (pp. 214–241). New York: Guilford.

PART II

INTERVENTION AND RECONSTRUCTION

INTRODUCTION

Eleven-year-old Kunda depicts the overpowering and violent nature of warfare. Illustration published with permission of Margarida Ventura.

Part II includes nine chapters that describe varied and innovative approaches to address the psychosocial needs of civilians exposed to war stress. In general, it is agreed that traditional individually focused interventions are not suitable to respond quickly and efficiently to the needs of large groups of civilians in a war or postwar situation. A very practical problem is that there are not enough psychologists or other mental health workers to respond on such a large scale. The programs described here are community-based approaches that address the psychosocial needs of individuals in their social context and that make use of all the social agents available. They are multifaceted, interdisciplinary, and culturally relevant. The integration of traditional healing practices with Western-based methods is a common component in these approaches. Individual healing is not considered separate from community healing and, as such, community empowerment is another key element in these programs. Finally, targeting children and families is a priority in several of these chapters, justified in our view by the fact that with them lies the key to a more peaceful and prosperous future.

Overall, these chapters illustrate how psychology can contribute in a creative and scientific manner to alleviating civilian suffering. Additionally, the authors of these chapters challenge Western psychologists to examine their assumptions about how healing takes place as and after violence disrupts individual and social development, especially in terms of an ethnocentered attitude. Finally, there is a call for social responsibility and collaboration among professionals in various cultures to promote peace through professional, social, and political intervention on behalf of civilian populations.

The first three chapters have a more individual focus in terms of intervention strategies to work through war trauma. Chapter 8, by Paulson, is a lead chapter that summarizes the various forms of trauma civilian victims of war experience and the main conceptual approaches in understanding this traumatization, such as psychiatric, developmental, and cognitive-behavioral. The author reviews the treatment strategies stemming from these theories and introduces an innovative cognitive approach that uses internal mythic structures as a strategy to reframe the traumatic experience in a constructive manner. In Chapter 9, Arons examines the therapeutic value of diaries and memoirs of the Holocaust as creations that express the victim's suffering but also push forward toward recreation and renewal. Next, in Chapter 10, Barrett and Behbehani focus on a very specific post-traumatic intrusive symptom related to exposure to war stress—nightmares. The authors review post-traumatic nightmare research, giving examples of dreams from Kuwait after the Gulf War. This chapter underscores the importance of taking into consideration the interface between trauma and cultural beliefs about dreaming, such as in Muslim and Arabic folk traditions, in designing effective interventions.

The remaining chapters describe several approaches to healing and reconstruction that are group and community based, focusing on psychological intervention in the former Yugoslavia. Edelman, Kersner, Kordon, and Lagos describe in Chapter 11 the use of reflection groups as a mode of intervention for victims of political repression in Argentina. The group format is considered ideal because it offers response to a large number of people while allowing the development of a social construction of a shared traumatic event, such as police violence or the kidnapping of a relative. In Chapter 12, Baráth reports on the psychological consequences of war in the former Yugoslavia and the concerted efforts that have been undertaken in the past 10 years to respond to the needs of this population, especially children and teachers. The author describes four public health oriented art therapy prevention programs, which were supported by UNICEF and had primary, secondary, and tertiary prevention aims. These programs model important aspects of large-scale psychological interventions in war situations, such as the use of existing public institutions (schools, refugee camps), the use of community agents and volunteers, and the involvement of local facilitators who can carry on and potentiate the intervention. Another important model feature of this work was the careful quantitative and qualitative outcome evaluation of the efficacy of these interventions. In Chapter 13, Ognjenovic, Skorc, and Savic, a group of developmental psychologists from Croatia, describe their response to mitigate the effects of war stress on refugee children and families in Serbia and the Srpska Republic over the past 8 years. Based on the Vygotskian sociocultural approach, they developed an innovative workshop program focused on promoting child-adult social interaction through play and creativity. These programs share Baráth's community orientation and emphasis on play as a source of individual and social healing. Again, these programs are aimed at children as the repositories of hope for a more peaceful future.

The last three chapters introduce interventions directed at three groups of civilian victims of war that have received public attention only in the last few years: child soldiers, survivors of torture, and youth forced into sex-trafficking. In Chapter 14, Wessells and Monteiro illustrate further the use of a community-oriented approach to promote psychosocial assistance directed at children and youth in war-torn Angola. These programs were based on the same principles as the ones described above but seem to make more explicit the empowerment of local communities through the use of key people, such as elders and folk healers, and recognizing the need to respect the local culture and use culturally relevant avenues for healing. Another differing aspect is the integration of material and psychosocial assistance as a condition for the psychological interventions to succeed. The programs described also tackle a delicate issue, the reintegration of child soldiers, which may be seen as a prevention strategy against continued violence. Chapter 15 is the transcription of an interview with Michael Korzinski that describes the history of the Medical Foundation, a London-based group that offers multidisciplinary assistance to survivors of torture and other forms of organized violence, such as asylum seekers. This chapter highlights the holistic nature of the experience of trauma, calling attention to the mind-body links in terms of how trauma affects the individual. Korzinski proposes a form of psychological intervention that addresses the somatic dimension of this experience—somato-psychotherapy. Finally, in Chapter 16, Graves examines the post-Vietnam War repercussions in Southeast Asia in terms of the phenomenon of sex trafficking of young girls. This chapter affirms once more the need to look at trauma as a social phenomenon and to consider the effects of structural violence as well as overt violence. The author offers an integrative approach for intervention with these youth, which is aimed at their social reintegration, and includes Qigong, narrative psychotherapy, and expressive art therapy as complements of group therapy.

Despite the diverse array of interventions proposed in this part, it is important to stress that these efforts can only be successful and have long-term effects within a context of economic, political, and social change that creates conditions for a peaceful existence. Part III, on prevention, presents some strategies that can aid in creating more peaceful societies and preventing conflict and dehumanization.

8

War and Refugee Suffering

Daryl S. Paulson

Most wars are conducted between states. However, in recent decades wars have started to take an ominous new direction, that of states conducting wars against civilians (Van der Veer, 1998; Whitaker, 2000). Often these civilian targets are both poor and from a minority group, having few or no allies either in their home country or abroad. Since the early 1980s and into the new millennium, wars against civilians have been and, in some cases, are still being carried out in such countries and regions as Afghanistan, Algeria, Angola, China, Colombia, El Salvador, Ethiopia, Guatemala, Indian Kashmir, East Timor, Israeli-occupied territories, Liberia, Mozambique, Nicaragua, Northern Ireland, Peru, the Philippines, Russian Chechnya, Rwanda, Sierra Leone, Somalia, South Africa, Sri Lanka, Sudan, Timor, the former Yugoslavia, and Zaire (Wright, 1999).

That these are "wars" is not an overstatement or hyperbole. Take the case of Rwanda, for example. Fourteen percent of its total population, representing a majority of the Tutsis, was killed within 3 months. In Bosnia, at least 200,000 civilians were killed in "ethnic cleansing" campaigns, with another 20,000 civilians missing and unaccounted for (Van der Veer, 1998).

A key strategic goal in this type of warfare is to create terror among the targeted civilian population (Blank, 1987; Clayton, Barlow, & Ballif-Spanvill, 1999). In creating a state of terror, normal economic, social, cultural, and political relations are disrupted, making it easy for the warring state to achieve its goal: control and subjugation of the civilian population. Further, the destruction of social and cultural institutions, which connect people to their past and provide shared values, meaning, and goals, has been extremely effective in disenfranchising civilian victims.

The goal of this chapter is to address the suffering of civilian victims of war and review some of the psychotherapeutic approaches to assisting the victims in dealing with trauma and unresolved issues. I have worked with civilian victims of war for more than 25 years. I have used internal mythic structure with this population, as well as with veterans of the Vietnam War, with positive therapeutic results. The results have often been in terms of integrating the negative effects of war into their psyche (Paulson, 1991, 1995).

CIVILIAN EXPERIENCE

A common thread binding present-day civilian victims of war is that, as a group, they have been unjustly persecuted and, as individuals, they have suffered immensely, with few individuals or groups coming to their aid. Their stark awareness of the world communities' apathy and indifference is shocking for them. Generally, their persecution does not happen overnight. Instead, it is progressive, and there are at least three stages to their experience (Bustos, 1990).

Increasing Political Repression

Initially, both social and political changes occur in the person's home country, resulting in ever-increasing levels of political repression and persecution (Van der Veer, 1998). These may include limits to freedom of speech and movement within the country, as well as general intimidation by police, army, or paramilitary groups. The usual response is passive acceptance, even indifference, because they do not understand what is happening. Denial, suppression, and repression are the common social psychological defenses erected to dismiss the unclear situation from concern (Daly, 1985; Whitaker, 2000).

Major Traumatic Experience

At some point, psychological defenses no longer work, as the political and social conditions worsen (Horowitz, 1998). The person witnesses friends and/or family members taken at night or even killed. Survivors have vividly described the psychological trauma of being arrested, being detained, and even being jailed for no substantive reason (Knudsen, 1991; Van der Veer, 1998). Both psychological and physical torture are typically brought to bear on these individuals. Some undergo brutal forms of torture immediately; others experience a more selectively applied torture, not only to break their psychological feelings of well-being, but also to humiliate and degrade their personhood. The torture takes place in an environment where the victim is helpless and completely at the mercy of the torturers (Dahl, 1989). Thus, torture can be used to promote and carry out a systematic policy of intimidating and destabilizing an entire ethnic community or group. The physical torture procedures not only are premeditated, but are creatively designed to produce the most pain and torment possible to the victim (Applegate, 1976).

Commonly, too, captives are further terrorized by having a towel placed over their faces as they are lying down and water steadily poured over the towel so they feel intense suffocation panic. Pouring salt or a strong acid into freshly incised wounds and inserting needles under the fingernails and heating them with a cigarette while a person hangs by wrists or ankles are extremely effective, fast-acting torture methods. There often are the added psychological torments of being constantly intimidated, of hearing the screams of other prisoners, of sleep deprivation, of solitary confinement, and of observing friends and family members killed, tortured, or raped.

Life in Exile

Those who escape to a safe haven in another country generally suffer many hardships, not the least being the escape process. Life in exile entails psychological and social adjustment issues (Curtis, 1982; Sue & Sue, 1999; Van der Veer, 1998). For example, people seeking political asylum generally experience extended periods of gut-wrenching anxiety as to whether they will be accepted by a host country or will be sent back to their home country to face imprisonment or death. Nevertheless, they generally feel deeply connected to their home country.

Probably the greatest trauma at this phase is the uprooting of their physical, psychological, cultural, and social past (Carson, Butcher, & Mineka, 2000; Horowitz, 1986). They are no longer in a comfortable, familiar setting but are trying to adapt to a new culture that is difficult and strange, and to a community that is often distant and even hostile. Many persons at this stage report feeling a sense of guilt for living, when others were killed, or for various acts committed in leaving their home country, or for having taken appropriate action (Daly, 1985; Knudsen, 1991; Pennbaker, & Beall, 1986; Van der Veer, 1998).

Difficulties faced from their complete personal uprooting and from living in exile have been characterized as "culture shock" (Sue & Sue, 1999). This means that a person undergoes intense and usually prolonged emotional upheaval, once they realize how "strange" their adopted new culture is and how difficult it is for them to adjust to it. As Sue and Sue state (pp. 258–265), the consensus of individuals characterizes this upheaval as feelings of insignificance and being lost in the world, in that:

1. They have lost the love and respect they formerly experienced with friends and family.
2. They have lost their former social and cultural status.
3. They have lost their cultural environment and the many obligations and dependencies that gave their lives meaning.
4. They are adrift among the values of the new cultural environment, those not recognized in their native culture, and those they bring with them that are not valued in the new.

There are both intrapersonal and interpersonal aspects of these phenomena. Intrapersonal conflicts usually relate to issues with regard to the cultural values and norms being at odds with their own. Intrapersonal conflicts lead to anxiety, which leads often to depression or, at least, avoidance. Avoidance prevents integration of the new culture. This engenders a second problem, interpersonal conflicts. Interaction with those outside of one's native culture is seriously impeded by differences in both verbal and nonverbal communication. In cases where the victims of war are still within the home country, a clear distinction between normal suffering of violence and war versus post-traumatic stress disorder (PTSD) must be identified. Only a small minority develop psychological dysfunction requiring psychological treatment. Trying to categorize a traumatic experience as a normal one is difficult. Generally, after the hostilities end, people tend to get on with their lives, often with no evidence of trauma. As long as they are reunited with their family, cultural group, and familiar surroundings, there is seldom a problem. But if a person goes to a different country, many problems may occur. As if this were not enough with which to contend, even the concepts and treatment of traumatic conditions of refugees are not uniform.

TREATMENT APPROACHES TO TRAUMATIC DISORDERS IN CIVILIANS

From my experience, there are six basic views of traumatic disorders and their treatments, which will be briefly described below.

Psychiatric Approach

The psychiatric approach, in its most basic presentation, views refugee traumatization in terms of a post-traumatic stress disorder (PTSD) as characterized in the *DSM-IV-TR* (2000). Additionally, PTSD is often linked with other disorders, particularly depression and meaninglessness. In fact, it stands to reason, if one continually experiences anxiety, it is not long before the quality of one's life disintegrates, thrusting one into a depressive state (Pine, 2000).

While it is generally agreed that the psychiatric approach is useful, particularly in characterizing symptoms, it tends to force a "medical" construction of reality onto the situation, ignoring the victim's subjective experience or shared interpersonal and social values, meaning, and goals, reducing these symptoms to mere biochemical reactions (Bandura, 1997; Shapiro & Astin, 1998). The psychiatric approach does not, in this author's view, present a convincing analysis of cultural uprooting (Cancelmo, Millan, & Vazques, 1990). It has cross-cultural limitations that can be considered normal under the circumstances (Sue & Sue, 1999). Yet treatment of certain classes of anxiety, depression, and phobia with pharmacologicals is often dramatic, with few negative side effects (Sheikh & Nguyen, 2000).

Developmental Approach

The ability of people to develop psychologically is often hampered by the trauma, as is the ability to remain at their current level of growth (Goleman, 1998). This is due, in part, to normal psychological defense mechanisms, perhaps better described as "protective factors," such as regression in the service of the ego, which forces one to act in ways that reduce tension and anxiety (Bandura, 1997; Commons et al., 1990; Mendelsohn, 1987). This is of even greater concern when the victim is a child or an adolescent, since normal development can be arrested. If development is hindered, a person is less likely to be able to integrate traumatic experience into his or her psyche (Kegan, 1994).

Psychodynamic Approach

The psychodynamic approach views trauma in terms of the interaction of the person with the environment. In this view, the traumatic experiences are beyond those that are normally experienced and, in essence, overwhelm the psyche, resulting in its numbing, and in the person's behaving passively (Blanck & Blanck, 1974; Stolorow, Brandchaft & Atwood, 1987). Sometimes, usually within hours or several days of the traumatic experience, one's emotions are stimulated by what has been called an "outcry" period. This is usually followed by a period of denial, with unwanted memory intrusions.

As an outcome of his treatment of World War I veterans, Sigmund Freud (1920) developed a theory on this subject. This view posits that it is the biologically felt tension of the so-called id that overwhelms the rational aspect of the ego. Undoubtedly, the so-called superego also exerts pressures of guilt and inadequacy on the psyche, often to the extent that the "ego" becomes immobilized. Usually, individuals repress a traumatic incident from conscious awareness successfully but, sooner or later, will relive it in their dreams. A major goal, from this perspective, is to work through the experience by building the "ego strength" necessary to allow for a conscious reexperiencing of the traumatic event, generally a repetitive process of gradually and consciously assimilating the experience into one's life.

A fundamental problem with this view is that it generally requires more than personal insight and reliving the experience in one's mind to work through it (Corey, 2001). It generally takes much time and a highly motivated patient in a committed therapeutic relationship to deal fully with the trauma. A careful reading of Freud would find that he called for "working through" psychoanalytically derived insights. The psychodynamic view of trauma has evolved a great deal since Freud, centering, to a large degree, in Object Relations Theory (Blanck & Blanck, 1974, 1986; Greenberg & Mitchell, 1983), as well as aspects of hypnotherapy (Brown & Fromm, 1987).

Family System Approach

A number of practitioners have reported using a family system approach to dealing with civilian victims of war. The dynamics of those relationships and the roles, rules, and taboos of the family system are evaluated and restructured to become more effective in meeting the needs of the family members (Corey, 2001; Teyber, 2000). Traumatization of one or all family members has particularly strong effects on the entire family system, including exacerbating any existing dysfunctional characteristics, communication disturbances, family secrets, over-protection of certain members, or blame directed toward specific members for actions allegedly committed.

The routine use of family system approaches in the treatment of war trauma can be exceptionally difficult to manage therapeutically and usually requires lengthy treatment periods. Once treatment begins, the facilitator often discovers that the war trauma issues are interwoven within a preexisting dysfunctionality, highly resistant to change (Corey, 2001; Pennbaker & Beall, 1986; Van der Veer, 1998).

Learning Theory Approach

Many of the reactions of the war victim can be viewed in terms of learned behavior or conditioning. That is, a person learns to avoid stimuli that are associated with trauma (Bandura, 1997; Wolpe, 1982). This, in itself, would probably not be problematic. What is problematic, however, is that the person generalizes avoidance to even the most benign situations. Much research and applied practice has been used successfully in desensitizing a victim of trauma, through realization that, in spite of one's conditioning, there is no real danger in certain situations. Biofeedback and other self-regulation control strategies have been developed to speed up the desensitization process (Moss, 1999). If the body can remain physiologically relaxed, as taught in biofeedback, the desensitization process is greatly enhanced. The goal is to let the body remain relaxed as one confronts the traumatic event psychologically in increasingly anxiety-producing doses. Over time, the victim can usually regain a sense of psychological well-being.

Note, however, that anxiety desensitization is not the same as dealing with one's experience (Bugental, 1965; Schneider & May, 1995). The learning theory approach is useful but usually also requires in-depth discussion of traumatic events, cognitively and emotionally. In other words, the phenomenology of the experience, as well as the overt symptoms and reactions, need attention.

Cognitive-Behavioral Approach

Much useful treatment of war trauma can be achieved via cognitive-behavioral therapy. The strategy of treatment is straightforward. The person is shown, by a therapist, that many injunctions such as "must," "should," and "ought" are irrational; that they are not grounded in the here-and-now (Ellis, 1971). Self-instructions, positive self-talk, and reframing are very useful to many victims (Beck & Emery, 1985). After this is done, refugees are shown how this thinking style continues to affect their lives negatively, and then, how to modify their thinking to remove and abandon illogical ideas. They are then in a position to construct a life philosophy rooted in the here-and-now, instead of the there-and-then (Bandura, 1997). However, for sophisticated individuals who exhibit emotional sensitivity and intelligence, it is important that the new belief system be grounded in a constructed view rooted in the person's own life experiences, values, meanings, and beliefs. Otherwise, individuals run the risk of accepting views to which they do not really relate.

Horowitz (1998) describes the role of defense mechanisms that preconstruct information processes that effect moods, transitional patterns, and general maladaptive behaviors. Depression can also be effectively treated with cognitive therapy of war refugees by instilling positive meaning (Beck, Rush, Shaw, & Emery, 1979).

Each of these viewpoints offers valuable potential for the therapist, but each must be used with appropriate balance and discretion, much as a mechanic chooses the right tool (Norcross & Goldfried, 1992). In my experience, perhaps the most damaging effect of war trauma is the frequent loss of the feeling that victims are in control of their life (Paulson, 1994). When individuals feel little control over the course of their lives, the negative effects of trauma are accentuated (Shapiro & Astin, 1998). Additionally, from an existential perspective, finding positive meaning in war experiences is often impossible (Paulson, 1994). For example, trying to help a young woman who was raped and now is carrying the fetus of an enemy to find positive meaning in the event is absurd. This situation makes her vulnerable to rejection by her community, not only because she is "tainted," but also because, in some way, she "brought on the event."

Treating refugees who have experienced these situations is extremely difficult. And worse, many victims feel they are being punished by God for some action they have committed, or that they are somehow the cause of the situation (Richards & Bergin, 1997). The therapist often is caught in a no-win dichotomy. If victims modify their thinking, they lose much of the cultural mythology that provides them with life-meaning. Yet, until they reframe this perspective, they remain victims not only of war, but of their own thinking.

Sometimes an existential perspective is helpful but rarely by itself (Paulson, 1994). War victims have, more than likely, experienced "too much reality" and, through this experience, are acutely sensitized to the brutality and sheer meaninglessness of not only their life, but of all life. A spiritual perspective has limited effectiveness because refugees could feel one of two ways. First, as previously suggested, refugees may feel as though they are being punished by God for some transgression. Often, the specific transgression cannot be identified by the refugee, or, because it seems to be so minor to the therapist, it is discounted or ignored. For example, not saying one's prayers or not praying enough can be viewed as the transgression that brought all the strife to one's life. The other common reaction is total hatred of the enemy for their actions and existence. While anger is often easier to work with than internalized guilt, it has a tendency to fester and grow, encompassing more and more of the victim's world-view. Neither the existential nor the spiritual approach will provide long-term therapeutic benefit in most instances (Richards & Bergin, 1997). However, existential and spiritual approaches, if life-affirming and positive, can be combined with other therapies, notably those based on learning theory and cognitive psychology.

Learning theory and cognitive-behavioral approaches are, in my experience, critically useful in the desensitization of a surface problem, but do not touch the deeper aspects of a victim's life (Paulson, 1994). While individuals can ultimately realize they are not physically in harm's way in the new country, no amount of desensitization is effective when they perceive their underlying psychic discord as grounded in reality. And the problem is that, all too often, it *is* grounded in reality.

TREATING TRAUMA IN OTHER GROUPS

Experience gained by this author through counseling Vietnam combat veterans, as well as Vietnamese, Middle Eastern, and Latin American war victims now residing in the United States, reveals a crucial aspect of psychotherapy. The person must be heard truly and be taken seriously by the therapist (Teyber, 2000). Victims need to tell their stories, express their pain, their rage, their despair, their guilt, and their hatred (Van der Veer, 1998). As they tell their stories, often over and over, they need to be reassured that they are heard, that they are valued, that they are respected, and that they are appreciated.

I have also used another therapeutic approach in the treatment of victims and refugees of war. It consists of a cognitive approach that reframes the situation into the perspective of a mythic *rite of passage* (Paulson, 1994). However, it is contraindicated in the early stages of therapy, when anxiety, depression, and feelings of loss are intensely experienced (Paulson, 1999). Later in the course of therapy, when the person has dealt, to some degree, with the traumatic experience and is somewhat desensitized to it, it is often beneficial to bring the rite of passage viewpoint to the fore (Paulson, 2001).

Rites of passage and the mythic structures that contain them are not legends or falsehoods when used in this context. Instead, they provide a cognitive map with which to reframe past war experience in positive, meaningful ways (Feinstein & Krippner, 1988). A rite of passage, from a "within" perspective, is a self-constructed, cognitive map that serves to organize one's traumatic life experiences in a coherent structure that clarifies and defines the meaning of one's unique experiences. These cognitive maps can provide meaning to the past, definition to the present, and direction for the future.

USING INTERNAL MYTHIC STRUCTURE

Campbell (1968, p. 3) identified three recurrent cross-cultural phases that are present in mythical rites of passage: separation; initiation; and return.

Separation Phase

The separation, or "call to adventure," signifies that destiny has summoned a person for a rite of passage. The separation in terms of civilian victims of war is their initial challenge to their former situation. For example, war victims did not choose the event but were "chosen by fate" for whatever reason in their home country. The event is then viewed as the motivating force behind the person's situation. It is the point where a transition begins between the former life situation and a passage to a new life. It is a liminal period in which the person is psychologically off balance and is "betwixt and between."

Initiation Phase

The initiation phase is the experience of being removed from one's normal surroundings, being arrested, and tortured, or having escaped. It is a very difficult period when one has little or no control of the events and their outcomes, a period of intense psychological and physical testing, which the person must survive (Paulson, 1997). The victim is essentially in an impossible situation and must endure. There appears to be no future, only a painful and present now.

Return Phase

The return phase includes the therapeutic phase in which victims deal with the traumatic experience (Paulson, 1991). It includes dealing with the traumatic experience as well as designating meaning to the experience that can be used as a source of new wisdom.

The return phase is the integration stage. Generally, the victims, while suffering horribly from the experience, can reach a greater level of psychological well-being than could have been achieved without the experience. In essence, they have derived value that is greater than they would have had they not experienced the war. Notable examples are Viktor Frankl (1992) and Elie Wiesel (1996), interned in Nazi concentration camps, both of whom gained much wisdom from their traumatic experiences.

As time goes on, refugees often can describe the traumatic war experience as horrible in many ways, but also as one of the most useful experiences or lessons in their lives. For example, had those victims not experienced the traumas, they would not have searched for meaning or found an intense purpose in life. It can be a momentous "wake-up call," one that can contribute to the benefit of humanity (Paulson, 1993). And, chances are, in dealing with war issues, that victims will also be forced to deal constructively with other intrapsychic issues that they would not have addressed, had they not been victimized. In this way, survivors of the horrors of war may have a clear purpose to help others in similar situations in their country and beyond.

REFERENCES

American Psychiatric Association. (2000). *Diagnostic and statistical manual of mental disorders* (4th ed., Text rev.). Washington, DC: Author.

Applegate, R. (1976). *Kill or get killed* (Rev. ed.). Boulder, CO: Paladin Press.

Bandura, A. (1997). *Self efficacy: The exercise of control.* New York: Freeman.

Beck, A. T., & Emery, G. (1985). *Anxiety disorders and phobias: A cognitive perspective.* New York: Basic Books.

Beck, A. T., Rush, A. J., Shaw, B. F., & Emery, G. (1979). *Cognitive therapy of depression.* New York: Guilford.

Blanck, G., & Blanck, R. (1974). *Ego psychology: therapy and practice.* New York: Columbia University Press.

Blanck, G., & Blanck, R. (1986). *Beyond ego psychology.* New York: Columbia University Press.

Blank, A. S. (1987). Irrational reactions to posttraumatic stress disorders and Vietnam veterans. In S. M. Sonnenberg (Ed.), *The trauma of war* (pp. 66–99). Washington, DC: American Psychiatric Association Press.

Brown, D. P., & Fromm, E. (1987). *Hypnosis and Behavioral Medicine.* Hillsdale, NJ: Lawrence Erlbaum.

Bugental, J. F. T. (1965). *The search for authenticity.* New York: Holt, Rinehart & Winston.

Bustos, E. (1990). Dealing with the unbearable. In P. Suedfeld (Ed.), *Psychology and torture* (pp. 143–163). New York: Hemisphere.

Campbell, J. (1968). *The hero with a thousand faces* (2nd ed.). Princeton, NJ: Princeton University Press.

Cancelmo, J. A., Millan, F., & Vazques, C. I. (1990). Culture and symptomatology: The role of personal meaning in diagnosis and treatment. *American Journal of Psychoanalysis, 50,* 137–149.

Carson, R. C., Butcher, J. N., & Mineka, S. (2000). *Abnormal psychology and modern life.* Boston: Allyn and Bacon.

Clayton, C. J., Barlow, S. H., & Ballif-Spanvill, B. (1999). Principles of group violence with a focus on terrorism. In H. V. Hall & L. C. Whitaker (Eds.), *Collective violence* (pp. 277–311). Boca Raton, FL: CRC Press.

Commons, M. L., Armon, C., Kohlberg, L., Richard, F. A., Gretzner, T. A., & Sinnott, J. P. (1990). *Adult development* (Vols. 1 and 2). New York: Praeger.

Corey, G. (2001). *Theory and practice of counseling and psychotherapy* (6th ed.). Belmont, CA: Brooks-Cole.

Curtis, A. J. (1982). Life-threatening indicators among Indochinese refugees. *Suicide and Life-threatening Behavior, 12*(1), 46–51.

Dahl, C. (1989). Some problems of cross-cultural psychotherapy with refugees seeking treatment. *American Journal of Psychoanalysis, 49,* 19–32.

Daly, R. J. (1985). Effects of imprisonment and isolation. In P. Pichot, P. Bernes, B. Wolf, & K. Thau (Eds.), *Psychiatry: The state of art* (Vol. 8, pp. 249–254). New York: Plenum.

Ellis, A. (1971). *Growth through reason: Verbatim cases of rational-emotive therapy.* Hollywood, CA: Wilshire Books.

Feinstein, D., & Krippner, S. (1988). *Personal mythology: The psychology of your evolving self.* Los Angeles: Tarcher.

Frankl, V. E. (1992). *Man's search for meaning* (4th ed.). Boston: Beacon Press.

Freud, S. (1920). *A general introduction to psychoanalysis*. New York: Washington Square Press.

Goleman, D. (1998). *Working with emotional intelligence*. New York: Bantam Books.

Greenberg, J. R., & Mitchell, S. A. (1983). *Object relations in psychoanalytic theory*. Cambridge, MA: Harvard University Press.

Horowitz, M. J. (1986). Stress response syndromes: A review of posttraumatic and adjustment disorders. *Hospital and Community Psychiatry, 37,* 241–249.

Horowitz, M. J. (1998). *Cognitive psychodynamics: From conflict to character*. New York: Wiley.

Kegan, R. (1994). *In over our heads*. Cambridge, MA: Harvard University Press.

Knudsen, J. C. (1991). Therapeutic strategies for refugee coping. *Journal of Refugee Studies, 4,* 21–38.

Mendelsohn, R. M. (1987). *The synthesis of self,* (Vol. 2). New York: Plenum Medical.

Moss, D. (1999). Biofeedback, mind-body medicine, and the higher limits of human nature. In D. Moss (Ed.), *Humanistic and transpersonal psychology* (pp. 145–161). Westport, CT: Greenwood.

Norcross, J. C., & Goldfried, M. R. (1992). *Handbook of psychotherapy integration*. New York: Basic Books.

Paulson, D. S. (1991, Spring/Summer). Myth, male initiation, and the Vietnam veteran. *Voices,* 156–165.

Paulson, D. S. (1993, Winter). Authentic integral living: The search for the real self. *Voices,* 58–65.

Paulson, D. S. (1994). *Walking the point: Male initiation and the Vietnam experience*. Plantation, FL: Distinctive Publishing.

Paulson, D. S. (1995). The shadow of war. In S. Hansel, A. Steldle, G. Zaczek, & R. Zaczek (Eds.), *Heart: Survivors' views of trauma* (pp. 189–191). Lutherville, MD: Sidram Press.

Paulson, D. S. (1997). Participation in combat perceived as a male rite of passage. In S. Krippner, & H. Kalweit (Eds.), *Yearbook of cross-cultural medicine and psychotherapy,* (Vol. 8) (pp. 53–68). Berlin: Verlag for Wissenschaft und Bildung.

Paulson, D. S. (1999, Fall). Courage to be oneself. *Voices,* 56–58.

Paulson, D. S. (2001). The hard issues of life. *Pastoral Psychology, 49*(5), 385–394.

Pennbaker, J. W., & Beall, K. S. (1986). Confronting a traumatic event. *Journal of Abnormal Psychology, 95,* 274–281.

Pine, D. S. (2000). Anxiety disorders: Clinical features. In B. J. Sadock & V. A. Sadock (Eds.), *Comprehensive textbook of psychiatry,* (Vol. 1) (7th ed., pp. 1476–1498). Philadelphia: Lippincott, Williams, & Wilkins.

Richards, P. S., & Bergin, A. E. (1997). *A spiritual strategy for counseling and psychotherapy*. Washington, DC: American Psychological Association.

Schneider, K. J., & May, R. (1995). *The psychology of existence*. New York: McGraw-Hill.

Shapiro, D., & Astin, J. (1998). *Control therapy*. New York: Wiley.

Sheikh, J. I., & Nguyen, C. T. M. H. (2000). Psychopharmacology: Anxiety drugs. In B. J. Sadock & V. A. Sadock (Eds.), *Comprehensive textbook of psychiatry,* (Vol. 3) (7th ed., pp. 3084–3096). Philadelphia: Lippincott, Williams, & Wilkins.

Stolorow, R. D., Brandchaft, B., & Atwood, G. E. (1987). *Psychoanalytic treatment: An intersubjective approach*. Hillsdale, NJ: Analytic Press.

Sue, D. W., & Sue, D. (1999). *Counseling the culturally different: Theory and practice* (3rd ed.). New York: Wiley.

Teyber, E. (2000). *Interpersonal process in psychotherapy* (4th ed.). Belmont, CA: Brooks-Cole.

Van der Veer, G. (1998). *Counseling and therapy with refugees and victims of trauma* (2nd ed.). West Sussex, England: Wiley.

Whitaker, L. C. (2000). *Understanding and preventing violence: The psychology of human destructiveness.* Boca Raton, FL: CRC Press.

Wiesel, E. (1996). *All rivers run to the sea: Memoirs.* New York: Schocken Books.

Wolpe, J. (1982). *The practice of behavior therapy* (3rd ed.). Elmsford, NY: Pergamon.

Wright, J. W. (1999). *The New York Times almanac.* New York: Penguin Books.

9

Self-Therapy Through Personal Writing: A Study of Holocaust Victims' Diaries and Memoirs

Sandrine Arons

This chapter discusses the psychological benefits of the diary and the memoir for the war crime victim by exploring personal writings from the Holocaust. I begin by clarifying the basic difference between the two genres and how such distinctions are made even more apparent in connection with the Holocaust. Then, an overview of recent research on the subject of Holocaust diaries and memoirs will be linked to my own findings, which indicate that diaries and memoirs help the individual cope with trauma and serve to support their transition back into a more normal life-state.

THE DIARY AND THE MEMOIR

The diary, or journal, can be defined as an ongoing, usually chronological, documentation of individual events, beliefs, and desires. Baldwin (1977), an expert researcher on diaries, explains that there is a dichotomy established between the self who reads and the self who writes, and "since the journal connection between the two parts is interior, it fosters an increased sense of awareness of personal psychology. It becomes a way of observing survival. It becomes an instrument of survival" (p. xiv). Diaries can be used as an outlet for frustration and as a sounding board for personal ideas and dilemmas. As Rainer (1978) explains, the "diary is a psychological tool that enables you to express feelings without inhibition, recognize and alter self-defeating habits of mind, and come to know and accept that self which is you" (p. 18). People often begin writing a diary during the most difficult moments of their lives and, henceforth, turn to their journals as an outlet for feelings such as guilt, depression, and fear (Arons, 1997; Bullough & Pinnegar, 2001). Rainer's (1978, p. 27) research identifies the diary as a place to release tensions, to explore future behaviors and attitudes, to explore problems, and as an opportunity to find solitude. Unlike the memoir, a diary is usually unedited, although many diarists feel that someone else may find their private writings and read them posthumously. Mallon (1984), the author of *A Book of One's Own*, reasons that the diary is actually a way to immortality. He states that "time is the strongest thing of all, and the diarist is always fleeing it" (p. xv). This, I believe, is a key to diary keeping during the Holocaust.

The memoir, an edited portrait of one's past, is defined by the *American Heritage Dictionary* (1981) as "a narrative of the experiences that the writer has lived through." To write a memoir one must be able to employ the same literary devices as the novel, such as structure, point of view, voice, character, and story (Rainer, 1978). In other words, the memoir is much more thoughtful than the diary. According to Frankl (1984, p. 24), a survivor of the Auschwitz and Dachau concentration camps, the basic difference between the memoir and any other historical text is that the memoir holds within it the memories of a person's (or a society's) experience.

Recent Research on Holocaust Memoirs and Diaries

The Holocaust diary and memoir nourish the same craving, representing an absolute desire and psychological need to express the horrific events that took place over the course of World War II, but for two separate reasons. Brenner (1997) supposes that the survivor who writes a memoir does so in an attempt to "return to the experience and relive it, often as an attempt to exorcise the haunting past" (p. 131), while the diarist records in order to gain distance from present suffering. Frankl's (1984) principal reason for writing his memoir *Man's Search for Meaning* was to answer the question "how was everyday life in a concentration camp reflected in the mind of the average prisoner?" (p. 21). The question is, in fact, the biggest difference between the memoir and the diary: the memoir *attempts* to illustrate what the prisoner may have experienced, while the diary is the illustration *itself*.

The Holocaust memoir, in consequence, has sometimes been perceived as neglecting certain facts. Appelfeld (1999), who survived the Transnistra camps in Ukraine, infers that memoirs are "burning testimonies that the survivors have sworn to write, but [that] the reader should not seek great innerness ... or a new worldview" from them. If anything, they are more like chronicles, "concealing more than they reveal" (p. 4). He also distinguishes between diaries written during and after the Holocaust, feeling that diaries written during the war have more "innerness" than those written after. The war diaries are "the most fiery outcries raised by the soul" (p. 4). Porat (1999) echoes Appelfeld's belief, stating that "unlike later memoirs ... the diaries do not display lapses of memory, for the writing occurred while the events were taking place" (p. 159). For Appelfeld, postwar diaries and memoirs could never compare to the contemporaneous writings during the war because the survivor does not have the power to relive what he or she underwent. "No one," he says, "willingly returns to Hell" (p. 4).

Because it is important for the survivor to describe the Holocaust in precise detail, many first writings about the Holocaust were essentially self-centered: writing about personal experiences (the reason why imaginative writing on the subject is considered provocative, if not insulting). With this in mind, the war diaries appear to best represent Holocaust experiences. Diaries, in a sense, are pure. They provide a perspective on the Holocaust that could exist only during the war. Diaries, however, are not always complete. Diarists often omit specific events or feelings in fear that, were the diary found, they would be held accountable for the writing. This is an advantage for memoir authors: Survivors have the opportunity to write free of fear.

DIARY AS THERAPIST/FRIEND

The diary is also liberating, and therefore therapeutic, in its capacity to offer a safe haven for emotions. For the Holocaust victim, who was devoid of any external freedoms, the diary became the embodiment of freedom, the place to create and explore a unique life.

It is certainly clear in reading World War II diaries that there is an "irreducible need to express the horror" (Brenner, 1997, p. 131). Although the main difficulty was accepting the situation, victims also struggled to find adequate means of expression. For example, Sierakowiak (1996) wrote in a journalistic form, trying never to omit any facts:

Monday, April 28, Łódź

The Germans win one victory after another. The fighting in Yugoslavia and Greece is coming to an end, and the last English groups are leaving in a hurry; in Africa, where Germans are arriving through France (using French ships to reach French Tunis), the English are beginning to take heavy losses. Although they talk again about tensions in German-Soviet relations. (p. 84)

In spite of the seemingly journalistic form of the diary, however, Sierakowiak also uses it to release negative feelings, especially in recording the dynamics of his family. In several entries he reveals that his father has been stealing food from the family, including from his very weak mother. Although he does not inscribe great emotional outbreaks on this subject, it is evident that his father's behavior toward his mother was tormenting him, because he consistently devotes time to mention it throughout his diary:

Oh, if only there weren't this situation with Mom. Poor, broken, weak, dear, unhappy creature! She has had enough trouble in the ghetto already, and quarrels and conflicts at home (there are many of them). According to Father, they're caused by my "indifference" to the family, or more precisely, to him. May we be able to save her! We will settle accounts with Father after the war. (p. 156)

Zelkowicz (in Dawidowicz, 1976) doubts the ability of language to represent the victim's situation. He writes, "there is simply no word, no power, no art able to transmit the moods, the laments, and the turmoil prevailing in the ghetto since early this morning"(p. 299). Nevertheless, his skepticism does not prevent him from attempting it in the very next paragraph.

Friday, September 4, 1942

Tears flow by themselves. They can't be held back. People know these tears are useless. Those who can help it refuse to see them, and those who see them—and they too shed useless tears—can't help themselves either. Worst of all, these tears bring no relief whatsoever. On the contrary. It's as though they were falling on, rather than from, our hearts. They only make our hearts heavier. Our hearts writhe and struggle in these tears like fish in poisoned waters. Our hearts drown in their own tears. But no one can help us in any way, no one can save us. (p. 299)

And then the very next day in this powerful description:

Saturday, September 5, 1942

People scream. And their screams are terrible and fearful and senseless, as terrible and fearful and senseless as the actions causing them. The ghetto is no longer rigid; it is now writhing in convulsions. The whole ghetto is one enormous spasm. The whole ghetto jumps out of its own skin and plunges back within its own barbed wires. Ah, if only a fire would come and consume everything! If only a bolt from heaven would strike and destroy us altogether! There is hardly anyone in the ghetto who hasn't gasped such a wish from his feeble lips, whether he is affected directly, indirectly, or altogether unin-volved in the events which were staged before his very eyes and ears. Everyone is ready to die; already now, at the very start, at this very moment, it is impossible to endure the terror and the horror. Already at this very moment it is impossible to endure the screams of hundreds of thousands of bound cattle slaughtered but not yet killed; impos-sible to endure the twitching of the pierced but unsevered thoughts, which let them nei-ther die nor live. (p. 311)

Hillesum (1984, p. 200) also writes that the situation is indescribable, yet she writes because she never doubts the diary as a place to express. She makes use of the diary to write away her depression: "I am tired and depressed. I still have half-an-hour and I would like to write for days, until all of my sudden depres-sion has been shaken off" (p. 202). What is unique in her relationship with her diary, however, is that she uses the diary as a vehicle to communicate with God. And this belief that God is reading her sorrows gives her a feeling of serenity. The diary (i.e., God) is the ever-open, ever-accepting entity that Hillesum rec-ognizes she can depend on.

And yet I am one of Your chosen, oh God, for You allow me to experience so many things and have given me enough strength to bear them all. Last night when I finally went up to Dickey's room at 2 o'clock and knelt down, almost naked, in the middle of the floor, completely "undone," I suddenly said, "I have been through such great things, today and tonight, my God, I thank You for helping me to bear everything and for letting so little pass me by." (p. 194)

The idea that there is no language to express the Holocaust did not deter diarists. The expression of emotions instead became a kind of resistance. Flinker, a 16-year-old who was eventually killed at Auschwitz after living in hiding for 2 years in Brussels, uses his diary to vent doubts and to contemplate the emptiness he feels:

What shall I do? The emptiness has spread within me and now fills me completely. For a few days now, no new thought or idea has come to me. I have tried various measures and nothing has helped. . . . Maybe these things will yet help, but so far I am completely in the grip of this nothingness, this lack of will and thought. I have tried to find a reason for all this, but I have been unable to settle on a life of peace and quiet while my brothers are in a situation so bad that God alone knows its full horror. Maybe this void will disappear soon; there are some signs of this, but I cannot be sure. (in Holliday, 1995, pp. 264–265)

May's (1953) belief that freedom is dependent on consciousness of self gives the diary an immense degree of power. He states that this "is shown in the fact that the less self-awareness a person has, the more he is unfree" (p. 161). Introspection, which comes from self-awareness, points to an inner power, what Hillesum would refer to as God. This inner strength is what sustains the diarists, and finding this power within the diary is not uncommon, as Progoff (1963) makes evident in the following:

When [someone] has encountered the inward principle working in the psyche and when he has recognized it as the effective power of his being, the framework of his experience alters and he can perceive the world in a new context. With this he becomes capable of meeting his anxieties and overcoming them by means of a superior inward power. (p. 36)

Brenner (1997) writes, "life narratives affirm individuality and personhood under the rule of terror that sought their dehumanization" (p. 5). Diaries give the silenced one a voice. The act of writing, the communication with oneself, immediately breaks the silence and moves the writer from a submissive to an assertive role. "At the time of the unbearable suffering the victim records the horror in an attempt to distance herself from it" (p. 131). In this way, writing gives a focus other than suffering and death, even if one is writing about suffering and death. "The menacing reality" explains Brenner, "is transformed into the subject of an artistic interest" (p. 137). None of the diarists can imagine how they would survive if they could not write. As Hillesum (in Brenner, 1997) states: "The worse thing for me is when I am no longer allowed pencil and paper to clarify my thoughts—they are indispensable to me, for without them I shall fall apart and be utterly destroyed" (p. 135). Frank (1995) exemplifies this same dependence on the diary in an entry written after a burglar broke into the annex where she was hiding with her family. "Not my diary" she exclaims, "if my diary goes, I go too!" (p. 256). Or, then again when Sierakowiak (1996) writes:

I, too, considered the possibility of leaving, but because of my weakness and lethargy caused by hunger, I don't think I have enough strength to go. Besides, I would miss my books and "letters," notes and copybooks. Especially this diary. (p. 174)

DIARY AS WITNESS

Up to this point I have discussed the diary's role as *liberator* and *outlet* for the expression of emotions. But the diary had another purpose as well, which was to narrate the facts. It attempted to be the voice that disclosed the realities of the situation. "Some diaries were written from fear that no Jews would be left alive when the war was over, and no one would be able to relate the history of their agony and death" (Shapiro, 1999, p. 159). In this sense, the diary became a sort of time capsule destined to be read by future generations.

Many of the diarists took on the role of historian. This is not surprising considering that many diarists came from the "ancient Jewish tradition in which records are the continuous responsibility of a scattered people" (Egan, 1987, p. 6). They felt it their duty to record events. Frank, for instance, rewrote her diary at one point in preparation for its future publication under the title *Het Achterhuis* (literally, "the back part of the house"). Each diary has its own focus. For Frank (1995) and Hillesum (1984), the focus tends toward emotional description. For Sierakowiak (1996), however, the emphasis is placed on details of the ghetto. He focuses mostly on food, politics, and weather. All his entries share the same structure, though not always in the same order. He gives a brief description of the weather, gives a detailed account of food shortages, and offers reports on the political climate.

Monday, April 27, Łódź

A ration for the first ten days of May was issued in the afternoon (15dkg of sugar, 25dkg of wheat flour, 10dkg of honey, 20dkg of salt, 10dkg of margarine, 20dkg of sauerkraut, soda, baking soda, matches, and citric acid). A ration of fuel has also been issued for all of May (8 kilos of briquettes per person, and 2 kilos of wood per family). It's cold again; constant clouds, wind, but no rain. In politics there is nothing new. (p. 160)

The fact that Sierakowiak recorded facts in such minute detail makes it evident that many of his journal entries were intended for future readers.

Zelkowicz (in Dawidowicz, 1976) also refers to the importance of bearing witness to the horrors of the Holocaust. He writes:

Be strong and don't let your heart break, so that later on you can give a thoughtful and orderly description of just the barest essentials of what took place in the ghetto during the first few days of September in the year 1942. (p. 300)

Many ghetto-dwellers like Zelkowicz kept diaries. Jews who lived in the ghettos were actually encouraged to keep a written record of the events of their day-to-day existence and were determined to leave a documentary of their lives. The following was written by a member of the underground ghetto organization

Oneg Shabbat and demonstrates the importance placed on the diary as relevant and necessary documentation:

I regard it as a sacred task ... for everyone, whether or not he has the ability, to write down everything that he has witnessed or has heard from those who have witnessed—the atrocities which the barbarians committed in every Jewish town. When the time will come—and indeed it will surely come—let the world read and know what the murderers perpetrated. This will be the richest material for the mourner when he writes the elegy for the present time. This will be the most powerful subject matter for the avenger. ... We are obligated to assist them, to help them, even if we must pay with our own lives, which today are very cheap. (in Dawidowicz, 1976, p. 6)

It is estimated that about 400 diaries from Holocaust victims have been traced. Of these 400, more than 200 were written in Polish ghettos. The slogan of the ghettos was "there is nothing minor ... everything is of historical value. ... We must observe everything and ... sketch all that occurs" (Shapiro, 1999, p. 99). Diaries provide a sober look at the Holocaust because they are without pretensions, judgments, or excuses based on the outcome of the war. Unlike memoirs, they are untainted representations of life as it was.

MEMOIRS: THE RESURRECTION OUT OF THE INVISIBLE

Memoirs, like diaries, have therapeutic value. Perhaps the most difficult tasks for the Holocaust autobiographer are writing to a public that has no concept of the horror victims endured, and forcing him- or herself to return to that place in memory, however grueling and anguishing the undertaking. Some historians, such as Appelfeld (1999), believe that no one has the strength to fully remember such hellish experiences. However, several schools of psychology support the idea that one must express unbearable memories in order to live an emotionally healthy life. Memoirs often alleviate the burden of memory and the guilt one feels for having survived when so many others perished. As Egan (1987) so clearly states:

What the writer has to deal with is a depraved and damaged self clinging to life beyond reason and at the expense of fellow victims. And that self is not a saint, did not die in mid-story, but has survived in fully human wretchedness with the burden of memory. (p. 8)

The memoir also defies invisibility by bringing the survivor back into life, via his role as narrator. But, according to Egan, the autobiographer's difficulty in making the experience comprehensible to others actually reproduces, or imitates, the invisibility he suffered as a victim.

Levi described the invisible, "emaciated man, with head dropped and shoulders curved, on whose face and in whose eyes not a trace of thought is to be seen" (in Egan, 1987, p. 8). The Holocaust autobiographer is able to draw the invisible out of the dark back into the light; to give him substance. Antelme (1992), who managed to survive Buchenwald, Gandersheim, and Dachau, relates this issue of invisibility in his memoir. A scene in which he describes the passing around of a mirror reiterates the idea of invisibility, speaking to the problem of anonymity and effacement.

Our face had, for us, finally become absent from our life. For even in our relations with other prisoners our life remained burdened by this absence; our life had almost become that absence. Of the same striped outfits, of the same shaved heads, of our progressive emaciation, of the rhythm of our life here, for each of us what finally appeared generally amounted to a collective, anonymous face. (p. 52)

The reaction against invisibility is also why Frankl (1984) chose not to make his memoir anonymous.

I had intended to write this book anonymously, using my prison number only. But when the manuscript was completed, I saw that as an anonymous publication it would lose half its value, and that I must have the courage to state my convictions openly. (p. 25)

Whether Frankl recognized this or not, what would actually have lost value had he used only his prison number would have been himself. It appears that he was so annihilated as an individual that, at the time he wrote the memoir, he still struggled with recognizing himself as Viktor Frankl and not as a number. It is not uncommon for memoirs to describe immunity to death and suffering, an imperviousness that devalues one's existence, as illustrated in the following passage:

He stood unmoved while a twelve-year-old boy was carried in who had been forced to stand at attention for hours in the snow or to work outside with bare feet because there were no shoes for him in the camp. His toes had become frostbitten, and the doctors on duty picked off the black gangrenous stumps with tweezers, one by one. Disgust, horror and pity are emotions that our spectator could not really feel any more. . . . I spent some time in a hut for typhus patients who ran very high temperatures and were often delirious. . . . After one of them had just died, I watched without any emotional upset the scene that followed, which was repeated over and over again with each death. (pp. 40–41)

MEMOIRS: A PURPOSEFUL ACTIVITY

To be invisible is nonexistence, and one way to exist is to give meaning to one's life. The creative powers of writing help to rebuild the person by giving him purpose. When personal purpose is taken away, as was done to Holocaust victims, the accumulation of traumatic memories makes emotional growth almost impossible. Writing a memoir relieves this condition, giving the survivor a noninhibiting and accessible reservoir for memories, and a resource for re-creative energies.

Part of re-creating oneself is facing death and recognizing that one did survive. Among the main differences between the memoir and the diary is that the memoir speaks much more of death. It seems clear that the diarist, although mentioning death or expressing a fear of it, rarely describes death in the kind of detail that the writer of a memoir does. To ponder death would be torture for the diarist. On the other hand, the autobiographer, who no longer faces death directly, can now confront it. Holocaust autobiographers' newly found freedom imparts a realization of strength, as the last paragraph of Frankl's (1984) memoir confirms: "The crowning experience of all, for the homecoming man, is the wonderful feeling that, after all he has suffered, there is nothing he need fear anymore—except his God" (p. 65).

Once Frankl and Antelme were free, they both recognized that the way to relieve some of their suffering was to record their experiences in the concentration camps. Frankl (in Egan, 1987) claims that "emotion, which is suffering, ceases to be suffering as soon as we form a clear and precise picture of it" (p. 12). Egan points out that the telling of facts alone is not enough to relate the experience of the victims. If someone were to look at a picture of an emaciated prisoner lying on his bunk, they might find the sight shocking. The narrator, however, may write that on that particular day, that prisoner was not so unhappy, because the sun was shining. A deeper experience is acquired through narrative, implying the idea of the memoir as an artistic, literary endeavor. The memoir is structured like a novel in that it has a narrator, characters, and a story to tell. The label *autobiography* is actually inappropriate because the memoir, although definitely relating one individual's story, also relates the stories of those who did not survive. It has already been expressed that the art of writing serves to alleviate suffering, but it also gives those who practice it a reason to live.

When the Holocaust survivors were freed, their entire life before the war was gone. Most of their family members, if not all, were dead. They had no house. They may not have even been able to return to their hometown. What was left? Only a human being, filled with suffering, confusion, and the burden of memories. Many survivors contemplated suicide. It may seem illogical that, having survived the concentration camps, one would, in freedom, take one's own life. But in the concentration camp, at least, one had the future to live for. When the prisoners were released and challenged with indifference, they often felt a sense of meaninglessness. Frankl comments (1984):

If each and every case of suicide had not been *undertaken* out of a feeling of meaninglessness, it may well be that an individual's impulse to take his own life would have been *overcome* had he been aware of some meaning and purpose worth living for. (p. 166)

The memoir becomes the purpose in the autobiographer's life. First, the idea of writing a memoir gives the survivor the title of "author," which imparts vocational meaning. Second, writing the memoir lends purpose to all the time spent in the concentration camp. The survivor has two roles: that of author, and that of bearing witness, both of which fill one's life with meaning and reason to live. Even though Holocaust autobiographers know they cannot speak for every individual, they feel obliged to speak for others, and for the human race as a whole. In his introduction, Antelme (1992) explains the following:

I relate here what I lived through. The horror in it is not gigantic. At Gandersheim there was no gas chamber, no crematorium. The horror there was darkness, absolute lack of any kind of landmark, solitude, unending oppression, slow annihilation. The motivation underlying our struggle could only have been a furious desire, itself almost always experienced in solitude; a furious desire to remain men, down to the very end. (p. 5)

It is common among most Holocaust autobiographers to write both to the specific and to the universal. They set off to write about their individual experiences as a camp victim, but in doing so they are inescapably led to wider questions about human nature. In fact, the titles of both Frankl's and Antelme's memoirs, *Man's Search for Meaning* and *The Human Race*, correspondingly, demonstrate the acknowledgment that their writings reflect on what it means to be human, and not only on what it means to be Viktor Frankl or Robert Antelme.

CONCLUSION

That the diary and the memoir are different, and that both can be therapeutic to the Holocaust victim, is clear. The diary's therapeutic value can be found in its consistency and function as an outlet for pent-up emotions. It is also useful in its ability to distance the author from existing situations, and to act as a time capsule for future generations. The memoir is therapeutic because it draws out of the shadows and strengthens the weakened individual, and because it speaks for the whole of a people who suffered during the Holocaust. Both the diary and the memoir are similar in terms of their intrinsic artistic value: They are both creations. With the ability to create a text comes the capacity for self-re-creation; ultimately rescuing the author from the depths of despair.

REFERENCES

American heritage dictionary of the English language. (1981). Boston: Houghton Mifflin.

Antelme, R. (1992). *The human race* (J. Haight & A. Mahler, Trans.). Evanston, IL: Marlboro Press.

Appelfeld, A. (1999). Individualization of the Holocaust. In R. M. Shapiro (Ed.), *Holocaust chronicles: Individualizing the Holocaust through diaries and other contemporaneous accounts* (pp. 1–8). Hoboken, NJ: KTAV Publishing House.

Arons, S. (1997). *Journal writing and self-growth: A four-phase process.* Unpublished master's thesis, State University of West Georgia, Carrollton, Georgia.

Baldwin, C. (1977). *One to one: Self-understanding through journal writing.* New York: M. Evans.

Brenner, R. (1997). *Writing as resistance: Four women confronting the Holocaust.* University Park, PA: Penn State University Press.

Bullough, R. V., Jr., & Pinnegar, S. (2001). Guidelines for quality in autobiographical forms of self-study research. *Educational Researcher, 30,* 13–21.

Dawidowicz, L. (Ed.). (1976). *A Holocaust reader*. New York: Behrman House.

Egan, S. (1987). The invisible Jew, the untellable story: Writing oneself into existence. *Literary Review*, 31, 5–16.

Frank, A. (1995). Achterhuis. (S. Massotty, Trans.). In O. Frank & M. Pressler (Eds.), *The diary of a young girl: The definitive edition*. New York: Doubleday.

Frankl, V. (1984). *Man's search for meaning*. New York: Washington Square Press.

Hillesum, E. (1984). *An interrupted life: The diaries of Etty Hillesum* (J. Cape, Trans.). New York: Washington Square Press.

Holliday, L. (Ed.). (1995). *Children in the Holocaust and World War II: Their secret diaries*. New York: Washington Square Press.

Mallon, T. (1984). *A book of one's own: People and their diaries*. New York: Ticknor and Fields.

May, R. (1953). *Man's search for himself*. New York: Bantam/Doubleday/Dell.

Porat, D. (1999). The Vilna ghetto diaries. In R. M. Shapiro (Ed.), *Holocaust chronicles: Individualizing the Holocaust through diaries and other contemporaneous accounts* (pp. 157–169). Hoboken, NJ: KTAV Publishing House.

Progoff, I. (1963). *The symbolic and the real*. New York: McGraw-Hill.

Rainer, T. (1978). *The new diary*. New York: G.P. Putnam's Sons.

Shapiro, R.M. (Ed.). (1999). *Holocaust chronicles: Individualizing the Holocaust through diaries and other contemporaneous accounts*. Hoboken, NJ: KTAV Publishing House.

Sierakowiak, D. (1996). *The diary of Dawid Sierakowiak: Five notebooks from the Lódź ghetto* (A. Adelson, Ed., K. Turowski, Trans.). New York: Oxford University Press.

10

Post-Traumatic Nightmares in Kuwait Following the Iraqi Invasion

Deirdre Barrett and Jaffar Behbehani

Research on post-traumatic nightmares finds consistent symptomatology across all populations exposed to a vast range of traumas. The attack on the World Trade Center and the U.S. military intervention in Afghanistan indicate both that such nightmares will continue and that understanding different cultural perspectives of an event is crucial to their interpretation. In this chapter, we will review post-traumatic nightmare research and discuss beliefs about dreaming specific to Muslim and Arabic folk traditions. Then we will present dreams from Kuwait after the Gulf War, describing how cultural beliefs interact with post-traumatic effects.

Nightmares (i.e., frightening dreams) are so ubiquitous after trauma (Terr, 1990) that they are listed as diagnostic criteria for post-traumatic stress disorder (PTSD) in the *Diagnostic and Statistical Manual of Mental Disorders* of the American Psychiatric Association (1994). Much nightmare research has centered on domestic violence. Nightmares follow childhood abuse in those who end up with formal PTSD diagnoses (King & Sheehan, 1996), dissociative disorders (Barrett, 1996), or more transient symptomatology not meeting formal diagnostic criteria (Belicki & Cuddy, 1996). Survivors of rape and battering as adults also have nightmares about these events (Herman, 1992; Muller, 1996).

Studies centering on war have reported mostly on soldiers' reactions. Nightmares were mentioned as a symptom of "shell shock" and "battle fatigue" during both world wars, but studies became more numerous after the Vietnam War. Van der Kolk, Blitz, Burr, Sherry, and Hartmann (1984) found nightmares most frequent in the youngest Vietnam combat veterans as well as those with other PTSD symptoms. Wilmer (1996) emphasized that Vietnam veterans reported more nightmares about killing and committing atrocities than they did about being the victims themselves. In other words, they were put in situations that violated their own ethical standards. This dream content suggests that such a violation is at least as traumatizing as the danger the soldiers faced in the field.

There are also some data on civilian nightmares following war. Aron (1996) found recurring chase nightmares among South American political refugees long after the traumatic events abated. Punamäki (1999) found a high rate of nightmares among refugee children living in the occupied territories of Israel.

These studies chart the most typical evolution of post-traumatic nightmares. They begin with fairly realistic re-creations of the worst parts of the experience, moving toward dreams of better outcomes—being rescued, mastery over attackers—as the person begins to recover from the trauma. However, people with a history of earlier traumas have a tendency for that content to become activated in nightmares associated with later trauma (King & Sheehan, 1996). Most report that nightmares, especially when discussed with others, serve as positive coping mechanisms, assisting the incorporation of the traumatic material. However, prolonged, unchanging dreams are both a sign of problematic adjustment and have a retraumatizing effect themselves (Barrett, 1991; Cartwright, 1996; Punamäki, 1999).

Interventions can facilitate this evolution of dreams if it is does not happen spontaneously. Brockway (1987) and Wilmer (1996) both emphasize that concerned listening to the nightmares—whether in an individual or group formats—is therapeutic in and of itself, tending to resolve the nightmares over time. The recovery process can also be facilitated by therapeutic interventions specifically coaching people on altering their dreams toward mastery of the frightening elements. Therapy for recurring nightmares typically involves plotting an alternate ending and rehearsing it with vivid waking imagery. As people fall asleep at night, they can remind themselves, "Tonight if I have the dream of (the rapist, Vietnam, etc.), I want to (have a weapon, freeze the action and speak to the Vietnamese boy, etc.)." Resulting dreams may be transcendent dialogues with one's attacker or one's victim. Also, simple goals such as revenge or flight serve to break the cycle of helplessness.

Many clinicians have succeeded in using this technique with a wide variety of traumatized populations (King & Sheehan, 1996; Zadra, 1996). These techniques not only reduce nightmares, but they also reduce waking PTSD symptoms. Krakow (2000) has documented this in carefully controlled studies with rape victims. Just as repetitive nightmares make people more afraid during the day, mastery dreams translate into a sense of strength or comfort.

Most of these nightmare studies have examined Western populations and, as is clear from research on cross-cultural aspects of dreaming (Bulkeley, 1995; Krippner & Faith, 2001), post-traumatic nightmares bear examining from other perspectives.

ARAB AND MUSLIM DREAM BELIEFS

Muhammad received his notice that he was "the greatest of all prophets" in a dreamlike vision of being guided by the angel Gabriel through the seven celestial spheres, conferring with Abraham and Jesus along the way, and returning to earth to write his 65-page *Nocturnal Journey*. Later, much of the Qur'an was also revealed to Muhammad, either in a literal flight with Gabriel or in his dreams, depending on which interpretation one chooses to entertain. In any event, each morning Muhammad and his disciples would share and interpret dreams. Muhammad ordered the practice of *adhan*—the central Islamic ritual of daily prayer—after one of his followers dreamed about it (Van de Castle, 1994). The split of Islam into the conflicting factions of Sunni and Shiite was based partly on a dream about Muhammad, which the Sunnis used to justify their rights as his successors (MacKenzie, 1965).

Secular Arab traditions have always emphasized the potential of dreams to foretell the future. It is believed that there is a great likelihood that they may literally come true, but there have also been elaborate constructions of symbolic translations of what dream symbols may foretell about waking life events (Von Grunebaum & Caillois, 1966). These were originally oral traditions but were set down by Achmet, a 10th-century scholar. In his *Oneirocriticon* (1991), seemingly traumatic dream events could foretell beneficial outcomes, for example:

If someone dreams that he died, he will serve a great source of power and be wealthy, although he will suffer from opthalamia because death cuts off the sight. (p. 140)

If someone dreams that he was decapitated in battle, he will receive beneficence from a powerful man. (p. 129)

Minor dream events could also denote waking tragedies:

If he dreams that a front tooth fell out, the closer of his kin will die. (p. 108)

If he dreams that his fingernails were pulled out, the misfortune will be even more severe, and this points to a short life. (p. 113)

Today, dream divination is taken very seriously among Muslims. The autobiographies of prominent Muslim figures often contain extensive dream diaries and examples of decisions ostensibly based on dreams. One example was when a shah of Iran was deciding whether to seek a loan from Russia. He dreamed that a famous theological figure dressed in primitive Muslim garb approached him and threw at his feet a sack containing gold and silver. The fairly obvious interpretation of this dream was that the shah shouldn't make any new loans with unbelievers but should trust that his subjects and fellow servants of the faith would restore his finances (Van de Castle, 1994). More recently, in December 2001, the U.S. government aired a videotape of Osama bin Laden discussing his foreknowledge of the September 11 attack. Bin Laden recounted several dreams of associates (who did not know of the impending attack), ranging from a soccer game in which the winning Arab players were pilots to a much more literal enactment of planes crashing into a tall building. He described having had some anxiety that these dreams could become so common as to give away the plan but mostly he took them as an omen that the attack would succeed.

DREAMS IN KUWAIT FOLLOWING THE GULF WAR

Kuwait is a small, affluent Muslim Arab nation, somewhat more Westernized than most of its neighbors. On August 2, 1990, the Iraqi army swept into Kuwait, with heavy fighting and causalities the first day and then complete military rule by the Iraqis, including a dusk to dawn curfew, for the next 6 months. Torture and executions were used to obtain information about resistance activities. Often family members were made to witness rapes and executions. Bodies were left in conspicuous public places with orders that they were not to be removed. Even those who experienced no direct harm to themselves or their families lived with a constant sense of danger.

Kuwait developed a prisoner-of-war situation similar to the one in the United States after the Vietnam War. Hundreds of Kuwaitis arrested by the Iraqis are missing. Families still cling to the hope that they are being held alive in Iraq. Kuwaitis are still being killed by the land mines hidden in the deserts and beaches of Kuwait. The survival of Saddam Hussein's regime in Iraq continues to fuel fears of future invasions.

Kuwait presented us with an opportunity to observe the effects of a specific trauma more directly than offered in other situations. Many war-traumatized areas have had multiple overlapping conflicts going on within their borders for decades, most experience extreme poverty and medical illness, and many are beginning to see a long list of social problems secondary to the war. Kuwait was secure, politically and socially stable, and had excellent medical care and education. Therefore, the effects of the occupation can be separated from the internal traumatic sources that characterize many other invaded countries.

Four years after the Iraqi invasion and occupation of Kuwait, 27 percent of Kuwaitis were still suffering from PTSD, and as high as 86 percent of an adult clinical population. Children were still experiencing a variety of behavior problems typical of trauma exposure (Staehr, Staehr, Behbehani, & Boejholm, 1995). A more recent survey found that 66 percent of those with diagnosable PTSD and 22 percent of nonclinical Kuwaitis were still dreaming about traumatic events of the occupation (Al-Hammadi, Makhawi, & Al-Shereedah, in press).

We discovered, in our interviews, that many Kuwaitis continue to have nightmares. One dreamer had a brother fighting in the resistance; after the war ended, he disappeared. Soon after this report, she had the following recurring nightmare:

We are at home and the Iraqis come to the house. They break the windows and storm in, searching everywhere and demand to know where he [the brother] is. My two little children are crying. One soldier is pointing a gun at each of our heads one by one, saying he will shoot us if we do not tell where he is hiding, we do not know. The soldier pulls the trigger and shoots my son, then my daughter. I wake up screaming. In real life, they came into the house almost like this, and did hold guns to everyone's head while they asked about my brother. But they never shot anyone, they finally left. My brother has never come home, I think they found him and shot him, but my mother believes he is a prisoner in Iraq.

Other people reported nightmares that are less realistic representations of their concerns. Some also demonstrated an evolution of mastery in their dreams such as described by Cartwright (1996). For example, one young woman told us about a recurring nightmare throughout the occupation in which she was riding in the elevator of a high-rise building along with many people. The elevator cord would break, the elevator plunging down several floors and then, dangling by a thread, the cord would break and she would awaken in terror. After the liberation, changes occurred with each repetition of the dream, with the final repetition ending in rescuers coming to help people climb to safety through a door in the top of the elevator.

The children we interviewed were even more likely to have repetitive nightmares. As has been observed among other traumatized children, during and shortly after the trauma their dreams were likely to contain material directly related to their ordeal. During the occupation, one 6-year-old boy whose father was being held prisoner by the Iraqis had the following dream as recounted by his mother:

He dreamed about the Iraqi soldiers attacking his father; they cut his ears and blood was everywhere. After that they threw him in a ditch and the father was calling out for his son to help him by pulling a rope to help his father out of the hole. But the boy could not help and his father fell back into the ditch screaming. He was so affected by the dream that whenever he would tell it, he would begin crying and feeling sad for his father.

The mother had attempted to reassure the boy by telling him of the Arab tradition that blood in dreams means they will never happen in waking life, and that dream events can sometimes predict their own opposite. She did not tell him, as a Western parent might, that it was "only a dream" or suggest that his concern about his father caused the dream. Instead, she reframed it as a potentially positive prediction. These nightmares ceased several months after his father was released, but returned 4 years later at the age of 10 when the Iraqi troops were again massing at the border.

Another boy, age 7, dreamed repeatedly during the occupation that Saddam Hussein was chasing him down a street with a knife trying to kill him; he would awaken screaming. After the occupation, he would have dreams that he and his father—sometimes with other Kuwaiti men and boys—would track down Saddam Hussein and fall on him with knives and kill him. These dreams would not frighten him; rather he would recount them with pleased excitement.

INTERVENTION AND CULTURE-SPECIFIC ISSUES

Muslim and Arab folk beliefs about dreams focus so exclusively on using them to foretell the future that few assumptions are made (such as those taken as a given in Western traditions) of dream content arising from the dreamer's past. Therefore, many classic repetitive post-traumatic dreams are likelier to arouse anticipation that the event will occur again and increase the survivor's anxiety level even more than they might in other cultures. Westernized Kuwaitis with some respect for social science are pleased to have information that people in other traumatized situations consistently have repetitive dreams about those traumas without a repetition of those events being preordained.

There is, of course, a positive side to this emphasis on dreams foretelling the future. These dreams have been a source of inspiration that has served to mitigate trauma in Islamic society, while in Western traditions they would be dismissed as "wish fulfillment" without a potential beneficial impact. One fundamentalist Islamic woman told us that she had seen the Iraqi invasion in a dream several days before it happened, hearing the voice of Allah telling her she would need to provide strength for her people during this time. She then dreamed of the invaders being driven out—specifically, getting up from a partially eaten meal and running out of a house. She told us that this is exactly what she eventually witnessed in the house across the street from hers, one that had been taken over by Iraqi soldiers during the occupation. Other Kuwaitis told us less dramatic stories of simply dreaming of the city functioning normally, of the Iraqis not being there, and taking comfort in this as a prediction that the occupation would end. Professionals seeking to intervene in war-torn Muslim countries would do well to be aware of the supportive role that positive dreams play in Islamic culture.

NOTE

The Association for the Study of Dreams maintains information on post-traumatic nightmares, both for professionals and the general public. Go to www.asdreams.org and click on "nightmares" to access this information. The association also runs a nightmare hotline, with an emphasis on post-traumatic nightmares. Persons who wish to discuss their nightmares may call toll-free in the United States, 1–866–DRMS911.

REFERENCES

Achmet. (1991). *The Oneirocriticon: A medieval Greek and Arabic treatise on the interpretation of dreams* (S. Oberhelman, Trans. & Ed.). Lubbock, TX: Texas Technological University Press.

Al-Hammadi, A; Makhawi, B., & Al-Shereedah, S. (in press). Behavioral abnormalities of Kuwaiti children due to Iraqi invasion. *Journal of Traumatic Stress.*

American Psychiatric Association (1994). *Diagnostic and statistical manual of mental disorders* (4th ed.). Washington, DC: Author.

Aron, A. (1996). The collective nightmare of Central American refugees. In D. Barrett (Ed.), *Trauma and dreams* (pp. 140–147). Cambridge, MA: Harvard University Press.

Barrett, D. (1991). Through a glass darkly: The dead appear in dreams. *OMEGA: The Journal of Death and Dying, 24,* 97–108.

Barrett, D. (1996). Dreams in multiple personality disorder. In D. Barrett (Ed.), *Trauma and dreams* (pp. 68–81). Cambridge, MA: Harvard University Press.

Belicki, K., & Cuddy, M. (1996). Identifying sexual trauma: Histories from patterns of sleep and dreams. In D. Barrett (Ed.), *Trauma and dreams* (pp.46–55). Cambridge, MA: Harvard University Press.

Brockway, S. S. (1987). Group treatment of combat nightmares in post-traumatic stress disorder. *Journal of Contemporary Psychotherapy, 17*, 270–284.

Bulkeley, K. (1995). *Spiritual dreaming: A cross-cultural and historical journey.* New York: Paulist Press.

Cartwright, R. (1996) Dreams and adaptation to divorce. In D. Barrett (Ed.), *Trauma and dreams* (pp. 179–185). Cambridge, MA: Harvard University Press.

Herman, J. (1992). *Trauma and recovery.* New York: Basic Books.

King, J., & Sheehan, J. (1996). The use of dreams with incest survivors. In D. Barrett (Ed.), *Trauma and dreams* (pp. 56–67). Cambridge, MA: Harvard University Press.

Krakow, B., et al. (2001). Imagery rehearsal therapy for chronic nightmares in sexual assault survivors with posttraumatic stress disorder: A randomized controlled trial. *Journal of the American Medical Association, 286*, 537–545.

Krippner, S., & Faith, L. (2001). Exotic dreams: A cross-cultural study. *Dreaming, 11*, 73–82.

MacKenzie, N. (1965). *Dreams and dreaming.* New York: Vanguard Press.

Muller, K. (1996). Jasmine: Dreams in the psychotherapy of a rape survivor. In D. Barrett (Ed.), *Trauma and dreams* (pp. 148–158). Cambridge, MA: Harvard University Press.

Punamäki, R.-L. (1999). The relationship of dream content and changes in daytime mood in traumatized vs. non-traumatized children. *Dreaming, 9*, 213–233.

Staehr, A., Staehr, M., Behbehani, J., & Boejholm, S. (1995). *Treatment of war victims in the Middle East.* Copenhagen, Denmark: International Rehabilitation Council for Torture Victims.

Terr, L. (1990). *Too scared to cry.* New York: Basic Books.

Van de Castle, R. (1994). *Our dreaming mind.* New York: Ballantine.

van der Kolk, B., Blitz, R., Burr, W., Sherry, S., & Hartmann, E. (1984). Clinical characteristics of traumatic and lifelong nightmare sufferers. *American Journal of Psychiatry, 141*, 187–190.

Von Grunebaum, G. E., & Caillois, R. (Eds.). (1966.) *The dream in human societies.* Los Angeles: University of California Press.

Wilmer, H. (1996). The healing nightmare: War dreams of Vietnam veterans. In D. Barrett (Ed.), *Trauma and dreams* (pp. 85–99). Cambridge, MA: Harvard University Press.

Zadra, A. (1996). Recurrent dreams: Their relation to life events. In D. Barrett (Ed.), *Trauma and dreams* (pp. 231–247). Cambridge, MA: Harvard University Press.

11

Psychosocial Effects and Treatment of Mass Trauma Due to Sociopolitical Events: The Argentine Experience

Lucila Edelman, Daniel Kersner, Diana Kordon, and Darío Lagos

The collective traumatic experiences that occurred in Argentina during the past quarter century, especially those experiences related to sociopolitical events and grave human rights violations, had a significant impact on Argentine society as a whole. These effects reach beyond the impact on those individuals and families most directly involved. For this reason, these effects constitute an important reference point in seeking to understand the emergence of new psychosocial and clinical problems in the mental health of contemporary Argentines.

While different theoretical approaches to these problems exist, there is little doubt that collective traumatic events such as those experienced in Argentina have a far-reaching impact on the society in which they occur for generations to come. This fact is supported by the experiences of Holocaust victims of the Nazi concentration camps and other populations affected by World War II, such as prisoners of war, the Japanese Americans interned in the United States, and Japanese survivors of the atomic bomb attacks. In addition, millions of individuals have been affected by repressive dictatorships in Argentina and many other countries. It can be said that the impact is multigenerational (i.e., several generations are affected simultaneously), intergenerational (i.e., the impact is translated into conflicts between generations), and transgenerational (i.e., the effects reappear in different ways in succeeding generations).

In this chapter, we report on our experience dealing with the problems encountered by those affected by Argentine social injustice, especially family members of the *desaparecidos*,[1] and on the implementation of "reflection groups" for the interpretation and treatment of traumatic effects and situations stemming from these sociopolitical events.

This approach evolved directly from our clinical work with people generally affected by political repression in Argentina and, specifically, those individuals most affected by the state-sponsored terrorism undertaken by the military dictatorship that held power between March 1976 and December 1983 and which persists, in a much less severe form, to the present day. This unfortunate period in Argentine history has been characterized by:

1. The illegal detention and "disappearance" of at least 30,000 people, the majority of whom were murdered after being tortured.
2. The illegal detention in public jails of an additional 10,000 people, also subjected to torture and inhumane conditions for prolonged periods.
3. The kidnapping of children, whose identities were frequently altered.
4. The hundreds of thousands of Argentine citizens who sought asylum outside the country in order to escape oppression.

PSYCHOLOGICAL CONSEQUENCES OF TRAUMATIC EVENTS

In 1976, a brutal dictatorship took power in Argentina. One result of the dictatorship was widespread oppression and victimization of Argentina's citizens. Thousands of individuals who were viewed by the dictatorship as a threat "disappeared." Obviously, these kidnappings and related acts of terror on the part of agents of the dictatorship caused misery and suffering to the *desaparecidos*, who were frequently tortured before being murdered by the government. But the wider impact on Argentine society and the immediate families, including the children, of these victims caused widespread psychosocial problems for Argentines stemming from the events themselves as well as their subsequent denial by the state.

These "survivors" of the drama—individuals affected, both directly and peripherally, by these traumatic sociopolitical events—commonly required a long time to recover. Through what might be called the psyche's "silent work," the victims' interpretation and experience of the trauma involved a complete process of bereavement and recovery. But due to the widespread public denial by Argentine authorities and other powerful institutions, the bereavement itself was often interrupted and postponed. In the case of the *desaparecidos* of Argentina, for example, the physical absence of the deceased body prevented appropriate funeral rites from being conducted, depriving family members and loved ones of the healing experience of psychological "closure." This factor made the natural processes of bereavement even more difficult for the Argentine survivors, adding a tragic complication to an already agonizing natural process of grieving and letting go.

Beyond this obstacle to the successful bereavement of the affected families, the events proved catastrophic—on a more general and public level—for the entire generation of people contemporary with the *desaparecidos*. Argentina, as a nation, suffered the loss of beloved public figures, community projects, and collective ideals. The disappearances created a high degree of psychological pain for all concerned and a profound alteration in the everyday experience of the affected groups. These effects have already been repeated in succeeding generations as frustrated expectations of social justice gave way to widespread personal experiences of skepticism, alienation, the loss of collective social values, and disillusionment with the authorities. When bereavements derived from traumatic situations are, for various reasons, left unresolved by the generation directly affected, these issues must be addressed by succeeding generations.

These traumatic effects were especially potent among individuals who actually witnessed first-hand the kidnapping of their child, a friend, or even a neighbor, and who later encountered a public denial of the reality of their perceptions. This official, public denial often generated a psychoticlike state in the survivors that was further aggravated by the persistent absence of reliable information concerning the nature of the traumatic events. This sense of "madness" in the affected persons mirrored the schizoid position of the dictatorship itself as it simultaneously denied the existence of the *desaparecidos* while pressuring the families to consider them dead.[2]

Adding to the official denial was the fact that the reality of a person being kidnapped by the government was simply "unbelievable" or "unthinkable" in Argentine society. For example, when their children were kidnapped, the relatives of the victims, in many cases, never suspected that the detention would actually end in a "disappearance" or a murder. Then, after a sustained effort invoking fruitless bureaucratic and investigative procedures to determine the whereabouts of their children, these concerned relatives were threatened by government agents in order to prevent knowledge of the disappearances from becoming publicly known. The survivors' silence and cooperation were secured under the pretext that further inquiries would increase the risks for the victim. While not yet contemplating the possibility that their loved one or missing person would never return, they began to sense that something terrible beyond anything they could have ever imagined was now possible. A system of political oppression had emerged, one in which the victims were literally "swallowed up by the earth."

In addition to the denial, and to some extent because of it, different types of conflicts occurred within families who were directly affected. These conflicts, in many cases, had definite consequences in terms of disruptions and modifications to the family dynamic and structure. The conflicts were related to the different positions individual family members assumed when faced with the actual situation, the terror that conditioned their behavior, and varying degrees of identification with the alienating propaganda issued by the dictatorship. Furthermore, instead of directing aggression to the appropriate object (i.e., the state terror), the denial deflected the anger and hostility to the family itself, where the misdirected aggression became embedded unconsciously within the family dynamic with devastating results.

To complicate the situation further, many families were reduced to the immediate nuclear family, reinforcing both internal reactions and the expression of hostility toward outsiders. These nuclear families became the sole source of support for their members in an isolated social environment. Many individuals had the unsettling personal experience of being viewed, even by family members, as "hot potatoes" with whom no one wanted to deal. Their anguish antagonized the very people they needed for support, which only exacerbated and prolonged their suffering.

In the ordinary course of events, each individual finds an important source of support in the greater social network required to buttress his or her personal sense of dignity and ability to function productively in society. In normal, everyday life, this support typically resides in the background of consciousness, tacit and mute, yet exists as a necessary condition to guarantee the healthy functioning of the individual. Situations of crisis, emergency, or trauma—whether endogenous or exogenous in origin—clearly demonstrate the importance of this support system or lack of it, because in traumatic situations the subject typically experiences the loss of habitual supports. Predictably, the internal family conflicts discussed above, compounded by the social isolation, led to a disturbing experience of the loss of conventional social support systems as the individual was subjected to powerlessness, isolation, abandonment, and fear of psychic disintegration.

PROBLEMS IN THE MANAGEMENT OF INFORMATION AND TRUTH

A separate but related set of problems emerged from the management of information concerning the traumatic events, both by government officials and by surviving adult family members thrust by the event into the role of substitute parents for the *desaparecidos'* children, many of whom had witnessed their parents' abduction first-hand.

Many families experienced great difficulty in informing children about the events that had overtaken their missing parents, especially during the first years of the dictatorship. Several factors help explain this difficulty. These include the official "mandate of silence" concerning everything that was going on in Argentine society; fear of what might happen to these same children, or their families, if the children mentioned the event in public; and, finally, the difficulty the adults had in accepting and dealing constructively with their own suffering and sense of loss, a difficulty projected onto the children disguised beneath the rationale that truthful information could harm the children and cause them further suffering.

As a result, the typical explanation given to children of the *desaparecidos* concerning the absence of their parents was false. In fact, the explanations frequently suggested the possibility of voluntary abandonment of the children by the missing parents. In the majority of cases, the children, especially those of school age, knew that the information they were being given was spurious, and, in some cases, they actually knew what had happened to their parents. Nevertheless, they co-conspired in keeping the family "secret," complying with the unspoken prohibition against speaking aloud of the terrible events that had overtaken the family.

Simultaneously, many therapists who were consulted on how to manage the children's situation were influenced by the alienating propaganda of the dictatorship. Because of the countertransference phenomenon, they needed to give a response that could solve the psychotic ambiguity of the situation, that is, the simultaneous "presence-absence" of the missing parent. These experts often advised adult family members to pass the *desaparecido* off as dead to the children, assuming that, in this manner, the family—and especially the children—could carry on their bereavement. It was also common practice to maintain vigilant silence outside the immediate family. In some cases, the event was confided to a friend as a secret to be held in strict confidence. In all scenarios, the children were effectively deprived of both the truth of what happened and the emotional support of their natural peer and family groups.

THE PSYCHOSOCIAL RESPONSE OF THE AFFECTED

A widespread collective social response—led by the families of the *desaparecidos*, those most affected by the disappearances—gradually took shape in Argentina. This occurred in spite of a widespread denial of social reality, imposed simultaneously by both internal and external mandates of silence, and in response to the emerging social crisis in Argentina.

When situations of social emergency occur, a spontaneous tendency may be observed in the affected population to form groups as a way of finding, on a social level, a response to—or even resolution of—the complex psychosocial problems derived from the catastrophe. This tendency to form groups, while acting on the sociopolitical level with the practical objective of confronting whatever provoked the crisis, represents an important psychological support mechanism in maintaining the functioning of the individual. It also functions as one of the supporting factors that may prevent the catastrophe from being internalized and transformed into a private, psychological problem.

In Argentina, this group-forming reaction to the mass trauma caused by the actions of the dictatorship took the specific form of the Movement of Mothers of Plaza de Mayo. This social movement consisted of family members who refused to participate in the denial. They banded together in mutual support and emerged from both public and private isolation, producing a mass social response in the face of the oppressive situation that exercised a socially constructive political effect within the larger antidictatorial struggle taking shape in Argentina. At the same time, it produced a psychosocial context that favored the social and personal reinterpretation of the traumatic situation and the treatment of problems caused as a result of the trauma and its denial.

The authors' work during the dictatorship evolved from the Movement of Mothers of Plaza de Mayo as the need to take action of a preventative nature, and to provide psychological assistance to those affected, became evident. The *Equipo de Asistencia Psicológica de Madres de Plaza de Mayo* (Mothers of Plaza de Mayo Psychological Aid Team) was established to respond to a demand for professional and technical support. This demand emerged not from private affected individuals or families seeking assistance, but from within the group itself.

REFLECTION GROUPS AS A PSYCHOSOCIAL TOOL

In our opinion, one of the most essential therapeutic functions, when working with such affected populations, is the honest confrontation and acceptance of the traumatic reality. This is necessary to overcome the internal (psychological) and external (sociopolitical) systems of denial by creating a receptive environment for the expression of the experience to emerge from behind the "wall of silence" brought about by the external and internal mandates. This opportunity is important to the healing process, even though the initial encounter with this condition may cause discomfort and require a period of conscious suffering.

In developing an appropriate intervention strategy, the authors observed that these affected individuals and families had found, in the meetings that they held in relation to the mothers' movement, a natural setting in which to discuss their problems. We also noticed that, apart from the movement, they might talk about the events at their natural meeting places. For this reason, we decided to work with participants in those places where mothers, fathers, and other family members were already meeting, and not in our private offices.

Another reason for meeting in public places rather than private offices was the nature of both the problem and the clients. The public group forum established for the meetings was a natural expression of our view of the clients; we considered these people, rather than being "sick" or "pathological," to be victims of dictatorial oppression and, therefore, in a situation of social emergency. They were people going through a situation of sociopolitical crisis that forced them into complex life alterations. Nor did we think that, just because they had been affected by this situation, they should undergo psychotherapeutic treatment. "Reflection groups" (described in detail in the following section) do not become therapeutic groups in the traditional sense, and their members are not "patients."

The authors applied basic principles of positive group dynamics and group process within the context of the forum. This was a response to the widespread and emerging need for assistance for the affected families, including the children of the *desaparecidos*, and was a natural extension of this group-forming tendency to respond to the mass traumatic phenomena of the *desaparecidos*. This strategy resulted in the formation of what we call reflection groups, implemented for this population of the affected as part of an array of social and psychological tools (Edelman & Kordon, 1994; Kordon, 1988; Kordon, Edelman, Lagos, Nicoletti, & Bozzolo, 1987; Lagos, 1994).

Both during the military dictatorship and, subsequently, in the succeeding period of constitutional government, the authors participated in numerous reflection groups with relatives of *desaparecidos*. When we considered the fact that these traumatic situations were common to a great number of Argentines, the group approach appeared to be the most efficient and effective modality. These groups, which came about from a direct demand by those most affected—principally, the Mothers of Plaza de Mayo—represented, in our opinion, the approach that most effectively facilitated the psychosocial reinterpretation of the traumatic situations.[3] As our work progressed with reflection groups, this approach was confirmed. We became convinced that, when dealing with mass or collective traumatic situations of social origin, the group approach offered the best possibility of a meaningful, personal interpretation of certain aspects of the problem that were not achieved using other approaches. In fact, they function as a means of mitigating the impact and preventing greater intrapsychic catastrophes.

Characteristics and Dynamics of Reflection Groups

Reflection groups are modeled after the characteristic principles of effective group dynamics and are characterized by the following features:

1. They are open groups, coordinated by two or more professionals. Attendance is voluntary.
2. The number of participants is unlimited. In our experience, group size has ranged from 15 to 80 people.
3. The group meeting lasts from 2 to 3 hours.
4. All members of the sponsoring institution may take part, independent of the position they hold within that institution.
5. The reflection group is offered as one of many options that the sponsoring institution provides to its members.
6. During a group meeting, many issues that spontaneously arise are discussed by participants. The topics may include personal, family, and institutional problems generated by the traumatic situations they have in common.
7. Discussion of these issues develops on the basis of sharing personal experiences among the members of the group.

In the reflection group process, different modalities for confronting the bereavement appear and new ideas are encountered. For example, the idea frequently occurs, in the context of facing the traumatic event and the situation of loss, that one "should" have done the opposite of what was actually done. Many survivors believe, mistakenly, that if they had only adopted the "right" attitude, the tragedy could have been averted. Within the group, such fantasies are checked as other members of the group intervene to express their views. Furthermore, opposite and extreme modes of facing the conflicts, as well as the irrational behaviors and ideas influenced by official propaganda, are confronted in the group. Through the group dramatization of shared needs a safe space is opened in the group for the emergence and discussion of the original traumatic situation. The group becomes a refuge, a healing space, in which it becomes possible for participants to respond appropriately to their need to reinterpret personal histories, grasp the context of the traumatic events that have occurred, and understand the role of the social group in which they participate.

The Role of Coordinators in Reflection Groups

Because reflection groups are based on principles of group dynamics, there is no need to discuss the actual techniques in any detail (see, e.g., Danieli, 1998; Jaranson & Popking, 1998; Marcelino-Protacio, 1989). However, a few features are worth mentioning as a guide to the implementation of similar groups.

The central role of the coordinators is to facilitate the activity of reflection, applying appropriate psychosocial tools and interventions toward the consistent objective of encouraging group members' own constructive attitudes and reflective capacities. We try, to the extent that is possible, to respect and stimulate communication among the members of the group. We attempt to favor all the processes of acknowledgement of each member toward the others. We recognize group members' similarities and differences, as well as their capacity to understand, and be understood by other members of the group.

Our forums have grown so rapidly that we have not been able to treat all group members ourselves. Therefore, we have trained several "coordinating groups," usually made up of teams of two people per group. The massive amount of suffering that accompanies traumatic problems and that is transferred to the group needs to be treated in depth by these coordinators. The diversity and number of group participants may evoke the reexperiencing of suffering and increase the need for a coordinator's intervention.

This use of a coordinating team takes into account the fact that transference may interfere with the therapeutic capacity of the individual coordinator. The presence of a team, moreover, allows the weight of the transference material to be more evenly distributed, so that if one of the coordinators is overwhelmed by his or her own anguish, the other coordinator can maintain the necessary distance and, therefore, the positive function of the group.

This two-member team approach has the added benefit that, within the coordinating team, the functions can be distributed in a programmed manner. For example, one of the coordinators can be the speaker and the other the observer. Another feature of the coordinating team is to facilitate exchange among all the members of the reflection group, avoiding a radial communication. There is a tendency, especially during the first few meetings of the groups and during moments of crisis, to establish a "radial modality," a process in which the coordinators are placed in the center. This modality reflects the initial dependence of each one of the group members on the coordinating team.

Beneficial Effects of the Groups

The following are examples of the beneficial psychosocial effects stemming from participation in the reflection groups:

1. The group gives the affected person an opportunity to speak about his or her personal experience of the traumatic events. Speaking about the experience has a cathartic effect as the contained and intense emotions are put into words and shared with others. This process helps the individual break through his or her sense of isolation and narcissistic obsession with such unanswerable questions as, "Why did this happen to me?"

2. The group allows for emotional expression and seeks the possibility of a shared interpretation of the *meaning* of the traumatic event. We found that the meaning that each person gives to the traumatic event is even more important than the effects that it produces in the psyche. This is one reason why an exact correlation between the intensity of the trauma and the effects it produces in each person does not exist. When the traumatic event is both catastrophic in scope and derives from social origins the discovery of its meaning requires a simultaneous social and psychological interpretation in which the group can play a vital role.

3. The group also plays the role of a "resupporting" forum. Great social catastrophes often produce a loss of social support. This function of support remains while the groups or institutions function normally, but when this habitual function is changed by traumatic events, the survivors are subjected to disturbing personal experiences that may result in panic or similar compulsive behaviors.

In Argentina, the military dictatorship imposed absolute suppression of the social norms that should be an integral part of the social fabric in every citizen's life. This included a suspension of the most basic human rights, including the right to life itself. This was accompanied by the loss of habitual supports within the traditional groups and institutions, as the functioning of these entities was either suppressed outright or profoundly altered. The fact that the constitutional government that succeeded the dictatorship guaranteed impunity to the masterminds behind these crimes against humanity, as well as their agents and accomplices, only contributed to the persistence of the negative affects of the trauma. Our reflection groups, as a new social organization with the shared, collective function of finding a solution to the traumatic problem on the level of social action, help restore this function of support by establishing new safe havens for its participants.

4. In these groups, both the "spaces of silence" and the "spaces of speech" can be regulated. It is necessary to differentiate between the need for personal, silent space, a frequent effect of the lived traumatic situation, from the type of silence imposed as a norm by those in power. In Argentina, the authorities attempted to impose a blanket of silence over everything in order to conceal their inhumane and illegal acts. They tried to deny the very existence of those whom they had victimized most directly, the *desaparecidos*. This mandate of silence was produced by the absolute control of the mass media and the use of terror, including direct threats that made people afraid to talk, and, often, afraid even to listen. This sociopolitical mandate was extended, with decreased effectiveness,

into the succeeding constitutional period as a requirement to guarantee the system of impunity for the criminals.

5. The interpretation of guilt feelings is another important function of the groups. Here, it is a question of differentiating between feelings of guilt that may naturally accompany a process of bereavement and feelings that are socially induced. In the case of the Argentine dictatorship and the constitutional period that followed, it is important to analyze the induced feelings of guilt that attempt to place the responsibility on the victims instead of the murderers, as the saying goes, "blaming the victims for the crimes." When referring to mass social catastrophes, the group approach provides a receptive and safe environment for the analysis and interpretation of these feelings. By directly observing these shared feelings, it becomes easier to compare them to the feelings conditioned by the hegemonic social discourse of the state.

6. The creation of "meaning" concerning the traumatic situation and the sharing of personal emotions with others reduces the anguish. This reduction of suffering, combined with the communal feeling of the group and the sense of not being the only one affected by the situation, promotes favorable conditions for an attitude of increased acceptance and tolerance toward the losses, painful feelings, and other frustrations derived from the trauma.

7. Frequently, the activities of the reflection group have therapeutic effects, as important individual changes are produced in some participants. In other cases, however, the participation in a reflection group generates a demand for psychotherapeutic assistance—either individual or family—when personal problems may exceed the scope of the group's task as well as its capability.

8. A positive effect of the groups is the mutual bonding and formation of a peer-support network within the group setting that often carries over into the lives of the participants as lasting friendships are formed among members.

CONCLUSION

During the past few decades, Argentina has undergone the collective experience of extraordinary mass trauma resulting from sociopolitical origins, primarily in the form of systematic kidnapping, torture, and murder of thousands of its citizens, including children (Lagos, 1994; Libby, 1998). Assailed simultaneously from within and without by mandates of silence, the families directly affected by these "disappearances" experienced many psychosocial problems, ranging from an inability to deal effectively with their private suffering, disillusionment, and grief to the complicity of surviving adult family members in misinforming affected children.

The relatives of the *desaparecidos* eventually found a way of individually and collectively tackling their problems by mutually supporting one another and assuming a proactive attitude toward the traumatic event by uniting under the auspices of human rights organizations with the intention of searching for their missing loved ones and demanding social justice. In the process, the families—

and the Argentine people affected by the greater tragedy represented by the phenomena of the *desaparecidos*—have articulated an effective social response against oppression and its various forms of denial.

NOTES

1. During the first years of the dictatorship in Argentina, no word existed to describe the status of abducted citizens. Eventually, this new term, *desaparecido* ("missing-detained") was coined. The term became crucial to the ability of Argentines to talk about the events taking place in their society without actually talking about them.

2. Frequently, in a traumatic situation, the affected person tends to produce equivocal interpretations that, internalized, reproduce within the interior of the psyche the paranoid field already present in the social context. In this manner, the murderer-victim dynamic tends to be reproduced internally.

3. Currently, we are using this same tool to approach the problems of people who have suffered police violence and impunity, and present-day sociopolitical oppression.

REFERENCES

Danieli, J. (Ed.). (1998). *International handbook of multigenerational legacies of trauma.* New York: Plenum Press.

Edelman, L., & Kordon, D. (1994). Algunos aspectos de la práctica y la teoría de los grupos de reflexión [Some aspects of the practice and theory of reflection groups]. *Revista de la Asociación Argentina de Psicología y Psicoterapia de Grupo, 1*(17), 191–203.

Jaranson, J., & Popking, M. (Eds.). (1998). *Caring for victims of torture.* Washington, DC: American Psychiatric Press.

Kordon, D. (1988). Presentation of psychological assistance to mothers of "Plaza de Mayo" group. *International Newsletter on Treatment and Rehabilitation of Torture Victims, 1*(1), 1–7.

Kordon, D., Edelman, L., Lagos, D., Nicoletti, E., & Bozzolo, R. (1987). *Psychological effects of political repression.* Buenos Aires, Argentina: Sudamericana-Planeta.

Lagos, D. (1994). Argentina: Psychosocial and clinical consequences of political repression and impunity in the medium term. *Torture Magazine, 4*(1), 13–27.

Libby, T. A. (Ed.). (1998). *War violence, trauma and the coping process.* Copenhagen, Denmark: International Rehabilitation Council for Torture Victims.

Marcelino-Protacio, E. (1989). Psychological help to child victims of political violence in the Philippines: The experience of the Children's Rehabilitation Center. *International Newsletter on Treatment and Rehabilitation of Torture Victims, 1*(2/3), 1–12.

12

Cultural Art Therapy in the Treatment of War Trauma in Children and Youth: Projects in the Former Yugoslavia

Árpád Baráth

War-related trauma in children may be of diverse origin, may be cumulative over time, and may endanger the child's healthy personal, social and moral development (Greenstone & Leviton, 1993; Pynoos & Nader, 1993; Ressler, 1992). Research from the former Yugoslavia on war-related trauma suggests that over 90 percent of children who lived in high-risk zones such as in Sarajevo were exposed to traumatic life events (Stuvland, Baráth, & Kuterovec, 1994). In 1999 the United Nations Children's Fund (UNICEF) estimated that 56 percent of the children who lived in the frontline cities of Croatia were in urgent need of professional help. Many children have suffered or witnessed horrifying acts of violence and aggression, and teachers and parents observed the symptoms of post-traumatic stress disorder (PTSD) in an alarmingly high number of children. These children needed lasting psychosocial aid programs to help them come to terms with their traumatic experiences, as well as the everyday activities, such as education and healthy socializing with peers, that would make life more "normal" for them (UNICEF, 1999; United Nations General Assembly, 1989).

Robert Oravetz (1993), a child psychiatrist from Slovenia, in his discourse-analysis of the trauma-related utterances of refugee children from Bosnia and Herzegovina found four major clusters of mental health issues: (1) sadness, (2) denial, (3) grieving, and (4) escapism. Nearly 1 million people were affected by the 1999 military crisis in Kosovo, of whom 500,000 were children (UNICEF, 1999). As part of one of the first psychosocial aid programs for Kosovo, the Center for Crisis Psychology (CCP) from Norway conducted a trauma assessment survey in July 1999 (Stuvland, 1999). The study was conducted with 58 refugee children from Kosovo, 9–15 years of age, who were living in Macedonia's

Neprosteno camp. The results showed that children who were forced to leave Kosovo during the war had experienced a wide range of traumatic events, in the following order of diagnostic significance:

1. 77% were forced to leave their homes due to violence or threat of violence;
2. 75% strongly believed they might be killed or seriously hurt;
3. 63% experienced enemy soldiers forcibly entering their residence;
4. 62% witnessed an act of physical assault on a loved one;
5. 52% lost a close member(s) of his or her extended family;
6. 51% saw a known person severely injured;
7. 48% believed they would starve or die of thirst;
8. 46% witnessed shooting from a very close distance;
9. 43% saw the body of someone who had been killed;
10. 41% were physically assaulted, i.e., hit or kicked by an unknown person;
11. 30% were personally threatened with serious injury or death; and
12. 21% were arrested, taken to prison, or confined in a detention camp.

PROBLEM STATEMENT

In the summer of 1991, at the outbreak of war in Croatia, several issues became the focus of our professional attention. First, it became obvious that the conventional, office-based human services were unprepared for emergency situations. The prewar system of professional training for those concerned with mental health did not offer any special training in so-called disaster work with large numbers of civilians. The level of disaster management skills and knowledge related to the war situation was as low among professionals as it was among the vast majority of the lay public, that is, close to nil. Second, a large number of mental health professionals were distressed about their personal problems and exhausted by the routine work they were expected to do at the time of this "national emergency." Few, if any, felt capable of and motivated for the initiation of large-scale outreach programs for trauma work. Finally, it soon became evident that the rates of distressed civilians, especially children, women, and the elderly, would surpass the number of staff available for providing professional services to these people. Therefore, it became necessary to train large numbers of paraprofessional helpers and volunteers so that the local self-help resources could be mobilized in the communities to which distressed children and their families now belong (e.g., schools, refugee camps).

These observations were important, but they were only one aspect of a full series of innovative approaches in treating hundred of thousands of children affected by war all over Croatia, and, later, in Bosnia and Herzegovina and Kosovo. Another striking observation for me was that children, as opposed to their parents, demonstrated the ability of developing an unusually healthy way of coping with their fear in life-threatening situations. The key element of these strategies was group play of all kinds, for example, storytelling, puppet shows, drawing and painting, and even certain basic forms of psychodrama. Most of these performances were spontaneous and were permeated by certain elements of "magic" (e.g., by candlelight). Children encountered a large and supportive audience, sometimes comprising an entire neighborhood. The flourishing of this grass-roots creativity in children appeared in epidemiological dimensions throughout the country, especially in the settlements under heavy and lasting military attacks, such as Osijek, Slavonski Brod, Karlovac, Zadar, Dubrovnik, Sarajevo, Mostar, and Tuzla (Djurok, Milivojevič, & Pörös, 1993; Pintarić, 1992).

SPECIFIC AIMS

Several therapeutic purposes are met by engaging children with art (Feder & Feder, 1984). Klingman, Koenigsfeld, and Markman (1987) were perhaps the first authors who called attention to the use of art as a crisis intervention modality that might enable an immediate response to the stress reactions of children in a community setting (e.g., a school). Of these, the following major benefits of artistic activity seemed important as a potential therapeutic tool: (1) lowering one's defenses, (2) tension release, (3) tangibility and permanence, (4) availability and ease of use, (5) reaching out, (6) expanding coping resources.

With these specific aims in mind, we undertook the task of expanding our earlier research experience in fostering creativity in children in prewar times in Croatia and other parts of the former Yugoslavia (Baráth, 1991; Karlavaris, Baráth, & Kamenov, 1988), and organizing these strategies under unusual (wartime) conditions. That meant:

1. To reach out to as many children as possible, using the existing and/or improvised public institutions (e.g., schools, refugee camps) as potential sites of early intervention.
2. To encourage schoolteachers, community workers, mental health professionals, and volunteers to adopt various forms of artistic expression as a crisis-intervention modality, both on a short- and a long-term basis.
3. To adopt and develop a specific "teaching of teachers" model for the dissemination of information and necessary basic skills in using expressive arts as a preventive crisis-intervention modality, including both verbally and nonverbally centered activities.
4. To make early art therapy intervention complementary to other modes of intervention (e.g., educational), open to adaptation according to local community needs.
5. To use the "best" human resources for program development in each single local community in order to ensure the continuity and sustainability of program activities both during and long after the acute wartime period.

METHODS

Intervention Programs

Before turning to a brief description of major intervention programs, four important methodological notes should be made clear: First, all these programs are part of the domain of public health action research and were undertaken in close collaboration with local teachers, community-oriented psychologists, social workers, and lay helpers (Stringer, 1996). Second, the programs should be considered as an open-ended sequence of interventions, starting with early crisis (trauma-focusing) interventions and moving toward the ultimate goal of promoting children's rights (Adams et al., 1972) and their positive coping via cross-cultural art therapy (Wadeson, Durkin, & Perach, 1989). Third, the programs were launched with deliberately prepared written instructions and educational materials for program facilitators (Baráth, 2000). Last but not least, all programs were organized within the paradigm of contemporary self-help and mutual aid (Katz & Bender, 1990), that is, training large numbers of local program facilitators who themselves went through the "hell of war," and who were able to cope with their own trauma before helping others.

Early Crisis Intervention Program: "Images of My Childhood"

In October 1991 we developed and offered to Croatia's Ministry of Education, Department of Schooling, a special series of creative visual art activities. We asked the school authorities to make room for this special-purpose program within the context of regular classroom activities, targeting elementary school age children (6–13 years of age), initially on a purely voluntary basis. The pilot program was first run in some 15 public schools in Zagreb, and later was extended to some 45 public schools all over Croatia. At the time of war in Bosnia and Herzegovina, it was extended to Sarajevo and Mostar. Table 12.1 provides the thematic outline of this first art-crisis intervention program.

Table 12.1
Thematic Flow and Specific Goals of an Early Crisis Intervention Program: "Images of My Childhood"

Workshop Item	Central Topic	Specific Goals
1	MEMORIES: "The paths of my life"	To recall positive prewar memories
2	SPACES: "Where am I? How do I feel?"	To develop security in here-and-now situations
3	TIME: "What has happened to me since . . . ?"	To correct biased attributions to traumatic events
4	WAR: "What is the smell, touch, and color of war . . . ?"	To promote metaphoric thinking about the war
5	FEAR: "What am I afraid of? How do I cope with it?"	To promote body awareness and acquire skills for stress reduction
6	MESSAGES: "My dove of peace"	To promote constructive feelings and the sense of community
7	WISHES: "If I had a magic wand. . . ."	To promote creative imagery and self-empowerment

Secondary Prevention Program: "Step by Step to Recovery"

This particular program was built upon the thematic structure and tradition of the 12-step approach to recovery from lasting stressful life events, including self-destructive tendencies. Many practitioners of the 12-step programs stress their prime effectiveness for moral and spiritual healing, including changing belief systems and regaining hope for the future. In our case, we organized a special version of this program, following Brende's (1991) approach to helping survivors of war. However, specific to our approach was the innovation that we removed the whole 12-step paradigm from the context of special group treatment. Instead, we transposed its core themes onto a series of creative activity workshops, and made it acceptable and flexible for large-scale use even by paraprofessional helpers and volunteers, such as teachers, art teachers, librarians, and independent professional artists. Table 12.2 provides the thematic outline of this program, launched first in some 28 public libraries in Croatia (1994–1995), and later in refugee camps in Slovenia (e.g., in Novo Mesto, Slovenia, 1995–1996).

Table 12.2
Thematic Flow and Specific Goals of a Primary Pilot Program: "Step by Step to Recovery"

Workshop No.	Central Topic	Specific Goals
1	POWER vs. POWERLESSNESS	To promote self-empowerment and self-control
2	MEANING vs. MEANINGLESSNESS	To promote active coping with mental confusion
3	TRUST vs. SHAME & DOUBT	Recovery from fear from unknown others
4	"GOOD ME" vs. "BAD ME"	To promote self-awareness and critical thinking
5	BENEVOLENCE vs. ANGER	To promote impulse control and prevent acting-out in anger
6	SAFETY vs. FEAR	To promote active coping with anxiety and fear
7	INNOCENCE vs. GUILT	To promote healthy moral reasoning
8	PLEASURE vs. PAIN & GRIEF	To promote subjective well-being in the here-and-now
9	LIFE vs. DEATH	To promote positive thinking about losses
10	JUSTICE vs. REVENGE	To promote the need for social justice
11	HOPE vs. HOPELESSNESS	To promote the search for personal purposes and goals
12	LOVE vs. HATE	To promote feelings of love and tolerance for others

Tertiary Prevention Program: "Paths to the Future"

This subsequent program emerged from our insight into the need of both children and their teachers to gain a positive outlook on the future, and most importantly, a need for specific cognitive and social skills for creative problem solving. The program was organized around the basic principles of creative problem solving (CPS) as a paradigm (Parnes, 1992) and combined with our rather rich practical experience from prewar times to adapt this paradigm to art education in Croatia. The program was launched in the same network of public libraries in Croatia (1996–1997), as well as in refugee camps in Slovenia. Table 12.3 summarizes the thematic structure and specific goals of this pilot program.

Children's Rights Art Program: "Step by Step to Children's Rights" (in Progress Since 1998)

This program rests on three major challenges regarding rights of children from war-torn areas and populations all over the world: (1) their right for mass communication, (2) their right for literacy and education, (3) and their right for self-determination. Table 12.4 summarizes the thematic structure and goals of this pilot program.

Table 12.3
Thematic Flow and Specific Goals of a Creative Art-Therapy Problem-Solving Program: "Paths to the Future"

Workshop No.	Central Topic	Specific Goals
1	PERCEPTIONS: "Order vs. Chaos"	To promote perceptive skills, including body awareness
2	FEELINGS: "Man vs. Machine"	To improve healthy emotional functioning
3	THINKING: "Known vs. Unknown"	To promote effective, integrative thinking
4	IMAGERY: "Dreams vs. Reality"	To improve cognitive skills for dream-work
5	IDEATION: "Abundance vs. Poverty"	To improve cognitive skills for idea-generation
6	CREATION: "Building vs. Destruction"	To promote motivation and skills for creative work
7	EVALUATION: "Success vs. Failure"	To promote value standards and active coping with judging values
8	HELPING: "Me vs. You"/"We vs. They"	To promote basic interpersonal and intergroup communication skills in creative problem solving

Table 12.4
Thematic Flow and Specific Goals of a Children's Rights Promotion Program:
"Step by Step to Children's Rights"

Workshop No.	Central Topic	Specific Goals
1	DISCOVERING THE SCRIPT	To promote visual communication and sharing
2	CURIOSITY & PLAY	To promote skills for constructive play
3	THE "MAGIC WORLD"	To promote imaginative feeling and understanding
4	THE ART OF READING	To promote comprehension of children's writing and artistic expression
5	THE ART OF STORYTELLING	To promote rhetoric and dramatization skills in storytelling
6	CHILDREN & THE MEDIA	To promote media awareness and mass communication focused on children's creative activities
7	CHILDREN FOR CHILDREN	To promote the basic values and skills for self-help and mutual aid

Intervention Strategies

Training Seminars and Population Coverage

The implementation of these programs rested on the basic principle of organizing special-purpose educational seminars for local action teams consisting of teachers, health professionals, and volunteers. All "teacher-to-teacher" seminars were based on the ground rule of participants' "working through" their own personal problems before working with children in distress. In this way, special attention was given to the issue of what is called in the contemporary self-help literature the "helpers' principle" (Riessman, 1995). Since 1992 over 30 training seminars with over 400 art therapy workshops were organized at different sites in Croatia, Bosnia and Herzegovina, and Kosovo (Baráth, Sabljak, & Matul, 1999; Stuvland, 1999). The approximate number of primary beneficiaries of these programs has been some 100,000 children. Table 12.5 shows the sites and coverage of the interventions.

Workshops

All programs were designed to be run in a sequential ordering of thematic workshops as outlined earlier (Tables 12.1–12.4), each lasting at least 120 minutes. The workshops included classroom-size groups of participants, with a maximum of 30 persons. Most workshops were run only with children, but at many

Table 12.5
Chronology and Population Coverage of Program Implementation

Year	Site	Program(s)	Number of workshops	Seminar participants	Approximate number of primary beneficiaries
1991	Zagreb, Croatia	I	7 workshops in 15 elementary schools	30 teachers	750 children
1992	Frontline cities in Croatia	I	30 workshops for teachers and school psychologists	120 teachers, art teachers, school psychologists	60,000 children
1993	Sarajevo, Bosnia	I	7 workshops in 15 elementary schools	30 teachers	750 children
1994	Mostar, Herzegovina	I	7 workshops in 15 elementary schools	30 teachers	750 children
1993– 1998	Novo Mesto, Slovenia	I–III	40 workshops with groups of refugee children and teachers	250 people	7,500 children
1993– 1996	Public libraries in Croatia	II–III	17 workshops with librarians from 28 library centers	425 librarians and local teachers	12,750 children
1997–	Public libraries in Croatia	IV	7 workshops with librarians from 28 library centers	425 librarians and local teachers	12,750 children
1999–	Kosovo	I–II	13 workshops with teachers and school pedagogues	150 teachers, school pedagogues, and volunteers	3,750 children
Total			422 workshops	1,460 people	99,000 children

sites (e.g., in refugee camps), teachers, parents, and local mental health professionals were also included. In principle, all workshops represented a mixture of different art media for creative self-expression and communication. The combination of (a) visual arts and craft activities, (b) literary activities, (c) music therapy—both active and passive—and (d) dramatic play activities was provided, under the direction of a multidisciplinary team of art therapists.

Material

Depending on circumstances, the materials actually developed for, and used in, different programs ranged from nothing or a minimum requirement (e.g., paper and pencil) to optimum aids. Wherever and whenever it seemed applicable, the group facilitators and participants were provided with printed materials (handbooks, handouts), art kits, puppets, masks, costumes, and simple music instruments (Orff-sets), or materials that were handmade on the spot. A special series of slides was prepared with famous artwork selected thematically (e.g., Marc Chagall's "War," Pablo Picasso's "Guernica") to promote aesthetic perception and reasoning. For the purposes of relaxation and visualization training, written or audiotaped texts were provided, accompanied by carefully selected background music. In optimal circumstances, such as the sites at public libraries with appropriate audio and video equipment, a series of thematically selected video material was prepared as well (e.g., cartoons). For a description of program supplements see Baráth and colleagues (Baráth, Matul, & Sabljak, 1996; Baráth, Miharija, Leko, & Matul, 1993).

Evaluation Design and Instruments

In principle, the evaluation research on the effectiveness of the previously listed programs was subject to a pretest/posttest design with repeated measurements on the same subjects and constructs, including controls (Campbell & Stanley, 1966). For this purpose, a special battery of evaluation instruments was developed beginning in 1992. This included standardized tests on cognitive functioning prior and after intervention (Karp, 1992), screening scales for PTSD (Stuvland & Kuterovec, 1992), coping styles inventories (Karp, 1992), and measures of family functioning (Karp, 1992). In addition, a special series of qualitative measures (e.g., semantic differential scales) was developed for recording changes in the quality of participants' art productions in the progress of each single program (i.e., workshop-based evaluation). Semantic differential scales were used to determine if the program facilitated a lowering of emotional defenses by the children and willingness for them to share their traumatic experiences with others.

RESULTS

This section summarizes the major empirical findings of our evaluation research conducted parallel with program implementation, at several different sites.

First-Wave Programs

Table 12.6 presents the major evaluation scores of the first-wave crisis intervention program in Croatia (1992–1993) with a nationwide representative sample of elementary school age children from both "high-risk" and "low-risk" areas. The results clearly show that these programs, in combination with other approaches (e.g., individual counseling), were able to induce relief in nearly one-third (35%) of children with initial high-level PTSD scores. These interventions were activated during the heaviest military attacks all over Croatia. Without these programs, a great many children would have been left, at best, "uncured" by the existing system of mental health services, and at worst, stigmatized as "sick" by both their own families and among peers.

Other empirical findings on the effectiveness of this first-wave intervention program include (Kuterovec, 1993):

Cognitive Functioning

Our early hypothesis was that children's cognitive functioning, as measured by standardized psychological tests, might become seriously impaired by traumatic experiences. This initial hypothesis and reasoning was not supported by the data.

Table 12.6
Population Rates of Children (N = 5,628) with High vs. Low PTSD Scores Before (T1) and After (T2) the Application of the First-Wave Crisis Intervention Program in Croatia (1992–1993)

Criterion groups in follow-up	Population rates (%)	Tests on change		
		Significance D-score*	t-test	p
High PTSD-Intrusion scores before (T1)	27.1			
High PTSD-Intrusion scores after (T2)	17.4			
Change		−35.8	23.7	.001
High PTSD-Avoidance scores before (T1)	20.5			
High PTSD-Avoidance scores after (T2)	16.4			
Change		−20.0	14.7	.001
Low PTSD-Intrusion scores before (T1)	9.7			
Low PTSD-Intrusion scores after (T2)	8.2			
Change		−15.5	10.3	.001
Low PTSD-Avoidance scores before (T1)	11.3			
Low PTSD-Avoidance scores after (T2)	12.7			
Change		+12.4	6.0	.001

*Change scores (D) = {Rates after T2} − {Rates before T1}/{Rates before TA}

Children from "high-risk" zones were found to be doing as well in the series of cognitive tests as their peers from "low-risk" zones. Nor was any significant difference found between children with "high-stress" vs. "low-stress" scores on the PTSD scale. Accordingly, further efforts to create and implement special cognitive skills training programs were omitted from subsequent program development.

Coping Strategies

It was found that highly traumatized children use a significantly greater variety of coping strategies, and that they use them more often than nontraumatized children. For the low-stressed groups the most efficient coping strategies were found in drawing, writing or reading something, watching television, or listening to music. In contrast, high-stressed groups of children were found to prefer praying as a coping strategy, followed by more outward-oriented communications and confiding in someone. It was also significant that high-stressed children, on the average, found their coping strategies more helpful than did low-stressed children. This early finding helped us to focus our further program development in the direction of empowering children, in a subtle and unobtrusive way, with as many active (object-centering) coping strategies as possible.

Semantic Analysis of Children's Art Productions

The initial hypothesis was that the effectiveness of art-crisis intervention programs would be demonstrated by children "opening-up" progressively, step-by-step. The ultimate therapeutic goal would be for them to confront even their most painful experiences and share them with others if they were provided a safe psychosocial environment, and the necessary tools and opportunities for creative self-expression. In the first wave of the crisis intervention program, a total number of over 30,000 artworks were produced at different school sites of program implementation. A sample of these works was subjected to semantic analysis by group facilitators themselves (e.g., teachers), according to carefully prepared instructions for the use of a series of semantic differential scales (see Table 12.7). As predicted, the principle of "gradual catharsis" was demonstrated, suggesting that children's art productions had been progressively loaded with trauma symbols. Apparently, the thematic workshops had been successful in asking, step-by-step, for the opening and sharing of painful experiences from the war, later providing a closing with reconciliation and a positive outlook on the future. Specifically, these statistics clearly suggest that children's artwork permeated with clinically significant visual signs and symbols had changed in the flow of the program, reflecting an inverted U-shaped "cathartic" learning curve of aesthetic expression. As far as the semantic differential scores were concerned, we found that the program had demonstrated its effectiveness on all three criterion scales of connotative meaning, in that children's art productions were progressively loaded with more positive emotions, greater self-empowerment, and an increase in active coping.

Second-Wave Programs

An additional set of findings demonstrates the effectiveness of the second-wave intervention programs at two different sites of their implementation. The first was at Novo Mesto (Slovenia), with mixed groups of refugee children from Bosnia (1994–1995) and mixed groups of local volunteers (Baráth, 1995, 1996).

Table 12.7
Frequency Distribution of Trauma Symbols and Teachers' Average Semantic Differential Ratings of Children's Drawings (N = 530, k = 3,710 Art Works) from the First-Wave Crisis Intervention Art Therapy Workshops

Workshops	Trauma symbols	Semantic differential measures (in z-scores)		
		Evaluation	Potency	Activity
1. MEMORIES	4.76	.37	0.54	.35
2. SPACES	5.47	.13	− 0.27	− .05
3. TIME	5.48	.29	− 1.37	− .06
4. WAR	7.19	.55	− 2.11	− .09
5. FEAR	7.19	.52	− 2.12	− .09
6. MESSAGES	3.87	.85	1.29	.74
7. WISHES	4.17	.58	1.32	.53

The second was in Croatia (1994), via a network of some 28 public library centers (Baráth & Stuvland, 1994).

The most salient finding drawn from the Slovenian study was that virtually all age groups invited to participate (from 6 to 60) benefited from the program, at an overall level of statistical significance. In contrast, the findings for the Croatian pilot studies were mixed. Specifically, in the Croatian study sample by far the greatest gains were recorded on the criterion scales of coping with "Hopelessness," "Powerlessness," "Guilt-feeling," "Grief," and "Meaninglessness." Virtually no improvement was recorded in another series of criterion measures, "Anxiety," "Distrust," "Revenge," "Death-concern," and "Hate."

We offer two possible explanations for these differential findings. One is that the two samples were really not comparable in many respects. While the Slovenian refugee sample was ensconced in a safe, caring environment far away from actual military operations and related traumatic events, the Croatian resident sample was exposed daily to both physically and psychological distressing life events. Hence it is no wonder that the Slovenian treatment groups may have benefited substantially more from the intervention program than their peer groups in Croatia living under harsher life conditions.

Another possible explanation may be grounded in methodological differences in the implementation of the same programs at these two sites. In Slovenia, the entire program was run under the personal responsibility and full engagement of the present author and his closest professional multidisciplinary team (visual art therapists, music therapists, social workers, etc.). Moreover, in the case of Slovenian implementation, the program turned out as a full-fledged community development project with the support of a great many local civil, nonprofit organizations, including local artists, local social workers, and schoolteachers. In contrast, the Croatian site of the program's implementation took a different path. From the beginning, it was planned as a two-step "teaching-of-teachers" action research program, at 28 public libraries throughout Croatia. Local teams of public librarians with quite different professional backgrounds were first trained for program implementation (by the present author and his working team), then asked to adapt and implement the program on their own, adjusted to local needs and circumstances. As one may assume, the program implementation in Croatia was subjected to looser methodological criteria than that in Slovenia. These two biasing factors probably were involved in the sharp differences in the program's effectiveness for the two sites.

DISCUSSION

The development and refinement of wide-band, public health oriented art therapy prevention programs beg for global implementation, especially in countries hit by civil disturbances and/or by war, because they have the potential of helping young victims in a creative and meaningful way. This is a call that has been echoed by many leading mental health professionals and specialists in trauma psychology (Bloch, 1994; Randall & Lutz, 1991).

In this paper four model art therapy programs were outlined, originating in the series of wars and civil disturbances in the former Yugoslavia, from their starting point in Slovenia (1991) to Kosovo (1999). The significance of these and similar programs should be measured and checked against five critical points: (1) originality, (2) acceptability, (3) applicability-replicability, (4) effectiveness, and (5) productivity.

Regarding originality, the previously mentioned programs called for fundamental changes in the entire system of elementary school education, for example, making more room for children's expressive art activities both in the school and in the community. Many school authorities, who viewed art therapy programs as unnecessary and incompatible with the regular school curriculum, forcefully opposed this program's goal.

Due to the overpoliticized policy making in education and cultural life throughout the nations of the former Yugoslavia, none of these programs was supported by governmental bodies or by local nongovernmental organizations (NGOs). The sole supporter of all these programs was the UNICEF Office for Former Yugoslavia. In spite of these unfortunate political circumstances, however, certain component parts of the previously listed programs remain viable and have found grass-root support thanks to local initiatives.

According to modest estimates, nearly 300 international NGOs have emerged in diverse areas of the former Yugoslavia, all with their own flags, symbols, and vehicles to provide psychosocial aid for children who had become war victims. During this period, however, we never saw any professional paper on the major objectives, roles, or achievements of these so-called humanitarian organizations in promoting children's rights and improving mental health. What we heard, instead, were rumors that the administrators and employees of these international NGO programs felt "quite comfortable" with their large salaries, while they paid miniscule wages to their local servants. In this respect, more evaluation research is badly needed to protect and promote children's rights and well-being throughout the former Yugoslavia.

In closing this discussion, it should be noted that we have moved away from treating war trauma per se, and that our research interests have shifted into three different directions. One is the effective use of bibliotherapy in public libraries throughout Croatia in promoting children's rights (Baráth, Sabljak, & Matul, 1999). Literary works appear to help distressed children, youth, their parents, and teachers build trusting relationships with one another and create a positive future outlook (Baráth & Sabljak, 2001).

The second direction combines small-group based social work methods with the principles of contemporary self-help and multicultural art therapy (Baráth, 1998). The rationale involves a public health model of intervention, as well as the importance of self-help and mutual aid.

The third line of action research leads us to work with populations and local groups of children and youth living and growing under rather harsh economic and social conditions, attempting to help socially isolated and abused children and youth within their own families and social environments. This is especially critical when neither social services nor large-scale social programs are available, except for reliance on local human resources (Baráth & Vastagh, 2000).

However, we have encountered three sobering obstacles at almost every site of our program implementation. First are the political obstacles blocking implementation of our "psychosocial aid" programs at local schools. Most educational authorities seem to be afraid of such programs. Second, the societies we deal with are still autocratic national states; therefore, any freewheeling, multiethnic creative art therapy projects may arouse suspicion by local governmental and school authorities. The third sobering obstacle is the rivalry of various subcultures and value systems. Therefore, we have found the most serious obstacles do not involve the unwillingness of ordinary local people to participate but, rather, the prejudices and wariness of the political leadership.

CONCLUSION AND RECOMMENDATIONS

Our work over the past decade, documented in this chapter, indicates that organized art activities with children, even at times of acute military operations, may be therapeutically valid and socially acceptable both by children and their local supporters. Large numbers of lay helpers and professionals may be mobilized and trained in a relatively short time for an integrative and effective use of creative therapies as tools for communication and education, helping large numbers of distressed children during wartime and following the cessation of hostilities.

More care should be taken for the planning and large-scale management of psychosocial aid programs in order to prevent their marginalization by governmental and political authorities. This study has demonstrated the usefulness of a multidisciplinary approach to war trauma in children. These programs deserve increased attention and support if young victims of war are to reclaim their lives and their future.

REFERENCES

Adams, P., Berg, L., Berger, N., Duane, M., Neill, A. S., & Ollendorff, R. (1972). *Children's rights: Toward the liberation of the child.* London: Panther Books.

Baráth, Á. (1991). *Patterns of creative growth during pre-adolescence: A cross-sectional study of public school children in Croatia.* Zagreb, Croatia: University of Zagreb Medical School.

Baráth, Á. (1995, May). *Sažetak iskustava i rezultata psihosocijalnog programa "Korak po korak do oporavka" u Sloveniji 1994–1995* [Summary of experience and results of the "Steps to Recovery" Program in Slovenia 1994–1995]. Unpublished manuscript.

Baráth, Á. (1996). Lepesről-lépésre a javulásig: Egy komplex művészet-trápiás program hatékonysága a háborús és egyéb traumák kezelésében Horvátországban és Szlovéniában [Step by step to recovery: The effectiveness of a complex art therapy program for treating war trauma in children in Croatia and Slovenia]. *Pszichoterápia, 7*(3), 25–33.

Baráth, Á. (1998). Kreatív terápiák szociális válságkezelésben [Creative therapies in social crisis interventions]. In J. Kozma (Ed.). *Kézikönyv a szociális munkásoknak* [A handbook for social workers] (pp. 179–201). Budapest, Hungary: Szociális Szakmai Szövetség.

Baráth, Á. (2000). Treating war trauma in children and youth from the former Yugoslavia. In N. Dimitrijević (Ed.), *Managing multiethnic communities in the countries of former Yugoslavia* (pp. 355–369). Budapest, Hungary: Local Government and Public Service Reform Initiative.

Baráth, Á., Matul, D., & Sabljak, L. (1996). *Korak po korak do oporavka: Priručnik za kreativne susrete s djecom u ratnim i poslijeratnim vremenima* [Step by step to recovery: A handbook for creative encounters with children at the time of war and after]. Zagreb, Croatia: Tipex.

Baráth, Á., Miharija, Z., Leko, A., & Matul, V. (Eds.). (1993). *Psihološka-pedagoška pomoč učenicima stradalim u ratu: Priručnik* [Psychological and pedagogical help for children affected by war: Guidebook]. Zagreb, Croatia: Ministartsvo prosvjete, Zavod za kolstvo, UNICEF.

Baráth, Á., & Sabljak, L. (2001). *Bibliotherapy for healing war trauma in children and youth: Experience in Croatia 1991–1999.* Newark, DE: International Reading Association.

Baráth, Á., Sabljak, L., & Matul, D. (1999). *Korak po korakj do prava djeteta: Priručnik za kreativne susrete s djecim u radionicimama djećjeg odjela narodne knjižnicve* [Step by step to children's rights: A handbook for creative encounters with children in public libraries]. Zagreb, Croatia: Knjižnice Grada Zagreba–Gradska Knjižnica.

Baráth, Á., & Stuvland, R. (1994). Projekti UNICEF-a za Republiku Hrvatsku. (UNICEF programs for Croatia). In N. Šikič, M. Žužul, & I. Fattorini (Eds.), *Stradanje djec u domovinskom ratu* [The suffering of children in the homeland war] (pp. 247–259). Zagreb, Croatia: Slap.

Baráth, Á., & Vastagh, J. (2000). *Önsegélyezéső csoportok támogatása a halmozottan veszélyeztetett gyermekek és fiatalok szociális gondozásában Villány város és aprófalvas környékén* [Support to children and youth self-help groups in Villány and its rural surroundings]. Pécs, Hungary: University of Pécs, Department of Sociology and Social Policy.

Brende, J. O. (1991). *A workbook for survivors of war: A twelve-step trauma recovery workbook supplement for group leaders and participants.* Columbus, OH: Trauma Recovery Publications.

Campbell, D. T. & Stanley, J. C. (1966). *Experimental and quasi-experimental designs for research.* Chicago: Rand McNally.

Đjurok, I., Milivojevič, S., & Pörös, B. (Eds.). (1993). *Rat kako to djeca vide* [War through the eyes of children]. Pécs, Hungary: Hrvatski Institut/Ifjúságért Egyesület.

Feder, E., & Feder, B. (1984). *The expressive arts therapies.* Sarasota, FL: Feders Publications.

Greenstone, J. L., & Leviton, S. C. (1993). *Elements of crisis intervention: Crises and how to respond to them.* Pacific Grove, CA: Brooks/Cole.

Karlavaris, B., Baráth, Á., & Kamenov, E. (1988). *Razvijanje kreativnosti u funkciji emancipacije ličnosti putem likovnog vaspitanja* [Promoting creativity as the process of emancipation in children through art education]. Belgrade, Yugoslavia: Prosveta.

Karp, S. A. (Ed.). (1992). *Kit of selected distraction tests.* Brooklyn, NY: Cognitive Tests.

Katz, A. H., & Bender, E. (Eds.). (1990). *Helping one another: Self-help groups in a changing world.* Oakland, CA: Third Party.

Klingman, A., Koenigsfeld, E., & Markman, D. (1987). Art activity with children following disaster: A prevention-oriented crisis intervention modality. *The Arts in Psychotherapy, 14,* 153–166.

Kuterovec, G. (1993). *Evaluation of UNICEF's psychosocial programme for Croatia: "Psychological and educational help to children affected by war."* Zagreb, Croatia: University of Zagreb, Faculty of Philosophy, Department of Psychology.

Oravetz, R. (1993). Menekült gyermekek traumás zavarai [Traumatic disturbances of the refugee children]. *Szenvedélybetegségek, 6*(2), 94–103.

Parnes, S. J. (1992). *Visionizing: State-of-the-art processes for encouraging innovative excellence.* Buffalo, NY: Creative Education Foundation Press.

Pintarič, A. (Ed.). (1992). *Duga moga djetinjstva: Literarni i novinarski radovi ucenika osnovnih skola i srednjih skola Slavonije i Baranje* [The rainbow of my childhood: Literary and journalist works of elementary and high school children from Slavonia and Baranja]. Zagreb, Croatia: Zavod za školstvo Ministarstva prosvjete, kulture i športa Republike Hrvatske.

Pynoos, R. S., & Nader, K.(1993). Post traumatic stress disorder in children. In J. Wilson & B. Raphael (Eds.), *International handbook of traumatic stress syndrome* (pp. 535–549). New York: Plenum Press.

Ressler, E. M., Tortoricim, J. M., & Marcelino, A. (1992). *Children in situations of armed conflict.* New York: UNICEF.

Riessman, F. (1995). The "helper" therapy principle. *Social Work, 10*(3), 27–32.

Stringer, E. T. (1996). *Action research: A handbook for practitioners.* London: Sage.

Stuvland, R. (1994). URT Snimak URL [URT/URL questionnaire]. In R. Đapić, M. Sultanović, & Š. Jahić (Eds.), *Psihosocijalna pomoć učenicima i roditeljima u ratu* [Psychosocial aid for children and parents in wartime] (pp. 53–54). Sarajevo, Bosnia and Herzegovina: Ministarstvo Obrazovanja Nauke Kulture i Sporta, Pedagoški Zavod Grada Sarajeva/UNICEF Sarajevo.

Stuvland, R. (1999, November). *Psychosocial project for children and women affected by violence in Kosovo: Project proposal to UNICEF Prishtina.* Bergen, Norway: Centre for Crisis Psychology.

Stuvland, R., Baráth, Á., & Kuterovec, G. (1994). A háború által érintett iskolás korú gyermekek: UNICEF programok a volt Jugoszláviában [Schoolchildren affected by war: UNICEF programs for former Yugoslavia]. *Szenvedélybetegségek, 2*(8), 197–205.

Stuvland, R., & Kuterovec, G. (1992). *Screening of children for traumatic experience from war in Croatia: Interim research report.* Zagreb, Croatia: UNICEF Zagreb.

United Nations Children's Fund. (1999, November 11). *Information brief.* New York: United Nations.

United Nations General Assembly. (1989, November). *Convention on the right of the child.* New York: United Nations.

Wadeson, H., Durkin, J., & Perach, D. (Eds.). (1989). *Advances in art therapy.* New York: Wiley.

13

Social Sources of Life: Rehabilitation in the Former Yugoslavia

Vesna Ognjenovic, Bojana Skorc, and Jovan Savic

When the war in the former Yugoslavia began, enormous human suffering pervaded the whole country, which for 45 years had been a common space inhabited by people of different ethnic and religious backgrounds. Many people were faced with death, threats, shelling, and ruin. Entire worlds, physical and social, fell apart. War in Yugoslavia did not only imperil the lives of people directly exposed to its brutality; the deleterious effects expanded the areas of armed conflict to spread over the whole social surrounding.

SOME FACTS OF LIFE IN SERBIA AND THE SRPSKA REPUBLIC

After the armed conflicts began in June and July 1991, the first wave of refugees from Croatia and Slovenia reached Bosnia and Serbia. In Bosnia and Herzegovina, the war started in spring 1992, instigating the second wave of refugees reaching Serbia. The armed conflicts ended in the summer of 1995, and the third wave of refugees from the Krajina area of Croatia reached Serbia. During the war, only the ex-republics of Serbia and Montenegro remained in the Federal Republic of Yugoslavia (FRY).

Serbia was exposed to NATO bombing for 78 days and nights, from March 25 to June 9, 1999. Early summer 1999 brought the fourth wave of internally displaced people, this time from Kosovo. New groups of people were settled in collective centers or tried to find shelter in private accommodations. Political instability, as well as feelings of uncertainty and despair, put great numbers of people into a passive position—that of war victims—and made them incapable of taking responsibility for their own lives and the lives of their children. By the end of 2000, approximately 1 million refugees and displaced persons, mostly Serbs, lived in FRY. In autumn 2000, significant political changes took place in FRY, including elections that produced a dramatic change in the government. After the war in 1995, Bosnia and Herzegovina transformed into two coexisting entities: the Bosnia-Herzegovina Federation, with a majority of Bosnians (predominantly Muslims) and Croats (predominantly Roman Catholics), and the Srpska Republic, with a majority of Serbs (most of whom were Serbian Orthodox Christians). Five years after the war, in the Srpska Republic, every third citizen was a refugee or displaced person, a total of some 40,000 people. During the NATO strikes in Serbia, about 12,000 displaced people arrived as refugees. War has taken away many lives and the search for those missing and killed is ongoing. The mass graves of people killed during the war are still being discovered.

OUR RESPONSE TO DISASTER

In 1991 our group of developmental psychologists in Belgrade became concerned about the effects of war on all children in the former Yugoslavia and, in particular, with the issues facing the growing number of children and families seeking refuge in Serbia. In November 1991 the Belgrade group met with the refugees from Croatia in one collective center in Belgrade. In January 1992 the main program activities were constructed and applied in collective centers for refugees in Serbia:

1. Life is valuable per se, and there is always energy to sustain it.
2. Life needs others who see, who hear, and who feel.
3. It is worth proclaiming that life is present, even when it seems that everything else is lost.

"Hi Neighbor" Community

In November 1992 our Belgrade group was invited to Banja Luka by the Association of Children's Friends to train the group of professionals working in schools and institutions of mental health. Since that time we have worked together in the "Hi Neighbor" ("Zdravo da ste") program, which became a social community consisting of two nongovernmental organizations with offices in Belgrade and Banja Luka. Each organization has developed networks covering many regions in Serbia and the Srpska Republic.

The Process of Reconstruction

After the intrusion of war, the meaning of people's lives was shattered. In our efforts to stay alive, internal resources were valuable. Social interaction was a powerful source of life, almost the only one left. The constructive alternatives were reduced by the fact that we belonged to the group of people labeled as "aggressors." In this chapter we have tried to narrate our common story about the joint efforts to reconstruct the meaning of our lives. This story has many authors, all of whom have experienced war, some of them more than once.

Being developmental psychologists, we found that the Vygotskian sociocultural approach was a promising source for initiating the process of reconstruction. The Russian psychologist Lev Vygotsky's general genetic law states that all higher psychological functions are internalized relationships of the social kind and constitute the social structure of personality (Vygotsky, 1962, 1990). The composition of higher psychological functions, including their genetic structure and ways of functioning, is social. Even when these functions become psychological processes their underlying nature remains social. This perspective helped us create meaningful and proper activities for the sake of preserving life (Valsiner, 1987).

CHILDREN AS THE SOCIAL SOURCE OF LIFE

Being a child during the war carries deep and hidden suffering: loneliness, anxiety, fear, nightmares, curiosity motivated by fears instead of by a desire to discover the surrounding world, stifled imagination, and frozen play. The joy of life has been disrupted, and normal childhood behaviors and experiences have been lost. Research carried out with young children in Belgrade (1991) and with schoolchildren in Banja Luka (1994) indicated the intrusion of war in the children's thoughts and feelings.

The impact of war was consistently manifested in the free drawings and free play of these children (Ognjenovic, Andjelkovic, & Skorc, 1995b; Savic, 2000). The children's spontaneous activities of drawing and playing lacked playfulness and imagination. The free drawings of schoolchildren changed in their content and use of color. They were dominated by war imagery and the use of colors was drastically reduced, with generally somber tones pervading many drawings. Black flowers and black suns appeared in the drawings of many children. For example, a young girl asked to draw a self-portrait drew herself as a princess with a black crown on her head, black spots on her face, a black flower on her clothes; in the middle of her room, a small black tank was shooting at her.

The children's images of war created through their play were realistic rather than imaginative. Role-playing with war content was more frequent than before the war, and it tended to interfere with or even dominate other play activities, transforming them into war play. Role-playing reflected realistic details of war that had not been seen before in previous children's behavior. Traditional war games were transformed into fights between real political enemies, with labels taken from actual "war vocabulary." Those children who were directly and severely affected by war did not play at all. It seemed as if they had forgotten how to play, expecting adults to teach them what to do.

The Vygostkian conception of play emphasizes its crucial value for future development. Vygotsky puts the matter in a very clear and simple way: "In play the child is always above his average age, above his usual everyday behavior. In play he is ... head-high above himself" (quoted in Valsiner, 1989, p. 64). According to Vygotsky (1990), play is "not simply a recollection of past experience, but a creative reworking that combines impressions and constructs from ... new realities addressing the needs of the child" (p. 87). In play the child develops his or her capacities for life experiences. Faced with the fact that war had intruded upon these play activities, the vital sources of children's development, we initiated efforts to restore playfulness.

The Program of Psychological Workshops

In considering the possible strategies of how to protect and promote development, we gave crucial relevance to social interaction. Under drastic and destructive changes of social context, the child's actual interactive field becomes an unknown and dangerous territory. Its ordinarily fine dynamic complexity is transformed into turbulent changes that cannot be controlled and understood. In order to build new relational activities, the whole potentiality of the interactive field needed to be reconsidered.

The model applied in workshop activities emphasizes the child's social capacity to initiate changes in adults. By saying that the "child may initiate the changes of adult and vice versa," we wanted to stress the child's active contribution to adults' development. The traditional adult-child dyads (e.g., parent-child, teacher-child) needed to be revised for the sake of mutual benefit. During an 8-year period child-adult interaction was analyzed. The main goal of the research was to reconsider the asymmetrical position thus far exclusively ascribed to adults. In the actual social field of the child both sides, not only adults, alternate the symmetrical-asymmetrical position. In the drastically changed social environment, the child was seen as initiator of adult changes and co-creator of social reality (Ognjenovic, Andjelkovic, & Skorc, 1995a). Family and community members may initiate relevant changes as well. Adults other than parents and teachers may have a decisive part in a child's development. Relatives, neighbors, and friends may play relevant and even decisive roles. The relevance of others in general becomes more obvious under war circumstances.

Workshop activities were developed as complex and open interactions involving elements of play and creativity. Interactive playlike patterns of activities were structured in order to evoke and integrate individual and group creativity. The activities were built on expressive sources through flexible and guided use of voices, words, gestures, movements, colors, lines, shapes, drawings, and so forth. The participants were expected to express the meaning of a word by nonverbal means, to find the voice for something that is ordinarily voiceless, to find a color for a voice or gesture and vice versa, to touch and sense the untouchable. There was a wide range of games, for example, "let's color our names," "let's express our feelings by movements," "let's exchange the first syllable of our names." Our assumption was that unusual and unexpected external activities with visual tools of expression would provide an opportunity for internal symbolic activity to occur, develop, and integrate.

From the very beginning, the responsiveness of all participants (children, teachers, parents) to the program was positive. It was amazing how easily individual feelings were evoked and transformed into a new common stream of activity that was beneficial for everyone. It is hard to explain, but it seemed as if laughing and crying joined to create a new alternative. It was astonishing how quickly and easily an eruption of creativity had been evoked in spite of recent destruction, violence, and social deterioration. The participation of many people of various ages, different backgrounds, and varied experiences was the main source of creating new guidelines and facilitating the process. Turning points in developing activities emerged within the activities themselves.

"Undiscovered Treasure" and "Human Beings" were the titles given by two young refugee boys to our relational activities. A 10-year-old boy living in an area directly affected by war reflected on the workshops, "I wondered what it could be. I felt the workshops to be gentle natural phenomena. The workshops remind me of the resources we have to build our future." This provided encouragement for what we were doing. We recognized the many benefits that could accrue from the joint activities of adults and children. From spring 1992 to the end of 2000, the children's sayings were collected to serve as guides for future activities.

It Is Always Time

We found out that the process of reconstruction is built on discovering the treasure hidden in human relations. In a social context deeply changed by war and its attributes (scenes of physical violence, victims, frightened people), hardly visible—but only one available source for changing it—was transformation through new human relations. This idea appeared from Vygotsky's theory, which sees human relations as a main constitutional element of social reality. The proper timing of intervention is assuming new dimensions. It is no longer either too early or too late, it is always time. A group of children in a 1995 workshop at Banja Luka wrote about "Life":

> Dark, gloomy, cold, sad! All of a sudden—a volcano. Fire! Fertile lava flows. A tree grows from it. Life begins! The sun smiles, a cloud bursts into tears. Birds start singing the song of love. The wind sows the seed of life. The fertile field of love flourishes, blossoming, into children happily playing. They sing as one:
> Life is the real thing when the gift of love is blossoming.

A group of adults in a 1997 workshop in Laktasi titled "My Hands" wrote a story titled "The Tree of Life":

The seed of life was sent as a divine gift.

For a long time, a man cherished it and carried it with him as the greatest treasure of all. Lonely, with the seed in his bosom.

And then he realized that unless he shared it with others it would never grow. As leathery hands caressed it, the seed grew. Drawing love, warmth, and strength from the depths of the earth, a beautiful tree had grown. In return, it bore us fruit.

And so, for centuries, we have been growing together, giving and taking.

Hands that are small and big, soft and hard, tender and tough, a mother's hands, friendly hands, my hands, a stranger's hands. They seek one another to share warmth, strength, resources belonging to childhood, like endlessly rippled rivers with stolen sun rays engulfed in them.

Hands, join together in the tree of life so that we all reach the sun and make the dream of goldfish come true.

The choice of the stories is deliberate. Our main intent is not to demonstrate or present what we were doing but to share with others the treasure we discovered. A multitude of meanings are involved in these stories, and each time we look at them there is a chance to discover a new one. In this meaningful complexity we see the opportunity to reconstruct the sense of everyday life. Through relational activities undiscovered resources could be reached and transformed into social treasures.

The Turning Point

The relevant turning point, which was based on international resources, was the work of the International Institute for Human Development and the East Side Institute for Social Therapy in New York presented in *Lev Vygotsky—Revolutionary Scientist*, a book written by Fred Newman and Lois Holzman (1995). In this book we found new guidelines for further developing our activities. The human capacity to perform is central to their practice and also became relevant for our work. According to Holzman (1997) the human capacity to perform is to be both who we are and who we are not at the very same time. She describes performance as the revolutionary activity by which human beings create their lives, qualitatively transforming and continuously reshaping the unity between them and their environment. The "performance of lifetime" concept focused our program activities, transforming them into workshops that were even more creative in nature.

In March 1999 NATO bombing began and disrupted our everyday life. Feelings of helplessness, loneliness, despair, anger, grief, and pain were very strong. We again saw the children's drawings and recreational activities losing playfulness. We even saw many of the young children stop playing. We again saw the toys on shelves or in boxes going untouched for days. We again saw overly realistic play. In two collective centers, we saw refugee children making real shelters rather than imaginative constructions. We saw, heard, and experienced again the hidden suffering of many children at risk for their lives. However, our activities continued to build on performance and helped us to rebuild our daily lives, step by step.

In July 1999 we met many children and adults from Kosovo in collective centers lacking basic conditions for decent living. We again initiated our workshop activities with children. Once again we began to build "Hi Neighbor" communities.

ALTERNATIVES

Are there any alternatives for those who experience war trauma in the form of helplessness, loneliness, despair, anger, grief, and pain? Our answer to the question is yes.

It is worth remembering that in play the child can be transformed. It is worth trying to discover whether in playlike activity the adult can be transformed as well. We believe that in play, the child can be transformed more easily than the adult can. We listen to what children are saying and grasp new meanings from their statements. Through the activity of listening we can hear voices of the future. Life is not somewhere else; life is where we are. There is no end.

"Hi Neighbor" has developed a network consisting of 18 teams in Serbia and 10 teams in the Srpska Republic. The first steps have been completed by a group of developmental psychologists in Belgrade in Serbia. By the end of 2000, the refugees and displaced persons (both children and adults) were active and creative participants in program activities related to social and cultural integration. After this 8-year period, a new sense of possibilities emerged. The process of building new relationships under war-affected circumstances created the vision of a better life in the future. Our activities with preschool children, schoolchildren, adolescents, and adults made the link between culture and development visible.

REFERENCES

Holzman, L. (1997, January). *The performance of a lifetime*. Paper presented at the conference Unscientific psychology: Conversations with other voices. Conference sponsored by the East Side Center, New York.

Newman, F., & Holzman, L. (1995). *Lev Vygotsky: Revolutionary scientist*. New York: Routledge.

Ognjenovic, V., Andjelkovic, D., Skorc, B. (1995a) *Child as initiator of an adult's changes: Elaboration of war events by refugee children involved in psychological workshops*. Paper presented at IV European Congress of Psychology, Athens, Greece.

Ognjenovic, V., Andjelkovic, D., Skorc, B. (1995b, October) *The drawings of the children living in war affected social context*. Paper presented at International Colloquium of the International Society for the Psychopathology of Expression (SIPE) , Budapest, Hungary.

Savic, J. (2000). The experience of war in children's paintings. In *Children in and after the war* (pp. 75–84). Banja Luka: National and University Library of the Srpska Republic.

Valsiner, J. (1987). *Culture and the development of children's action*. New York: Wiley.
Valsiner, J. (1989). *Human development and culture*. Toronto: Lexington Books.
Vygotsky, L. (1962). *Language and thought*. Cambridge, MA: MIT Press.
Vygotsky, L. (1990). Imagination and creativity in childhood. *Soviet Psychology, 28,*
    87–92.

14

Healing, Social Integration, and Community Mobilization for War-Affected Children: A View from Angola

Michael Wessells and Carlinda Monteiro

Over the past several decades, the nature of armed conflict has changed, and the consequences for children, defined under international law as people under 18 years of age, have been catastrophic. At the turn of the previous century, most wars were fought between states (Wallensteen & Sollenberg, 2000), and nearly 90 percent of their casualties were combatants. Now wars are fought mostly within states, mostly along ethnopolitical fault lines, and nearly 90 percent of their casualties are noncombatants, mostly women and children (Garfield & Neugut, 1997; Sivard, 1991). In addition, children are important actors in political violence (Wessells, 1998), as there are an estimated 300,000 child soldiers worldwide. In situations of armed conflict, children are subjected to attack, loss of home and future, landmines, and normalization of violence at the levels of family, community, and society (United Nations, 1996). Of the approximately 40 million refugee and internally displaced people in the world, approximately half are children.

Western-trained psychologists working in war zones have focused primarily on trauma, and the eruption of a large-scale emergency is usually followed by an influx of counselors and clinicians. In many situations this may not be the most effective use of scarce resources (Wessells, 2000). In complex emergencies such as that in Angola's 40-year-old war, however, trauma is only a small part of a much larger set of psychosocial burdens carried by war-affected children and families. In particular phases of the war, children became separated from their parents, placing them at risk of abduction by the military, sexual abuse, and other problems. This made family tracing and reunification a high priority for child protection, prevention, and psychological well-being. Similarly, many displaced children grew up in a context of severe poverty without having access to education, job training, and basic life skills. For them, poverty and hopelessness were more powerful issues than trauma was.

In addition, people in rural areas reported that their greatest emotional burden had spiritual origins and socially constructed meanings that did not fit readily within the trauma idiom. An 11-year-old girl reported, for example, that following the attack on her home, in which her parents had died, the main problem was that she had been unable to complete the culturally appropriate burial rituals. She believed that her parents' spirits could not make transition to the world of the ancestors, leaving them in a state of agitation in which they might visit misfortune on her or members of her community. In this and related war contexts, programs that focus narrowly on trauma fail to meet children's needs in the holistic, culturally sensitive manner that is needed.

For psychologists interested in supporting children and preventing further abuses of children, it is important to examine strategies for more comprehensive, integrated psychosocial assistance in war zones. The purpose of this chapter is to illustrate a community-based strategy for providing psychosocial assistance involving elements pertaining to healing, reintegration of underage soldiers, and youth development. The work described below was conducted by Christian Children's Fund in Angola (CCF/Angola), through the leadership of an all-Angolan team in the period 1995–2001 and with generous support of the United States Agency for International Development (USAID). Because the purpose is to illustrate the application of a wider approach to psychosocial assistance, the emphasis will be on summarizing diverse program strategies and elements, and their connection with the core issue of preventing violence. The importance of respecting local culture will be emphasized throughout.

COMMUNITY-BASED HEALING

From 1961 to 1975 Angolans fought for independence from Portugal. Independence, however, soon became a space in which two primary actors, the socialist government and the main opposition group, UNITA (the National Union for the Total Independence of Angola), struggled for power. The war became a superpower proxy struggle in which the former USSR and Cuba backed the government while the United States and South Africa backed UNITA out of fear that communism would spread through southern Africa. With surges and pauses, the war continues today, and several generations of children have grown up with war as a daily feature of their social reality. Highly destructive fighting occurred between 1992 and 1994 as large numbers of civilians, mostly women and children, were subjected to direct attack, community destruction, displacement, landmines, and sexual violence. By 1994 and the signing of the Lusaka Protocol, the international community provided extensive material assistance, but little had been done to address emotional wounds, which, left unhealed, spark cycles of violence. The Angolan government, noting the depth of the psychological suffering, invited CCF to provide psychosocial assistance.

Beyond issues of security, three key challenges were scale, sustainability, and community empowerment. In a country of over 11 million people, there were large numbers of war-affected children yet few professional psychologists. CCF decided to use a training of trainers approach in order to cover a wide geographic area that included eight of the most severely war-affected provinces: Benguela, Bié, Huambo, Luanda, Malanje, Uíge, Huíla, and Moxico (in the latter two provinces, CCF collaborated with the United Nations Children's Fund). In each province, a three-person team of trainers who were respected and knew the local language and culture was constructed and trained by a national CCF team. These trainers conducted week-long training seminars aimed at building local capacity to assist children and to mobilize communities around children's needs.

Sustainability was challenging in that counseling and Western psychological interventions have no cultural basis in Angolan society. Too often, outsider interventions simply collapse when the period of funding has ended, even though healing and social integration processes may require longer periods of time. Because rural villages had traditional healers who applied sustainable, useful practices such as burial rites and healing rituals, CCF approached training not as a one-way transfer of knowledge and skills but as an opportunity for mutual learning. In training seminars, local people brought to the table local understandings of children, how people had been affected, and tools for supporting children emotionally. CCF trainers brought to the table a variety of mostly Western concepts and tools such as the use of drawing to enable children to express their feelings and come to terms with their experiences of violence. Through dialogue, local community people and CCF trainers decided collaboratively what kinds of activities could best be used on an ongoing basis to support children.

Community empowerment was a key part of the strategy because the program would be sustainable only if there was a sense of community ownership. Amidst traumatic experiences and hopelessness, it is vital for people to regain a sense of control over their circumstances. In addition, CCF also learned that local communities viewed the wounds of war as communal, and they sought communal solutions. Shattered and distraught by war, many communities had no venue for collective planning and action, and traditional values were under assault from modernization, urbanization, and colonialism. Traditions, however, can provide a sense of continuity, social meaning, and support under difficult conditions. Accordingly, CCF worked with local traditional leaders to build a jango, an open community hut where meetings could occur in a manner that honored the ancestors believed to be the foundation for the living community. Working as partners, the community donated the labor to build the jango, while CCF donated the materials. The respect that CCF showed for local cultural beliefs and practices had enormous value in boosting the self-esteem of people who during the colonial era had internalized a sense of inferiority about their own culture and doubted their ability to construct a positive future.

Work in the provinces by the trainers began in 1995 and included seven steps (Green & Wessells, 1997). First, the team conducted a local situation analysis to identify the areas of greatest need. Second, the team visited local communities, meeting with and demonstrating respect for local *sobas* (traditional chiefs), elders, influential women, and caregivers. If they expressed having strong material needs, the CCF trainers worked with other NGOs and local agencies to meet the material needs. Third, the trainers conducted sensitization dialogues with community groups. Many local people viewed problems such as children's aggression as signs of disobedience rather than as impacts of war experiences of violence. The sensitization dialogues helped local people understand children's behavior and activated them around assisting children. They also helped to map the community groups, which could later be supported and worked through as part of the community mobilization process. Fourth, using the community networks identified in the first two stages, the trainers selected well-respected adults such as organizers of youth groups or teachers who were in a good position to assist children. Fifth, the trainers conducted week-long training seminars for groups of approximately 20 adults. The curriculum included children's healthy psychosocial development, the impact of war and violence on children, local belief and rituals surrounding loss and bereavement, activities for assisting children, and nonviolent conflict resolution. The seminars also provided a space in which adults could take stock of how they themselves had been affected and consider how to build bridges between past, present, and future. The activities for assisting children consisted of expressive arts such as drawing, song, dance, storytelling, drama, and other tools for improving emotional integration. Follow-up support was provided through regular site visits. Sixth, the trainees implemented activities on behalf of children. As the project evolved, trainees included more activities such as soccer teams and drama groups for increasing social integration. Because local people needed to see tangible improvements in their circumstances, the teams also began a program of giving small grants for community-planned projects such as school construction or building community huts. Seventh, the work was evaluated using a mixture of qualitative and quantitative methods and indicators.

Over 3 years, the project trained more than 5,000 adults, who in turn assisted nearly 300,000 children. The impacts on children included improved child-child and adult-child relationships, improved behavior and cooperation in the classroom, less evidence of war-related games and toys, diminished isolation behavior, reduced violence and aggressive behavior, fewer concentration problems, decreased hypervigilance, increased hope, and improved school attendance. Adults, too, reported discernible benefits. Many reported that the training seminars had for the first time provided space in which they could begin coming to terms with their own war experiences.

The impacts on community development had significant psychosocial implications. Local *sobas* and elders reported that communities had become more active and hopeful as a result of the project. The rebuilding projects turned out to be necessary complements to the training and child-focused activities, as communities reported that they needed to see tangible improvements in order to feel hopeful and continue working on behalf of children. Schools reconstruction had a significant impact because as schools were built, the physical structures became tangible symbols of communal healing and monuments to people's hope and resilience. In war zones, healing cannot be reduced to counseling or expressive activities—rich connections exist among healing, physical reconstruction, and hope (Wessells & Monteiro, 2000).

REINTEGRATION OF FORMER CHILD SOLDIERS

Reintegrating former child soldiers back into civilian society is a key prevention issue because former soldiers are at risk of continuing cycles of violence. Because former child soldiers are primary targets for reabduction, effective reintegration programs are primary means of child protection. Some youth, however, choose to continue military activity in the absence of obvious coercion. Fearful of returning home, where someone might remember what they had done and seek revenge, they often see military activity or other forms of violence as their main options (Wessells, 2002). Even following demobilization, their developmental pathways reflect their immersion in a system that honors and teaches violence. Postconflict activities of youth often serve to blur the lines between war and peace, as former child soldiers may have difficulty reentering civilian life. Young people who have no education or job skills but who have learned the power associated with wielding a gun often turn to violence to meet their basic needs. In fact, waves of political violence tend to be followed by waves of criminal violence and banditry, much of which is committed by youth.

In Angola as in many African countries, troop shortfalls, widespread availability of light weapons, and failures to protect children have led military commanders to exploit children under 15 years of age, in violation of the United Nations Convention on the Rights of the Child (Boothby & Knudsen, 2000; Brett & McCallin, 1996; Wessells, 1997, 2002). Of the more than 9,000 underage soldiers registered for demobilization under the Lusaka Protocol, 520 came from the government forces while 8,613 came from UNITA forces (Verhey, 1999). In UNITA-controlled areas, where people live under a reign of terror, most children had entered the military via abduction. Typically, a UNITA group would tell the *soba* to turn over a particular number of recruits or the entire village would be destroyed. Of the registered children, the median age was 13–14, the median length of time spent in combat areas was 2 years, and over 75 percent reported that they had shot someone (Christian Children's Fund, 1998). Children report that they served various roles—cooks, porters, spies, and bodyguards as well as combatants. Very little is known about the role of girls, though anecdotal evidence suggests that they served multiple roles including that of "soldiers' wives," a euphemism for sexual slavery. Although much remains to be learned about girl soldiering (Mazurana & McKay, 2001), this pattern seems to be prevalent.

In assisting former soldiers, CCF grappled with the problem that Western, universalized views of childhood do not fit the local context. In rural Angola, a 13-year-old who has completed the culturally scripted rite of passage is regarded as an adult. It would have been disrespectful of local culture to have called someone a youth who was a demobilized "child" soldier. At the same time, CCF wanted to ensure enforcement of international legal safeguards for people under 18 years of age. Since local chiefs agree that people under 18 should not be involved with the military, a compromise was reached to use the term "underage soldiers."

In designing the Reintegration of Underage Soldiers program (RUS), CCF decided to take a community-based rather than a center-based approach. Although center-based programs may be useful in providing a transition space and basic counseling services, centers tend to become long-term residences, and little attention is typically given to follow-up and community integration. In addition, Western counseling can be damaging in some contexts. In many Bantu cultures, for example, rural peoples believe that children who kill in combat are contaminated by the unavenged spirits of the people they have killed. Trauma is less of a problem than the breach between the living community and the community of the ancestors. A traditional purification ritual may be more appropriate in this context than Western counseling. In fact, many people believe that talking about one's war experiences invites the bad spirits to reenter (Honwana, 1997).

In the RUS program conducted in 1996–1998, the CCF province-based teams, collaborating with UNICEF, assisted former underage soldiers through a network of approximately 200 *activistas* (activists). Many of the *activistas* were connected with the local church and were recognized by their communities as being in a good position to assist returning youth. The provincial teams trained the *activistas* on the psychosocial impacts of child soldiering and on methods of enabling the integration of former soldiers. The program strategy was to reunite youth with their families when possible; to prepare families and communities to reconcile with and to work effectively with the former soldiers; and to build positive life options through vocational training, job placements, and small business activities.

Following the training, the *activistas* conducted their work in three steps: preparation, reentry, and reintegration. While the former soldiers were in quartering areas, the *activistas* traced and notified their families. The *activistas* listened to family members' concerns, educated them about the situation of child soldiers, and advised them on how to aid family and community reintegration. They also worked to increase understanding that problems such as disobedience might stem not from bad character but from war experiences. In the community, *activistas* worked to raise awareness of the needs of former child soldiers, to reduce stereotypes, and to hear concerns about their return. They also worked to gain support of local officials by conducting meetings with *sobas*, government leaders, and community influentials.

The reentry work was very dangerous because Angola remained a divided country, and strong pressures existed in UNITA-controlled areas to continue fighting and to reabduct former soldiers. There were reports that groups of demobilized youths had been rerecruited, and some youth had disappeared en route to meeting their families. Further complications included last-minute changes in transportation dates and destination points, route changes, and difficulties of family travel in dangerous conditions. Recognizing that family reunification is one of the most basic forms of psychosocial assistance to children, the *activistas* provided extensive logistical and transportation support, accompanying the child soldiers to their rendezvous points and arranging temporary foster care when it was impossible for the families to meet the children. Of the 4,104 youths demobilized into the CCF/UNICEF project areas, over 50 percent were successfully reunited with their families. The *activistas* also arranged community receptions, which were important in reconciling former child soldiers with their communities. Families and communities greeted the returning youths with great relief and joy that occasioned singing, dancing, and traditional reentry rituals in which adults sprinkled the youths' faces and heads with flour or water.

To aid social reintegration, the CCF teams worked extensively with local cultural resources. With the aid of ethnographic training from Alcinda Honwana, a Mozambiquan social anthropologist, the teams documented traditional healing practices and their surrounding belief systems regarding life and death, illness and health (e.g., Honwana, 1997, 1998). This documentation was a key part of the mobilization process because it valorized local practices and boosted the self-esteem of people whom colonialism had taught to regard their own culture as inferior. Although the evidence is preliminary, traditional purification rituals appear to have powerful effects on individuals and communities. If a returning child soldier is deemed to be spiritually contaminated, the local healer arranges a communalized purification ritual to restore spiritual harmony with the ancestors. The rituals vary according to ethnic group, situation, and other factors. Typically, the rituals include a purifying diet; demarcation of a space that the bad spirits cannot enter; use of special herbs for fumigation and bathing; ritual offerings to the bad spirits; and a symbolic action such as stepping across a threshold and not looking back. Such actions indicate a break with the past, and the healer may announce as it is performed that the young person's life as a soldier has ended and that he is now part of the community. The conduct of this type of ritual enables community reconciliation wherein the community accepts the young person back without fear of spiritual reprisal. Although long-term follow-up studies of psychological adjustment have yet to be conducted, the youths who participate in these rituals seem to function remarkably well. There is great need of multicultural action research on these and related issues.

Social reintegration requires having a positive role and a means of meeting one's basic needs. In communities, *activistas* assisted by helping to identify school, job, and vocational training placements. These are vital for building hope for the future and giving young people skills that will enable them to support themselves. In addition, participation in culturally appropriate patterns of activity provides a sense of normalcy, continuity, and social meaning (Gibbs, 1997). Unfortunately, many youths chose not to return to school due to embarrassment over having to take classes with young children in primary school. Because many youths will return to agricultural life, CCF/Angola, with the aid of funding from the World Bank, provided small grants for land purchase and quick-impact projects such as starting a small business. This approach underscores the importance of linking psychosocial healing with economic reconstruction in an integrated effort.

Unfortunately, these efforts were scuttled by the reeruption of war in December 1998. In this most recent phase of war, there have been significant numbers of underage soldiers, creating the need to replicate and institutionalize similar programs. The reeruption of war provides a sober reminder that psychosocial assistance alone cannot build peace, and efforts toward healing and integration need to be vertically integrated with wider programs of political and economic reconstruction.

YOUTH DEVELOPMENT

In rural areas of Angola, as in many war zones, teenagers have enormous constructive or destructive potential. If they have developed positive values and learned appropriate skills and knowledge, their energy, intellectual competencies, and willingness to try new ways make them powerful assets for community development and emergency response. In reality, however, many youth who have grown up in a situation of war, normalized violence, and poverty may have values pertaining mostly to individual survival. Many Angolan teenagers have only 3 or 4 years of formal education, are out of school, and have few skills needed to function as contributing members of the community. In many villages teenagers are often regarded as troublemakers or as disrespectful toward authority, and many teenagers feel marginalized. Struggling with difficult problems ranging from poverty to sexually transmitted diseases, youths often receive little social and emotional support because they are regarded as old enough to care for themselves. Spending significant amounts of time idling and desperate for money, many youths are at risk of involvement in crime, violence (including child soldiering), and prostitution. Surprisingly, relatively few programs have focused on the needs of youth (Women's Commission for Refugee Women and Children, 2000).

To support youth, CCF organized a 4-year project that began in late 1998. Initially conducted in Benguela, Huíla, Luanda, Uíge, and Moxico Provinces, the project included a mixture of long-term work on youth and community development, and emergency psychosocial assistance to people displaced by the renewed fighting. The focus here is on the youth elements of the project and the assistance supports that had developed by the project midpoint. The project strategy was to support adolescents (12- to 18-year-olds) by (a) increasing teenagers' social integration and life skills and (b) giving teenagers a positive role as agents of community development. Consistent with the overarching strategy of community empowerment, youth were regarded not as beneficiaries but as participants who helped to mobilize their peers and communities.

To increase teenagers' social integration and life skills, the project included several elements, including literacy training. Angola's literacy rate is over 40 percent, and the educational system is characterized by a crumbling infrastructure, scarcity of qualified teachers, and high failure rates. Accordingly, the project provides basic literacy training outside of school settings, in the local communities where people live and work. A decision was made to include adults in the literacy training because many adults need literacy skills. Also, adult participation often serves to motivate youth. At the midterm, 836 people participated in the literacy training, and approximately two-thirds of them were adolescents.

A training methodology similar to that which had been used in the project on healing described above was used to prepare adolescents to act as mobilizers and positive change agents in their communities. The adolescents were selected according to criteria of leadership, communication skill, motivation, and respect by the local community. In groups of approximately 20 people, adolescents took part in week-long seminars that used the previously described curriculum, adapted for adolescents. For example, discussions of psychosocial development included material on adolescence, including the physical and psychological changes, sexual awakening, and factors in the family, peer group, and community that influence healthy development. Regarding violence, the training focused on physical and verbal violence; causes and manifestations of violence between adolescents and children, other adolescents, and adults; individual reactions to violence; and nonviolent conflict resolution. By the midterm, 426 adolescents had participated in the training and were receiving periodic follow-up visits by trainers for support purposes. The training itself helped to increase social integration. Because youths were relatively unfamiliar with traditions, the trainers required the youths to interview their parents about traditions, beliefs, and practices. This dialogue increased social integration across generations and earned adolescents new respect in the eyes of adults.

Following the seminars, the trainees helped to organize community dialogues and youth meetings on topics such as drug abuse, prostitution, sexually transmitted diseases, education, traditions, and life preparation. The youths themselves choose the topics of these meetings and dialogues, and they also choose the methodologies, which often include improvisational drama, role-plays, and other participatory approaches. Regarding the meetings with other youths, the trainees reported that the peer dialogue helped to build a sense of solidarity, reduced feelings of isolation and of not being listened to, and enabled them to cope more effectively with the stressors they encounter. The community dialogues also had positive impacts. Adult participants reported that as a result of the dialogues they had become more aware of the issues young people faced. In addition, community leaders reported increased appreciation of adolescents' skills and talents.

Working with other adolescents in the community, the youth trainees facil-itated integration via recreational activities such as soccer, sewing, and commu-nity drama. Outsiders sometimes wonder why recreational activities are included in psychosocial programs, since people can play soccer without any psy-chosocial preparation. This project stood on the assumptions that structured, su-pervised activities are an antidote to idleness and support child protection; because adolescence is a peer-oriented time, it is vital to build norms of peer in-teraction that emphasize positive values; and recreational activities, if arranged in an effective manner, can serve as venues for increasing life skills of teamwork, communication, and nonviolent conflict resolution. Over 3,000 youths have par-ticipated in recreational activities, and many have said that this participation has increased solidarity, peer respect, and willingness to handle conflict nonviolently. Between communities, soccer games that do not place excessive emphasis on winning are powerful tools. People in impoverished, rural communities often suffer boredom, lack access to clothing and other goods, and the press of meet-ing daily needs leads many families to look out for themselves. Community spirit and identity is often lacking. In such settings, soccer games between teams wearing uniforms bring people together, elicit much excitement, and set the oc-casion for discussions of youth and how to support them.

Youth activities also related to education and employment. In communities, the trained youth served as promoters of formal schooling and encouraged chil-dren and families to stay involved in education. To enable income generation in a situation of abject poverty, the project organized small groups of youths into solidarity groups that receive training on basic aspects of small business and keeping track of money, and that borrow small funds to conduct petty business. This aspect of the project has been hampered by rampant inflation (its rate often exceeds 100 percent per month), which makes loan repayment very difficult. Still, some youths have found their way to set up small business activity, and the project team remains enthusiastic about this project element because youth who cannot earn at least a subsistence-level income will be at risk. The project team is also establishing vocational and professional training venues for youth in areas such as agriculture, carpentry, masonry, baking, sewing, locksmithing, and metalworking.

Perhaps the most important activities of youth pertained to community de-velopment. Following the psychosocial training, youths helped to mobilize their communities around collective planning and action on behalf of children. Many communities felt they could function as communities only if they built a *jango* where they could talk and plan in a manner that respected tradition and enabled harmony with the ancestors. Youth participated in the construction of these *jangoes*, thereby showing their respect for tradition and contributing to community-defined development.

Another set of development projects that youth enabled was the construction of small community playgrounds. Before the project had begun, few rural areas had well-defined areas for children's play or play facilities. Often children played without adult supervision and engagement, and there was little dialogue between parents in the context of play. Sometimes children played alone. When children played together, the dominant themes were often war or fighting. People in the community commented that they felt inferior to city-dwellers because they lacked such basic facilities as swings and playgrounds for their children. In this context, building small playgrounds enabled not only healthy play but also child protection and supervision, social integration among adults, and increased community esteem. Typically, the playgrounds consisted of a small area of 10 square meters in which there were swings, space for jumping rope and playing hopscotch and traditional games, some beach sand, and materials such as old tires on which children could climb. Some playgrounds included small huts in which children could read, play with dolls, or act out various roles. Having participated in building the playgrounds, the youths helped to staff them by providing volunteer oversight of the children and facilitation of healthy play.

Two unexpected results emerged in the context of the playgrounds. First, the playgrounds stimulated extensive activity by adults, as parents came to the playground. The positive side of this was that some parents spent more time playing with their children than they had previously. The drawback initially was that the adults themselves wanted to play on the swings and other facilities to which they had never had access but had always wanted in their own childhoods. Fortunately, this situation subsided following the initial excitement and the establishment by the community that the children had primary access during particular hours. Second, in some cases the playgrounds provided a means of reducing conflict and improving relations between neighboring communities. In Cambila, Uíge, neighboring but segregated communities experienced significant tensions, a not uncommon situation in a country where displaced people move close to and compete for resources with more stable communities. The solution in this case was to plan jointly a playground built midway between the neighborhoods. By bringing the neighborhood leaders together for dialogue and enabling the conduct of reconciliation rituals by elders on both sides, the project significantly improved intercommunity relations.

Because the project is in progress, it is possible at this point only to sketch the preliminary results discerned at the midterm review. For youth, main results include the acquisition of important life skills, increased hope and sense of solidarity, reduced fighting, better relations with adults, improved relations between boys and girls, and achievement of greater respect within the community. For communities, main results include increased collective planning and action on behalf of youth, improved attitudes toward youth, and increased respect for local traditions that provide a sense of continuity and support amidst difficult circumstances. These preliminary results suggest that program approaches that link youth development with community mobilization are useful tools for peacebuilding and conflict prevention.

CONCLUSION

The three psychosocial programs described in this paper are part of wider efforts by the CCF/Angola team. In fact, CCF/Angola has conducted three additional programs that are important in their own right. The first provides emergency psychosocial assistance to recently displaced people, while the second provides help for the helpers. Helping the helpers is crucial in a situation in which the teams are themselves affected by the war, carry enormous emotional and social burdens, and are at risk of burnout and related difficulties. Third is work on child survival that aims to reduce Angola's under-5 mortality rate, which is among the highest in the world. This innovative program integrates medical and psychosocial elements, the latter of which have increased care-seeking behavior by mothers, provided household support for overwhelmed mothers, and helped to handle difficult cases in which children are severely ill.

Collectively, these programs illustrate the ways in which psychologists can make positive contributions in war zones through work that is framed not by the trauma idiom but by an emphasis on community empowerment and enabling communities to build positive futures for their children. Even this diverse array of program elements, however, does not exhaust the psychosocial applications that are needed desperately in a war-torn country. Extensive psychosocial assistance is needed for displaced people because nearly one-third of the Angolan population is displaced. In addition, psychosocial work is needed to promote tolerance. For decades Angola has essentially been a country inside a country, as UNITA-controlled communities have been isolated and subjected to heavy doses of indoctrination, propaganda, and terror. To build peace at the community level, steps to increase tolerance and a sense of common ground are essential.

Further, violence has become so systemic and normalized in Angola that much work on peace education and nonviolent conflict resolution are badly needed. Sadly, the word *peace* has dropped out of the local discourse because many local people have never experienced peace, only know how to survive in war, and fear that if war ends they may fare more poorly. Ultimately, psychosocial programs ought to be gauged in part by the contribution they make to peace, which is essential for the protection of children's rights and well-being.

REFERENCES

Boothby, N., & Knudsen, C. (2000). Children of the gun. *Scientific American, 282*(6), 61–66.

Brett, R., & McCallin, M. (1996). *Children: The invisible soldiers.* Vaxjo, Sweden: Radda Barnen.

Christian Children's Fund. (1998). *Final report: Project of reintegration of child soldiers in Angola.* Luanda, Angola: Author.

Garfield, R. M., & Neugut, A. I. (1997). The human consequences of war. In B. S. Levy & V. W. Sidel (Eds.), *War and public health* (pp. 27–38). New York: Oxford.

Gibbs, S. (1997). Postwar social reconstruction in Mozambique: Reframing children's experiences of trauma and healing. In K. Kumar (Ed.), *Rebuilding war-torn soci-*

eties: Critical areas for international assistance (pp. 227–238). Boulder, CO: Lynne Rienner.

Green, E. G., & Wessells, M. G. (1997). *Mid-term evaluation of the province-based war trauma team project: Meeting the psychosocial needs of children in Angola.* Arlington, VA: USAID Displaced Children and Orphans Fund and War Victims Fund.

Honwana, A.M. (1997). Healing for peace: Traditional healers and post-war reconstruction in southern Mozambique. *Peace and Conflict: Journal of Peace Psychology, 3*, 293–306.

Honwana, A.M. (1998). *"Okusiakala Ondalo Yokalye": Let us light a new fire.* Luanda, Angola: Christian Children's Fund/Angola.

Mazurana, D., & McKay, S. (2001). Child soldiers: What about the girls? *Bulletin of the Atomic Scientists, 57*(5), 30–35.

Sivard, R. L. (1991). *World military and social expenditures 1991.* Washington, DC: World Priorities.

United Nations. (1996). *Impact of armed conflict on children: Report of the expert of the Secretary General of the United Nations Ms. Graca Machel.* New York: United Nations Publications.

Verhey, B. (1999). *Lessons learned in prevention, demobilization and social reintegration of children involved in armed conflict: Angola case study.* New York: UNICEF.

Wallensteen, P., & Sollenberg, M. (2000). Armed conflict, 1989–99. *Journal of Peace Research, 37*, 635–649.

Wessells, M. (1997). Child soldiers. *Bulletin of the Atomic Scientists, 53*(6), 32–39.

Wessells, M. G. (1998). Children, armed conflict, and peace. *Journal of Peace Research, 35*, 635–646.

Wessells, M. (2000). Trauma, healing, and psychosocial assistance: The case of East Timor. In Government of Canada (Ed.), *Background papers for the International Conference on War-Affected Children.* Winnipeg, Manitoba: Government of Canada.

Wessells, M. (2002). Recruitment of children as soldiers in sub-Saharan Africa: An ecological analysis. *The Comparative Study of Conscription in the Armed Forces, 20,* 237–254.

Wessells, M. G., & Monteiro, C. (2000). Healing wounds of war in Angola: A community-based approach. In D. Donald, A. Dawes, & J. Louw (Eds.), *Addressing childhood adversity* (pp. 176–201). Cape Town, South Africa: David Philip.

Women's Commission for Refugee Women and Children. (2000). *Untapped potential: Adolescents affected by armed conflict.* New York: Women's Commission for Refugee Women and Children.

15

Somato-Psychotherapy at the Medical Foundation in London

Michael Korzinski (an interview by Stanley Krippner)

Stanley Krippner: You've been working on the frontline, treating torture victims in a London clinic associated with Amnesty International. Can you provide us with a brief history of this clinic?

Michael Korzinski: The Medical Foundation is an independent charity founded in December 1985 to continue the work first carried out by volunteer practitioners, primarily physicians, under the auspices of Amnesty International. It was founded by Helen Bamber who, at the age of twenty, was a member of one of the first rehabilitation teams to enter the Bergen-Belsen concentration camp at the end of World War II. This event was to initiate five decades of work with survivors of torture and other atrocities.

In 1961 Helen joined Amnesty International and was instrumental in establishing its first Medical Group. Its aim was to document evidence of torture and, along with the World Medical Association, examine the role played by physicians in the torture process. However, it was never a part of the medical group's mission to provide a specialized rehabilitation service for the survivors of torture. Helen, along with others, recognized that it was not enough to simply document the injuries for forensic purposes. What was needed was a specialized service that could meet the long-term rehabilitation needs of people who had survived torture and other forms of organized violence. With Amnesty's support, Helen set up the Medical Foundation as an independent human rights organization that works exclusively with these survivors.

Since 1985 the Medical Foundation has received close to thirty thousand referrals. In 2001 there were five thousand thirty-one new referrals from eighty-nine countries, including the United Kingdom. The vast majority of the Medical Foundation's clients have not only been systematically tortured but have suffered other traumas associated with war, such as ethnic and communal violence, genocide, and forced migration.

Furthermore, since 1996 asylum seekers in the United Kingdom have been subjected to increasingly punitive policies that have further stigmatized them and left them vulnerable to increased levels of racist attacks and exploitation. It's within this context that the Medical Foundation aims to offer a multidisciplinary service (i.e., psychological, medical, and social) embracing crisis intervention, long-term rehabilitation, and practical assistance. As a nongovernmental organization, we are also involved in campaigning on behalf of the rights of asylum seekers, raising the public's awareness about torture and its consequences, and writing reports that identify offending governments and perpetrators. It is my understanding that, in light of the events on September 11, 2001, and the subsequent "War on Terrorism," the United States is reopening the debate about the advisability of using torture to make suspects talk (Alter, 2001). It is important to remember that making people talk is only one, and often not even the most important, aspect of torture. Torture, as Helen once said, aims to "kill" a person without his or her actually dying, and serves as a reminder of the omnipotent destructive power of the state. I am reminded of the ancient proverb, "Choose your enemy wisely, for it is he you are mostly likely to become."

Krippner: What is the history of your own involvement with the Medical Foundation?

Korzinski: I began working at the Medical Foundation in 1990. At that time there was a high percentage of patients who were presenting with physical symptoms in the absence of any clear-cut medical diagnosis that would explain their symptoms. A common factor of the group was that they were all refugee survivors of torture. They all shared a preoccupation with those bodily feelings for which conventional medicine was unable to find a physical cause and which could not be explained by any known physical conditions. The attempts by physicians, counselors, psychologists, and others suggesting that the causal explanation for the pain might be due to social stressors or have a psychological basis were rejected outright. I remember some members of the staff would argue, "Of course these clients are going to present with physical symptoms. After all, we are called the Medical Foundation and it is only logical that they would present with physical symptoms."

In addition, many clients come from cultures where it is not safe to speak about what really happened to their body. An Algerian patient of mine laughed when I asked if he had ever spoken openly with his family doctor following nearly eight years of detention in a military prison. "The nature of our society is such," he said, "that you do not know if your family doctor is linked to the very forces that had you tortured." He continued, "You learn to speak in a kind of code. You tell people that your bodily trauma happened when you fell down a flight of stairs or were in a fight or some other kind of serious accident, like being hit by a bus. Likewise, the doctor is suspicious of you and that you might be spying on him. He gives you a tablet to ease the pain, and does not ask too many questions. That is the way it is. The lucky ones are the people who have family members who love them. They will attend to your injuries and pain. They know what happened without asking any questions."

However, it is important to remember that physical torture aims to gain access to the psyche through the abuse of the soma; as a result, the links between body and mind become disrupted. I started to listen more carefully to what these patients were actually saying about their bodies and came to believe that they were communicating something incredibly profound about the nature of their experience and that perhaps the pain did reside in the body, but not in the way that doctors or psychologists have traditionally been trained to identify. These patients often feel trapped between the reality of their bodily feelings, on the one hand, and the absence of an explanation and treatment they can comprehend, on the other. What treatment actually means for these clients, or what they recognize or are prepared to accept as treatment, is complicated by all kinds of factors including the particular nature of their experience of torture, their cultural background, their understanding of the context in which they are seeking help, and their previous experiences in the ways in which physicians and other practitioners function.

My own view is that torture has a profound and disturbing effect on a person's felt sense of his or her body. Torture is a shameful, degrading, guilt-ridden experience that is a perversion of all that is positive in human relationships. It savages one's earliest sense of self, the sense of being in one's own body. What I call "somato-psychotherapy" is an attempt to address this dimension of a person's experience of torture. I derived somato-psychotherapy from my training in psychology, psychotherapy, sensory awareness, and psycho-physically based processes such as the Alexander technique, Dalcroze Eurythmics, and Robert Masters's Psychophysical Education. Anyone wishing to undertake such work must be able to combine a firm grasp of the anatomy and physiology of human movement with an understanding of traditional views of psychopathology such as post-traumatic stress disorder, reactive psychosis, depression, hysteria, hypochondria, somatization, illness behavior, dissociation, splitting, and depersonalization, as well as the possibilities and limits of rehabilitation.

Krippner: What are the basic elements of your therapeutic approach?

Korzinski: I typically work with individuals whose bodies have been brutally assaulted under torture. The anatomical body is extraordinarily resilient, with an enormous capacity to heal, and no significant physical damage is sustained by many of these patients. What is far less resilient, defying reassurances both medical and psychological, is the person's fragile sense of the integrity of the somato-psyche. The objective in these cases is always the same: the restoration of the integrity of the damaged body percept to a healthy state. The methods employed to achieve this vary but the core principle remains the same.

Somato-psychotherapy is essentially a process of finding a method to open the pathways of communication between the therapist and the patient's tortured body and mind. This allows the healing potential inherent within the therapeutic relationship to be realized. The therapist's use of touch, movement, and speech provides both patient and therapist with the opportunity to explore the problem in all its individual complexity. The client is free to communicate through whatever medium seems appropriate because he or she knows that the therapist will be able to understand and respect the communication as valid. This sets in motion a process of development and growth through which the client's shattered sense of wholeness can be restored.

The starting point of somato-psychotherapy is essentially determined by the client's sense of where and how the damage is experienced. In my view, the client's initial preoccupation with bodily experiences is a natural response to the catastrophic violence perpetrated against the body under torture. It is, however, the clients' changing understanding of their feelings about the effects of their previous trauma that directs the course of treatment, and this understanding is followed closely throughout. The therapist is required to move with the client's shifting somato-psychic presentation, whether the clients are expressing their trauma in words or in symptoms relating to their damaged sense of the body. Each is a valid form of communication needing an appropriate response. If, for example, a therapist attempts to make a psychological interpretation of a person's symptoms, suggesting that it means "something else," when in fact the client is really communicating something about his or her damaged body percept, the client is left confused and disoriented. The body percept is an emotional construct, one which may need to be responded to verbally, somatically, or in various combinations of the two.

The client's sense of the reality of his or her body, and ability to safely test this reality in the presence of the therapist, is crucial to the overall course of the client's rehabilitation. The somato-psychotherapist accepts the person's bodily communication in its own right even though he or she operates with the awareness that there are deeper emotional issues involved. In this approach, the therapist is not simply a blank screen upon which the patient projects his or her unconscious fears or fantasies. The somato-psychotherapist has a far more active role to play in the therapeutic process than is often associated with classical psychoanalytic theory where, for example, the use of touch and movement is considered a taboo.

Before the trauma can be integrated with a person's whole life experience the damaged parts need first to receive the attention, acceptance, and care of the therapist. It is the therapist's acceptance and process of care that validates and helps restore the person's damaged bodily sense. Without this, a trusting therapeutic relationship can rarely be achieved. When the therapist disregards the client's clear physical and psychological signals about his or her experience, and the course of the healing process, it casts doubt on the client's frail sense of what is real. This engenders a sense of "madness" that reminds clients of their experience under torture and could exacerbate their symptoms. The therapist must be able to respond appropriately to the unconscious communications of the client. This requires that the therapist have sufficient understanding of the link between bodily awareness and emotional expression in order to sensitively respond to the client in both somatic and psychological terms. If the therapist does not have sufficient self-awareness in all these areas the possibility for open-ended exploration so crucial to the success of this particular form of intervention cannot take place.

The therapist is not passive. He or she plays a highly active role in knowing when and how to intervene as the emphasis shifts for the client. This approach requires special skills and strategies enabling the therapist to respond flexibly to the client's shifting presentation over the entire course of his or her rehabilitation.

Krippner: Can you give an example of how the client's presentation might shift during treatment?

Korzinksi: For example, a person initially presenting with a totally fragmented body percept, needing extensive rehabilitation in that area of the somato-psychic continuum, may eventually abandon the need for somatic work and choose to work exclusively in words and on issues not directly related to their bodily feelings. It is equally possible that the client may need a combined approach throughout the entire course of their rehabilitation, neither working exclusively in words nor in somatic techniques. Furthermore, it also might occur that someone who is not able to work somatically, but whose symptoms are in need of validation, understanding, and acceptance may, in time, address his or her body in physical terms. It may be enough in such cases for the therapist to accompany and occasionally guide the patient through the morass of feelings he or she is experiencing in the body.

So, the therapeutic process is not simply a linear progression from A to Z. There is no predetermined starting or ending point imposed by the therapist on the client, and there are many potential variations around the basic somato-psychotherapeutic approach. The therapist will need to be continually alert and correspondingly shift his or her approach to the client's changing needs and presentation.

Krippner: Can you describe the typical background of your clients?

Korzinski: For the past eleven years I have been working in an organization where the vast majority of my patients are Muslim. One of my colleagues actually practices "Islamic counseling." However, I've found that torture and atrocity have ways of deconstructing one's belief systems, whether they are political, cultural, or religious. For example, a person who holds a fundamental-ist Islamic worldview is unlikely to present for psychological treatment. He or she would first seek help from an imam, a Muslim holy man. However, when his or her worldview doesn't stem the flow of nightmares or enable him to func-tion sexually, that individual often finds himself or herself in trouble and might seek medical treatment.

Krippner: How do you adapt this approach for specific cultures, such as your work with Muslim clients?

Korzinski: Part of the difficulty with cross-cultural treatment can be seen in the relativism of certain key terms, like *torture* itself. Torture as a concept is firmly rooted in a myriad of contexts. Each person who hears the word will have a different perspective on its meaning.

At a 1992 seminar in London entitled "Torture: Perpetrators and Bystanders," Professor Mika Haritos-Fatourous recalls commenting on her experience while attending a conference on human rights where she confronted an Iranian gov-ernment official in attendance at the conference on his country's use of torture. He told her simply that Iranian "practices cannot be defined as torture because they are an integral part of our religious tradition and beliefs."

His reaction illustrates the complexities of defining torture in certain parts of the world. The word *torture* in this case is perceived through the frame of fun-damentalist Islamic ideology and beliefs. This problem was explained to me by an Iranian client of the Medical Foundation who was a lecturer in sociology at Tehran University before he was imprisoned, brutally tortured, and forced to flee his country.

"The Qur'an along with various resalah is cited as legitimizing such atroci-ties. *Resalah* in Persian means 'essay.' They are written by the mullahs, i.e., peo-ple who speak for God. For example, there is one resalah that describes all the ways in which an individual can praise Allah. There is a short sentence on every aspect of his or her life, what they should and shouldn't do, and the punishments for disobeying. The mullah speaks for Allah, so these books are considered God's law. Anyone who speaks against a mullah must be 'punished' and put to death. Since Khomeini came to power in the 1978 revolution over five thousand writ-ers, researchers, and artists have been tortured and murdered."

So the Iranian government, despite being considered by the international community as having an appalling human rights record, insulates itself from the reality of its actions by the incorporation of torture into its ideology and re-ligious beliefs (U.S. Department of State, 1992). That is just one example of the complex conceptual problems encountered when treating Muslim patients. To a greater or lesser extent, such culturally specific definitions of "torture" may be characteristic of cultures in which the teachings of Islam play a dominant role, though this sort of denial is common to many non-Islamic cultures as well.

By way of contrast, within our own culture one can easily imagine a case in which a woman who was systematically and repeatedly beaten and humiliated by her husband might use the word *torture* to describe the years of domestic violence she survived. Or an animal rights activist could argue that the use of non-human subjects in certain types of scientific research results in the "torture" of defenseless animals. In both cases the meaning of the word carries with it the nuances of the particular context in which the word is used. The pain, agony, and suffering reflected in both of these cases is irrefutable. However, in each of these situations, the use of the word *torture* is informed by the context in which it is used. In such cases, "abuse" must be distinguished from "torture," since all torture contains abuse, but not all abuse is torture. So, our understanding of the concept of torture is reflected in how the people in these cases use the word to describe their experiences. The Iranian example is different in that it represents an outright denial of the concept. No one other than another Islamic fundamentalist would suggest that torture is a normal activity for punishing disobedience.

The important point is that practitioners working with refugee populations need to be cognizant of how the client's culture is shaping his or her illness behavior. Mollica and Lavalle (1988) observed that refugees will often present with somatic rather than emotional or psychological complaints, even though the patient clearly meets the diagnostic criteria for depression. The patient doesn't view his or her psychological problems as warranting psychiatric attention. They may come from a background where it is socially and culturally acceptable to talk about bodily complaints, but if they were to talk about their psychological distress they would risk being stigmatized within the community whose support is so important for their recovery. Problems that are seen as psychological in nature may result in the person being seen as mentally weak or damaged. So, in some cultures, somatization is not only the accepted but the *expected* form of expressing psychological distress. The practitioner is faced with an extremely complex treatment picture when working with refugees from other cultures, including Islamic cultures, who have been tortured.

To give you a better sense of this complexity in terms of actual therapeutic method, the use of touch is important in my approach since it allows the therapist to "speak" and "listen" to the person's body with his or her own hands. The touch used in these cases is distinct from the way a medical doctor would touch a patient to diagnose a specific condition or the touching that occurs in social situations. Touch communicates the therapist's concern and respect for the client's damaged body percept coupled with his or her intent to "understand" and help "repair" that damage. It is through the skin that, as infants, we receive our primary understanding of the world. Touch is the foundation upon which our experience and understanding of reality is constructed. So torture can be understood as a massive and catastrophic assault directed against the very foundations of a person's earliest bodily experiences.

For many of my clients, words only provide a partial answer. It is only through the therapist's direct somatic interventions, through touch, that the reality of their damaged feelings about their bodies is responded to and ultimately affirmed. This approach has worked well with many of my clients, including a number of Muslim men for whom a psychological approach to somatic complaints would seem threatening. After all—and they would be the first to tell you this—they're not "crazy." However, the therapist must always be alert to the *meaning* that the individual client is giving to his or her touch. This meaning may be cultural-specific or it may have more to do with the traumatic experience or other factors.

This complexity was demonstrated to me in the case of a female client, an Iraqi Muslim who had experienced the most brutal and traumatic experiences including sexual torture, where it was patently clear that direct somatic interventions would have been inappropriate. She presented with a number of physical complaints for which an organic basis couldn't be found. She was also concerned that she would be unable to have a child although nothing could be found that would physically prevent her from having one. As the therapy began she made it clear that she felt that talking was her best way forward even though, at this stage, she probably didn't fully understand how that could help her bodily symptoms. She clearly didn't want to explore the idea of movement or touch and seemed to struggle just to be a "body" in the room with me. I had already considered that the use of movement and touch as the cornerstone of her therapy might not be appropriate given her previous history of sexual torture, so we proceeded without somatic interventions.

This case also demonstrates that it's possible for the somato-psychotherapist to make contact with a person's damaged sense of soma through words, physical presence, and understanding. In this case, happily, the treatment has been successful, and the client continues to attend sessions regularly and reports that her physical symptoms are no longer a problem. Finally, she and her husband have been approved as foster parents for a young Iraqi boy with cerebral palsy.

REFERENCES

Alter, J. (2001, November 5). Time to think about torture. *Newsweek*, p. 45.

Mollica, R., & Lavalle, J. (1988). Southeast Asian refugees. In L. Comas-Diaz & E. H. Griffith (Eds.), *Clinical practice in cross-cultural mental health* (pp. 262–304). New York: Wiley.

U.S. Department of State (1992). *Country reports on human rights practices.* Washington, DC: Author.

16

Post-Traumatic Stress Syndrome and Related Disorders Among Civilian Victims of Sexual Trauma and Exploitation in Southeast Asia

Glenn Graves

During the past century, the nations of the earth have undergone a terrible and disturbing transformation in the global evolution of warfare. To cite one shocking and devastating trend, about 85 percent of all victims killed in World War I were combatants. Today, some 90 percent of all people killed in wars are innocent, civilian women and children (Ehrenreich, 1997; Kolb-Angelbeck, 2000). Machal (2001) writes:

Modern wars are exploiting, maiming and killing children more ruthlessly and more systematically than ever.... Millions of children have been killed as deliberate targets in warfare or drawn in as fighters. And millions more have fallen victims to malnutrition, disease, sexual violence, and the depredations of forced flight.... Currently, approximately 20 million children have been uprooted from their homes, either as refugees or internally displaced. (p. 4)

The original motivation for this research began with my interest in exploring therapeutic methods that might lead to improved emotional well-being, specifically, for children forced into prostitution in Southeast Asia. These victims, by various means, have escaped from the sex industry but continue to experience the lingering effects of sexual trauma in the form of various psychological sequelae. In Southeast Asia today, millions of girls and young women are being exploited and traumatized through both voluntary and involuntary prostitution, sexual slavery and trafficking, and related forms of sexual abuse associated, at least initially, with war and its immediate aftermath.

Between 1998 and 2002, I interviewed several dozen former female prostitutes from Nepal, Thailand, Cambodia, Vietnam, and Laos as well as social workers involved in helping them to rehabilitate. Additionally, in my role as a documentary filmmaker, I interviewed U.S. veterans of the Vietnam War. During these interviews, I was struck by the similarities between civilian victims of what the Vietnamese call "the American War" and U.S. combatants in both the original traumatic situation and the psychological aftereffects.

By illustrating some of these similarities—focusing primarily on parallel symptoms of post-traumatic stress disorder (PTSD) and dissociation—the reader will begin to appreciate that some wars do not just take place on the "battle-ground," but may also occur—and persist within the affected society in the aftermath of war—in the lives of civilian noncombatants as well, and with no less devastating effects than those experienced by the combatants.

Article 39 of the United Nations Convention on the Rights of Children reads:

State parties shall take all appropriate measures to promote physical and psychological recovery and social reintegration of a child victim of armed conflicts. Such recovery and reintegration shall take place in an environment [that] fosters the health, self-respect and dignity of the child. (United Nations, 2000)

My intention is to describe how children in civilian populations—especially girls and young women—may be traumatically affected by sexual practices associated with war and its consequences, using Southeast Asia as my example, specifically, Vietnam. We will also consider promising therapeutic approaches for these civilian victims of war-related trauma, including models adapted from successful approaches applied to assist combatants.

WAR AND THE SEX TRADE IN SOUTHEAST ASIA

Since the end of the Vietnam War, a great deal of attention has been focused on the lingering psychological aftereffects of various forms of war trauma. During the war, tens of thousands of U.S. soldiers experienced and witnessed extremely brutal and violent events. The experiences of many of these young men and women were so intensely horrifying that many returned emotionally damaged. Some of them witnessed torture or were victims of torture; others committed unspeakable acts themselves. The overall experience left numerous U.S. veterans physically and/or psychologically wounded.

As a result, many combatants who returned from the war developed classic symptoms of dissociation and PTSD, a condition of great concern to psychiatrists throughout the last century. In earlier 20th-century wars, U.S. psychiatrists referred to PTSD by such terms as *shell shock* and *combat neurosis*.

While a great deal of interest has attended throughout the last century on the effects of war trauma on returning combatants, relatively little concern has focused on secondary and derivative mass traumas affecting civilian victims of war. This is especially true of children forced into sexual slavery and prostitution as a direct or indirect result of wartime socioeconomic factors. For example, one of the long-lasting effects of the war in Vietnam and its aftermath was a huge economic boom for the sex industry in Southeast Asia. Although prostitution existed in Vietnam prior to the Vietnam War, the presence of U.S. troops led to a rapid increase in the number of sex workers during the war. Kuo (2000) reports that prostitution during the Vietnam War grossed $16 million in U.S. dollars for the Thai economy alone. As one South Vietnamese observer put it at the time: "The Americans need girls; we need dollars. Why should we refrain from the exchange?" (p. 42). Kuo similarly points out that between 1957 and 1964, when the United States established seven military bases in Thailand, the number of prostitutes in that country rose from an estimated 20,000 to 400,000.

History demonstrates that armed conflict brings with it the demand for sex-oriented facilities. The presence of the U.S. military in Southeast Asia, for example, has created a demand for sexual entertainment centers located near military bases. All too frequently, this demand for sex has been met by local business interests who have supplied the women by coercing and exploiting females, including young girls, mostly from poverty-stricken rural areas. The conditions of war create a need for sex, and with it a demand for women. When demand outstrips supply, as occurred during the Vietnam War, brothel owners are forced to search for girls, whether or not they are willing. While war, by itself, does not necessarily *cause* sexual trafficking, research indicates that local socioeconomic conditions, both during and after a war, do lead to a higher number of persons being exploited by the industry.

Both Olongapo, Philippines, home of the U.S. naval base at Subic Bay since World War II, and Angeles City, Philippines, where the U.S. Air Force operated a large base at Clark Field, have a well-established history in the trade of underage girls catering to U.S. service personnel both during and after the war in the Pacific. The sex trade in Angeles and Olongapo continues to thrive up to the present day, due to aggressive marketing by Filipino entrepreneurs even after the U.S. military departed in 1992 (Satchell, 2000). According to Satchell, a social worker interacting with girls as young as 9 years of age reported that "the kids said they had been used by American sailors, but the naval authorities told us to keep quiet so they could catch the perpetrators. However, it has been reported by the organizations that the Navy shipped out suspects to avoid prosecution."

During my interviews with two U.S. veterans of the Vietnam War—a colonel and a squad leader in the infantry—in October 2001, both witnesses described a government-sponsored encampment called "Sin City." During the war, more than 70 "hooches"(shacks for drinking, taking drugs, and prostitution) were located within this single fenced compound. These hooches were operated by pimps who cooperated with the U.S. government in an effort to provide a safer means for sex-based rest and recreation (R&R). Each member of the military entering this compound had to show identification papers. The girls providing sex were examined weekly by the U.S. military physician and, if free of sexually transmitted diseases (STDs), wore a patch designating them as "safe." Eventually someone wrote to a U.S. congressional representative to complain, and Sin City was shut down.

In Vietnam, as elsewhere in Southeast Asia, the society's vulnerability to socioeconomic conditions favoring the sex trade continued long after the end of the war itself. During war, a host country's economy is severely affected by the increased need for food and supplies to meet the increasing demands of the war population. For example, the authorities often impose rules forcing people to turn over a share of their crops, income, businesses, and/or skills to the state or its agents in order to help the war effort. During the Vietnam War, it became easier for traffickers to negotiate the market for the sex trade as the war-ravaged civilian population struggled to overcome mass shortages of money and food. In this period, a markedly increased likelihood of family involvement in sexual trafficking existed because of the family's desperate economic circumstances combined with the relatively high pay being offered by the traffickers (Kelly & Duong, 1999; Mayor, 1995).

When the war ended, however, the major source of clients disappeared, and brothel owners were left with the challenge of replacing their source of income. In an effort to increase the customer base, brothel owners continued seeking girls from rural areas who were desperate to help their families (Kuo, 2000). Within a community that has recently been involved in an armed conflict, many individuals are vulnerable and desperate for any type of income, including earnings from prostitution. This was apparent in Vietnam, Cambodia, and several other Southeast Asian countries (United Nations Children's Fund, 1995). The pay for sex workers during this postwar period of economic recovery is typically affected because the client base predominantly consists of locals. This leads to further exploitation and, in many cases, sexual slavery without any compensation for the sex worker.

In general, even today, Southeast Asian governmental policies restricting the sex industry are met, most often, with apathy. The practice of women and children being forced into prostitution has been an integral and traditional part of some Southeast Asian cultures for centuries. While, officially, prostitution in most parts of the region is illegal, the authorities generally do not enforce these laws and, in many cases, actively sponsor the industry as patrons, allowing brothel owners and traffickers to operate without fear of prosecution. This further exacerbates a situation in which sex workers are vulnerable to violence from both brothel owners and patrons while threatened with criminal arrest by the authorities. In short, they lack any effective justice system to protect them. Equally disturbing is the growth of demand for child prostitutes within the region. A 1999 United Nations report estimated that over 1 million Southeast Asian children are currently working in the sex trade (Kelly & Duong, 1999).

CIVILIAN TRAUMA AS A RESULT OF THE SEX TRADE

A composite "case profile," or scenario, drawn from interviews with several victims will serve to illustrate the trauma typically experienced by girls forced into prostitution both during and after the war in Vietnam. These descriptions apply to sex workers who were either forced or coerced into prostitution, many as children, and were recorded during my interviews with social workers and former prostitutes in Vietnam and Thailand.

Typically, the scenario begins when a brothel worker cruising the area, looking for potential prospects, observes a girl from a poor family. A family member, family friend, or even boyfriend may also target the victim. The girl is either abducted outright, coerced, or seduced with the promise of a well-paying domestic job, such as seamstress or hotel service worker, to help support her family. Then, she is taken to a second party by the recruiter, frequently being smuggled into another country with passage secured by bribes to border patrols and falsified travel documents. This second party may be either the brothel owner or the owner's representative. Once established in her new residence, the victim is told by her new employers/owners that they have incurred expenses in bringing her to her new home and that she must work until she has paid off her debt. She is also told that her room and meals, as well as any other bills—for example, for medical care—will be added to her debt. The room and board charges are so exorbitant that the girl will, in fact, never be able to pay off the debt, which continues to grow at an astounding rate. It is explained that she will have to service the sexual demands of each customer, which may involve as many as 12 or more men each day. As one victim reported, "We had to serve sick old men, schoolboys, and sexual perverts." If she resists, she may be repeatedly raped and/or gang-raped, drugged, burned, tortured, deprived of food, or subjected to various other methods at the hands of her "trainers," as they are called, in an effort to break her spirit and resistance to her enslaved condition. These are children who are being raped before they have experienced their first kiss.

In the course of my inquiries, I received numerous accounts of torture, including the torture of a blind girl who had been sold to a brothel and was gang-raped by six men in an effort to make her submit to her new life. I elicited an equally shocking account of a girl who had been shackled to her bed because she kept trying to escape. Eventually, she even had to service her customers while shackled. In Thailand, I was told that 12 girls burned to death in a fire because they had been shackled to their beds and were abandoned by the owner when the fire broke out in the brothel.

Phuong is a former sex worker who had run away from home, was raped, had no money and was tricked into the sex industry by an acquaintance. She recalled,

My boss kept almost all of my earnings. She was a monster! After four months I was able to save only 200,000 Vietnamese dollars ($15). I finally escaped. I decided even if I earned less selling goods on the street, I would be happier. (Research Center, 2000)

Huong, a 13-year-old, described her first sexual encounter:

I met a new friend. She was 14. She asked me to come to her uncle's house. When we got to his house, she put me in a room and locked the door. After a short time, a Vietnamese man came into the room. He was about 50 years old. I held on to my clothing and started to cry, but he tore at my clothes and ripped them off. He slapped me for crying. When he finished raping me, I was lying on the bed and I felt like I couldn't see or feel anything. I looked up and saw my blood all over the bed. The man was dressed and standing near the door and told someone on the other side that it was okay to open the door. After he left, someone came in and washed me and put my clothing back on. (Research Center, 2000)

Between customers, the new recruit typically stays in a crowded room and usually is not provided with the means to wash. Most customers refuse to use condoms, so the girls can be easily infected with STDs very early in their new career, including HIV. They are also more susceptible to other contagious diseases, for example, tuberculosis. Once the girl has contracted an incurable disease, she is released from the brothel. Frequently, she is literally dumped in the street. As she most likely finds herself in a foreign country with no money and no means to navigate—and faced with serious language barriers—she almost invariably ends up at a police station where she is arrested for lacking the proper papers. She is typically held in a home for juveniles, in most cases for several years. The only possible means of help may be from agencies looking for missing girls. If she is brought back to her country, which often takes years of legal proceedings, she typically enters a "reformation center," where she will spend 2 or more years learning new skills to help her to reintegrate back into the community.

The goal of these reformation centers is to allow these girls to be reunited with their families. This aim is often unsuccessful, however, as the family members may themselves have been involved in the original trafficking or may fear the shame and social stigma attached to having someone in their family who has worked in the sex trade. In one case, for example, a girl was returned to the mother who had originally sold her into sexual slavery. After her return, her mother sold her a second time, a common practice. Girls are frequently resold during their career because, by moving the girls around, they always appear "new" to the next brothel's customers.

PTSD IN COMBATANTS AND CIVILIAN VICTIMS OF SEXUAL ASSAULT

Even when the girl is eventually able to escape, the lingering and often devastating psychological effects of the trauma can persist for long periods of time. When I compared these effects among U.S. combatants of the Vietnam War and Vietnamese victims of prostitution, both during and immediately after the war, it was clear to me that the effects of the trauma are similar in both populations.

Within the two groups, many returned to their countries and/or their homes experiencing similar psychological symptoms. The most noteworthy similarity between the two groups is that they both have members who exhibited classic symptoms of dissociation and PTSD, frequently accompanied by drug and alcohol abuse and/or addiction. These disorders are due not only to the trauma suffered in the field but also to the emotional trauma he or she typically experienced upon return when rejected by his or her community and/or family members.

For the purposes of this chapter, I will focus on the similarities between the two populations in terms of PTSD. During the Vietnam War, many U.S. soldiers witnessed and experienced brutal situations and, as a result, suffered emotional trauma. The symptoms they displayed were similar to those of the young girls who were able to make it out of the sex trade alive (Herman, 1992; Walker, 1979).

Much has been written in recent years concerning PTSD. The 4th edition of the *Diagnostic and Statistical Manual of Mental Disorders (DSM-IV)* defines PTSD as an anxiety disorder (American Psychiatric Association, 1994). The condition is generated when a person has experienced, witnessed, or faced a stressor involving death, the threat of death, serious bodily injury, or risk to the physical integrity of the self or of another person. It produces reactions characterized by intense fear, feelings of helplessness, and/or terror (p. 427). PTSD was unrecognized as a diagnostic category until the publication of the *DSM-III* in 1980. Although, as previously mentioned, there were various descriptions for these symptoms as they applied to combat veterans of previous wars, the condition has been described most completely during and after the Vietnam War (Albuquerque, 1992).

The important point, for purposes of this chapter, is that PTSD is not limited to former combatants but is also found in victims of sexual assault (Echeburúa & Corral, 1997; Greening, 1997). The highest levels of PTSD are found in ex-combatants and in female victims of sexual assault (Echeburúa & Corral, 1997). In fact, not until "the advent of the women's liberation movement in the 1970s was it recognized that the most common PTSD sufferers are not men in war but women in civilian life" (Herman, 1992, p.28). Furthermore, approximately 50–60 percent of sexual assault victims are at risk of developing PTSD (Corral, Echeburúa, Sarasúa, & Zubizarreta, 1992). One of the most common symptoms is a heightened state of arousal as well as a generalization of fear including of places previously considered to be safe, with nightmares being relatively secondary (Echeburúa & Corral, 1995; Herman, 1992). Generally, the symptoms of PTSD include depression, loss of self-esteem, feelings of guilt and/or shame, avoidance behavior in interpersonal relations, expressive deficits, and sexual dysfunction (Echeburúa & Corral, 1995).

The female victim of sexual assault first passes through a period of generalized psychological distress characterized by anxiety, fear, and feelings of vulnerability, stress, and behavioral confusion. After this comes a period of time characterized by anxiety, phobic behavior, and changes in sexual functioning, which tend to become chronic. In fact, the initial stress is a good predictor of future stress. It is important to distinguish, when designing the treatment, between recent victims and not-so-recent victims because after this initial period has passed, symptoms tend to become chronic.

THERAPEUTIC APPROACHES FOR VICTIMS OF SEXUAL ASSAULT AND TRAFFICKING

Few psychological services have been established for either Vietnam veterans or victims of sexual trafficking since the war. In particular, few agencies in

Vietnam offer assistance to girls and young women who have left the sex trade. For the most part, assistance consists of providing immediate medical care, shelter, food, and a safe environment. The goal of these shelters is to offer the former prostitutes an opportunity to reassimilate into society.

My own observations have led me to conclude that not much is being done for these girls in the area of psychological assistance, including therapy. It was also clear that most of the girls I observed were suffering from PTSD and dissociative disorders. In many cases, their symptoms have been documented, but I found little or no information on available therapeutic procedures for assisting them. However, a number of therapeutic approaches shown to be effective for the treatment of similar populations (e.g., Vietnam veterans, sexually abused children) may prove equally effective in the treatment of female victims of sexual trauma in the brothels of Southeast Asia.

For example, therapeutic modalities utilized in the treatment of PTSD among U.S. Vietnam War veterans include behavioral (e.g., systematic desensitization and exposure), cognitive-behavioral (e.g., stress inoculation), cognitive, abreaction-based, and hypnotically facilitated therapy, and family or group therapy procedures. Of these treatment methods, group therapy seems to me the most practical for victims of sexual trafficking in Southeast Asia. Group therapy, as described by Walker (1979), may help alleviate a victim's sense of isolation or loneliness, reminding her that she is not the only one to have experienced such a trauma.

A combination of group therapy and other available treatment modalities may have an added positive effect. For example, *Qigong* and other types of movement meditation for mind/body integration have been used in Southeast Asia for centuries (Krippner & Colodzin, 1989). Cohen (1997) claims that Qigong cultivates a sense of integrity and unity and may be a powerful adjunct to therapy for overcoming fragmentation and/or dissociation. He cites studies that demonstrate the effectiveness of Qigong in behavioral and attitudinal change (Cohen, 1997, pp. 225–226, 232–237).

Narrative psychotherapy (see, e.g., Beels, 2001) allows the participant to create a framework of meaning for life experiences using words and cultural symbols familiar to them. In this approach, the participant may be asked to take imaginary journeys and reinterpret past experiences, but there are no requirements that these journeys fit into a particular mold. The goal of narrative psychotherapy would be to help the girls establish and change false beliefs about their experiences. Some victims have formulated personal myths that hold that they are valued only as prostitutes. If these beliefs aren't challenged, they will continue to consider prostitution a viable alternative even during their quest for self-worth.

In at least one study (Volker, 1997), expressive art therapy demonstrated a reduction in PTSD symptoms after only 10 weeks of group treatment. Art therapy may be used as a means of expressing inner experience. Malchiodi (1997) illustrates how art can be used as a therapeutic tool, pointing out that this modality permits nonverbal expression of thoughts and feelings, facilitates healthy communication, restores psychological equilibrium, and alleviates fear and anxiety. As a therapeutic tool, expressive art therapy appears to be a very effective approach for working with children exposed to violence and abuse.

Dance therapy gives children an opportunity to express themselves without using words. Before young children learn to speak, they utilize movement and nonverbal communication. Through the medium of dance, trauma victims can learn to relax, express themselves spontaneously, and make contact with other people. Tolfree (1996) reports that dance therapy has been successful with Bosnian refugee children in camp situations (p. 178).

Finally, dreamworking has been used successfully with combat veterans of the Vietnam War and could be a powerful adjunct to group therapy for victims of sexual trafficking. According to Brockway (1987):

Group dreamwork can offer hope of mastery of symptoms previously viewed by veterans with fear, apprehension, and uncertainty. Traumatic dreams were like night ambushes; sleep was the path for the patrol to be hit. A group can pool the meanings when the painful parts are not avoided. Dreams lay forth the meanings, and the group provides the cohesive support to explore them. The exploring leads to new meanings and finally the dreamer returns to a reality that he can accept. (p. 285)

Following a 2-year follow-up study, Brockway concluded that group dreamwork with combat veterans provided almost universal relief from nightmares and frightening dreams (p. 278).

All of these therapeutic procedures work to reestablish a sense of self, build self-esteem, and create an outlet for expression so that the trauma can begin to be addressed, interpreted, and understood. They possess the added advantage that they can be used in several cultures or are already practiced in Southeast Asia.[1] However, there are few studies with rigorous controls that demonstrate the effectiveness of one psychotherapeutic approach over another, not only for victims of sexual assault but for PTSD sufferers in general. Therefore, more well-designed studies comparing the effectiveness of various currently available psychotherapeutic techniques are needed before we know which approach works best for a particular type of patient, including former prostitutes in Southeast Asia.

CONCLUSION

As we examine war and its persistent traumatic effects more closely, it becomes readily apparent that armed combat can, and often does, perpetuate forms of mass trauma that have long-standing effects on civilians within the affected society as a whole. Even now, nearly 3 decades after the end of the Vietnam War, a quiet "war" continues, experienced every day by the girls and young women forced or manipulated into prostitution throughout Southeast Asia. The experiences of these young women, while different in many respects from those of

U.S. soldiers in Vietnam, are in many cases no less horrifying or traumatic. Unfortunately, while promising therapeutic approaches currently exist for the effective treatment of these victims of sexual abuse and trauma, few psychological services have been established to assist them.

NOTE

1. While beyond the scope of this chapter, cultural considerations in the treatment of trauma are important and, although some insight may be gained by surveying the success of various treatments for Americans who, for example, served in the Vietnam War, major cultural differences exist between these victims of trauma and civilian victims in Southeast Asia.

REFERENCES

Albuquerque, A. (1992). Tratamiento del estrés postraumático en ex-combatientes [Treatment of post-traumatic stress in ex-combatants]. In E. Echeburúa (Ed.), *Avances en el tratamiento psicológico de los trastornos de ansiedad* (pp. 51–68). Madrid, Spain: Pirámide.

American Psychiatric Association (1994). *Diagnostic and statistical manual of mental disorders* (4th ed.). Washington, DC: Author.

Beels, C. C. (2001). *A different story: The rise of narrative in psychotherapy.* Washington, DC: Zeig & Tucker.

Brockway, S. S. (1987). Group treatment of combat nightmares in post-traumatic stress disorder. *Journal of Contemporary Psychotherapy, 17,* 270–284.

Cohen, K. (1997). *The way of Qigong. The art and science of Chinese energy healing.* New York: Ballantine Books.

Corral, P., Echeburúa, E., Sarasúa, B., & Zubizarreta, I. (1992). Estrés postraumático en ex-combatientes y en víctimas de agresiones sexuales: Nuevas perspectivas terapéuticas [Post-traumatic stress in former combatants and in victims of sexual aggression: New therapeutic perspectives]. *Boletín de Psicología, 35,* 7–24.

Echeburúa, E., & Corral, P. (1995). Trastorno de estrés postraumático [Treatment of post-traumatic stress]. In A. Belloch, B. Sandín, & F. Ramos (Eds.), *Manual de psicopatología* (pp. 132–151). Madrid, Spain: McGraw-Hill.

Echeburúa, E., & Corral, P. (1997). Avances en el tratamiento cognitivo conductual del trastorno de estrés postraumático [Advances in cognitive behavioral treatment of post-traumatic stress]. *Ansiedad y Estrés, 3,* 249–264.

Ehrenreich, B. (1997). *Blood rites: Origins and history of the passions of war.* New York: Henry Holt.

Greening, T. (1997). Post-traumatic stress disorder: An existential-humanistic perspective. In S. Krippner & S. M. Powers (Eds.), *Broken images, broken selves: Dissociative narratives in clinical practice* (pp. 125–135). New York: Brunner/Mazel.

Herman, J. (1992). *Trauma and recovery: The aftermath of violence from domestic abuse to political terror.* New York: Basic Books.

Kelly, P. F., & Duong, B. L. (1999). *Trafficking in humans from and within Vietnam.* Hanoi, Vietnam: United Nations Children's Fund.

Kolb-Angelbeck, K. (2000, October 2). Winona speaks: An interview with the Green Party candidate. *In These Times,* pp. 12–13.

Krippner, S., & Colodzin, B. (1989). Multi-cultural methods of treating Vietnam veterans with posttraumatic stress disorder. *International Journal of Psychosomatics, 36,* 79–85.

Kuo, M. (2000, Summer). Asia's dirty secret [Electronic version]. *Harvard International Review, 22*(2), 42.

Machal, G. (2001, April). The war against children. *Share International,* p. 4.

Malchiodi, C. (1997). *Breaking the silence: Art therapy with children from violent homes,* 2nd ed. Bristol, PA: Brunner/Mazel.

Mayor, S. (1995). *Children and the commercial sex industry.* Phnom Penh, Cambodia: Youth with a Mission Survey.

Research Center for Gender, Family, and Environment. (2000). *Interview documents.* Hanoi, Vietnam: Author.

Satchell, M. (2000, May 8). Fighting the child sex trade [Electronic version]. *U.S. News and World Report, 128*(18), 32.

United Nations. (2000). *Sexually abused and sexually exploited children and youth in the Greater Mekong subregion.* New York: Author.

Tolfree, D. (1996). *Restoring playfulness: Different approaches to assisting children who are psychologically affected by war or displacement.* Falun, Sweden: Swedish Save the Children Foundation.

United Nations Children's Fund. (1995). *The trafficking and prostitution of children in Cambodia; A situation report.* (1995). Phnom Penh, Cambodia: Author.

Volker, C. A. (1997). *Treatment of sexual assault survivors utilizing cognitive therapy and art therapy: Self esteem, post-traumatic stress disorder, victimization.* Unpublished doctoral dissertation, California Institute of Integral Studies, San Francisco.

Walker, L. E. (1979). *The battered women.* New York: Harper and Row.

PART III

PREVENTION

INTRODUCTION

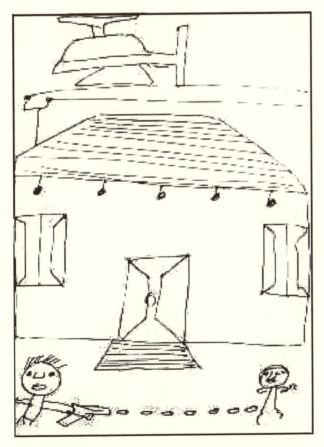

This drawing by an Angolan boy demonstrates that there is no safe place during wartime, especially for a child. Illustration published with permission of Margarida Ventura.

Whereas Part II covered strategies for primary, secondary, and tertiary prevention directed at war-afflicted civilians, in this part the focus is on detailing primary prevention approaches. The five chapters in Part III tackle the difficult challenge of preventing war and conflict in the world and, specifically, in regions that are characterized by ethnic and religious diversity.

Chapter 17, by Fisher, presents an organizational response to a pressing problem on the part of professionals trying to provide assistance in various war scenarios—the lack of specialized training in war trauma relief and ethnopolitical conflict resolution, as well as the lack of materials to implement this work. Fisher describes the development of an innovative ethnopolitical warfare (EPW) curriculum sponsored by the Canadian and American Psychological Associations, with the aim of enabling a deeper understanding of the causes of EPW and increased expertise in its treatment and prevention. Broughton, in Chapter 18, adds to these efforts describing the implementation of several conflict prevention and reconciliation activities in Kosovo and Macedonia, which attempt to increase tolerance for ethnic and religious diversity and are ultimately aimed at preventing war and promoting social integration of minorities, such as the Albanians. Along the same line, in Chapter 19 Dane presents a brief report on the work of a Sufi psychiatrist in the Middle East as an inspiring agent of change toward conflict resolution and peace. She describes a fruitful collaboration between Western and Middle Eastern professionals in terms of promoting training of local practitioners in mediation and conflict resolution strategies. Chapter 20, written by Abu-Saba, is unique in its presentation of several peacebuilding programs supported by NGOs in Lebanon. These programs illustrate how women in Lebanon, who are often targets of various kinds of direct and structural violence, can move beyond powerlessness to a place of self-determination, and become an inspiration to other marginalized women in the promotion of a more fair and peaceful society. In Chapter 21, Balzer describes the plight of the shamans seeking to preserve their culture and practices in the post-Soviet period. As in Lebanon, this persecuted group was able to find creative ways to face adversity and contribute to a more eclectic and diverse society, bearing testimony to the power of resilience in the face of religious repression.

Overall, these chapters show that the paths of preventing conflict and war are complex and difficult but nevertheless possible, encouraging further efforts. The common thread seems to be the need to promote social change as the means to impact individual and collective attitudes as well as social policy. We take the stand that constructing a culture of peace is a mission that each person must embrace, although greater responsibility lies in those who are leaders and presume to control the destiny of nations.

17

Toward a Graduate Curriculum in War Trauma Relief and Ethnopolitical Conflict Resolution

Ronald J. Fisher

THE ETHNOPOLITICAL WARFARE INITIATIVE

This chapter describes an effort to produce a generic curriculum for a 1-year professional training program for trauma relief and conflict resolution in ethnopolitical warfare (EPW), which capitalizes on the basic training that psychologists and other professionals have in mental health and in conflict resolution. The curriculum can be utilized as a 1-year post-masters or postdoctoral program, or it can be blended into existing graduate programs in specialities such as clinical, health, community, or applied social psychology. The curriculum may also be useful for graduates from a variety of disciplines and professions who have the basic expertise to address the many personal and social problems created by EPW.

The effort to develop this graduate curriculum was sponsored by a joint initiative created in 1997 by the two presidents-elect of the American and Canadian Psychological Associations (APA and CPA), Martin Seligman and Peter Suedfeld. These organizations represent tens of thousands of psychological scientists and professionals engaged in research and service directed toward the understanding of human social behavior and the improvement of human welfare. The initiative was based on the realization that the nature of warfare had shifted since the end of the cold war, and that a response was required in terms of both scholarship and the training of professionals for appropriate intervention (APA/CPA, 1997).

The Presidential Initiative on Ethnopolitical Warfare grew from the concern that destructive international conflict in the post–cold war era had entered a new and chilling phase of expression. Rather than engaging combatants in organized warfare with limited "collateral damage," these "total wars" between distinct identity groups (defined in ethnic, racial, religious, or cultural terms) vying for political power destroy the very fabric of governments, institutions, communities, and families. Civilian casualties are commonplace; child soldiers are forced to kill; human rights are violated on a massive scale; and all types of atrocities, including torture, rape, and murder, are committed. Extreme violations against communal groups in the form of ethnic cleansing and genocide are the ultimate expressions of EPW. In the aftermath of such terrible inhumanities, physical, social, and psychological problems are both widespread and deep-seated. Populations are uprooted, communities devastated, and individuals left in a state of post-traumatic stress on a large scale. The legacies of these conflicts include mistrust and hatred between communal groups, and a strong sense of mutual victimization that typically feeds future cycles of mass violence across generations. The needs for all kinds of services are very high at a time when the physical and social infrastructure for providing them has been destroyed or severely debilitated.

In the face of the incredible human problems brought about by EPW, the APA/CPA presidential initiative considers it urgent that psychologists collectively and systematically broaden and apply their knowledge and skills to understand and deal with the social and psychological elements that relate to their areas of expertise. Although many clinical, social, peace, and other psychologists have worked as individual professionals, some for many years, on the problems associated with EPW, the initiative is a direct organizational response to what can be seen as the world's number one social issue. Thus, the mission of the initiative is to apply the tools of psychology to EPW, with the goals of stimulating scholarship on the causes and prevention of EPW and encouraging the training of psychologists in trauma intervention and conflict resolution (APA/CPA, 1997). To work toward the mission, the two presidents-elect invited a number of APA and CPA members and others with relevant expertise to form a steering committee, which began meeting in mid-1997. At the time of this writing, the cochairs of the steering committee were Peter Suedfeld of the University of British Columbia and Daniel Chirot of the University of Washington (see Appendix A for the membership of the committee). In addition, a cadre of experts was formed through further invitations and indications of interest, and electronic mailing lists were developed to connect members in each group.

The goal of stimulating scholarship was addressed by sponsoring an interdisciplinary scholarly conference on the causes and expressions of EPW, held at the Initiative on Conflict Resolution and Ethnicity (INCORE) in Northern Ireland in July 1998. The conference, chaired by Daniel Chirot and supported by an anonymous donor, brought together 50 of the world's leading experts on EPW to provide a conceptual and empirical base for further development. A conference report was issued and an edited collection of selected contributions has been published (Chirot & Seligman, 2001).

In parallel with the EPW Initiative, the University of Pennsylvania established the Solomon Asch Center for the Study of Ethnic Conflict (SACSEC), and with funding from the Mellon Foundation and the National Institutes of Health was able to offer a 10-week summer training program in both 1999 and 2001, at the postgraduate level, for professionals interested in the mental health problems associated with ethnic conflict. The Asch Center is an interdisciplinary effort to prepare psychologists and other social scientists to pursue research on ethnic group violence and its mental health consequences, and to contribute to the development of interventions for reducing ethnic conflicts and promoting psychosocial recovery. In addition to the summer training institutes, the center sponsors graduate seminars in topics related to EPW, and is working toward a concentration in ethnopolitical conflict in the doctoral psychology program at the University of Pennsylvania. The center has also established international links with like-minded professionals and institutions in Northern Ireland, South Africa, Israel/Palestine, and Sri Lanka (see SACSEC Web page). Through its work, the Asch Center is serving as a clear expression of the EPW initiative and as a prototype for the development of a larger EPW institute. The curriculum described here has benefited from the experience of the summer program at the Asch Center and will be valuable in informing further educational developments at the University of Pennsylvania and other training sites. In addition, the curriculum may be useful in acquiring major, long-term funding, such as that provided by the National Institutes of Mental Health, for the development of full, 1-year postdoctoral or post-masters training programs. It may also be useful in providing components to existing graduate programs that may want to develop a specialization in trauma relief or conflict resolution in EPW.

THE CURRICULUM DESIGN CONFERENCE

Within the context of the EPW initiative, the goal of training psychologists in trauma intervention and conflict resolution was initially addressed through an interactive conference to design a generic graduate curriculum, initially conceived to be at the postdoctoral level. A concept proposal was developed by a task force charged by the steering committee and provided seed money to develop the conference agenda and seek funding for the event. The task force, chaired by the author, was composed of other steering committee members and additional volunteers chosen for their relevant expertise in trauma intervention and/or conflict resolution (see Appendix B for the list of task force members).

The task force was successful in obtaining support for the curriculum design conference from the United States Institute of Peace (USIP) under its solicited grants program in the topic area of conflict management training. Psychologists for Social Responsibility (PsySR), through its office in Washington, D.C., with Anne Anderson as national coordinator, served as the sponsoring organization and secretariat for the grant, and the author was the project director. The task force partnered with the Institute of World Affairs (IWA), an applied conflict resolution organization based in Washington, D.C., to use its conference center in Salisbury, Connecticut, for the event. Additional sponsorship was provided by APA Divisions 9 (Society for the Psychological Study of Social Issues) and 48 (Society for the Study of Peace, Conflict and Violence: Peace Psychology Division).

The conference was held on August 12–15, 1999, with approximately 30 professional psychologists in attendance, in addition to 5 task force members, who served as conference facilitators. The participant list speaks to the stature, competence, and diversity of the attendees, from the United States, Canada, Northern Ireland, South Africa, and elsewhere (see Appendix C for the participant list).

The methodology of the conference was a fusion of adult education or workshop training with curriculum design and development. The design was highly interactive, with plenary sessions used to organize and supplement the primary activity of small teams working intensively on different elements of the curriculum. Four "design teams" were formed in the areas of (1) cross-cultural psychology, (2) conflict analysis/prevention and peace education, (3) trauma relief and psychosocial healing, and (4) conflict resolution and reconciliation. This approach produced workable teams in terms of numbers of members (seven or eight) and also provided for considerable diversity in each team.

The overall flow of the design, following introductory panels on the challenges of trauma work and conflict intervention in EPW zones, involved the design teams' producing one major element of the curriculum, and reporting this back to a plenary session for comment before proceeding to the next element. Sequentially, the teams worked first to identify the competencies (knowledge, skills, and attitudes/values) required in their domain; second, the components (courses, training modules) necessary to train those competencies; and third, the resources (publications, faculty, internship settings) required to support the training process. Midway through the conference, the facilitators formed "cross-over teams" of volunteer participants—one to integrate the total curriculum, and others to deal with specific issues that had been identified, for example, how to blend trauma work and conflict resolution into a process of intercommunal reconciliation.

A significant change in the intended curriculum as a result of the conference is that it is now cast as a graduate-level training experience, which could be incorporated into existing programs in modular form or mounted as a 1-year postdoctoral or post-master's experience. Participants believed that this change would increase the potential for implementation, particularly in areas of the world where a master's degree rather than a doctorate is the required level for professional practice.

THE CURRICULUM

Following the design conference, the project director produced a draft curriculum based on the notes and newsprint sheets, and the draft was then distributed to the members of the task force and the participants for review and comment. The responses were largely supportive of the manner in which the draft curriculum captured the work of the conference. In addition, a number of useful suggestions for improvement and elaboration were received. The draft curriculum was then distributed to a wider review list, consisting of invitees to the conference who could not come, the EPW steering committee, and members of the EPW cadre of experts who have volunteered to provide comments.

Subsequent to the conference, a volunteer effort led by David Hart of the University of British Columbia, with support from CPA, resulted in the creation of an electronic mailing list for participants and a Web page dedicated to the EPW initiative (http://www.cpa.ca/epw/epw/). The EPW Web page currently houses a history of the initiative, a description of the curriculum design conference, and links to related entities, such as the Asch Center at the University of Pennsylvania. The full curriculum document is now available from the EPW Web page, as well as from the Web pages of PsySR, Divisions 9 and 48 of APA, and the International Page of APA's Web site.

The complete curriculum document includes a number of major sections, which are described here in abbreviated form. The Introduction provides an overview of the EPW initiative and the curriculum design conference. The Objectives of the curriculum are juxtaposed with the significant Challenges of working in trauma relief and conflict resolution in zones of EPW, as identified by experienced conference participants. The Pedagogical Approach of the curriculum is emphasized as a participative, experiential, and adult education one, which blends conceptual understanding with practical experience and application. The elements of the curriculum include the Parameters (time, resources) within which it is designed; the Competencies (knowledge, skills, attitudes) that are required for the work in both areas; the Classes, including the internship, in an integrated sequence; and the Resources (mainly print materials) required to support curriculum implementation. A number of Additional Considerations also receive comment, including the institutional resources and constraints that will affect implementation, the level of training (M.A. or Ph.D.), the importance of partnership and empowerment in working with local professionals, and the critical process of selecting learners to undertake the curriculum. The draft thus presents a broad and deep description of a serious and systematic approach to professional training in the two domains of trauma relief and conflict resolution.

Objectives and Challenges

Given the disciplinary base in psychology, the focus of the curriculum in the first instance is to provide supplemental training to individuals in appropriate specialties. In the second instance, the curriculum is addressed to professionals and social scientists in related disciplines in order to extend their expertise in trauma relief and/or conflict resolution. Thus, the objectives of the curriculum are articulated as follows:

1. to capitalize on the basic training of psychologists and other professionals in mental health or applied social science to train scholar-practitioners who can provide services in trauma intervention or conflict resolution in zones of EPW;
2. to infuse cross-cultural knowledge and sensitivity, and collaborative strategies of empowerment and partnership into the training process;
3. to blend trauma relief work and conflict resolution intervention into training scholar-practitioners who can facilitate reconciliation at the interpersonal, group and intergroup levels of societies divided by EPW.

The challenges of working in EPW zones, either during or following extensive destruction and violence, are immense and can be identified in the following domains:

1. Cultural: Working in different societies requires an understanding of one's own culture and the cross-cultural sensitivity and respect not to impose one's values and approaches on others who will be the primary service providers.
2. Ethical/Strategic: Ethical questions arise around whose purposes are served by intervention and what the negative effects might be. There is a need to be transparent about the work, to consult widely, and to build local capacity and ownership through mentoring, partnership, and succession.
3. Methodological: Flexible, adaptive, and elicitive methods of information gathering are necessary to understand local perceptions and concerns, and understanding of methods of social change is necessary beyond the ability for service provision.
4. Systemic: Intervenors need to take a holistic view of the social and political context of their work, and develop multilevel programs that will support change rather than leading to disappointment through unrealistic expectations.
5. Personal/Operational: Working in zones of EPW presupposes a critical analysis of one's self and the personal qualities to operate effectively in chaotic and dangerous environments in an impartial and security-conscious manner.

Pedagogical Approach

The educational approach of the curriculum needs to engage learners in interaction with others, in response to real problems, and in ways that parallel fieldwork. Interacting in a diverse learning community, participants require facilitators of their learning who model the values, strategies, and skills being taught, and need to engage in self-reflection that supports their professional development. The goal is to train individuals who have the capacity to transform theory into practice in ways that are collaborative and transformative. Thus the curriculum needs to follow a team-based, problem-centered approach, in which learners engage one another in case studies, simulations, role-plays, and field experiences that require the application of knowledge and skills to various types of reality.

Parameters

The parameters specify the time and other design boundaries within which the curriculum is intended to operate. These are based mainly on the U.S. education system and need to be translated into other systems for appropriate implementation. The curriculum is envisaged as a 1-year, stand-alone program, or the equivalent if integrated into an existing program of longer duration. Thus the elements involve two teaching terms of 3 to 4 months, with three or four courses offered per term, each of which would be weighted at 3 credit units. An internship of 4 to 6 months is recommended following the teaching terms, yielding a total of approximately 30 credit units for the program. A final parameter is the recommendation that courses on cross-cultural relations and conflict analysis/prevention precede courses in trauma intervention and conflict resolution, followed by capstone courses of an integrated nature.

Competencies

In the curriculum design process, competencies were first specified in terms of the knowledge, skills, and attitudes required to operate effectively in the areas of: (1) cross-cultural interaction, (2) conflict analysis/prevention and peace education, (3) trauma intervention and psychosocial assistance, and (4) conflict resolution and reconciliation. This extensive list was then distilled into a set of integrated competencies under three headings:

1. Knowledge of Theory
   - Culture Theory
   - Identity Development
   - Macro Context of Conflict
   - Conflict Processes and Dynamics
   - International Organizations
2. Knowledge of Practice
   - Conflict Assessment and Monitoring
   - Models of Addressing Psychosocial Trauma and Healing
   - Group and Community Processes
   - Educational and Structural Prevention Methods
   - Conflict Resolution
3. Skills
   - Interpersonal and Social Skills
   - Group and Organizational Skills
   - Intervention for Prevention and Healing
   - Intervention for Conflict Analysis and Resolution
   - Information-Gathering Skills
   - Self-Care and Self-Reflection

Classes

To train learners in the competencies required for intervention in trauma relief and conflict resolution, the curriculum is structured around several courses over two terms of study, some of which are recommended for those in both areas of practice, and some for only those in one or the other. In the following list of classes, the two streams of the curriculum are identified as TI for trauma intervention and CR for conflict resolution. The intent of the curriculum is to expose learners in each stream to knowledge and skills from the other, so that each can operate more effectively in a holistic and integrated fashion toward reconciliation among former enemies in EPW zones. However, it is essential that learners in the TI stream build on requisite competencies in individual-level clinical service, and those in CR build on their competencies in social-level, group, and community intervention. The curriculum does not pretend that fully trained professionals in either stream can be produced in a 1-year post-degree or supplementary educational experience.

Cross-Cultural Knowledge and Perspectives (Term 1; TI and CR). This course begins with an intensive 2-week immersion experience in cross-cultural sensitivity and interaction followed by a continuing element that runs throughout the first term of study. The rationale is to deepen learners' personal understanding of culture and to build their understanding of the cultural context and issues that are involved in trauma relief and conflict resolution work.

Conflict Analysis (Term 1; TI and CR). This course provides conceptual tools for understanding the causation, expression, and escalation of social conflict, particularly of a violent nature at the intergroup level. A practicum component involving a team-based case study of an ongoing violent conflict provides a linkage between classroom and field experience.

Traumatic Stress: Impact, Assessment, and Assistance (Term 1; TI and CR). This course takes a systems perspective for understanding the psychosocial impact of violence and traumatization and provides an overview of methods of assessing and responding to traumatic stress. Learners are exposed to skills in psychological assessment and to a range of intervention methods from crisis response to long-term service provision.

Violence Prevention (Term 2; TI and CR). This course considers how conflict can be prevented from escalating to violence, both through primary prevention at the societal level and through interventions that deescalate conflicts approaching violence. A team-based practicum examines how early warning and prevention can be applied, and how programs for deescalation can be mounted.

Intervention Design (Term 2; TI and CR). This course provides the conceptual foundation for creating, implementing, and evaluating interventions in trauma relief and conflict resolution in societies ravaged by widespread violence. A team-based project involves the design of an intervention through all of its stages, with attention to the importance of collaboration and partnering with local professionals.

Psychosocial Programs (Term 2; TI). This course covers the development, implementation, and evaluation of psychosocial programs to address the effects of traumatic stress in war-torn societies. Through working in program design teams, learners will address logistical, cultural, ethical, and political issues over the full cycle of program functioning.

Conflict Resolution (Term 2; CR). This course covers the concepts, strategies, and skills for addressing conflict that has escalated to extensive violence. Strategic models, such as the contingency approach to third-party intervention, provide a context for integrating a range of behavioral skills at the individual, interpersonal, group, intergroup, and community levels.

Peacebuilding and Reconciliation in Divided Societies (Term 2; TI and CR). This integrative seminar serves as the capstone for the residential training, and considers how trauma relief and conflict resolution can be integrated toward reconciliation in divided societies that have experienced ethnopolitical violence. The multiple roles of intervenors are considered in relation to the local and cultural context and the necessity of coordination among multiple actors in post-conflict reconstruction and peacebuilding efforts.

Internship (T3; TI and CR). This element is an intensive, full-time, minimum 4-month field experience in providing trauma relief or conflict resolution services in an active or postconflict war zone. The experience is of a cross-cultural or multicultural nature and is organized through local or international organizations engaged in service provision, with oversight provided by a program committee through an internship contract.

Resources

The classes in the curriculum are supported by a list of print resources in two parts. First, with each course are listed several books that could serve as texts for the course. Second, an appendix to the curriculum provides a list of books and a list of selected articles in each of the four areas of Cross-Cultural Interaction, Conflict Analysis/Prevention and Peace Education, Trauma Intervention/Psychosocial Assistance, and Conflict Resolution/Reconciliation. While not completely comprehensive, these lists provide a useful base of conceptual material for those who are interested in implementing the curriculum.

Additional Considerations

There are many challenges of program development in mounting a groundbreaking curriculum, only three of which are mentioned here. Selection of learners is a critical process in professional training, and selectors must consider both the attributes of individuals and the gender balance and multicultural diversity of the cohort. Interest and ability to work in teams and to engage in intensive, experiential learning, along with relevant life experience, are criteria that should be considered along with standard professional requirements. Institutional support in terms of finances, physical resources, and faculty is an immense challenge in a world of secondary education characterized by limited budgets and numerous demands. Partnerships among universities, research and training institutes, government programs, and philanthropic foundations will likely be required to support curriculum implementation. Evaluation is the final challenge, and given the innovative nature of the curriculum, requires a serious effort in each case of implementation. The usual methods of program evaluation need to be applied, with an emphasis on process evaluation in order to assure that the experiential and integrative aspects of the curriculum are being implemented as intended. In addition, an elicitive and qualitative approach to information collection with all involved parties is more likely to lead to sustainable improvements in program functioning than reliance on quantitative assessments and data would.

CONCLUSION

The efforts of the task force, the participants, and the reviewers have produced a generic graduate curriculum that addresses the training goal of the EPW initiative. The process of dissemination of the curriculum is now critically important and will be carried out largely through the voluntary efforts of the task force and the sponsoring organizations through their various Web sites. A limited number of hard copies will be made available to selected institutions and programs. The hope is to make the curriculum, with supporting rationale and resources, available to interested nonprofit institutes and university departments around the world. This hope will only be realized if individual professionals committed to reducing the destructive effects of EPW bring the curriculum to the attention of those with the mandate and the resources to implement it. We hope that you the reader can join us in this effort.

APPENDIX A

Original Members of the Steering Committee of the Joint Initiative on Ethnopolitical Warfare of the American and Canadian Psychological Associations

Anne Anderson, MSW
National Coordinator
Psychologists for Social Responsibility
Washington, DC

Ed Cairns, Ph.D.
Psychology Department
University of Ulster at Coleraine
Coleraine, Northern Ireland

Daniel Chirot, Ph.D., *Co-Chair*
Jackson School of International Studies
University of Washington
Seattle, WA

Ronald Fisher, Ph.D.
Department of Psychology
University of Saskatchewan
Saskatoon, SK, Canada

Jane Mocellin, Ph.D.
C/UN Disaster Management Training
Programs
Geneva, Switzerland

Corann Okorodudu, Ed.D.
Psychology Department
Rowan University
Glassboro, NJ

Martin Seligman, Ph.D.
(Former president, APA)
Department of Psychology
University of Pennsylvania
Wynnwood, PA

Barbara Smith, Ph.D.
Vice President
International Rescue Committee
New York, NY

Peter Suedfeld, Ph.D.
(Former president, CPA)
Department of Psychology
University of British Columbia
Vancouver, BC, Canada

Henry Tomes, Ph.D.
Public Interest Directorate
American Psychological Association
Washington, DC

Michael Wessells, Ph.D., *Co-Chair*
Department of Psychology
Randolph-Macon College
Ashland, VA

Staff Support:
Joan Buchanan, Director
International Affairs Office
American Psychological Association
Washington, DC

Student Scribe and Support:
Derek Isaacowitz
Department of Psychology
University of Pennsylvania
Philadelphia, PA

APPENDIX B

Ethnopolitical Warfare Curriculum Conference Planning Task Force

Anne Anderson, MSW
Psychologists for Social Responsibility
Washington, DC

Leila Dane, Ph.D.
Institute for Victims of Trauma
McLean, VA

Ronald Fisher, Ph.D., *Chair*
School of International Service
The American University
Washington, DC

Corann Okorodudu, Ed.D.
Psychology Department
Rowan University
Glassboro, NJ

Tamra Pearson d'Estree, Ph.D.
Institute for Conflict Analysis and
Resolution
George Mason University
Fairfax, VA

Henry Tomes, Ph.D.
Public Interest Directorate
American Psychological Association
Washington, DC

Gary Weaver, Ph.D.
School of International Service
The American University
Washington, DC

APPENDIX C

EPW Curriculum Design Conference, August 12–15, 1999, Salisbury, CT,
Participants' List

Inger Agger, Ph.D.
Consultant
Copenhagen, Denmark

Anne Anderson, MSW
National Coordinator
Psychologists for Social
Responsibility, Washington, DC

Carol (Corky) Becker, Ph.D.
Public Conversations Project
Watertown, MA

Ed Cairns, Ph.D.
Professor of Psychology
Centre for the Study of Conflict
University of Ulster at Coleraine
Coleraine, Northern Ireland

Cynthia Chataway, Ph.D.
Assistant Professor of Psychology
York University
North York, Ontario, Canada

Lillian Comas-Diaz, Ph.D.
Washington, DC

Leila Dane, Ph.D.
Institute for Victims of Trauma
McLean, VA

Andy Dawes, Ph.D.
Associate Professor of Psychology
University of Cape Town
Cape Town, South Africa

Tamra Pearson d'Estree, Ph.D.
Institute for Conflict Analysis
and Resolution
George Mason University
Fairfax, VA

Morton Deutsch, Ph.D.
International Center for Cooperation
& Conflict Resolution
Teachers College, Columbia
University
New York, NY

George Everly, Jr., Ph.D
Severna Park, MD

Ron Fisher, Ph.D.
Department of Psychology
University of Saskatchewan
Saskatoon, SK, Canada

Mari Fitzduff, Ph.D.
Initiative on Conflict Resolution
and Ethnicity
Derry, Northern Ireland

David S. Hart, Ph.D
ECPS, Faculty of Education
University of British Columbia
Vancouver, BC, Canada

Gerald Jackson, Ph.D.
President
New Arena Consultants
Somerset, NJ

Karen A. Jehn, Ph.D.
Wharton School
University of Pennsylvania
Philadelphia, PA

Loraleigh Keashly, Ph.D.
Graduate Program in Dispute
Resolution
Wayne State University
Detroit, MI

Katherine Kennedy, Ph.D.
Annandale, VA

Paul Kimmel, Ph.D.
Los Angeles, CA

Peter Levine, Ph.D.
Lyons, CO

Jane Mocellin, Ph.D.
United Nations Consultant
Crozet, France

Linden L. Nelson, Ph.D.
Psychology and Child Development
California Polytechnic State
University
San Luis Obispo, CA

Corann Okorodudu, Ed.D.
Psychology Dept.
Rowan University
Glassboro, NJ

Laurie Anne Pearlman, Ph.D.
Research Director, TSI/CAAP
South Windsor, CT

Dean Pruitt, Ph.D.
University at Buffalo
State University of New York
Bethesda, MD

Randa Slim, Ph.D.
SLIM & Associates
Kettering, OH

Ervin Staub, Ph.D.
University of Massachusetts
Amherst, MA

Peter Suedfeld, Ph.D., FRSC
Dept. of Psychology
University of British Columbia
Vancouver, BC, Canada

Harry Triandes, Ph.D.
Department of Psychology
University of Illinois
Champaign, IL

Gary Weaver, Ph.D.
School of International Service
The American University
Washington, DC

Nomfundo Walaza, Ph.D.
Director & Clinical Psychologist
The Trauma Centre for Survivors of
Violence and Torture
Woodstock, South Africa

Michael Wessells, Ph.D.
Department of Psychology
Randolph-Macon College
Ashland, VA

NOTE

The author was previously in the Department of Psychology at the University of Saskatchewan, Saskatoon, Canada, and the Division of Peace and Conflict Studies at Royal Roads University, Victoria, Canada. The author expresses appreciation to the members of the Curriculum Design Conference Task Force and the 30 other scholar-practitioners who attended the conference that produced the initial curriculum design. The contribution of the United States Institute of Peace through Grant No. SG-33–99 for the design conference is gratefully acknowledged. This chapter is a revised and enlarged version of a paper presented at the Annual Scientific Meeting of the International Society of Political Psychology, Seattle, Washington, July 2000.

REFERENCES

APA/CPA (1997). *Ethnopolitical warfare: Origins, interventions and prevention.* Joint presidential initiative of the American Psychological Association and the Canadian Psychological Association. Unpublished manuscript.

Chirot, D., & Seligman, M. E. P. (Eds.). (2001). *Ethnopolitical warfare: Causes, consequences, and possible solutions.* Washington, DC: American Psychological Association.

EPW Web page. http://www.cpa.ca/epw/epw/.

SACSEC Web page. http://www.psych.upenn.edu/sacsec.

18

Before and After Trauma: The Difference Between Prevention and Reconciliation Activities in Macedonia

Sally Broughton

For the first 10 years of its independence Macedonia was often touted as an example of "successful conflict prevention." However, when violence broke out in this small country in February 2001, the world saw that conflict in Macedonia had not been prevented. Now Macedonia's citizens find themselves in need of reconciliation instead of prevention. This is not to say that there were no attempts to solve the social, political, and economic problems contributing to the long-running underlying conflict in Macedonia. Perhaps they were not sufficient, but they did exist. Now, as military and paramilitary groups seem to have quieted their weapons, various efforts focus on rebuilding and reconciliation. The same actors that engaged in prevention activities before the outbreak of violence are those that are now beginning recovery efforts. Nevertheless, there is a marked difference in the procedures being employed.

The communities are the same. The locations are the same. The level of trauma experienced by the society, especially the communities involved in the fighting, is the major element that defines the difference between previolence, prevention activities and postviolence, reconciliation activities. This chapter will examine some of the types of intervention that made up the prevention effort in Macedonia before February 2001 and will compare them to the intervention activities that are being used to help the country recover since the Framework Peace Agreement was signed in August 2001. At the same time it will compare the problems and challenges that characterize these two periods to illustrate why these activities are being tailored differently now that the society has been traumatized.

PREVENTION

Characteristics

Most societies are marked by some kind of underlying conflict. In Macedonia the major underlying conflict, after its independence from Yugoslavia was finalized in 1991, was the tension between the Macedonian majority and the largest ethnic minority, the Albanians. According to the last census, conducted in 1994, Macedonians make up 67 percent of the population and Albanians, 23 percent (Bureau of Statistics, 1994), though Albanians claim their number is much higher.

Negative stereotyping was and still is common among Macedonia's ethnic groups. Macedonians often regarded Albanians as disloyal and aggressive (Ackerman, 2000). Albanians, when surveyed, viewed Macedonians as weak and dishonest (Petroska-Bekša, Popovski, & Kenig-Bogdanovska, 1998). These stereotypes are primarily the result of lack of information and contact between people. Macedonia's ethnic groups have lived in relatively segregated communities, mixing with each other in the markets, sometimes in the workplaces, but rarely socially. Social integration has usually occurred only in the mixed neighborhoods of urban areas and, somewhat, in the mixed villages in parts of western Macedonia. Even in those areas actual integration has been hindered by the fact that the education system is segregated by language (Petroska-Bekša et al., 1998). Macedonians and Albanians speak different languages, practice different religions, and have a variety of different cultural characteristics. These differences leave a lot of room for the kind of misinterpretation and misunderstanding that fuels negative stereotyping and prejudice. The fact that Macedonia's media outlets are divided by language and, therefore, cater to one ethnic group or another, only solidified the barriers between groups and exacerbated misunderstanding. Most of the Albanians in Macedonia understand the Macedonian language and, therefore, know what opinions and events are reported in the Macedonian media. However, most Macedonians do not understand Albanian and, therefore, do not have access to the thoughts or perspectives being published and broadcast by Albanians. Strong divisions in the media were a significant factor in the creations of suspicions and latent fear leading up to the violence.

The dire economic situation that Macedonia has faced since its independence has also exacerbated interethnic tensions (Lumsden, 1997). Having suffered an embargo by Greece, sanctions against Serbia (its main trading partner), and the war in Kosovo, Macedonia reached an unofficial unemployment rate of about 50 percent in 2000 (Fraenkel, 2001). In times of economic difficulty people tend to want to blame someone for their condition. That someone can often be a minority, especially if members of the minority are perceived as having a higher economic status than others. In the case of Macedonia, resentment over economic success has existed for many years among both Macedonians and Albanians. Macedonians see the wealth that some Albanians have accumulated by working abroad or in successful private businesses, and Albanians view the

Macedonians as better off because they have more access to state positions and state-owned enterprises (Lumsden, 1997).

Before the outbreak of violence the conflict in Macedonia could be characterized by a preponderance of negative stereotypes, suspicion, and jealousy. These things did not, however, impede cooperation between the communities in business, participation in politics, and, in some naturally integrated areas, daily social contact. Although there was a latent feeling of insecurity, people generally felt safe in their homes and traveling throughout the country.

Interventions

The most well known preventive intervention in Macedonia was the United Nations Preventive Deployment (UNPREDEP). This preventive deployment of just under 1,000 Scandinavian and U.S. troops was first dispatched as a part of a United Nations Protective Force (UNPROFOR), in December 1992, primarily to deter incursions from Serbia (Ackerman, 2000). While the UNPREDEP was high profile and considered effective, there were many nongovernmental initiatives, both local and international, conducting prevention activities in the 10 years prior to the outbreak of violence. Most were relatively small initiatives and many, especially local ones, suffered frequent funding difficulties. Even so, most of these activities found the society receptive and generated positive effects.

The Ethnic Conflict Resolution Project (ECRP) is a local initiative that conducted a variety of prevention activities designed to address the problem of stereotypes and prejudice in the society as well as develop positive capacity for dealing with conflicts (ECRP, 2000). One ECRP project was directed at high school students in mixed ethnic areas. Because they had not yet been traumatized by war and imbued with the type of hate that one can attribute only to enemies in a violent conflict, teenagers in Macedonia were able to come together and discuss the fundamental problems in their society and how to solve them. In this program, called Appreciating Differences, Albanian and Macedonian high school students, who attend the same schools but are in completely segregated classrooms, spent a week together speaking about stereotypes and prejudice in their society and how it affects them. They learned about each group's cultures and beliefs and finished by planning several projects in their schools through which they could introduce their classmates to the subjects covered during that week. Students responded enthusiastically to the program (ECRP, 2001).

Another program specifically geared toward youth was spontaneously organized by a mixed ethnic group of young people from Skopje, Kumanovo, and Tetovo. This group was called ALMATUROBO, using the first two letters of the ethnicities involved, and was created to promote contact among young people from different ethnic communities. As with the Appreciating Differences program, the goal of ALMATUROBO was to break down the social barriers, stereotypes, and misperceptions that contributed to ethnic tension. The organizers faced little difficulty in attracting young people to these activities (Skender & Dimovski, 2000).

Even the International Committee for the Red Cross (ICRC), which usually deals with humanitarian problems, was running an extensive program in the school system called the Promoting Human Values project. The project engaged teachers in using a locally designed curriculum for discussing values, culture, and morality in an effort to make a "contribution towards the neutralization of the factors which influence the generation of conflicts" (Simovska, Garber, & Jordanov, 1998). Teachers from all over Macedonia were involved in this program.

Search for Common Ground (SCG), another international nongovernmental organization, worked for several years to break down the ethnolinguistic divisions in the media in Macedonia. SCG projects included joint reporting efforts that engaged print journalists from different language media in producing a single piece or series, which was then published in their newspapers (Lumsden, 1997). Using a similar technique with television stations, SCG also organized an exchange of programming and even jointly produced programs among various stations broadcasting in different languages. Stations not only participated eagerly, but some began to cooperate without facilitation by the organization.

Although Macedonia's economic situation could not be significantly improved without major reforms and capital investment, some groups did have a positive impact with smaller-scale projects such as technical assistance and micro–credit lending. One example is the organization Možnosti, which offers small loans to help people start business in various parts of the country. As of 1998, its small grants had created 1966 new jobs in small, privately owned businesses (Možnosti, 1998). Creation of new jobs and improvement of the economic situation encourages cooperation and reduces jealousy among citizens of different ethnic groups in mixed communities.

Before the violence began in 2001, various groups were conducting prevention activities and documenting their successful impact. Program organizers found the people of Macedonia to be interested and eager for activities that brought them together and had the potential to improve both their individual lives and their relations with each other. Now, more donor dollars than ever are flowing into Macedonia. The World Bank, for instance, will be providing $35 million in postconflict interest free loans (World Bank, 2001). Nevertheless, the organizations that are engaging in recovery intervention now face a more difficult environment and additional problems in executing their activities.

VIOLENCE

Fighting broke out in Macedonia at the end of February 2001 and escalated during the course of the spring. At one point the National Liberation Army (NLA), the Albanian rebel group, occupied a village only 5 kilometers outside of the capital city of Skopje. Shelling of the village by the government security forces could be heard from the center of town. For 6 months, televisions and newspapers in all languages were filled with images of fleeing refugees, burning houses, and other destruction. Roads were blocked at various times and borders were closed for 6 weeks. On August 13, 2001, Albanian and Macedonian political parties within the government signed a framework for a peace agreement, and shortly afterward NATO began disarmament of the NLA. Though at the time of this writing the elements of the framework agreement had not yet been passed by the parliament and there is still sporadic shooting, recovery and reconciliation activities have already begun.

RECONCILIATION

Characteristics

The United Nations High Commission for Refugees (UNHCR) estimates that 135,000 people in Macedonia were either internally or externally displaced and fewer than half of them have returned (UNHCR, 2001). No definite information exists as to how many houses have been damaged or destroyed, as some areas remain inaccessible. Schools, mosques, churches, and factories need to be rebuilt, and systems for electricity, water, and sewage need to be repaired. Many areas are still inaccessible because of the presence of mines or unexploded artillery. The most difficult damage to repair will be that done to the relations between Macedonians and Albanians.

Whereas before the violence, negative stereotypes and latent suspicion were pervasive, there is now outright hatred and strong feelings of betrayal on both sides. A focus-group study of Macedonians and Albanians conducted after violence broke out showed that few Macedonians could attribute any positive characteristics to Albanians. Similarly, Albanians felt that Macedonians had "removed the masks" of civility that they had been wearing and allowed themselves to show their "true feelings" toward their Albanian neighbors (International Republican Institute, 2001).

Hatred and extremism have grown across the country because the whole population has been traumatized by fear, uncertainty, and continual images of the conflict. The situation is most acute in the areas where the fighting took place. Goran, from a village near Tetovo, described a highly representative situation.

One family that is still there told us that the Macedonian and Albanian elders in the village are trying to talk again and go on with their daily lives together, as much as possible. But they also told us that members of the younger generation are a lost cause. The anger that they have for each other is just absolutely frightening. (Reality Macedonia, 2001)

Both Macedonians and Albanians feel they are victims of violence at the hands of the other. Feelings of victimization are caused by violent traumatic aggression, a belief that the aggression was unjustified, and a fear that it will be repeated (Montville, 1993). Both the NLA and the Macedonian government's security forces used violence that traumatized civilian populations, creating equally strong feelings of victimization on both sides. Both Macedonians and Albanians fear that the violence will begin again, or at least that it will continue at a low level for some time. With each side feeling they are victims of the other, restoring trust and reconciling the two communities will be a difficult task.

Intervention

One of the first initiatives for reconciliation came from two local groups, Nansen Dialogue Center (NDC) and Multikultura. Shortly after the signing of the framework peace agreement, they began holding meetings in Tetovo, the location of the heaviest fighting between Albanian and Macedonian high school students. Whereas during the previous fall ECRP had no trouble bringing together groups from this same population and talking freely, NDC and Multikultura found the discussions difficult. "They are emotional and it is difficult for them to be productive," said Alexander Petkovski, one of the facilitators from NDC. Petkovski told me that during the discussions there were some very harsh reactions from the participants, but that in the end they did want to have another meeting adding, "now they know what the alternative is" (A. Petkovski, personal communication, October 22, 2001).

Teenagers in Tetovo are living under a curfew and with continued feelings of insecurity. ECRP has not yet attempted to reach the former participants in its Appreciating Differences program from Tetovo. However, it has tried to gather the teenagers from Kumanovo, which also experienced heavy fighting just outside of the city limits and is now under a curfew. ECRP project assistant Igor Ugrinovski told me that the students no longer see each other in town or hang out together. "Some Albanians are even afraid to speak Macedonian on the telephone in front of their families," he added (I. Ugrinovski, personal communication, October 23, 2001). ECRP will continue to try to organize small group meetings with the students.

Although some teenagers may want to restore relationships with their friends of other ethnicities, they experience strong pressure from their communities not to. Families and teachers have significant influence over youth, particularly in smaller towns and villages. In Tetovo, parent and teachers groups have refused to let their children study in schools also attended by students of the other ethnicity, sending messages of fear and hatred to their children (C.T., 2001). ICRC has had to redirect resources and staff away from its program on human values. This program had trained teachers to talk to their students about tolerance and community. According to Darko Jordanov and Herbi Elmazi, they are now concentrating on a program to train teachers to tell their students about mines and unexploded artillery (D. Jordanov & H. Elmazi, personal communication, October 19, 2001). Such programs are extremely necessary in a post-conflict situation to avoid further deaths or injuries; however, they may not prevent teachers from passing the hatred and feelings of victimization on to their students. The human values will be continued in some schools in which teachers have already been trained, and ICRC will return staff to the program in the future, but at the moment, the mine awareness program must take priority.

CONCLUSION

Conflict prevention methods include reducing inequalities and increasing integration among potential adversaries so that common interests can be identified (Kriesberg, 1995). Such activities are possible in a society in which people from the different groups are still willing, albeit reluctant, to socialize and to communicate about shared problems. This was the case in Macedonia until February 2001. Macedonians and Albanians were relatively segregated from each other and each group was suspicious of the other's character and motives. Yet people were able to cooperate, and many organizations demonstrated significant progress in terms of building positive interethnic relations.

It was not enough. Now in Macedonia the trauma of war has created a society of victims. Both Macedonians and Albanians live with the continual fear that despite peace agreements and international intervention, violence will start again. Each community perceives the other to be the cause of the violence and of the trauma its members have suffered. Reconciliation requires forgiveness and restoration of trust between those who perceive each other as aggressors (Montville, 1993). Organizations before the war had to overcome prejudices in order to get people to work together, but now they must build trust between groups who feel completely betrayed and victimized. This requires a different set of tools and expectations. These tools need to consist of simple activities, such as the ones started by NDC and Multikultura, designed to deal with the trauma and emotional reactions to what happened. In Macedonia, as in most postconflict areas, there are limited resources for dealing with the aftermath of the conflict. This means that many organizations, like ICRC, must deal first with the humanitarian and logistical problems of cleaning up after the war.

Healing Macedonia will take a considerable amount of time and will require a significant investment in reconciliation intervention. Perhaps if this same investment had been made in prevention efforts, and in building on those activities demonstrating success, there would have been no need to invest in postconflict healing and rehabilitation.

REFERENCES

Ackerman, A. (2000). *Making peace prevail: Preventing violent conflict in Macedonia.* Syracuse, NY: Syracuse University Press.
Bureau of Statistics of the Republic of Macedonia. (1994). *National census.* Skopje, Macedonia: The Government of the Republic of Macedonia.
C. T. (2001, October 7). Makedončinjata od O.U. Bratstvo-Migjeni ke učat vo srednoto ekonomsko vo Tetovo [Macedonian elementary school children from the Migjeni Brotherhood will study in economic high school in Tetovo]. *VEST* (no. 376). Skopje, Macedonia.

Ethnic Conflict Resolution Project. (2000). *Programs and activities 1994–2000*. Skopje, Macedonia: University of Saints Cyril and Methodius.

Ethnic Conflict Resolution Project. (2001). *Počituvanje na razlikite: Respektimi I dallimeve* [Respecting differences]. Skopje, Macedonia: University of Saints Cyril and Methodius.

Fraenkel, E. (2001). Macedonia. In A. Karatnycky, A. Motyl, & A. Schnetzer (Eds.), *Nations in transit 2001: Civil society, democracy, and markets in East Central Europe and the newly independent states* (pp. 260–271). Washington, DC: Freedom House.

International Republican Institute. (2001). *Focus groups conducted in the Republic of Macedonia*. Report, International Republican Institute, Skopje, Macedonia.

Kriesberg, L. (1995). Applications and misapplications of conflict resolution ideas in international conflicts. In J. A. Vasquez, J. T. Johnson, S. Jaffe, & L. Stamato (Eds.), *Beyond confrontation: Learning conflict resolution in the post–Cold War era* (pp. 87–102). Ann Arbor: University of Michigan Press.

Lumsden, M. (1997). *Peacebuilding in Macedonia: Searching for common ground in civil society*. Oslo, Norway: International Peace Research Institute.

Montville, J. (1993). The healing function in political conflict resolution. In D. Sandole & H. van der Merwe (Eds.), *Conflict resolution in theory and practice* (pp. 112–127). Manchester, England: Manchester University Press.

Možnosti. (1998). *Annual report, 98*. Skopje, Macedonia: Humanitarian Organization Možnosti.

Petroska-Bekša, V., Popovski, M., & Kenig-Bogdanovska, N. (1998). *Ethnic stereotypes among future pre-school and primary school teachers*. Skopje, Macedonia: University of Saints Cyril and Methodius.

Reality Macedonia. (2001, September 26). Macedonian refugees: Help from no one. Retrieved from: http://www.realitymacedonia.org.mk/web/news_page.asp?nid = 532.

Simovska, E., Garber, N., & Jordanov, D. (1998). *PHV: Coexistence, tolerance*. Skopje, Macedonia: International Committee of Red Cross, Macedonian Red Cross, and Norwegian Red Cross.

Skender, S., & Dimovski, S. (Eds.). (2000). *Let's get to know each other*. Skopje, Macedonia: Almaturobo.

United Nations High Commission for Refugees. (2001, October 16). *Refugee returns to former Yugoslav Republic of Macedonia remain slow*. Geneva, Switzerland: UNHCR News Stories.

World Bank. (2001, September 13). *FYR Macedonia: World Bank to provide post-conflict assistance*. (Press release 2001/080/ECA)

19

Change Agentry in an Islamic Context

Leila F. Dane

The old adage "necessity is the mother of invention" reminds us that practice precedes theory. Theory refines practice, and so goes the wheel of change. My interest in facilitating a shift away from human violence was already strong in my early adult years. Looking back, I can see that my volunteer work promoting change within the foreign service community solidified my self-image. More important, it was studying Thomas Kuhn (1962) that led me to understand how to explain conflict transformation, and it was working with organization development specialists in large-scale systems change that helped me develop cross-culturally effective group guidelines. These are: (1) focus on team building, (2) trust in the process, (3) promoting flexibility, (4) attending to human needs, and (5) fostering experiential learning to maintain a reality orientation. When I work cross-culturally I live by these guidelines, and I look for others who appear to do so as well. Gamal was one who did.

TEAM BUILDING WITH PSYCHIATRISTS IN THE MIDDLE EAST

It was in Cairo, 1987, that I first met Gamal Abou El Azayem. He was just starting a 2-year presidency of the World Federation for Mental Health, and I was giving exposure to the objectives of the newly established Institute for Victims of Trauma (IVT), a nonprofit organization I direct. Founded under the original name Institute for Victims of Terrorism, IVT was created to mediate attitude change in the Middle East by victim advocacy, and by linking violence and threat with traumatic stress reactions. We undertook to call international attention to the social, behavioral, and psychophysiological consequences of trauma resulting from violence and threat.

IVT specifically sought attention and understanding from health professionals, the media, and victims, as relevant mediators to more cooperative behavior patterns. We promoted research and training in conflict resolution at all levels of society to facilitate the shift from violence to accommodation. Our message was linked to a vision of an overpopulated world where distribution of food and water is crippled by human resistance to interacting cooperatively, a likely vision if major changes in human behavior fail to occur. Our target population was mental health professionals in view of their role as caregivers attuned to human needs. Our major forum and support structure was the World Federation for Mental Health (WFMH), because of its status as a nongovernmental organization of the United Nations.

Gamal and I had been working together almost 4 years when the Persian Gulf War broke out. Together, we had drafted and secured the approval of a Resolution for Mental Health Services to Victims of Community Violence, which introduced the principles of conflict resolution as effective deflectors of violence.[1] We also had identified crisis intervention techniques that were adaptable to local crisis response practices. Gamal recognized that the aftermath of the Gulf War was a real opportunity for constructive action. He immediately called for exercises and resource packets on mediation and conflict resolution. From these his assistants drafted articles for the Arabic-language journal *Mental Peace*. He was thus able to capture the attention of the grand mufti of Egypt, whose endorsement of our work was singularly important to its acceptance in the Middle East (see Appendix B for the grand mufti's endorsement).

Gamal's energetic behavior exemplified Charles Tart's (1986) concept of *consensus trance*. He was awakened to a greater understanding of how he could express his commitment to human needs in terms of prevention. These new academic foci were a stimulating challenge to his creativity. In the early 1980s Kenneth Boulding (1983) observed that "if the human race is to survive, it will have to change its ways of thinking more in the next 25 years than it has in the last 25,000" (p. 136).

From the time I met Gamal in 1987 until his wife died shortly after the Hebron Massacre in 1994, he was a leader of proactive change. This elderly Egyptian psychiatrist had helped found the World Islamic Association for Mental Health (WIAMH) and was editor-in-chief of its quarterly journal *Mental Peace*. He was also mideast regional director of Pride International, and mideast director of the Joint Program on Conflict Resolution. A Sufi whose father and grandfather were highly respected Egyptian imams and whose worldview demonstrated a superior education and the sophistication of a world traveler, his consulting skills were in demand throughout the Middle East to government, religious authority, police authority, resident diplomats, and private individuals.

SUFISM AND CHANGE AGENTRY

I had lived several years in Islamic countries, but knew little about Sufism and its potential for change agentry before I met Gamal. The brief description of Sufism below highlights this potential. The passage that follows discusses recent research on the personality of the policy entrepreneur and the use of collective power. This reflects my understanding of how Sufi leaders of the WIAMH fit the model of change agents.

Sufism

Sufis are schooled from early childhood to trust in the healing power of positive, harmony-seeking actions, and to promote them with patience and restraint. It is the practice of Sufi leaders to meditate, meet, discuss, and meditate again on all community issues, holding constant to the spiritual principles behind Sufism.[2] Whereas the *Shariya* is regarded as the exterior path of law, addressing the life of the individual and the community in terms of duties and rights, Sufism is the interior path of spiritual discipline (Dane, 1992). Sufis are found in both the Sunni and the Shia sects of Islam, but they represent an extremely small minority.

Carol Gilligan's (1982) theory of a female moral ethic, as distinct from a male moral ethic, is quite relevant to these differences. The *Shariya* can be equated with the ethic of justice and Sufi with the ethic of care; the tension between the two sustains the dialectic of human development. A Sufi not only follows God, but gets to know him by practicing a lifestyle that focuses less on the material world, and more on meditation, prayer, and fasting (Esposito, 1991).

Sufis are mystics, celebrating their union with God and with each other through this internal path. Their appeal to love as the way to know God is what keeps them closer to the religion of the common people than does the orthodox leadership (Lippman, 1990). This sense of connectedness is a major reason why the orthodox leadership seeks consultation with Sufi leaders. Sufism is the most important representation of the discipline of contemporary Arab thought that contributes to the development of knowledge by inner revelation and insight (Boullata, 1990).

The Personality of the "Policy Entrepreneur"

The recent work of Nancy Roberts (1992) focuses on the personality of change agents working outside government. For those who feed their narcissistic fantasies with a self-image of altruistic commitment, Roberts clarifies that the relevant literature refers to change agents and policy entrepreneurs alternatively. She notes that some researchers call attention to the prominent "dark side" of the identified entrepreneurial personality that is manipulative and ethically questionable in its misuse of people and resources (Lewis, 1984; Ramamurti, 1986).

In her attempt to examine whether entrepreneurship of necessity leads to a lack of accountability and abuse of power, Roberts developed a typology of public entrepreneurs she defined as "social actors." These entrepreneurs are involved in three phases of the innovative process—the creation, the design, and the implementation of innovative ideas in public sector practice (Roberts, 1992, p. 7). Using a variety of methods including in-depth interviews, archival research, surveys, and psychometric tests, she studied six persons working outside government. From this data she developed a profile of the "policy entrepreneur" personality. Then, renaming the dark-side type the "executive entrepreneur" in acknowledgement of the government paycheck, she looked for similarities and differences between the two personality types.

Roberts found that both types are achievement-oriented change agents with leadership and managerial potential. Both are recognized innovators and critical, analytical thinkers. The differences lie in the following domains. (1) In terms of *interpersonal style*, policy entrepreneurs are described as generally respectful, tolerant, ethical, and open, whereas executive entrepreneurs tend to treat subordinates as objects. (2) In terms of *expression of power*, policy entrepreneurs express their power in a collaborative manner, working with others, whereas executive entrepreneurs tend to amass their positional power, sometimes reaching their goals by way of Machiavellian strategies. (3) In terms of *actualization of higher-order values and ideals*, policy entrepreneurs showed congruence of expressed core values and day-to-day actions, whereas executive entrepreneurs appeared to pay only lip service to higher-order values.

For a closer look at expression of power, Roberts's earlier work addressed a developmental perspective of power (see, e.g., Roberts, 1987). Referring to the "definitional chaos" surrounding this concept, she deduced that power is "a projective test on which individuals impose their frame of reference, and their worldview to give meaning to their actions and the actions of others around them" (p. 3). Choosing Loevinger's (1976) work on ego development as the theoretical foundation for her analysis, she concludes that individuals from the higher stages of ego development tend to conceptualize and manifest power more as a collective than a competitive process. Of the five work styles she studied, the two that were found in collective power were consensual and charismatic work styles (Roberts, 1986).

To relate these concepts to a cohesive whole, I turn to Ernest Gellner's (1988) essay "Trust, Cohesion, and the Social Order." A social anthropologist, he describes Ibn Khaldun's analysis of 14th-century Muslim society to show how anarchy engenders trust and cohesion, and government destroys it. In his own analysis of modern Muslim society, Gellner describes how modern life has taken the hierarchical relationships out of the religious structure and put them into the political structure. Religion has thus become egalitarian and politics has become patronage ridden. Islamic universalism was acting as a "fortifying agent to the collective trustworthiness of clan cohesion" (p. 152). In 1988, Gellner wrote, "High Islam, which proscribes mediation, is now invoked more consistently" (p. 154).

That was in 1988. In 1991, a Sufi psychiatrist who fit the profile of a change agent, who had the ear of the grand mufti of Egypt, and who masterminded the writing of *Mental Peace,* opted for a modern version of mediation and conflict resolution in all of its ramifications. With the endorsement and close collaboration of the highest religious authority, Gamal managed to introduce the concepts into society, not only in Egypt, but throughout the Middle East, as necessary skills for mental health practitioners, educators, and community leaders.

From the 1991 Persian Gulf War until his death a few years after the Hebron Massacre in 1994, Gamal Abou El Azayem and I were codirectors of the Joint Program on Conflict Resolution. The program's mission is to bring conflict resolution experts to the Middle East for lecturing and consulting to promote the development of a core group of local practitioners with the requisite skills for family mediation, adolescent peer counseling, international negotiations, and conflict management. It is through these groups, and many others, that psychologists and members of allied professions are able to play a focal role in using psychological principles and practices in the quest for world and regional peace.

APPENDIX A

Resolution on Mental Health Services to Victims of Community Violence

The 1988 Cairo Working Conference of the World Federation for Mental Health on Mental Health Services to Victims of Community Violence recommends to the board the adoption of the following resolution:

The Board of the World Federation for Mental Health Recalling the recommendations of the Working Group on the Psychosocial Consequences of Violence, which was held under the combined auspices of the World Health Organization and the Netherlands Ministry of Health and Environmental Protection at the Hague, April 6–10, 1981, and which agreed on a working definition of violence as "interhuman infliction of significant and avoidable pain and suffering."

Further recalling the final report of the American Psychological Association Task Force on the Victims of Crime and Violence, November, 1984, as well as the Research and Evaluation Colloquium on the Aftermath of Crime: A Mental Health Crisis, coordinated by the National Organization for Victim Assistance, February 28–March 3, 1985,

Bearing in mind the adoption of the Declaration of Basic Principles of Justice by the United Nations General Assembly on November 29, 1985, defining victims as "persons who, individually or collectively, have suffered harm, including physical or mental injury, emotional suffering, economic loss or substantial impairment of their fundamental rights,"

Recognizing that the problem of community violence is a multi-faceted one which calls for examination within the context of both historic and current socioeconomic and cultural circumstances,

Acknowledging that a mental health professional's confusion of political identity with his delivery of professional services is a disservice to victims and their advocates,

Mindful of the effects of reward and punishment on human behavior,

Concerned that the socio-economic circumstances which may contribute to violence will continue to intensify in the foreseeable future,

1. Takes note with appreciation of the report of the 1988 Cairo Working Conference on Mental Health Services to Victims of Community Violence;

2. Enjoins Member Organizations to take specific actions to address community violence by advocacy for victims thereof;

3. Urges Member Organizations to encourage research on the origins and effects of community violence from a psychosocial perspective, and to formulate action-oriented strategies which could serve as a basis for policy formulations and to request reports thereon to the 1991 World Congress of WFMH;

4. Encourages Member Organizations to adopt specific measures with a view to making community leaders and the general public more sensitive in their understanding of and response to community violence, including the following steps related to services for individual victims, resolution and prevention of community violence, research and networking:

(a) Within the professional community, Member Organizations should encourage the development of expertise and professional networking through the utilization and dissemination of knowledge obtained from evaluation and research efforts in crisis intervention and emergency treatment, to facilitate the diagnosis and treatment of the psychological consequences of community violence;

(b) Member Organizations should encourage support and counseling to community members in order to improve their abilities to opt for peaceful solutions of conflict and to resist the choice of revenge-motivated violence;

(c) Member Organizations should encourage the development and widespread use of educational materials which address the principles of human behavior, conflict management, mediation and conflict resolution;

(d) Member Organizations should take leadership in various activities which contribute to the utilization and dissemination of information to the general public, such as giving lectures, publishing articles, encouraging interviews with members of the media to identify victim issues;

(e) Member Organizations should promote continuing dialogue with media persons to encourage sensitive rather than inflammatory dissemination of news concerning community violence;

(f) Member Organizations should make it a practice to remind members of their professional community that the promotion of mental health is in the practice of behaviors which are incompatible with community violence;

(g) Member Organizations should encourage research design and data collection on: 1) contingencies surrounding perceived frustration which leads to conflict and that which leads to conflict resolution; 2) the differences between the victim who becomes a perpetrator of violence, and the victim who remains oriented toward conflict resolution; 3) immediate and long term stress effects among the traumatized, including Post Traumatic Stress Disorder (PTSD), as recognized by the Working Group on the Psychosocial Consequences of Violence sponsored by WHO; 4) approaches to understanding and handling the perpetrator and the victim;

(h) Member Organizations should appoint a liaison or committee to maintain contact with their professional communities and with their local authority structures in a manner which will identify the Member Organizations as centers for sharing information at all levels of crisis-oriented training, and to encourage reports on preventive, interventive and rehabilitative programs as they are evaluated.

Amended and approved by conference participants, April 7, 1988, Cairo, and formally adopted as policy by the WFMH Board April, 1992, Sydney.

APPENDIX B

Opening Remarks: Welcoming Address of the Grand Mufti of Egypt

Dr. Mohammed Tantawi

In the name of God the most Merciful, most Compassionate, and thanks be to Him the Lord of all creation. Prayer and Peace to our master, the messenger of God, his House, companions, followers, and believers to the Day of Judgement.

It is a pleasure for Dar Al-Iftaa [The highest religious authority in a Muslim country] of Egypt to host this conference whose objective is the service of our religion and our nations as well. Doubtlessly, among the most effective means for the progress of nations is the cooperation among their sons, each in his field, for the sake of virtue and good deeds, not for sin and aggression.

This conference on psychological health and conflict resolution attempts to study how to solve problems that face individuals and communities. When we read the Holy Koran, we find that one of the most established laws recognizes the differences among people in their thinking and tendencies. The Holy Koran refers to this diversity in many verses. In one of these verses are the following words of God: "If your God willed, He would have made people One Nation. People will be in conflict except those on whom he has mercy. This is why He created them. This is the Word of your God. I will fill Hell with people and other species." In another verse: "If God willed, He would have brought them together on the Right Path in which nobody is ignorant." This idea is found in other verses as well. "If your God willed, they would not have done it. Look at them and how they quarrel. If He willed everyone would have been a believer. Do you force people to become believers?"

Koranic verses show that differences among people are taken for granted. If the difference is aimed to reach the truth and to direct to the right path, then it is a good and accepted difference. The forbidden difference is one based on hatred and mistrust; its aim is either fulfilling individual aims, or just whims to which God forbids us to surrender.

When we read the Holy Koran, we find many examples of conflicts that occurred among people; the result of some of these differences is regret and remorse. For example, we read the story of the two sons of Adam [Cain and Abel (Arabic: *Kabil* and *Habil*)]: "Recite to them the story of the two sons of Adam who both presented to God a token. It was accepted from one of them only. The other said 'I will kill you.'" That was a difference and a conflict between two brothers who had the same father and the same mother. The Brother answers: "God will accept the tokens of the virtuous. If you extend your hand to kill me, I will not do the same. I fear God, the Lord of all creation. I do not want to indulge our names in this, or else you will be sent to Hell. This is the punishment to aggressors." It was expected that this admonishment would be met by Cain with acceptance and understanding. However, these wise words of Abel were not earnestly received by his brother. The Holy Koran reveals to us the result of that conflict: "His conscience allowed him to kill his brother. Thus Cain became a loser." Not only did he kill his brother, the Koran tells us, but Cain who lost his brother, his ability to discern things, and his happiness, had left his brother bleeding in the open. Then God sent a raven to show Cain how to cover the body of this brother. Seeing that, Cain said: "'Shame on me, I am less able to do right than this raven'; thus Cain became a regretter."

This is an example of a conflict in which the motives of one side are whims, spite, egocentrism; it is a conflict that ends with remorse as God told us.

The Koran tells us of conflicts that erupt between the People of the Right and the People of the Falsehood. These conflicts end with the victory of the People of the Right. There are dozens, even hundreds of examples. All the stories that the Koran relates of Prophets and their societies tell of discussions and "negotiations." Let us listen to this discussion between our master the prophet Ibrahim [Abraham] and a ruler. It is a story of the conflict between right and falsehood. Ibrahim said: "My God gives life and takes it back." The tyrant answers: "I give life and take it back." Cleverly, our master Ibrahim responded with an argument that defeated the tyrant: "God brings the Sun from the east, will you bring it from the west?" The unbeliever was silent as a result.

All the conflicts which the Holy Koran report to us end with the revelation that right will eventually win, and that this life is a conflict between right and falsehood, a pristine conflict between the good and the bad. Falsehood may win for a period of time, but it cannot be for long. Right will restore its position. Everything in this Universe declares that right will never turn into falsehood even if the righteous are few; falsehood will never turn into right even if the false are many. This is the fixed law of God.

If this is the issue of Life; conflict, difference, discussions, arguments, how can we end these conflicts and differences with a Good result for individuals and nations as well? Again the Holy Koran reveals to us many ways and means to diminish these conflicts. Conflict in this Life will never end. As long as there is life, there is a conflict. What we need to achieve is that those who fight for Falsehood will not win over those who cling to right. The People of Right must cooperate and help each other. If the People of Falsehood agree to defend their stance, it is the duty of the People of Right to come together to defend what is right.

When the Holy Koran reveals to us the ways to reduce conflict or make it end with the victory of Right and virtues and the defeat of sins, it [the Koran] also shows us the means to do this; of which are the good word, trusting people, open-mindedness to listen to the arguments of others. All these means were revealed in the lessons of the Koran. The Holy Koran asks us to discuss things using calm words: "Call to the path of your God using wisdom and lessons, and argue with them for the best. God knows better of those who lose his path, and of those who follow that path."

Scholars of religion have mentioned that the Koran in the above passage has characterized this calling by wisdom, that is by truth and exact proof that only religious scholars understand. So one should argue with these scholars logically to convince them. It is also characterized by good lessons which are for the ordinary people nice polite words that will find in them listening ears and receiving hearts.

As for the phrase: "argue for the best," it is mentioned that this is directed for those who disagree with your thought and religion. You should also argue with nice words. God says: "Do not argue with the People of the Book ["People of the Book" are Christians and Jews] but for the best, except with those who are unjust. And say we believe in the Word sent to us and to you. Our God and yours are but one God, and to Him we surrender."

The Koran also tells us the story of the prophet Yunis [Jonah] and his people. He called upon them to believe in the Oneness of God, and to be virtuous for some years. When he warned them that they will be punished if they do not respond to what is Right, they believed in what he said because of his way of revealing the truth.

The means to solve conflict are many: one is the good word which works with both friends and enemies; with friends because it enhances their love and brotherhood: "Say to my believers: 'He says for the best. Satan is a staunch enemy of Man.'" With enemies the good word reduces their animosity.

As it is mentioned in the Koran and in the words of our master and prophet Muhammad (peace be upon him) there are many ways to solve problems between people. One is to mediate between people to prevent hostility among them.

Brothers and sisters, we in Dar Al-Iftaa are very pleased with this meeting that brings scholars of different fields, specialists in legal issues, medicine, social sciences, theology, Shari'a [Islamic Law], and psychology. Such meetings, based on sincerity and righteousness, are welcomed. All of you are welcomed.

The rich vocabulary of Arabic is not enough to express one's feelings when he meets such honorable colleagues who have dedicated themselves to spread the word of God with no fear, all for the good of individuals and societies. One is also pleased to find himself among virtuous friends. Again, Dar Al-Iftaa thanks you for attending this conference. We ask God Almighty to credit our meetings to our good accounts when we all meet Him. Peace of God, His mercy and blessings be with you. Thank you.

NOTES

1. This resolution became WFMH policy in 1992. See Appendix A for entire text.

2. In this manner, the Palestinian mental health leaders, in preparation for the Oslo Talks, attended a retreat that first covered cursory training in conflict resolution, peace making, and traumatology. This was followed by remarks from the grand mufti of Egypt, Dr. Mohammed Tantawi (1992), on the merits of conflict resolution as an academic discipline. They then met to discuss the pros and cons of the Oslo peace proposals. According to Gamal Abou El Azayem's son (1992, personal communication), who convened the group, fully half of these mental health practitioners refused to entertain the idea of peace initiatives until the principles of traumatology and the endorsement of their spiritual leader were made clear to them.

REFERENCES

Boulding, K. (1983). Preface: The application of therapeutic intervention on a global level. In D. W. Cole (Ed.), Conflict resolution technology (p. 136). Cleveland, OH: Organizational Development Institute.

Boullata, I. J. (1990). *Trends and issues in contemporary Arab thought*. Albany: State University of New York Press.

Dane, L. (1992, July). *Introducing concepts of conflict resolution in an Islamic context*. Paper presented at the annual convention of the International Society of Political Psychology, San Francisco.

Esposito, J. L. (1991). *Islam: The straight path*. New York: Oxford University Press.

Gellner, E. (1988). Trust, cohesion and the social order. In D. Gambetta (Ed.), *Trust: Making and breaking cooperative relations* (pp.142–157). Oxford, England: Basil Blackwell.

Gilligan, C. (1982). *In a different voice*. Cambridge, MA: Harvard University Press.

Kuhn, T. W. (1962). *The structure of scientific revolutions*. Chicago, IL: University of Chicago Press.

Lewis, E. (1984). *Public entrepreneurship: Toward a theory of bureaucratic political power*. Bloomington: Indiana University Press.

Lippman, T. W. (1990). *Understanding Islam: An introduction to the Muslim world* (Rev. ed.). New York: Penguin Books.

Loevinger, J. (1976). *Ego development: Conceptions and theories*. San Francisco: Jossey-Bass.

Ramamurti, R. (1986). Public entrepreneurs: Who they are and how they operate. *California Management Review, 28*, 142–158.

Roberts, N. C. (1986). Organizational power styles: Collective and competitive power under varying organizational conditions. *Journal of Applied Behavioral Science, 22*, 443–458.

Roberts, N. C. (1987, July). *A developmental perspective on power: Some preliminary findings*. Paper presented at the annual convention of the International Society of Political Psychology, San Francisco.

Roberts, N. C. (1992, July). *The psychology of public policy change agents and entrepreneurs*. Paper presented at the annual convention of the International Society of Political Psychology, San Francisco.

Tantawi, M. (1992). Opening remarks: Welcoming address of the Grand Mufti of Egypt. In L. F. Dane (Ed.), *Examining the merits of conflict resolution as an academic discipline: Applications to everyday real life situations in the Middle East* (pp. 5–8). McLean, VA: Institute for Victims of Trauma.

Tart, C. T. (1986). *Waking up: Overcoming the obstacles to human potential*. Boston: Shambhala.

20

Peacebuilding by Women in Lebanon

Mary Bentley Abu-Saba

As therapy for nation-states' pathological violence throughout the world, and to build a culture of peace, Galtung (1998) has enjoined peacebuilders to direct more attention and energy to other world actors such as nongovernmental organizations (NGOs) working for peace, human rights development, women, and the environment. During Lebanon's 17 years of violent confrontations between diverse communities, there were quiet, persistent calls and endeavors toward sanity, humanness, and peace. Though frequently unheard, or heard and forgotten, those voices were raised, often by women (Makdisi, 1990). The purpose of this chapter is to present several peacebuilding programs offered by NGOs involving women leaders in Lebanon. These programs are directed at ameliorating the effects of direct violence (civil war, foreign occupation, and terrorism) and also of structural violence (poverty, hunger, inadequate education, child abuse, domestic violence, and disregard for women's human rights) (Galtung, 1969).

Peace activists, including feminist activists, have incorporated structural violence into the task of peacemaking, calling not just for "negative peace" (an end to direct violence), but rather, "positive peace," a reconstruction of social and political structures so that well-being, security, and opportunities for development in life are shared equally (Alonso, 1993; Brock-Utne, 1989; Reardon, 1993). In addition to feminist writers examining the psychological foundations of human rights (Abu-Saba, 1996; Peters & Wolper, 1995), they have also made the connections among the problems of militarism, famine, and environmental limits and sexual, racial, social, and economic injustices throughout the globe; and have linked institutionalized violence with all forms of violence against women (McKay, 1995, p. 71). The International Conferences on Women established as their motto "Equality, Development and Peace" in Nairobi in 1985 and adopted a blueprint for women's future work in the "Forward Looking Strategies for the Advancement of Women in the Year 2000" (Osseiran, 1996).

Lebanese women have worked valiantly on peacebuilding projects through years of civil strife and foreign occupation. The examples cited here are envisioned as seeds of equality, development, and peace, which are being planted now in Lebanon. The women who are the gardeners of this fragile growth aimed at satisfying basic human needs are very aware that they are working for succeeding generations; they do not expect, necessarily, to see the fruits of their labor in this lifetime. The projects presented here are worthy examples for international peacebuilders' attention.

SISTERHOOD IS GLOBAL INSTITUTE

Basic human needs are seen to lodge within the individual, whereas human rights are located between individuals (Galtung, 1994, p. 56). However, in order to maximize the possibility of basic human needs being served, that is, for human rights to be claimed and provided for, individuals must become aware of the rights that are already proffered them within their society, as well as the accepted norms of human rights worldwide.

The Sisterhood IS Global Institute (SIGI) is an international organization established in 1984 that has developed a human rights educational manual entitled "Claiming Our Rights: A Manual for Women's Rights Education in Muslim Societies" (Afkhami & Vaziri, 1998) aimed at promoting consciousness-raising among women, specifically in Muslim societies. (The manual is available in Arabic, Azeri, Bangla, English, Hindi, Malay, Persian, Russian, Urdu, and Uzbek.) The method used is to involve small groups of women within their local settings to examine the sayings, proverbs, and attitudes in their own faith and culture that benefit women, and those that do not. In the process of their asking questions about women's rights within their own culture, they are also introduced to the universal human rights concepts contained in major international human rights documents such as the United Nations (UN) Universal Declaration of Human Rights.

The major premise of the human rights educational manual is that there is no contradiction between human rights and Islam. Muhammad the Prophet offered rules that elevated women's status above the accepted norms of his contemporary society. So SIGI members insist that the Qur'an be interpreted within the context of its original intent and correspondingly, within the context of present-day human rights values. In the process of women's becoming aware of their existent rights, the extent to which these rights serve their basic needs, and how their own rights compare to universal human rights, they are actively involved in the first step of building democratic societies. The steps that follow pertain to enlarging the scope of proffered rights within their society, and ensuring that these rights are egalitarian and sufficient to meet their basic human needs.

The structural violence of the legal system in Lebanon is thus being confronted by a massive consciousness-raising process among women, instigated by an organization (SIGI) that encourages women to seek validation for their rights within their own religious tradition. In addition, because of the 1993 UN World Conference on Human Rights in which the Global Campaign button declared "Women's Rights Are Human Rights" (Peters & Wolper, 1995), and the publicity surrounding the Fourth World Conference for Women held in Beijing in 1995, other women's organizations in Lebanon began to promote awareness of women's rights.

Affifa Arsanios, advisor to the minister of culture at the time of this writing, is the Lebanese representative for SIGI and vice president of International SIGI. She meets regularly with groups of local women in discussions about their own rights as Lebanese women, and how these rights correspond to, or differ from, universal human rights upheld globally. Under the leadership of Arsanios, local Lebanese women are meeting weekly to collect local folk practices, traditions, proverbs, sayings, and attitudes that support women's civil emancipation.

International meetings of SIGI are held yearly in world capitals, and its headquarters is in Montreal. In addition to the training manual "Claiming Our Rights," SIGI has also published two manuals targeting domestic violence, entitled "Safe and Secure" and "Strategies for Safety" (available from www.SIGI.org). Moreover, they have published a manual for training trainers. The international plan is to integrate these manuals into the educational system in Muslim countries, so girls from an early age will begin thinking about women's rights.

PEOPLE'S RIGHTS MOVEMENT

Galtung (1994) has posited that the basic need of security (survival) demands an avoidance of violence. In the education of children, it is imperative not only to treat children nonviolently, but also teach them alternatives to violence with each other. In addition, the need for identity implies an acceptance and validation of the child in terms of gender, class, and the specific religious group to which he/she belongs.

The People's Rights Movement (PRM) promotes nonviolence; nonauthoritarianism; and tolerance for gender, sect, and class in Lebanese schools. PRM is becoming a productive movement for peacebuilding: Its leaders are forming grassroots collaborations, targeting the training of teachers of young children, and writing curricula for schools on specific activities that promote nonviolence and human rights. Founded in 1986 and funded by European and Canadian sources, by 1995 PRM and its leaders had begun to implement its curriculum, generically entitled "Humanistic Education." The curriculum provides specific methods for implementing these principles.

PRM has been addressing the issue of violence directed at children in the schools. Corporal punishment is still an acceptable means of disciplining students in Lebanon, and PRM staff work with the principal to convince him or her that this method may only teach more violence and is not successful in creating a climate conducive to learning. In order to succeed in changing structural violence in the school system itself, PRM's position is that this direct violence must stop. The leader of PRM and one of its founders is Ugarite Younan. She has been invited to be on the National Committee for Curriculum Reform to modify the educational program in Lebanon and is working on the preparation of educational textbooks for teaching history and civics. Younan and her PRM colleagues have also worked with UNESCO and International Peace Research Association to publish a guidebook entitled "Teaching as a Promotion for Human Rights and Conflict Resolution in a Democratic and Peaceful Environment" (Osseiran, 2000). It has been translated into four languages and distributed in Lebanon and the Arab world. Younan has been a trainer for teachers throughout Lebanon on how to apply these guidelines on human rights and conflict resolution in educational settings.

Based on surveys on the number of students spanked at the beginning and end of training, Younan reported a 60 percent success rate in reducing violence with children among the principals with whom she worked (personal communication, June 1998). The PRM staff worked in 15 schools in the 1996–1997 academic year, with an enrollment of approximately 650 students, and trained about 500 teachers in 120 schools in 1997–1998. The leaders of PRM have a vision for a Lebanon of the future that encourages egalitarian relationships, beginning with children; a society tolerant of sect, class, and gender; and peaceful settlements of all conflicts, large and small.

YOUNG WOMEN'S CHRISTIAN ASSOCIATION

Individuals must be actively involved in the process of meeting their basic human needs. Avenues for self-determination must exist so that individuals in return can assert themselves to change the society to meet needs more equally and sufficiently. Unfortunately, women have been thrust into circumscribed roles that have truncated their avenues for leadership in determining their own life goals, and how their needs will be met. In addition, because of domestic violence, a threatening force to maintain the submission of women, they have not been assured of the basic need for security.

The Young Women's Christian Association (YWCA), active in Lebanon since 1900, has consistently supported women's self-determination and safety from violence in their homes. The YWCA has a long tradition of helping women find vocations to become more financially independent, and worked diligently through the first part of the 20th century for the right for women to vote, a right obtained in 1953. It was active in the preconvention summit and postconvention follow-up of the Fourth World Conference for Women in 1995 (King-Irani, 1995). Mona Khauli has been the national director of the YWCA since 1977.

Among the many programs of the YWCA, two projects are related to human needs and women's peacebuilding in Lebanon. The first is their Women's Leadership Training Program, which seeks to make each woman who completes the program capable of becoming a parliamentary deputy. As part of the training program, every month there is a presentation "Women and the Law in Lebanon" in which trainers focus not only on the current law, but also on ways and means each specific law could be changed for the benefit of women. The YWCA programs help to raise consciousness about the need for women in the parliament and other areas of politics. Here we see the need for self-determination being asserted by a group of women under the auspices of an internationally recognized organization.

After their training, the women leaders participate in the YWCA's ongoing programs. One of these is the legal counseling services for women, which is the YWCA's second focus toward peacebuilding. This program has active groups dealing with domestic violence, divorce, and women's awareness of their legal rights. The domestic violence counseling sessions and group support have widened in their impact as public awareness has grown. As in other parts of the world, secrecy, shame, and denial surround the topic of domestic violence. And, similarly, there is a snowballing effect to awareness of domestic violence: The more that is said about it publicly, the more those suffering are likely to step forward to seek help. As cited previously, feminist peaceworkers have frequently made the connections between domestic violence and war. The twin saplings of peacebuilding in the YWCA make powerful change agents: training women as leaders, and raising awareness to combat domestic violence.

UNITED NATIONS IN LEBANON

Identity and self-determination needs are basic to humans and can easily be repressed whenever people are rejected or discriminated against because of their race, creed, gender, or class (identity), or disallowed the choice of lifestyle or consciousness-formation, or a choice in receiving and expressing information and opinions (self-determination, or freedom) (Galtung, 1998). The history of the Middle East is replete with instances in which people of different creeds and cultural traditions have lived side by side in harmony. Lebanon has served as a refuge for many persecuted peoples such as Jews, Armenians, Kurds, Egyptians, and others (Harris, 1997).

However, there are also significant times of internecine violence. Beginning in 1975 the political structure broke down in such a way as to make people vulnerable to one another based simply on their religious sect, or their social class, or their identification with a particular political party. Lebanese citizens' sense of security was threatened because of collective violence; also, their sense of identity was threatened because they could not safely go to parts of the country in which the dominant sect or political party was at variance with their own.

A United Nations Children's Fund (UNICEF) program called Education for Peace (EFP) was initiated in 1985 in Lebanon. Its purpose was to offer young people the opportunity to meet others from different sects, to experience their differences and similarities. They trained 6,000 children, from age 7 and above, both Palestinians and Lebanese, in training camps lasting 8–10 days. The aim was for young people to see that although the violent world around them made no sense, they could have a life of their own that did make sense because of their commitment to peace and justice. With direct violence all around them, and rampant intolerance of others because of sect and class, the children were being offered another vision.

Over 100 NGOs coordinated with UNICEF in this program, and the majority of the collaborators were women. The young instructors were equal numbers of men and women, and an equal number of male and female young people attended. Young females, especially, had to pressure their families to allow them to attend, because it is not a usual part of the culture for young girls to attend a training camp. In 6 years, during some of the most intense warfare, 175,000 young people were involved in this program (A. Mansour, personal communication, June 22, 1997). The purpose of another UN development project, "Fora for Peace," was to support other NGOs in human development, peace, and reconciliation. "Fora for Peace" was widely recognized during the war years as a valuable conduit for peace activities, and it won a national Lebanese award (the Laurie Mughaizel Peace Award) for its benefits in Lebanese culture.

Ana Mansour has been a leader in these UN programs, which have focused on training young people and adults to tolerate those different from themselves. Her vision for human needs of security and self-determination has led her from organizing hundreds of youth peace education camps, to managing an umbrella of organizations working for peace at all levels. At present, she is director of the Lebanese Parliamentary Forum, an NGO that provides policy analyses about human rights issues to parliamentarians so that they have a heightened awareness of these issues. In this evolution, Mansour has been an active leader in protesting the direct violence in her culture, and then, when the war stopped, she turned her attention to influencing the dismantling of the structural violence as expressed in Lebanese laws and institutions.

INSTITUTE FOR WOMEN'S STUDIES IN THE ARAB WORLD

The basic need for well-being or the opportunity to be employed adequately to sustain oneself and one's family is a constant concern for most of the world (Schwebel, 1997), and this is certainly true in Lebanon. Women have the double jeopardy of not being as well educated as men, and not having adequate skills or similar opportunities for employment. In addition, they frequently do not have an awareness about their human rights to help them confront the endemic structural discrimination that leaves them without employment.

The Institute for Women's Studies in the Arab World (IWSAW) of the Lebanese American University is a catalyst for change for women's benefit and for the promotion of peacebuilding in Lebanon. Established in 1973, two years before the wars began, and originally funded by the Ford Foundation, it sponsors many projects and local, regional, and international conferences whose purpose is to improve the quality of life of Arab women and children. A particular focus in this chapter is on the institute's projects that combine income-generating training along with increased awareness of women's human rights, and tolerance for people from other sects. These projects serve as prime examples of development programs and peacebuilding working hand-in-hand in Lebanon.

The first income-generating project of IWSAW was to assist war-affected women. Beginning in 1988, the project brought together women from East and West Beirut, Christians and Muslims, to learn skills in handicrafts and sewing that could bring them income. Built into the program was training on the topics of tolerance, understanding, mutual respect, and friendships among the different sects. From their experience with these groups, IWSAW (1985b) developed a Peace Education Curriculum that was then used in each of its development programs. In addition, a "Basic Living Skills" program (IWSAW, 1985a) was integrated with the income-generating projects. It included family planning, nutrition information, environmental awareness, and the awareness of women's rights.

The first groups to participate in these IWSAW programs were women displaced from the war; they were extraordinarily marginalized, and lacked access to basic resources and social/moral support. By 1990–1991 there was another deluge of 15- to 21-year-old women who were forced to leave school because of the war and their displacement. These women were seen as a financial burden to their already impoverished families.

Another income-producing program has been sequin embroidery training implemented in 1999 at the Baabda Prison for women. This has been the biggest challenge, because, common to these women, the most marginalized of society, were feelings of utter failure and powerlessness.

Women in several targeted villages were also selected for IWSAW projects. One example is Akaar, a very poor region of northern Lebanon, where the women learned carpet weaving and how to produce bio-gas, in which excrement is converted to gas for burning.

The IWSAW staff provided counseling for all of these women, displaced or imprisoned, targeting their self-defeating attitudes that impeded their sense of autonomy. In addition, consciousness-raising classes in "Knowing Your Rights" were provided for all participants. Thus IWSAW has developed a sharply focused program for women that emphasizes three areas: marketable skills acquisition, personal development and human rights awareness, and cognitive reformation of self-defeating thoughts. The institute's work, which originates in Lebanon but has influence throughout the Arab world through its conferences, workshops, and publications, empowers women to become more self-reliant in meeting their needs for self-determination and well-being, and in so doing, challenges the existing societal structural violence.

CONCLUSION

A growing peacebuilding network can be envisioned and implemented through attempts of programs to raise the consciousness of women regarding their rights for meeting the basic needs of security, identity, well-being, and self-determination; to help them find a vocational place for themselves in their society; and to acknowledge the damage done to communities from direct and indirect violence. The efforts addressed here on the part of the Lebanese, a people who have greatly suffered from violence, can be upheld as dignified and hopeful examples for others faced with similar situations.

REFERENCES

Abu-Saba, M. B. (1996, Summer/Fall). The psychological underpinnings of women's human rights. *Al-Raida, 13*(74/75), 55–57. Beirut: Lebanese American University, Institute for Women's Studies in the Arab World.

Afkhami, M., & Vaziri, H. (1998). *Claiming our rights: A manual for women's rights education in Muslim societies.* Montreal, Quebec, Canada: Sisterhood Is Global Institute.

Alonso, H. H. (1993). *Peace as a woman's issue.* New York: Syracuse University Press.

Brock-Utne, B. (1989). *Feminist perspectives on peace and peace education.* New York: Pergamon Press.

Galtung, J. (1969). Violence, peace and peace research. *Journal of Peace Research, 3,* 167–191.

Galtung, J. (1994). *Human rights in another key.* Cambridge, England: Polity Press.

Galtung, J. (1998). On the genesis of peaceless worlds: Insane nations and insane states. *Peace and Conflict: Journal of Peace Psychology, 4,* 1–11.

Harris, W. W. (1997). *Faces of Lebanon: Sects, wars, and global extensions.* Princeton, NJ: Markus Wiener.

Institute for Women's Studies in the Arab World (1985a). *Basic living skills program* (In Arabic). Beirut: Lebanese American University.

Institute for Women's Studies in the Arab World (1985b). *Peace education curriculum* (In Arabic). Beirut: Lebanese American University.

King-Irani, L. (1995, Summer/Fall). The world is in need of women's qualities and skills. *Al-Raida, 12*(70/71), 25–27. Beirut: Lebanese American University, Institute for Women's Studies in the Arab World.

Makdisi, J. S. (1990). *Beirut fragments: A war memoir.* New York: Persea Books.

McKay, S. (1995). Women's voices in peace psychology: A feminist agenda. *Peace and Conflict: Journal of Peace Psychology, 1,* 67–84.

Osseiran, S. (1996). Peace studies. In M. L. Kearney & A. H. Holden (Eds.), *Women and the university curriculum: Towards equality, democracy and peace* (pp. 231–244).London: Jessica Kingsley Publications.

Osseiran, S. (Ed.). (2000). *Teaching as a promotion for human rights and conflict resolution in a democratic and peaceful environment.* Beirut, Lebanon: Education Center for Research and Development.

Peters, J., & Wolper, A. (Eds.). (1995). *Women's rights, human rights: International feminist perspectives.* New York: Routledge.

Reardon, B. (1993). *Women and peace: Feminist visions of global security.* Albany: State University of New York Press.

Schwebel, M. (1997). Job insecurity as structural violence: Implications for destructive intergroup conflict. *Peace and Conflict: Journal of Peace Psychology, 3,* 333–351.

21

Legacies of Fear: Religious Repression and Resilience in Siberia

Marjorie Mandelstam Balzer

Antireligion campaigns of officials in the Soviet Union against Indigenous peoples of the North were among the most striking and least understood forms of cultural repression in the 20th century. These Marxist "propaganda wars," begun in the 1920s and continuing into the 1980s, extended beyond clashes of ideology into widespread religious persecution of spiritual leaders, shamans, and their communities. While the campaigns were meant to destroy whole Indigenous ways of life, defined as "backward" and "primitive," they had unintended consequences. As with the politics of most wars and colonizing, Soviet violations of human rights had extensive and complex ripple effects.

Shamans were arrested, jailed for extended periods, forced to give up their religious and healing practices, they had their drums burned, and in massive numbers they were pushed politically underground. But they were never fully destroyed. In some dramatic cases, they were protected by the very communities tasked with turning them in to the Soviet authorities. In pre-Soviet times, shamans and their followers were besieged by Russian Orthodox missionaries. Whether Orthodox or Soviet, outsiders railed against shamanic beliefs while shamans themselves modestly limited their own advertising campaigns. The adaptability of shamanic practice has led to its survival and diversity, before, during, and after the Soviet period. Indeed, the nonmissionizing eclecticism of shamanic practice has provided fertile ground for debates within shamanic studies over whether shamanism is truly a cohesive "ism," a religion, or a set of folk healing premises and practices. One way to resolve this debate is to more closely examine patterns of shamanic responses to major sociocultural upheavals, such as Soviet repression. In the process, we can better understand the diversity of what shamans do, in and for their communities, as well as what they and their followers say about it.

It is useful to consider Siberian shamanism as a widespread complex of religious and medical beliefs, centered on a community or family shaman, who is usually perceived to be a mediator between spiritual and human worlds for specific purposes. The mediation is often chaotic and painful, for the mystical forces shamans describe themselves as negotiating in ritual are fraught with danger and easily misused (Balzer, 1997a, 1997b; Humphrey & Unon, 1996; Shirokogoroff, 1935; Siikala & Hoppal, 1992).[1]

This chapter incorporates anecdotes and life histories into an analysis of shamanic practice and human resilience, enabling greater respect for shamanic beliefs in the current post-Soviet, multicultural context. My assessments are based on field research in various cultural milieus, especially the Khanty (Ostiak) of West Siberia, and the Sakha (Yakut) of East Siberia. Relevant fieldwork was begun in 1986–1987 and continued periodically from 1991–2000. As a cultural anthropologist, I suggest a framework for understanding diverse shamanic strategies for survival under difficult circumstances. This historical context of current practices is significant and relevant to accurate interpretations of psychological healing of social trauma. I argue that how shamans responded to potential and often very real devastation in Soviet times influenced the uneven 1990s recovery of shamanic practices and beliefs (see Table 21.1).

RESPONSES TO REPRESSION

One relatively positive model of shamanic response was interethnic cooperation. This method of self-preservation runs counter to cases where outsiders' violence has stimulated ripples of interethnic enmity in colonial contexts. Interethnic solidarity is exemplified by the friendship of the famed Sakha shaman Tokoyeu with the Yukagir shaman Kurilov during the 1920s, and their mutual aid in crisis. Because Tokoyeu and Kurilov had the same spiritual teacher, they were close enough for Kurilov to hide Tokoyeu's drum when authorities tried to confiscate it. Another example is the cooperation of one Sakha shaman with a Russian doctor, whose daughter the shaman cured in the 1950s. The Russian doctor gave the shaman his village's first television, and helped protect him against Soviet authorities far removed from local realities.

Such cases point to flexible, nonpolarized indigenous approaches to ethnic relations, despite a general consolidating of ethnic identities in the Soviet period. Interethnic cooperation may surprise researchers focused on the study of shamanic complexes within one culture or cultural area, or those aware of the often-justified reputation of many shamans as competitive and territorial. Traditional seances done with the support of loving family members and community participants, broadly defined, frequently contained elements of group therapy.[2]

More recently, those shamanic curers who have also acquired Soviet or European-style medical degrees, such as Alexandra Konstantinova Chirkova of the Sakha Republic (see Balzer 1996, 1999a), exemplify a trend in shamanic re-

Table 21.1
Repression of Traditional Medicine and Shamanic Resilience (A Sociocultural Approach)

RESPONSES TO REPRESSION IN SIBERIA
Interethnic Cooperation SAKHA/EVENK/YUKAGIR/RUSSIAN,
                           e.g., Tokoyeu *oiuun* (shaman)
Organized Resistance   KHANTY (and through the North)
Situational Response   SAKHA, e.g., Konstantin *oiuun*
Perform on Demand   versus missionaries, versus Soviets (plus
                           initiation)
Go Underground   SAKHA, e.g., Nikon *oiuun*
Feminization   throughout the North, more female healers,
                           herbalists

CULTURAL REVITALIZATION
Solitary forest drumming, private rituals
Official support in Sakha (fluctuating), Tuva, Buryatia
       e.g., 1992 Conference on Shamanism in Yakutsk
       e.g., Yhyakh festival throughout Sakha, annual, public
       e.g., many conferences and rituals in Tuva, Buryatia
Spiritual revival groups and programs in Sakha Republic
       e.g., KUT-SIUR, philosophy of "heart-soul-mind-spirit"
       e.g., school program AIYY-YOREGHE "benevolent spirit teaching"
Healing Centers in Sakha Republic
       e.g., Association of Folk Medicine (V. A. Kondakov)
       e.g., Center for Traditional Medicine (Y. S. Prokopiev)
          (Polyclinic for Eastern Medicine)
Strong individuals with healing reputations, "gifted"
       e.g., A. K. Chirkova, M. K. Chirkova (SAKHA, Belaia Gora)
       e.g., Dora I. Kobiakova (SAKHA, Kobia region)
       e.g., Fedot P. Ivanov (SAKHA, Viliuisk region)
       e.g., Sobei (EVEN, southern Sakha)
Strong individuals with specialist reputations
       e.g., Vitaly Nikiforov antialcohol (SAKHA, Megino-Kangalask)

*Debates about republic-level laws regulating folk healing

silience that may well be the cutting edge of 21st-century interlinked medicine and spirituality.[3]

A second, contrasting response style is organized shamanic protest, far more widespread across the North in the 1920s and 1930s than acknowledged in official Soviet propaganda. The most significant example is the Kazym "rebellion" of 1931–1933, led by Khanty shamans but also including Nentsy leaders. To call this tragedy, which culminated in the hostage taking and ritual killing of an eight-member Soviet brigade, a "rebellion" or "uprising" implicitly aligns the analyst with official views. Field interviews on the protest and its brutal, massive aftermath enable Indigenous views of this painful, destructive on all sides, interethnic conflict to be heard. The granddaughter of one of the important leader-shamans explained to me that when the men of her family were arrested "two came into the yurt, one armed Russian and one well-dressed, non-local Khant in furs. Already, on their many sleds, sat Khanty, tied up two by two." Her grandmother had had premonitions of trouble when their clan spirits had refused an offering. See Balzer (1999a, pp. 110–119) on this underreported conflict.

One of the most important ramifications of the protest was the arrest and killing not only of most of the shamans in the community, but also of most of the men. Families were scattered and little was left of those aspects of healing traditions that were most linked to seances and an "altered consciousness" appeal to spirit helpers. Demoralization was rampant, with women, less likely to be arrested, carrying on what had been considered in earlier times "lesser" healing arts associated with herbal knowledge and dream interpretation.

Other Soviet period protests, for example in the North of the Sakha Republic, also can be compared and placed in the context of classic and more recent theoretical literature on cultural revitalization movements and attempts (Golovnev, 1995; Trott, 1997; Wallace, 1956). These cases all point to the important role of shamans as not only healers and psychologists, but also leaders of their communities in times of social, cultural, and political strife.

A third, and particularly common, kind of shamanic response can be termed the ad hoc, or situational, response. It is beautifully illustrated by an account concerning the famed Sakha *oiuun* (shaman) Konstantin Chirkov, Alexandra's father. In the 1960s he reputedly managed to divert a military plane flying near his village so that a young girl with appendicitis could be transported to a regional hospital. At this period in his life, the aging Konstantin had been forbidden to practice his widely acknowledged healing gifts. He went into "altered consciousness" communication with his spirit helpers in secret during emergencies. In this case, according to the niece who helped him, he used every ounce of his energies, donning his cloak and drumming solo by his hearth in order to cause the plane to make an emergency landing in their village. Konstantin collapsed after sending his niece to village leaders, warning them to be ready with the girl at the landing field well before they saw the plane. The niece added that the pilot emerged from his plane looking dazed, saying that something had caused him to lose control and land in the village.[4]

Descriptions of shamanic competitions with Soviet doctors also fall into this ad hoc response category, as do semifantastic, anomalous accounts of shamanic resistance to arrest and incarceration. In one case, from the Khanty of West Siberia, a Soviet doctor himself fell ill after he had played with and mocked a shaman's drum without permission. This clearly enhanced the reputation of the shaman involved, while sidelining the terrified doctor. In a narrative widespread among the Sakha of East Siberia, a shaman was said to have flown out of jail as a bird. Another shaman, worried about the safety of his family if he absconded entirely, simply proved he could escape his bars by constantly removing himself to the street in front of the jail, where his jailers could see him calmly reading.

A related, yet analytically separate, category may be called the "show off on demand" shamanic response. Much more than tricks or superficial sleight-of-hand, shamanic seances performed on demand or under duress are famed throughout the North. In relatively traditional contexts, shamans of some communities needed to prove themselves during their first seance, their debut after an initiatory bout of "shamanic sickness," their "calling" by the spirits. But more hostile show-off contexts developed during competitions with Russian Orthodox missionaries. And in the Soviet period, especially but not only in the Far East, believers repeated with awe reports of seances held in Communist Youth League halls, where conditions were set for shamanic failure. Such stories, surviving today, depict shamanic success and reinforce local respect for shamans as curers and miracle workers. At minimum, they are couched in the language of psychology: that powerful shamans could hypnotize audiences of skeptical Soviet atheists into believing the shamans had turned into bears, for example. At maximum, the accounts become symbols of ethnic pride and rekindled spirituality. I maintain they are subversive narratives that enabled Siberians to claim, at least among themselves, that their shaman leader-healers could outwit even the Soviet-Russian authorities.

A particularly astonishing variation on this theme is the shaman who journeyed to Moscow to try to recover his confiscated drum. On arrival at a Russian bureaucrat's office, he was challenged to prove his powers. "We have not seen meat for months," the bureaucrat allegedly said. "Could you produce some?" The shaman "conjured" a live pig running around the office. But still the bureaucrat balked at finding the drum. So the shaman blinded the pig and mentioned that he could inflict the same kind of harm on the bureaucrat. The stammering man managed to promise he would try to find the drum, not an easy feat, given that many drums were burned.

In Siberian shamanic traditions, spiritual prowess normally is expected to be low profile. Shamans are not supposed to boast of spirit control or communication, lest they lose their powers. Thus another common shamanic strategy in the face of Soviet repression, ironically in harmony with shamanic values, was the modest "go underground" response. In extreme cases, this led to seances in the forest or spirit invocation without drums, after drums were confiscated, hauled off to museums, or burned. One Sakha curer had to improvise using a frying pan for a drum. The underground response is well exemplified by the belatedly valorized career of Nikon-*oiuun* of the Viliuisk region (Yakutia, today's Sakha Republic). His gentle laying-on-of-hands healing and quiet chanting became renowned throughout the republic, on a need-to-know basis. Unlike previous practice, he had to develop his following with a minimum of information about his patients, to envelop them and himself in a careful veil of secrecy.

A related ramification of secrecy led to the feminization of shamanic practice throughout the Soviet North, not only among the Kazym Khanty. Because famed "big-man" shamans were more likely to be arrested or pressured, it was often the women who carried on the basics of shamanic traditions within their communities. This "gender transfer" response meant that much esoteric and important knowledge was lost, in cultural environments where male shamans had previously passed on their clients, prayer chants, and sometimes specific spirit-helpers to male protégés. While women had often been strong healers and dream interpreters in many communities, given refined traditions of curing divisions-of-labor, their significance was magnified. Women took over shamanic practices on an unprecedented scale yet with debilitating handicaps in northern communities, including Khanty, Nentsy, Sakha, Yukagir, Even, Evenk, and Amur River. This kind of gender transfer needs to be further and better investigated in diverse areas, for it concerns both changes in gender status, and the question, crucial for recovery of shamanic knowledge, of whether human apprenticeship needs to be part of the inheritance or acquisition of spirit power, supplementing the usually involuntary calling by spirits.

RECOVERY OF SHAMANIC KNOWLEDGE

In the post-Soviet period, and for about a decade prior to it, at first cautious and then exuberant revitalization of shamanic traditions occurred throughout the Siberian North and Far East. Yet recovery has been spotty, sometimes appearing to be haphazard or capricious. It has depended in part on the unpredictability of particular strong personalities living in certain areas and not others. In addition, some political, cultural, and interlinked psychological trends can be discerned.

In West Siberia, especially in northern Khanty territories, recovery of shamanic knowledge has been slow and halting. One young reindeer-breeder, who later became a folklorist, mourned to me that he feels the urge to explore his shamanic roots but still fears the psychological dangers and community suspicions that seances entail. He goes into the forest and drums by himself, and he has the potential to rekindle his family's curing legacy. But he has no viable teacher nearby and feels uncomfortable training with the few nonkin, elder-shamans left in remote eastern Khanty territories.

In the Far East, especially the Sakha Republic and the Republic of Tuva, prospects for recovery are much better. Indigenous leaders have been elected presidents in these republics, enabling respect for a wide range of rejuvenated traditions. An explosion of local interest in shamanic healing, spirituality, and seances has occurred. In the Republic of Tuva, presidential support of shamans has been open and consistent. In the Republic of Buryatia, although shamans compete with Buddhist as well as Russian Orthodox priests, shamanic prestige has been raised. In the Sakha Republic, presidential support has been uneven, but widespread spiritual hunger has led to considerable experimentation. In the 1990s some critics in Moscow sneered that shamanism had become the official "state religion" of the indigenous-led Sakha Republic. This reputedly embarrassed the republic's president, who withdrew most official sponsorship of shamanic clinics and associations. Nonetheless, several groups advocating a return to indigenous philosophy and shamanic healing have become popular.

One group sponsoring cultural revival calls itself *Kut-Siur*, meaning "heart-soul-mind-spirit." It has been active in performing annual public rituals, advocating integrative medicine, and promoting a new program of self-defined Sakha traditional philosophy, *aiyy yoreghe*, roughly glossed as "benevolent spirit(ual) teaching." Since 1993 concepts of multiple souls; of a multileveled cosmology inhabited by specific gods of the upper and lower worlds; and of kinship, ecology, and morality have been taught under the rubric of a republicwide *aiyy yoreghe* elementary and secondary school program.[5] Success thus far has depended on the skills and enthusiasm of specific teachers, and many are learning the program themselves. While children enjoy it, reactions of their elders range from pleasure to shock and even anger.

Other groups are more specifically oriented to recovering shamanic traditions. The Association of Folk Medicine, founded in Yakutsk in 1990 by Vladimir A. Kondakov, has focused on curing, broadening, and syncretizing its repertoire of techniques. A range of specialists serve in Kondakov's clinic. Kondakov, who many consider a "white shaman" (*aiyy oiuun*) has a degree from V. M. Kandyba's "extrasense" institute in Kiev. He has added aspects of Eastern religion and acupuncture to his shamanic spirit mediation, knows a range of herbal medicines, and is by training a historian. His association sends curing teams to villages, where they set up temporary clinics and perform seances. The results and social resonance of his work are mixed, as with all healing practices, but many Sakha defend his right to offer a tradition-based healing option for patients disgusted with standard, mostly Soviet-style, impoverished clinics and hospitals. Shamanic practice itself has historically been highly syncretic, so Kondakov's supporters can argue his innovations are within a shamanic tradition of creativity and flexibility.[6]

A multitude of other healers and groups have also formed small clinic practices, working in what can loosely be considered Sakha shamanic traditions and a more Russian-influenced "extrasense" context. A leading competitor to Kondakov is sports-medicine-trained Yuri Prokopiev, who has founded the Center for Traditional Medicine, outside Yakutsk. His center makes room for acupuncture, acupressure, and other aspects of Eastern curing traditions, with his healers discussing chakras, "chi," mineral baths, homeopathy, aromatherapy, "vito-therapy," and "bio-energy" with the passion of the converted. They have led a drive to have a controversial law on traditional folk medicine drafted by the Sakha parliament, to limit and license healers. Prokopiev estimates that about 240 people claim to be healers in the republic, while 30–50 have real talent.

Several indigenous practitioners focus on music therapy, especially the use of the Sakha *khomus* (jaw harp) for curing. Others use the more renowned drum and chanting of spirit-calling communal seances. Some are specialists in herbal cures, massage, or bone setting, while others practice telepathy and counseling.

Traditional Sakha healers also were specialized, so such divisions are not new. But relatively new problems have emerged, exacerbated by increasing poverty and social strife. A few healers focus on antialcoholism seances, while others try to ameliorate, if not cure, cancers derived from nuclear accidents and industrialization in smog-filled Siberian towns.

The most striking change is that indigenous spirituality is being revitalized in a politicized context of rekindled confidence in the potential of traditional cures, after intense propaganda to the contrary. This is reinforced by new styles of group therapy and cooperation among curers. Some indigenous doctors and psychologists trained in Moscow have been able to incorporate folk healing, support groups, and group seances (including group trances) into their practices. When it occurs, the partnership of therapists has had a positive, synergistic effect and has helped counteract traditions of competition and "turf-based" jealousy. However, thoughtful Sakha shamans warn their followers not to be overenthusiastic about the revival, because they are aware of aspects of shamanic knowledge that have been lost. For example, one shaman of the Upper Kolyma area was reputed to have been able to cure tuberculosis. A young Soviet doctor stumbled on evidence that this shaman was helping patients that the doctor could not cure. But in the 1930s, the shaman and the doctor were forbidden friendly contact, much less rapport. Years later, the doctor returned to the village hoping to work with the shaman as a colleague, but it was too late. The damage of lost knowledge and mutual suspicion takes more than a generation to cure.

CONCLUSION

Siberian shamanism is at once a nonmissionizing religion and a complex bundle of practical healing and hunting oriented spirituality. I have avoided directly addressing the debate on whether shamanism is better seen as multiple shamanisms or is a transcending cross-cultural faith, "the complex of beliefs, rituals and myths that has developed around the shaman" (Hultkrantz, 1993, p. 8), because I see both as valid.[7] When the spiritual power of shamans has been acknowledged, or ignored by the authorities, shamans have been able to provide great succor to their communities. Shamanic practice, as a kind of interlinked personal and community healing, has been hard to kill but was frequently driven underground. Shamanic recovery in new forms, as part of broader processes of cultural revitalization, has begun to help heal the wounds of social trauma caused by Soviet policies.

In 1997, after a short and chaotic period of religious liberalism, a new law on religion in the Russian Federation was passed, privileging the Russian Orthodox Church. Within the framework of this law and subsequent rulings, shamanic spirituality is valid unless it becomes the basis of an aggressive "cult." Post-Soviet Russians rarely consider eclectic, "exotic" indigenous religions as major competitors to Russian Orthodoxy. Debates inside several republics (including Tuva, Buryatia, and Sakha) have centered on restricting shamanic practices with laws and licenses focused on folk medicine. Such debates, while sharp and Russian-influenced, are led by indigenous intellectuals and are thus a major improvement over Soviet-era repression and persecution.

Analysts today are in an exciting, though bittersweet, position to review a broad range of responses to cultural repression and revitalization. The listing of models is only one step toward understanding a new, potential mutual synergy of shamanic communities. Such communities are not always neatly congruent with politically defined ethnic groups, making analysis of changing cultural values problematic and requiring attention to multiple levels of community organization. In the post-Soviet period, increased opportunities to abuse or fake shamanic knowledge must also be acknowledged. Yet cautious conclusions can be suggested, concerning which shamanic strategies met with the greatest success and provided the best conditions for a recovery of shamanic practices when post-Soviet spiritual revitalization became politically possible.

Those groups with greater numbers of Indigenous leaders, greater numbers of Indigenous philosophers, and more diverse historical responses to repression, especially the quiet, modest "underground" responses; the creative ad hoc responses; and the interethnic cooperation responses, eventually were able to bring shamanic practice out from secrecy, into public display and discourse more easily and more quickly than those in which violent protest was met with violent reprisal. Those larger Indigenous groups that have attained their own republics within the Russian Federation have been in the best position to recover their wounded self-images and spirituality. Thus it is no surprise that shamanic healing and reconfigured cosmologies have become part of an adapted, eclectic, popular cultural revival in the Sakha Republic, in Tuva, and in Buryatia, while in most Khanty, Yukagir, Nentsy, and Evenk territories, shamanic practices have been harder, but not impossible, to recover.

NOTES

I am indebted to the International Research and Exchanges Board (IREX); the Social Science Research Council (SSRC); Yakutsk University; the Academy of Sciences Institute of Languages, Literature, and History in Yakutsk (AN IIaLI, now the Humanities Institute); the Sakha Republic Ministry of Culture; and the Kennan Institute of the Smithsonian's Wilson Center for fieldwork and/or research support. I am deeply thankful to my Sakha language teacher, Klara Belkin, with whom I began studying in 1983, and to many Sakha friends and colleagues, especially Zinaida and Vladimir Ivanov for often sharing their home in 1992–2000.

1. On Soviet repression, see Bourdeaux (1995), Ramet (1992), and Slezkine (1994). On the peoples of the North, see Balzer (1999b).

2. Compare Taussig (1987) with Romanucci-Ross, Moerman, and Tancredi (1995). In times of crisis, such as epidemics, some shamans also worked with each other to communicate with a greater number of spirits (Gogolev, 1983).

3. On Sakha shamanism, see Alekseev (1984); Gogolev, Reshetnikova, Romanova, & Sleptsov (1992); and Ksenofontov (1928/1992).

4. On repression of Sakha shamans, including Konstantin, see Il'iakov (1995).

5. For Indigenous perspectives on Sakha worldviews, see Afanas'ev (1993), Kolodesnikov (2000), and Utkin (1996).

6. Kondakov has written several guides for his followers. On him, see Balzer (1993).

7. Atkinson (1992) stresses multiple shamanisms. Debates about whether shamanic faith and practice constitute a religion or a more practical, healing and hunting oriented "technique of ecstacy" (Eliade, 1951/1964) also seem limiting (cf. Hamayon, 1990).

REFERENCES

Afanas'ev, L. A. (1993). *Aiyy yoreghe* [Teachings of the spirit]. Yakutsk, Russia: Ministry of Culture.

Alekseev, N. A. (1984). *Shamanizm tiurkoiazychnykh narodov Sibiri* [Shamanism among the Turkic-speaking peoples of Siberia]. Novosibirsk, Russia: Nauka.

Atkinson, J. M. (1992). Shamanisms today. *Annual Review of Anthropology, 21,* 307–330.

Balzer, M. M. (1993). Two urban shamans. In G. Marcus (Ed.), *Perilous states: Conversations amid uncertain transitions* (pp. 131–164). Chicago: University of Chicago Press.

Balzer, M. M. (1996). Flights of the sacred: Symbolism and theory in Siberian shamanism. *American Anthropologist, 98,* 305–318.

Balzer, M. M. (Ed.) (1997a). *Shamanic worlds: Rituals and lore of Siberia and Central Asia.* London: M. E. Sharpe.

Balzer, M. M. (1997b). Soviet superpowers. *Natural History, 106*(2), 38–39.

Balzer, M. M. (1999a). Alexandra Konstaninovna Chirkova: Grenzuberschereitende heilerin und chirurgin [Alexandra Konstaninovna Chirkova: Folk healer and surgeon]. In C. Gottschalk-Bascus (Ed.), *Wanderer zwischen den welten* [Wanderer between the worlds] (pp. 57–62). Murnau, Germany: Reichert Verlag.

Balzer, M. M. (1999b). *The tenacity of ethnicity: A Siberian saga in global perspective.* Princeton, NJ: Princeton University Press.

Bourdeaux, M. (Ed.). (1995). *The politics of religion in Russia and the new states of Eurasia.* London: M.E. Sharpe.

Eliade, M. (1964). *Shamanism: Archaic techniques of ecstasy* (W. R. Trask, Trans.). Princeton, NJ: Princeton University Press. (Original work published 1951)

Gogolev, A. I. (1983). *Istoricheskaia etnografiia Yakutov: Narodnye znanie i obychnoe pravo* [Historical ethnography of the Yakuts: Folk knowledge and customary law]. Yakutsk, Russia: YaGU.

Gogolev, A. I., Reshetnikova, A. P., Romanova, E. N., & Sleptsov, P. S. (Eds.). (1992). *Shamanizm kak religiia: Genezis, rekonstruktsiia, traditsii-tezisy dokladov mezhdunarodnoi konferentsiia* [Shamanism as religion: Genesis, reconstruction, traditions. Abstracts of international conference papers]. Yakutsk, Russia: YaGU.

Golovnev, A. V. (1995). *Govoriashchie kul'tury: Traditsii Samodiitsev i Ugrov* [Speaking cultures: Samodeic and Ugrian traditions]. Yekaterinburg, Russia: Akademiia Nauk.

Hamayon, R. (1990). *La chasse a l'âme: Esquisse d'une théorie du chamanisme Sibérien* [Chasing the soul: Exploring a theory of Siberian shamanism]. Nanterre, France: Société d'ethnologie.

Hultkrantz, A. (1993). Introductory remarks on the study of shamanism. *Shaman, 1*(1), 1–14.

Humphrey, C., & Unon, U. (1996). *Shamans and elders: Experience, knowledge, and power among the Daur Mongols.* Oxford, England: Oxford University Press.

Il'iakov, P. N. (1995). *Bor'ba s shamanizmom in Yakutii (1920–1930)* [The struggle with shamanism in Yakutia]. Yakutsk, Russia: Dom Narod Tvorchestva.

Kolodesnikov, S. (2000). The person in the traditional Yakut [Sakha] worldview. *Anthropology and Archeology of Eurasia, 39*(1), 42–79.

Ksenofontov, G. V. (1992). *Shamanizm: Izbrannye trudy* [Shamanism: Collected works] (A. N. Diachkova, Ed.). Yakutsk, Russia: Sever-Iug for Museum of Music and Folklore. (Original work published 1928.)

Ramet, S. (Ed.). (1992). *Religious policy in the Soviet Union.* Cambridge, England: Cambridge University Press.

Romanucci-Ross, L., Moerman, D., & Tancredi, L. (Eds.). (1995). *The anthropology of medicine: From culture to method.* New York: Praeger.

Shirokogoroff, S. (1935). *The psychomental complex of the Tungus.* London: Kegan, Paul, Trench, Trubner.

Siikala, A. L., & Hoppal, M. (1992). *Studies on shamanism.* Helsinki: Finnish Anthropological Society.

Slezkine, Y. (1994). *Arctic mirrors: Russia and the small peoples of the north.* Ithaca, NY: Cornell University Press.

Taussig, M. (1987). *Shamanism, colonialism, and the wild man: A study in terror and healing.* Chicago: University of Chicago Press.

Trott, C. G. (1997). The rapture and the rupture: Religious change among the Inuit of North Baffin Island. *Étude Inuit, 21*(1–2), 209–228.

Utkin, K. D. (1996). The Kut-sur philosophy. *Anthropology and Archeology of Eurasia, 35*(2), 33–56.

Wallace, A. C. (1956). Acculturation: Revitalization movements. *American Anthropologist, 58,* 264–281.

PART IV

INTEGRATIVE SUMMARIES

INTRODUCTION

A child who was an eyewitness to death, injury, fear, and destruction drew these images. Illustration published with permission of Margarida Ventura.

The final part of this book provides a more theoretical reflection upon the individual and collective motives that fuel war and its vicious assaults on humanity, such as genocide, rape, or repatriation. Part IV also brings together in an integrative manner clinical, health, developmental, social, and cultural views of war-related phenomena.

Olweean, in Chapter 22, offers the first integrative summary, calling for the need to address the communal wounds caused by war, which tend to fuel conflict across generations, as a means to prevent war and conflict. He describes a project dealing with Catastrophic Trauma Recovery (CTR), an integrative and multifaceted training program that intends to offer a new model of promoting healing in large civilian populations. The CTR program trains local professionals in the Balkans and the Middle East trying to address the needs of both professionals and civilians to promote communal healing at various levels. Chapter 23, by Pappas, brings to light one of the most degrading and widespread tools of subjugation used in wartime—the rape of female civilians. He describes the psychological response of these women, focusing on the use of dissociation as a defense against traumatic rape, which transforms the victim in a dissociative container. In Chapter 24, Marvit examines the process of adaptation of Southeast Asian refugees in terms of both the risk for maladaption associated with their previous trauma and their potential for survival and positive coping. This chapter offers an understanding of how war refugee and migration experiences interact with developmental and cultural issues in youth psychosocial adjustment, proposing an ecocultural model to conceptualize ethnic minority adaptation. In the last chapter, Solomon, Greenberg, and Pyszczynski, experimental social psychologists, embrace the challenging task of discussing the human motives behind war, supporting their claims with convincing experimental evidence. In a thought-provoking style, they propose that existential fears regarding vulnerability and death fuel death-denying social constructions, such as the tendencies toward cultural identification and scapegoating of outgroups. Their seemingly pessimistic view of humanity is counterbalanced in the last section of the chapter, in which the authors propose some directives toward a more peace-building society. We would certainly agree with them that, as several other chapter authors have proposed, promoting worldviews that value tolerance, providing a context for self-actualization and self-worth, and facing our limitations as individuals and cultures are paths to a more humane and peaceful coexistence.

22

When Society Is the Victim: Catastrophic Trauma Recovery

Steve S. Olweean

Psychological and emotional injuries may be the most enduring effects of war, yet historically, they may be the least addressed in terms of rebuilding a society and preventing future violence. Perhaps there is a relationship here. Large-scale recovery efforts commonly have focused on more visible needs such as food, shelter, clothing, and physical health, as well as economic aid. Psychological trauma has been overlooked or minimized, leading to its becoming part of the psyche of a society that extends into future generations.

In recent world conflicts, terrorism has often been purposely utilized against civilians as a means of attacking the self-esteem and morale of "the enemy," as well as simple retribution. Ironically, perpetrators have frequently justified these actions based on past, unresolved emotional wounds of their own.

This psychological paradox of victims becoming perpetrators has long been examined in the field of psychotherapy relative to individuals, yet the parallel transformation on the societal level has been studied far less. For in-depth healing to occur on both levels, actions must be judged separately by their universal quality of being humane or not, rather than by the identity of who does them. When two societies in conflict each carries the deeply rooted identity of "victim," there is the greatest danger of blind, brutal treatment toward a dehumanized and demonized "other." Conversely, such inhumane actions against members of a society can further validate that society's demonized view of the perpetrators. The cycle of violence contributes to the cycle of trauma.

Whether in the Balkans, the Middle East, or elsewhere, in modern times or in the past, regardless of the original motivation of conflict, unresolved communal psychological wounds are one of the most—if not the most—powerful fuels of war and violent conflicts. The underlying insecurity and pervasive distrust, on the part of both individuals and groups, only intensify and validate fear of "the other" and contribute to dehumanizing stereotypes. Lack of understanding of these wounds can account for the seemingly incomprehensible dynamics of a conflict when viewed from afar. Efforts at maintaining peace and avoiding war are seriously handicapped if they do not address such current and historical wounds and create the means to prevent future traumas.

Treating large civilian populations experiencing catastrophic psychological trauma at all levels of a society due to war and violence poses unique challenges not typically focused on in the therapeutic literature or conventional clinical practice. When the society is one in which human services are seriously underdeveloped or absent, and where the integrity of the existing social support system itself is critically compromised, this challenge can become overwhelming.

What is needed are new models oriented toward treating large populations. These models must incorporate an integrated flow of services and supports designed to respond to both immediate and long-term effects of trauma. They should instill in the local community the capacity to provide and expand these services on an ongoing basis. It is imperative that any model also be sensitive to the cultural context of both the trauma experience and the treatment. Thus, in addition to adaptations of standard mental health treatment methods, it is important to enlist traditional aspects of the society itself, such as its cultural and spiritual resources (Olweean & Friedman, 1997).

Beginning in 1999 and during the recent Balkan conflicts, a series of special roundtables on the Balkans was held at the Annual International Conference on Conflict Resolution (ICCR) in St. Petersburg, Russia, sponsored by Common Bond Institute of the United States and Harmony Institute for Psychotherapy and Counseling of Russia. Representatives of nongovernmental (NGO) relief and conflict resolution organizations from Albania, Serbia, Kosovo, Bosnia, and Croatia participated. The first such roundtable occurred the afternoon of the bombing of the Chinese embassy compound in Belgrade. What was striking about these dialogues was the consensus that the most urgent and neglected need throughout all societies in the region was for healing from pervasive psychological trauma. Additionally striking was that all participants agreed this trauma was linked to not only recent but also past occurrences of violence, terror, and loss, many dating back for generations, and some going back for centuries. In subsequent discussions with key participants from each of these Balkan countries, trauma recovery needs were continually accented as the largest threat to future peace and reconciliation in the region.

Although in 1999 the United Nations Inter-Agency Needs Assessment Mission had also assessed this need to be widespread and relatively unattended to, there was little in the way of adequate direct services or local training being provided in trauma treatment (United Nations Security Council, 1999). It can be reasoned that at least part of this lack of action has been due to an absence of workable models for undertaking such an immense task.

In response to requests for such new models, and in cooperation with local Balkan NGOs and an international network of training organizations, Common

Bond Institute developed the Catastrophic Trauma Recovery (CTR) project. Its purpose was to design an intensive training program to provide on-site practical training in crisis intervention, trauma resolution, and support skills to large groups of local professionals and relief workers in the Balkans currently working directly with refugees and victims of violence. This program has subsequently been expanded to include trainees in the Middle East. The goals of this "training of trainers" are the following:

1. To create an extensive, permanent pool of local health professionals and paraprofessionals equipped with skills to assist the large number of people throughout the region suffering from psychological trauma;
2. To provide self-help skills and resources to the general population;
3. To make an investment in the quality of future health services of the region; and
4. To encourage cross-border cooperation among service providers.

The CTR model is presented here as one example of a comprehensive, integrated treatment and training model designed to be culture-sensitive and particularly suited to regions experiencing violent turmoil where health services are underdeveloped and the society's infrastructure has broken down. Trainees are instructed in each aspect of the model.

THE CATASTROPHIC TRAUMA RECOVERY (CTR) INTEGRATED MODEL

There are eleven major components of the CTR integrated model:

1. *Brief Therapeutic Intervention Process.* For immediate symptom relief, a number of highly effective, new, brief therapies are useful in alleviating psychological trauma symptoms. For the purposes of this model we have selected Eye Movement Desensitization and Reprocessing (EMDR). Major factors in selecting EMDR for this component of the model are that it provides quick results and can be learned in a relatively short time by both professionals and paraprofessionals. It is also felt to be easily adapted culturally (Shapiro, 1989).

2. *Survivor Support Groups.* Ongoing, programmed groups can be designed to be self-run and offer support, safety, and acceptance to victims, as well as to augment direct therapeutic services. The role of survivors support in providing contact for as many people as possible can not be emphasized enough due to the sheer size of the victim pool, the limited capability of mental health services in the regions, and the demonstrated benefit of this type of assistance in a variety of applications and settings.

3. *Crisis Phone Lines and Drop-in Centers.* The development of existing crisis phone line and drop-in center services, or the establishment of new ones where they are absent, is necessary for providing immediate crisis intervention and support, as is referral to available area services for ongoing treatment.

4. *Triage and Assessment.* For both immediate and long-term treatment, it is necessary to prioritize the severity of need and appropriate available treatment

resources. It is also necessary to identify those who need more extensive follow-up services in the future. During this time, an assessment is made of currently available mental health services in the area, with suggestions for developing essential components and networking with outside organizations and resources to support this development.

5. *Stress Management Training for Workers.* Self-help skills are needed to help workers manage the anticipated stress of this work and reduce burnout potential. Direct contact with relief workers cooperating on the project confirms that burnout is not only a high possibility; it is, unfortunately, an inevitable occupational hazard for many who continue to do this relief work. There is obvious need for effective mechanisms to assist with burnout recovery as well as prevention.

6. *Counselor/Trainer Support Groups.* Counselor/trainer support groups are needed for ongoing support in managing stress, peer consultation, and to help develop a cohesive pool of mentors in the region. Laying the groundwork for local professionals to eventually take on primary responsibility for providing these services, training, and supervision of others is emphasized.

7. *Community Support, Advocacy, and Intervention for Victims.* The community needs to be mobilized to assist with nurturing community acceptance and support for victims, and to avoid retraumatizing experiences. An orientation to the culture and predominant religions of the region is provided to project trainers to ensure sensitivity in applying training within this context. Teams work with community and spiritual leaders to encourage and aid them in taking an active role in developing community support for victims, particularly of rape and sexual abuse—some who may have given birth as a result—to reduce the social isolation and shunning that often occurs. Representatives of like cultural and religious traditions from other regions are enlisted to cooperate in meeting with local counterparts and offer assistance in sensitizing the general population to the need for acceptance, support, and reassurance of victims. In general, it is essential that the indigenous cultural and religious institutions that hold the society together are enlisted wherever possible to ensure long-term success in healing trauma.

One of the most under-reported and lamentable dynamics of trauma where rape, sexual abuse, and torture occur is the revictimization of individuals who are rejected, accused, and alienated by their family members and/or community. Shame and fear of such unfair oppression by those already victimized causes many to deny their trauma and refuse treatment. The added presence of children born from rape who are themselves rejected, oppressed, or even punished by their society only further carries and imbeds victimization into the next generation.

8. *Public Education.* There are many benefits to providing general education to the lay public relative to psychological health, common symptoms of trauma, and available services. Local resources, such as media outlets, educational institutions, hospitals, and religious organizations are utilized to disseminate this information.

9. *Mediation and Dispute Resolution.* As there is often some degree of increased domestic and community conflict in regions victimized, invariably workers may encounter such situations in their work. The mediation and dispute resolution component provides basic skills and helpful guidelines for coping and assisting with conflicts arising within the community being served. An extensive list of ICCR alumni is often utilized as a resource to draw on for trainers in this area.

10. *Training Resource Library.* It is essential to establish and maintain a growing on-site and Internet-based archive of video and audio programs, taped training sessions, and written manuals and program materials, for the purposes of continuing education, review, and utilization by local trainers conducting future sessions.

11. *Ongoing Consultation and Team Support.* Ongoing consultation and team support can be provided by training-team members and by establishing an international network of cooperating organizations. These organizations can help local workers and trainers in the region via e-mail, other Internet-based communications, fax, and telephone. All trainers agree to be available for ongoing consultation between and after training sessions. Following initial training visits, brief refresher courses are built into subsequent sessions to help maintain and advance the skills of previous trainees. For example, a core group of higher-skilled professionals from throughout the Balkans has been identified to receive more in-depth instruction to promote a permanent local pool of mentors who can carry on training at the local level. An added benefit of such a regional mentor pool is to build regular contact and encourage cooperation and mutual support among professionals and relief organizations across borders in healing their respective societies. As one outcome of this emphasis, there is a current effort by professionals involved in the CTR project to establish a regionwide Balkan psychological association.

A core concept in treating trauma at the societal level is a transfer of skills to both indigenous service providers and the general population as a means of giving the society the means to heal itself. A comparison can be made here with the manner in which telephone crisis intervention has been taught to paraprofessionals, and in which cardiopulmonary resuscitation, emergency first aid, and stress management have been taught to the general public in the United States.

The CTR model offers one example of an integrated approach to promote the psychological healing of a society. Further research and development are required to construct and use more models like this to treat large population trauma. We must meet this challenge if we are to assist immediate suffering and prevent future generations from inheriting trauma and the archetypal role of victim as part of their ethos.

REFERENCES

Olweean, S., & Friedman, S. (1997). Sharing tools for personal/global harmony. *Journal of Humanistic Psychology, 37*(1), 64–70.

Shapiro, F. (1989). Efficacy of the eye movement desensitization procedure in the treatment of traumatic memories. *Journal of Traumatic Stress, 2,* 199–223.

United Nations Security Council. (1999, June 9). *Report of the Inter-Agency Needs Assessment Mission dispatched by the Secretary-General of the United Nations to the Federal Republic of Yugoslavia.* Retrieved (June 2000) from: http://www.reliefweb.int/files/rwdomino.nsf/.

23

Poisoned Dissociative Containers: Dissociative Defenses in Female Victims of War Rape

James D. Pappas

The impact of rape on civilian women in the hostile climate of war is not only evident in wartime, but in peacetime politics as well. This political reality has alienated, decentralized, and marginalized women's access to power, equality, and gender expression. The sexual hostility toward women, specifically in wartime, may represent what Hayden (2000) refers to as a "polluted body" and what deMause (1998) calls a "poison container." DeMause uses this term to refer to the sexual subjugation of children by adults in history, specifically as "receptacles into which adults project disowned parts of their psyches, so they can control these feelings in another body without danger to themselves" (p. 217).

DeMause's metaphor is appropriate, as it represents female victims of rape as "poison containers" or receptacles in a gender-based hegemonic relationship and calls attention to how an oppressive militant consciousness has dominated women during wartime. According to Olujic (1998), "wartime transforms individual bodies into social bodies as seen, for example, in genocidal rapes or ethnic cleansing, which are thought to purify the bloodlines" (p. 31). Copelon (1995) argues that Bosnian soldiers used rape as a means of ethnic cleansing, not only to delimit procreation within an ethnic community, but also as a tool to intimidate combatants. This suggests that rape is used as a war tactic (Rojnik, Andolsek, & Obersnel, 1995) to demoralize (Swiss & Giller, 1993). This is evident in the estimated 20,000 to 60,000 women who were raped in Bosnia in 1992 (Jensen, 1998).

Furthermore, Shanks, Ford, Schull, and de Jong (2001) report that among the consequences of rape during the 1994 genocide in Rwanda were the births of 5,000 babies. This was followed by their abandonment and infanticide, as these children represented terrible memories in the form of "poison containers." Chelala (1998) indicates that in Algeria, many of the 1,600 women (aged 13–20) who were raped by members of the Armed Islamic Group became pregnant, which alienated these women from mainstream Algerian society. In preserving traditional practices, female victims of war rape are now allowed by the Algerian Islamic Supreme Council to have abortions in order to be accepted as respectable members of their society (Chelala, 1998).

In view of these notions, I concur with deMause (2000), who suggests that war and its accompanying violence are psychogenic in origin and represent regressive acts by a nation for the purpose of self-purification. Nikolic (1999) further adds that such nationalism and militarism have no proper place in any moral and ethical democratic society, as they leave women extremely susceptible to domination and trauma in times of peace and war. For Gordon (2000), the high incidence of rape among Kosovar Albanian women by Serbian forces, as well as of women and girls by Russian soldiers in Chechnya, suggests that the crime of rape during war may be marginalized under the Geneva Conventions. Accordingly, soldiers receive minimal punitive measures, which inadvertently legitimates the practice of rape (Valentich, 1994). Not only does this social arrangement expose the androcentric dominance prevalent in wartime, but it also constrains the victims of rape to function as "dissociative containers," as will be explained below.

DISSOCIATION AS A WEAPON AGAINST RAPE

As an extension of the notion of deMause's "poison container," the term *dissociative container* describes the inner-contained reality of experiences of a female victim during wartime rape as disowned, fragmented, and compartmentalized. In other words, during rape, a victim may suspend and withdraw from external reality by becoming preoccupied and contained by an inner fabricated reality to the extent that she no longer owns—or rather, disowns and denies—the traumatic experience. She may withdraw as a means to safety, protection, or integrity, and to avoid conscious awareness and responsibility.

Moreover, she may feel helpless and detached, in that her freedom is capitulated and assimilated by the traumatic experience in the form of a dissociative container, which may remain implicit, thereby dividing consciousness. In other words, victims who become so absorbed in the traumatic experience may "lose touch with their present surroundings [and] are able to dissociate memories and feelings, as well as memories from bodily sensations" (Maldonado & Spiegel, 1998, p. 58), leaving them disconnected from their bodies (Marmar, Weiss, & Metzler, 1998). When this occurs, the victim is using her dissociative ability to deflect trauma, which causes a failure in cognitive-affect integration and a diminished psychoemotional awareness.

These conditions have also been observed in post-traumatic stress disorder (PTSD) in such symptoms as "diminished cognitive functioning" and "emotional numbing" (Carlson, Armstrong, Loewenstein, & Roth, 1998, p. 221). According to van der Kolk (1996a), sensations experienced in peritrauma may be retrieved as emotional states, somatic sensations, or perceptions such as feelings of detachment, numbness, or flashbacks, all of which are common in PTSD (Herman, 1997). Van der Hart, van der Kolk, and Boon (1998) suggest that symptoms of dissociation resemble PTSD because they "consist of expression of the dissociated traumatic memory, such as reexperiencing the event in the form of intrusive recollections, nightmares, and flashbacks and concomitant emotional constriction (numbing, detachment, and feelings of isolation)" (p. 255).

Farley and Keaney (1997) concur that dissociative experiences from exposure to trauma are similar to symptoms of PTSD. The connection between dissociation and PTSD is that traumatic defense is accompanied by feelings of "horror, intense fear, and helplessness [and] symptoms include reexperiencing of the trauma in various forms, efforts to avoid stimuli which are similar to the trauma, a general numbing of responsiveness, and symptoms of physiologic hyperarousal" (p. 34). Pope and Brown (1996) suggest that "frequently, a trauma survivor experiences both hyperamnesia and posttraumatic amnesia as the individual cycles in and out of the numbing and intrusive phases of the posttraumatic response pattern" (p. 55). Such notions are consistent with the findings that traumatic events disrupt normal information processing of memory, and that there is a posttraumatic adjustment in the integration of emotions and memories (Brown, Scheflin, & Hammond, 1998).

However, temporarily suspending the direct experience of the external world, with an inner attentional involvement impervious to the traumatic event, may lead to distortions in identity, memory, and consciousness (Maldonado & Spiegel, 1998; Putnam & Carlson, 1998; Vermetten, Bremner, & Spiegel, 1998). In addition, the traumatic experience may narrow the field of consciousness to the point where somatosensory information may be registered and embedded in memory as body memory (Herman, 1995). Pierre Janet (1965) hypothesized that, in trauma, the psyche lacks sufficient strength to integrate the overwhelming nature of extremely intense emotions and memories. This suggests that there is a diminished ability to cohesively process and synthesize information, leading to a failure to cope in such an intense negative environment (Janet, 1965; Nemiah, 1998; Nijenhuis & Van der Hart, 1999; Van der Hart & Horst, 1989).

For protection, then, the victim may dissociate through experiencing an overall numbing sensation or a lack of pain perception, enabling her to detach from the abusive situation and escape to a bodily experience—a freezing response. This freezing or numbing response may lead to an insensibility to conscious sensations of emotional and physical pain, which suggests a loss of normal feelings due to the embodiment of trauma (Nijenhuis, Spinhoven, Van Dyck, Van der Hart, & Vanderlinden, 1998; Nijenhuis & Van der Hart, 1999; Nijenhuis, Vanderlinden, & Spinhoven, 1998). In such cases, numbing leads to the experience of depersonalization, such as feelings of estrangement or alienation, which may be accompanied by a somatic paralysis, such as difficulties moving limbs (Nijenhuis & Van der Hart, 1999). Barnes (1996) writes that "numbing serves as a protection from feeling too much, from being overwhelmed during the stress" (p. 412).

Nijenhuis, Vanderlinden, and Spinhoven (1998) suggest that trauma-induced dissociation resembles an animal defense response in a predacious environment. In physically threatening situations involving traumatic rape, the sexual predation triggers predatory responses such as fear and survival reactions. Levine (1990–1991) states that there are instinctive defensive responses in "posttraumatic and other panic dissociative reactions [that] show striking similarities to the behaviours and physiology of prey animals when they perceive themselves to be trapped by predators" (p. 18). In other words, these numbing responses, when compared with those of animals facing life-threatening events, suggest that responses to overwhelming experiences are survival mechanisms. Vermetten, Bremner, and Spiegel (1998) argue that this could be related to the "freezing response of animals confronted with a predator or other life-endangering threat or could be related to other primitive coping styles against fearful situations" (p. 119).

The claim here is that pathological symptoms of dissociation may develop as a consequence of traumatic rape because trauma is a trigger that causes a discontinuity between mind and body—a fragmentation between cognizant reality and mind-body awareness or between conscious and unconscious systems (Frankel, 1998; Kihlstrom & Hoyt, 1990; Maldonado & Spiegel, 1998; van der Kolk, 1996b; Waites, 1998). Thus, during traumatic rape, the mind-body splits into parallel experiences, disconnecting the victim from the external world and transforming her into a dissociative container.

CONCLUSION

This chapter discussed how sexual hostility during wartime rape turns its victims into poisoned containers with dissociative affects. Exploited, alienated, and dissociated from their personhood, female victims of wartime rape are assimilated to the demands of a combatant's predatoric impulses. This militant androcentric authority has become a convenient cultural edifice that predominates during wartime and, as such, has constrained, marginalized, and oppressed female freedom, leaving women feeling poisoned, numbed, detached, and estranged. More specifically, liberty and the power of will are reduced and dissolved for the purposes of a predator's exploitive needs, which transforms the victim of wartime rape into a "poisoned dissociative container."

The ideology and practice of wartime rape are thereby revealed in the subjugation and fragmentation suffered by thousands of civilian victims of rape. It is evident that wartime rape is an unethical acculturated practice that undermines a female's freedom of will and reduces her to the product of militant coercion. For the victim of wartime rape, what is human becomes dissolved into a dissociative container, poisoned by the immoral consciousness that concerns itself with alienating humanity from itself.

In light of these considerations, I believe that treatment interventions (psychoanalytic, cognitive-behavioral, and humanistic) would significantly benefit by reintegrating fragmented cognitions and affects within a victim's cultural context (worldview, acculturation, traditions, norms, and practices). This means synthesizing Eurocentric positivist practice with reformative pedagogical approaches (liberation-, gender-, or culturally sensitive therapies), which exposes acculturated attitudes in relation to prevailing sociocultural systems. In other words, a culturally sensitive approach would guide victims to phenomenologically acknowledge their traumatic experiences in relation to their ethnic identity and sociocultural traditions, as dissociative behaviors also represent trauma through ethnic and cultural traditions, themes, and metaphors. This is important to the consciousness-raising process in therapy, given that remembering a traumatic memory can be intensified from the way we phenomenologically and culturally understand ourselves and interact with others in our culture.

Thus, such a culturally sensitive approach would potentiate cathartic effects through recognizing how such narratives are continually constructed and through understanding and reorganizing of the embodiment of trauma within a cultural and political context. Endorsing such a practice leads to cultural integration and unification and not to fragmentation and differentiation between a victim and her cultural identity and culture. Most importantly, the implementation of such a therapeutic modality develops into a personalized and shared experience connecting a victim to her ethnic community and, as such, attenuates the poisoned dissociation between society and being.

REFERENCES

Barnes, M. (1996). *The healing path with children: An exploration for parents and professionals.* Kingston, NY: Viktoria, Fermoyle & Berrigan.

Brown, D., Scheflin, A., & Hammond, D. (1998). *Memory, trauma treatment, and the law.* New York: W.W. Norton.

Carlson, E., Armstrong, J., Loewenstein, R., & Roth, D. (1998). Relationships between traumatic experiences and symptoms of posttraumatic stress, dissociation, and amnesia. In D. Bremner & C. Marmar (Eds.), *Trauma, memory, and dissociation* (pp. 205–227). Washington, DC: American Psychiatric Press.

Chelala, C. (1998). Algerian abortion controversy highlights rape of war victims. *The Lancet, 351,* 1413.

Copelon, R. (1995). Gendered war crimes: Reconceptualizing rape in time of war. In J. Peters & A. Wolper (Eds.), *Women's rights, human rights: International feminist perspectives* (pp. 197–214). New York: Routledge.

deMause, L. (1998). The history of child abuse. *Journal of Psychohistory, 25,* 216–236.

deMause, L. (2000). War as righteous rape and purification. *Journal of Psychohistory, 27,* 356–445.

Farley, M., & Keaney, J. (1997). Physical symptoms, somatization, and dissociation in women survivors of childhood sexual assault. *Women and Health, 25,* 33–45.

Frankel, J. (1998). Ferenczi's trauma theory. *American Journal of Psychoanalysis, 58,* 41–60.

Gordon, N. (2000, July/August). Sanctioned rape. *The Humanist, 60,* 3.

Hayden, R. M. (2000). Rape and rape avoidance in ethno-national conflicts: Sexual violence in liminalized states. *American Anthropologist, 102*, 27–41.

Herman, J. (1995). Crime and memory. *Bulletin of the American Academy of Psychiatry and Law, 23*, 5–17.

Herman, J. (1997). *Trauma and recovery.* New York: Basic Books.

Janet, P. (1965). *The major symptoms of hysteria.* New York: Hafner.

Jensen, S. (1998). Mass rape: The war against women in Bosnia-Herzegovina. *Archives of Sexual Behavior, 27*, 315–317.

Kihlstrom, J., & Hoyt, I. (1990). Repression, dissociation, and hypnosis. In J. Singer (Ed.), *Repression and dissociation: Implication for personality, theory, psychopathology, and health* (pp. 181–208). Chicago: University of Chicago Press.

Levine, P. (1990–1991, Autumn/Winter). The body as healer: A revisioning of trauma and anxiety. *Somatics, 18*–27.

Maldonado, J., & Spiegel, D. (1998). Trauma, dissociation, and hypnotizability. In D. Bremner & R. Marmar (Eds.), *Trauma, memory, and dissociation* (pp. 57–106). Washington, DC: American Psychiatric Press.

Marmar, C., Weiss, D., & Metzler, T. (1998). Peritraumatic dissociation and posttraumatic stress disorder. In D. Bremner & R. Marmar (Eds.), *Trauma, memory, and dissociation* (pp. 229–247). Washington: DC: American Psychiatric Press.

Nemiah, J. (1998). Early concepts of trauma, dissociation, and the unconscious: Their history and current implications. In D. Bremner & R. Marmar (Eds.), *Trauma, memory, and dissociation* (pp. 1–26). Washington, DC: American Psychiatric Press.

Nijenhuis, E., Spinhoven, P., Van Dyck, R., Van der Hart, O., & Vanderlinden, J. (1998). Degree of somatoform and psychological dissociation in dissociative disorder is correlated with reported trauma. *Journal of Traumatic Stress, 11*, 711–730.

Nijenhuis, E., & Van der Hart, O. (1999). Forgetting and reexperiencing trauma: From anesthesia to pain. In J. Goodwin & R. Attias (Eds.), *Splintered reflections: Images of the body in trauma* (pp. 39–65). New York: Basic Books.

Nijenhuis, E., Vanderlinden, J., & Spinhoven, P. (1998). Animal defensive reactions as a model for trauma-induced dissociative reactions. *Journal of Traumatic Stress, 11*, 243–260.

Nikolic, V. (1999). Living without democracy and peace: Violence against women in the former Yugoslavia. *Violence Against Women, 5*, 63–80.

Olujic, M. (1998). Embodiment of terror: Gendered violence in peacetime and wartime in Croatia and Bosnia-Herzegovina. *Medical Anthropology Quarterly, 12*, 31–50.

Pope, K., & Brown, L. (1996). *Recovered memories of abuse: Assessment, therapy, forensics.* Washington, DC: American Psychological Association Press.

Putnam, F., & Carlson, E. (1998). Hypnosis, dissociation, and trauma: Myths, metaphors, and mechanisms. In D. Bremner & R. Marmar (Eds.), *Trauma, memory, and dissociation* (pp. 27–55). Washington, DC: American Psychiatric Press.

Rojnik, B., Andolsek, L., & Obersnel, D. (1995). Women in difficult circumstances: War victims and refugees. *International Journal of Gynaecology and Obstetrics, 48*, 311–315.

Shanks, L., Ford, N., Schull, M., & de Jong, K. (2001). Responding to rape. *The Lancet, 357*, 304.

Swiss, G., & Giller, J. (1993). Rape as a crime of war: A medical perspective. *Journal of the American Medical Association, 270*, 612–615.

Valentich, M. (1994). Rape revisited: Sexual violence against women in the former Yugoslavia. *Canadian Journal of Human Sexuality, 3*, 53–64.

Van der Hart, O., & Horst, R. (1989). The dissociation theory of Pierre Janet. *Journal of Traumatic Stress, 2*, 397–412.

Van der Hart, O., van der Kolk, B., & Boon, S. (1998). Treatment of dissociative disorders. In D. Bremner & R. Marmar (Eds.), *Trauma, memory, and dissociation* (pp. 253–283). Washington, DC: American Psychiatric Press.

van der Kolk, B. (1996a). The complexity of adaptation to trauma: Self-regulation, stimulus discrimination, and characterological development. In B. van der Kolk, A. McFarlane, & L. Weisaeith (Eds.), *Traumatic stress: The effects of overwhelming experience on mind, body, and society* (pp. 182–213). New York: London Guilford Press.

van der Kolk, B. (1996b). Dissociation and information processing in posttraumatic stress disorder. In B. van der Kolk, A. McFarlane, & L. Weisaeith (Eds.), *Traumatic stress: The effects of overwhelming experience on mind, body, and society* (pp. 302–327). New York: London Guilford Press.

Vermetten, E., Bremner, J., & Spiegel, D. (1998). Dissociation and hypnotizability: A conceptual and methodological perspective on two distinct concepts. In D. Bremner & R. Marmar (Eds.), *Trauma, memory, and dissociation* (pp. 107–159). Washington, DC: American Psychiatric Press.

Waites, E. (1998). *Trauma and survival: Post-traumatic and dissociative disorders in women.* New York: W.W. Norton.

24

Challenges and Opportunities for Southeast Asian Refugee Adolescents

Roben A. Marvit

Southeast Asian refugees have received very little attention in spite of their increasing numbers over the past 2 decades. These victims of persecution have experienced profound trauma and yet often appear to be coping well in multicultural societies (Pipher, 2002). Most research has centered on the adult experience with only scant attention to the experience of refugee children (Coll & Magnuson, 1997). Children develop coping skills in learning how to deal with a variety of challenging situations as they grow up, but there is very little known about the coping strategies of refugee youth. There are many similarities and differences between the challenges facing the Southeast Asian refugee adolescent and those that face other minority groups such as the urban African American adolescent. This chapter focuses on the diverse influences that may account for the adaptation patterns of refugee youth. By examining the risks, the protective factors, and the adaptive responses of diverse minority groups, a contextual model of resilience emerges.

There are several forces at work that place the Southeast Asian adolescent refugee at risk of maladaptation. Southeast Asian adolescents must cope with the stresses of migration and the losses that they experience in that process. They also carry memories of wartime trauma. The flight experience of the refugee usually entails the trauma of being victim to or witnessing cruelty and violence. Besides the residual effects of traumatic experiences, refugee children must adapt to cultural and language differences within an environment of prejudice and discrimination. This is complicated by the fact that Southeast Asian refugees often serve as a reminder of U.S. involvement in the unpopular Vietnam War.

Many refugee families arrive penniless and rely solely on public assistance. Contributing to the acute and chronic family disruption is the generational schism that occurs in refugee families due to the more rapid rate of acculturation for children than for adults (Gay, 1978; Kinzie, 1986). Cultural discrepancies and expectations often contribute to the adolescents' overreliance on peers, placing them at risk for gang involvement. Finally, there are gender differences in the types of challenge facing these adolescents. For example, particular efforts are required for adolescent girls in this group, who must seek a rounded identity in spite of profound cultural conflicts (Markstrom-Adams & Spencer, 1994).

A recent model emerging from minority research looks at the dynamic interaction of the forces at work in the adaptation of African American youth and provides a useful framework for the examination of the resilient patterns of other minority groups such as Southeast Asian refugee adolescents. Spencer and colleagues (Connell, Spencer, & Aber, 1994; Spencer, Cunningham, & Swanson, 1995; Spencer, & Dornbush, 1990) apply an interactive systems perspective in their examination of the social, environmental, and cultural differences experienced by minority youth. They base their model on evidence that suggests that ethnic minority adolescents use new coping strategies in the process of identity development. These researchers propose an "ecocultural character" model of development. They consider political, cultural, economic, and social forces to interact in complex ways with such developmental concerns of adolescence as identity and self-image, increased autonomy, relations with peers, school achievement, and career goals (Spencer & Dornbush, 1990). This life-span model recognizes the complex interactions of the political, economic, and social forces that interact with the developmental needs of minority adolescents and the dynamic sets of relationships and pathways that occur continuously across the life course, comprising a developmental "ecocultural character."

Resilience is often understood as the ability of some children to be competent and "well-adjusted" despite being in an "at-risk" situation. An *at-risk situation* means living in stressful, chaotic environments and/or generally experiencing some form of adversity, trauma, or deprivation. In spite of their risk status, successful coping has been noted in refugee youth who have experienced trauma and stress. A study by Sack, Angell, Kinzie, & Rath (1986) revealed that neither trauma nor the stress of migration seem to compromise school performance for refugee youth. The Cambodian adolescents who were exposed to Pol Pot's persecutions in Sack and colleagues' study were found to be comparable in academic performance, school absences, and disciplinary incidents to those refugees who were not directly exposed to the persecutions. However, as we will see, the Pol Pot survivors suffered other psychological sequaelae as a result of their wartime experiences. Rutter and colleagues (1974) also report resilience in the face of the stresses of migration. In their study immigrant children demonstrated very little behavioral disturbance despite the stresses of migration.

Jablensky et al. (1994) suggest that the resilient capacity of refugee youth can be explained by a number of cultural, social, and political factors that serve a protective function. Among these various factors are the extended family structure; the visibility of human rights organizations; the continuation of cultural traditions, beliefs and customs; and the ability of individuals and groups to frame their status and problems in terms that transcend the immediate situation and give it meaning (e.g., ethnic identity, cultural history).

Several authors point out that ethnocultural and religious traditions have a significant influence on the subjective experience and psychological appraisal of stressful events (Boehnlein, 1987; Westermeyer, 1987). Bruner (1990) has shown that the significance, interpretation, and metaphors that are attached to specific events are culturally determined. Indeed, language itself will determine how events are characterized and how such characterizations are communicated within each ethno-cultural setting.

It is not known what specific culture-bound belief systems provide a resource for coping for the Southeast Asian refugee. An alternative framework is necessary in order to fully understand the experience of traumatic events for the Southeast Asian refugee who holds, for example, the Buddhist belief of suffering as an inescapable part of life and the belief that "all worry about the self is vain"; that the self is "like a mirage, and all the tribulations that touch it will pass away ... vanish like a nightmare when the sleeper awakes" (Stryck, 1968, p. 64).

Because Southeast Asian refugees represent a broad and multifaceted group, the following discussion will be limited to youth who were part of the "second wave" of refugees arriving in the United States during the early 1980s. This group immigrated in order to reunite with their families who had left earlier. The discussion is arranged chronologically in order to address the stresses of premigration and migration (including loss of family and familiar surroundings) as they differ from postmigration stresses associated with culture change (economic standing, language, group subordination).

Trauma and stress begin at premigration and continue during migration. The postmigration challenges fall within the domains of acculturation, family issues, identity development, minority status, peer influences, poverty, and education. The experiences and conditions within each of these domains are discussed as they interact with political, cultural, economic, and social forces.

PREMIGRATION AND MIGRATION CHALLENGES

The traumatic and stressful events that lead up to a refugee's arrival are drastic. Refugees often have little time for preparation as they leave their home. They are in a desperate plight, living moment to moment in despair, fighting poverty, pestilence, and disease. They often carry very little with them except their fragile links to their extended family, their belief systems, and their values.

The effects of trauma and the stresses of migration are major psychological factors for refugees. The traumas that many refugees encounter include exposure to war-related violence, sexual assault, torture, incarceration, genocide, and the threat of personal injury and annihilation. The physical and psychological trauma suffered by many refugees contributes strongly to the appearance of psychopathology in this population (Friedman & Jaranson, 1994). Even considering the difficulties of a cross-cultural diagnosis, a higher than expected rate of depression, anxiety, and post-traumatic stress disorder (PTSD) is found among refugee populations (Orley, 1994). Trauma is only one aspect of the complex experiences of refugees. Besides life-endangering situations, the dislocation created by leaving one's country under uncertain conditions can also have a great impact (Espin, 1992), including serious problems in physical health and untreated chronic illness (Orley, 1994).

Refugee trauma and stress have a multifold impact on children. Children and adolescents are affected directly and indirectly by the trauma and stresses of migration. Krupinski and Burrows (1986) found that the rates of psychiatric disorder among Southeast Asian refugee children, adolescents, and young adults arriving in Australia were twice that of Australians of the same age. Beyond direct effects, there are indirect effects of trauma and stress. For example, it is possible that the symbolic or "imprinting" effects of trauma (e.g., witnessing violence being inflicted on family members) is more traumatic to children than suffering injuries themselves is (Jablensky et al., 1994). Additionally, parental mental disorder (resulting from trauma and stress) place children at risk for emotional disturbance (Rutter, 1985). The effects of parental chronic stress of refugee families can be traced to events in premigration when parents begin to anticipate the war's devastation on their way of life and face the threat to the family's safety (Cole, Espin, & Rothblum, 1992). There are the secrecy and tension associated with planning an escape and the need to carefully monitor the family assets. The flight itself is fraught with danger and losses.

Krupinski and Borrows (1986) noted developmental differences in response to escape-related stress. They found that escape-related stress has the least effect on children, intermediate effect on adolescents, and greatest effect on young adults. In adolescent refugees the direct experience of trauma has a greater effect than the experience of nontraumatic stressful situations. In their survey of Cambodian adolescents, Sack, Angell, Kinzie, & Rath (1986) showed that those who survived 4 years of the Pol Pot persecutions were more apt to meet criteria for a psychoactive diagnosis and to have more deviant schoolroom behaviors compared with those leaving Cambodia before these persecutions.

POST-MIGRATION CHALLENGES

Upon arrival, refugees share many of the same challenges that face other minority groups in the United States. Although the experiences of wartime violence are behind them, they face language barriers, overt discrimination, and economic limitations (Lin, Masuda, & Tazuma, 1982). In adolescence, the refugee child reaches a new stage of development in a new country. Like all adolescents, the Southeast Asian adolescent refugee is concerned with an emerging identity, self-image, and increased autonomy. These youth will face the same social, environmental, and cultural forces that effect other minority youth in a new country. However, the impact of the interactions of these forces will be different (Carlin, 1986). The meaning attached to the events will be influenced by this group's unique history and culture. Their flight experience, their history of trauma, and their newcomer status set them apart from other ethnic minorities. Family disruption caused by losses and the effects of trauma and stress on parents adds to the severe generational rift caused by the process of acculturation. Future perceptions, belief systems, and family traditions promote the development of coping strategies unique to this group, such as an unusual ability to endure setbacks and persevere toward long-term goals and to be resourceful in the face of adversity (Johnson, 1995; Marvit, 2000).

ACCULTURATION, FAMILY STRESS, AND PROTECTIVE FEATURES

The refugee family must face a variety of challenges in adapting to a new society. Most Southeast Asian refugee families come from a traditional rural or village setting where the values of interdependence and family lineage are stressed (Keller, 1975). They arrive in a secular, urban environment where they are suddenly forced to make their own decisions and rely on a radically different educational and health care system. Now, family members must venture out of the home on a daily basis to either visit a clinic, shop, or go to school or work. Traditional social patterns often become confused during this period (Stein, 1986). In their home countries, women were responsible for the family and the home. Adult females of refugee families often remain in the home and never learn the new language (Cole et al., 1992). These conditions lead to special challenges for the adolescent.

There seems to be an inevitable intergenerational conflict that accompanies the acculturation process. Generational differences begin with the children's forced school attendance and their quick acquisition of English. In a 5-year study, researchers found that children of Southeast Asian refugees in San Diego, contrary to the fears of antiimmigration groups, quickly embrace English (Rumbaut & Portes, 1997). The adolescent member of the family often serves as the interpreter and as the interface between cultures (Carlin, 1986). This responsibility can be perceived as an onerous or distracting burden for the adolescent who is focusing on his or her own adjustment and issues of identity. The generational rift deepens as parents maintain their cultural expectations in spite of the social norms that draw the refugee youth away (Nidorf, 1985).

Alienation from the family is particularly difficult for girls (Gilligan, 1982). The complex interaction of the demands of acculturation and the adolescent's identity development are particularly challenging for the female refugee. Gender role issues are a major concern for all adolescents, but these issues are complicated for the refugee girl when role expectations clash and become a source of conflict in the family. Most major theories suggest the important role of parents as models in gender-role development (Kagan, 1958; Kohlberg, 1966). However, there may be little continuity between the gender role model provided by the refugee parent and the gender role models seen in Western culture. Most refugees in the United States come from third world cultures in which there is clear separation between men's and women's workday worlds, and in which adolescent girls are expected to assume many of the same responsibilities as the adult females.

While family relationships present serious problems for the adolescent refugee, there are also opportunities provided by the values instilled by Southeast Asian parents. Family values serve as a source of positive coping in the face of the multitude of challenges that face the refugee youth. Case studies document the importance of early correlates of later attitudes. A Vietnamese refugee woman credited her "appraisal process" as well as the "values learned in her younger years" for her ability to withstand the many transitions. She counted her strong commitment and loyalty to family as a strong coping resource (Cole, Espin, & Rothblum, 1992).

In many Asian cultures, the role of the family is central to the survival of the individual. One's sense of wholeness comes from belonging to a family (Kuoch, Miller, & Scully, 1992). Religious beliefs and traditions serve to reinforce the importance of family with age-old customs and rituals that provide meaning and comfort in times of change or distress.

THE IDENTITY TASK, MINORITY STATUS, AND FUTURE PERCEPTIONS

The identity task is particularly complex for Southeast Asian refugee adolescents who question whether they will be foreigners forever. Will he or she ever become an American? Does he or she want to be identified as an American? Would that be a denial of one's real origin, family, and country? What does U.S. society expect from him or her in terms of gratitude and success? Or is he or she supposed to be inconspicuous and unnoticed so as not be a reminder of the unpopular wars in which the United States engaged?

Refugees, like all adolescents, have biological and acquired cognitive abilities that allow them sufficient awareness of the social pressures around them. They share the social needs of fidelity, intimacy, and the need for a sense of a trustworthy world. But the social context in which these developmental needs are met is different. Their minority status places them in a society that does not value and support them. Yet they have a need to feel competent and have a healthy, developing cognitive awareness. Unfortunately, this combination often leads to "turning off" the environment in which they find themselves, and they may become socially maladaptive.

Coles (1986), in his study of how children form political beliefs, stressed the role of social crisis in stimulating a precocious moral development in some children in some settings. Erikson (1989) maintained that identity development must be considered within the context of the historical time and place. In his autobiographical notes, Erikson—himself an immigrant—writes that "migration means cruel survival in identity terms ... for the very cataclysms in which millions perish open up new forms of identity to the survivors" (p. 21).

The identity task for adolescent refugees is complicated by their transition to minority-group status in their host country (Carlin, 1986). Perceptions of group status and identity needs influence the development of coping strategies (Spencer et al., 1995). The coping process can include both effective and ineffective mechanisms. For example, when a young refugee faces family alienation due to transgenerational culture conflict, his or her coping strategies might include turning toward gang membership or, more adaptively, seeking out culturally similar peers for comfort and support. Maladaptive coping can also be transient and contribute to a later resolve to pursue positive behaviors that are more congruent with the values of one's family (Marvit, 2000).

For minority-group adolescents the question of "Who am I?" expands to "What does my minority-group membership mean?" Adolescents have a "self-consciousness" and a strong desire to "fit in" but they are well aware of differences in skin color and speech patterns as well as unchallenged stereotypes. Their growing cognitive skills make them sensitive to subtle expectations and biases that surround group membership. DeVos (1982) defines group membership identity as a belief in a shared origin, common beliefs and values, and a shared sense of survival or "common cause." The development of negative or positive coping strategies is based on their group status perception. Adolescents who conclude that they are failures (and that their group is not as good as the majority) may fulfill their own prophecies. On the other hand, there is evidence that those who demonstrate a cultural identity that is accepting of their own group appear more stress-resistant and have higher achievement outcomes (Spencer, 1988).

Future perceptions and gender issues are additional considerations of group membership that also play a part in the development of coping strategies for minority adolescents (Spencer et al., 1995): "Future oriented perceptions include awareness of the expectations, privileges, restraints, and social responsibilities that accompany that membership" (p. 32). In the identity process adolescents must integrate "selves or identifications" with perceptions of future development (McCandless & Evans, 1973). Gender-role expectations demand a synthesis of multiple identifications for refugee adolescents. Spencer et al. (1995) point out that gender-linked effects of behavioral and physical differences between males and females are exacerbated by ethnicity and racial stereotypes. African American males, for example, are confronted with the dilemma of the expected role of economic provider in the social context of racism, which affects their ability to carry out that expected role. The Southeast Asian refugee female, on the other hand, often faces ethnic barriers and classroom gender discrimination that would place obstacles to the American promise of upward mobility. She may rebel against her family, whose traditional values stand in the way of the social freedom seen for majority adolescent girls.

An additional and unique feature of the Southeast Asian minority group is its function as a reminder of the United States' unpopular war. Government policies reflected discriminatory practices based on this negative association during the first wave of immigration, reflected in the assignment of mental health workers to treat traumatized refugees who usually lacked any background or training in Southeast Asian culture. A hostile environment based on this negative association plays a part in the experiences of refugee adolescents exploring job opportunities in a limited marketplace (Westermeyer, 1986).

POVERTY

Most refugees arrive in the United States with little or no money and depend on limited federal assistance. They easily become caught in the cycle of poverty (Friedman & Jaranson, 1994). The psychological stress associated with poverty and unemployment has been found to adversely affect parenting behaviors, increasing the incidence of impaired socioemotional functioning among the youth in these families (McLoyd, 1990). Poverty creates circumstances that place poor and minority youth at a severe disadvantage in their attempts to resist self-destructive behaviors such as teen pregnancy, delinquency, and drug abuse.

Refugees are likely to face the same chronic poverty that is typical in African American families where children grow up in the crowded, hostile atmosphere of inner-city life.[1] For the African American youth, family financial troubles stemming from unemployment or sustained poverty may be experienced as uncontrollable and pervasive. But for the Southeast Asian refugee youth, these circumstances may be perceived as temporary—a new beginning in a new country. As previously mentioned, Erikson maintained that identity development must be considered within the context of historical time and place. For new or recent refugees, the future may appear hopeful with the promise of opportunity in their resettlement country. This optimism may contribute to an ignorance of discriminatory practices and limited opportunities to which minority youths more familiar with our culture may be sensitive and for whom the future appears less hopeful.

PEER INFLUENCES

Cultural discrepancies between generations in a refugee home force the adolescent to rely on peers. Although most adolescents increasingly turn to their peers for support, Spencer and Dornbush (1990) note a particular need for refugee adolescents. Refugee adolescents become aware of the differences among their own expectations, those of their parents, and those of the majority culture. They may begin to distrust their parents as they observe that their parents lack power and competence in the new society (Nidorf, 1985). The language discrepancy further strengthens the peer group, which replaces the parents. "The desire to be accepted, which is compelling among teenagers, is especially strong among refugee adolescents. For them the greatest threat is not the feeling of belonging to two cultures but the feeling of belonging to none" (Lee, 1988, p. 173).

Peer influences can serve as a protective factor providing rewarding experiences and opportunities for social comparisons. While peers provide support to the adolescent they can also become maladaptive with gang membership occurring as a result of complex emotional forces that are part of the refugees' experience. Peer groups may form to oppose majority mores and to provide adaptive social supports that reduce feelings of isolation. Many refugee youth are living apart from their family in foster homes. Gangs act like substitute family in which roles such as "protective older sister," "older brother," and "father" are played out (Messer & Rasmussen, 1986; Nidorf, 1985). There is additional risk for gang membership with the accompanying aggression, violence, and crime for refugees who have themselves been victims of violence.

EDUCATIONAL ISSUES

Minority youth typically achieve lower levels of academic performance than do majority adolescents (Spencer & Dornbush, 1990). However, like Asian American youth in general, Southeast Asian refugees appear to be achieving academic success despite their minority status. Rumbaut (1991) found that Vietnamese and Chinese adolescent refugees in the San Diego metropolitan area had levels of education higher than native-born Anglo students. Models that consider cultural, historical, and political contexts are necessary to understand such discrepancies.

The model put forward by Ogbu (Boykin, 1986; Ogbu, 1986) emphasizes "minority response to perceived hegemony of white middle-class values in the educational system" (Spencer & Dornbush, 1990, p.141). The model differentiates between African Americans and Mexican Americans in the United States and recent immigrants; the former groups are "far more likely to reject characteristic American attitudes and behaviors than [the latter] ... who seek economic and political opportunities in the United States" (p. 141). According to Ogbu, minority opposition to the educational system stems from a lack of trust in the American social structure (1987a, 1987b). The role of a promising perspective is key to the Southeast Asian refugee's educational success.

SUMMARY AND CONCLUSION

Southeast Asian refugee adolescents in the United States represent a vulnerable group at risk for maladaptation. Yet many have become healthy and productive individuals despite their adversity (Coll & Magnuson, 1997). These successes point to the development of positive coping skills as seen by their success in school and demonstrated by the numbers who have become healthy and productive individuals despite adversity. Their resilience bears similarities to evidence of resilience in refugee children who have been exposed to violence, a widely noted fact observed among diverse ethnic groups (Angel, Hjern, & Ingleby, 2001; Chikane, 1986; Krupinski & Burrows, 1986; Sack et al., 1986). Most of these studies link the persistent strength of family bonds and religious values to successful outcome. It also appears that Southeast Asian adolescents benefit from cultural values laid down early in the context of family life. In all cases, family environment is considered to be a mediating factor that strongly shapes the development of minority youth (Spencer & Dornbush, 1990). The Southeast Asian refugee family relies heavily on its belief system and, like the African American family, an extended kin network. The apparent resilience of this group suggests future research on the link between family belief systems and successful coping outcomes.

The neglect of minority-focused research in developmental science reinforces a pattern that omits minority youth from a normal human developmental framework. The dilemma contributes to patterns of simplistic, noncontextual, one-dimensional, and monocultural analysis of human development. There is a need for an alternative model that recognizes that development consists of dynamic sets of complex interactions that occur throughout the life span. More specifically, refugee adolescents are developing coping strategies in the context of diverse political, cultural, economic, and social forces that interact with the developmental needs of identity, self-image, increased autonomy, relations with peers, school achievement, and career goals. What is needed is a greater understanding of the specific coping mechanisms within this context. What are the strategies that interact with the diverse forces to make the difference between those who overcome their difficulties, becoming healthy and productive individuals with unique sets of strengths, and those who fail?

The intent of this chapter has been to broaden the current understanding of adolescent development in its cultural context. A cross-cultural, transactional model of ethnic minority adaptation has been used as a basis for examining the challenges and opportunities for Southeast Asian refugee adolescents and for understanding some of the social, environmental, and cultural forces that might explain the successful adaptations of many of these refugees. Their resilience in the face of multiple adversities underscores the need to view the interaction of the person and the environment within the context of the person's view of life, experience, beliefs, cultural practices, patterns, and traditions. It is hoped that this review will contribute to the development of a model of resilience specific to their experience.

NOTE

1. Statistics drawn from studies of inner-city populations reflect in large measure the experience of poor black youths, who constitute 45 percent of all blacks under the age of 18. However, these data are often uncritically assumed to hold true for all black youths, although the majority (55 percent) of African-American youths are not poor (Spencer & Dornbush, 1990).

REFERENCES

Angel, B., Hjern, A., & Ingleby, D. (2001). Effects of war and organized violence on children: A study of Bosnian refugees in Sweden. *American Journal of Orthopsychiatry, 71,* 4–15.

Boehnlein, J. (1987). Clinical relevance of grief and mourning among Cambodian refugees. *Social Science and Medicine, 25,* 765–772.

Boykin, A. W. (1986). The triple quandary and the schooling of Afro-American children. In U. Neisser (Ed.), *The school achievement of minority children* (pp. 57–92). Hillsdale, NJ: Erlbaum.

Bruner, J. (1990). *Acts of meaning.* Cambridge, MA: Harvard University Press.

Carlin, J. E. (1986). Child and adolescent refugees: Psychiatric assessment and treatment. In C. L. Williams & J. Westermeyer (Eds.), *Refugee mental health in resettlement countries* (pp. 131–139). Washington, DC: Hemisphere.

Chikane, F. (1986). Children in turmoil. In S. Burman & P. Reynolds (Eds.), *Growing up in a divided society* (pp. 333–344). Johannesburg, South Africa: Raven Press.

Cole, E., Espin, O. M., & Rothblum, E. D. (Eds.). (1992). *Refugee women and their mental health: Shattered societies, shattered lives.* Binghamton, NY: Harrington Park Press.

Coles, R. (1986). *The political life of children.* Boston: Houghton Mifflin.

Coll, C. G., & Magnuson, K. (1997). The psychological experience of immigration: A developmental perspective. In A. Booth, A. C. Crouter, & N. Landale (Eds.), *Immigration and the family: Research and policy on U.S. immigrants* (pp. 91–131). Mahwah, NJ: Erlbaum.

Connell, J. P., Spencer, M. B., & Aber, J. L. (1994). Educational risk and resilience in African American youth: Context, self, action, and outcomes in school. *Child Development, 65,* 493–506.

DeVos, G. (1982). Ethnic pluralism: Conflict and accommodation. In G. DeVos & L. Romanucci-Ross (Eds.), *Ethnic Identity: Cultural continuities and change* (pp. 5–41). Palo Alto, CA: Manfield.

Erikson, E. H. (1989). Autobiographic notes on the identity crisis. In G. Holton (Ed.), *The twentieth-century sciences* (pp. 3–32). New York: W.W. Norton.

Espin, O. (1992). Roots uprooted: The psychological impact of historical/political dislocation. In E. Cole, O. M. Espin, & E. D. Rothblum (Eds.), *Refugee women and their mental health: Shattered societies, shattered lives* (pp. 9–20). New York: Haworth Press.

Friedman, M., & Jaranson, J. (1994). The applicability of the posttraumatic stress disorder concept to refugees. In A. J. Marsella, T. Bornemann, S. Ekblad, & J. Orley (Eds.), *Amidst peril and pain* (pp. 207–227). Washington, DC: American Psychological Association.

Gay, G. (1978). Ethnic identity in early adolescence: Some implications for instructional reform. *Educational Leadership, 35,* 649–655.

Gilligan, C. (1982). *In a different voice: Psychological theory and women's development.* Cambridge, MA: Harvard University Press.

Jablensky, A., Marsella, A. J., Ekblad, S., Jansson, B., Levi, L., & Bornemann, T. (1994). Refugee mental health and well-being: Conclusions and recommendations. In A. J. Marsella, T. Bornemann, S. Ekblad, & J. Orley (Eds.), *Amidst peril and pain* (pp. 327–339). Washington, DC: American Psychological Association.

Johnson, A. C. (1995). Resiliency mechanisms in culturally diverse families. *The Family Journal: Counseling and Therapy for Couples and Families, 3,* 316–324.

Kagan, J., (1958). The concept of identification. *Psychological Review, 65,* 296–305.

Keller, R. T. (1975). Role Conflict and Ambiguity: Correlates with Job Satisfaction and Values. *Personnel Psychology, 28,* 57–64.

Kinzie, J. D. (1986). The establishment of mental health outpatient services. In C. L. Williams & J. Westermeyer (Eds.), *Refugee mental health in resettlement countries* (pp. 217–231). Washington, DC: Hemisphere.

Kohlberg, L. (1966). A cognitive-developmental analysis of children's sex-role concepts and attitudes. In E. E. Maccoby (Ed.), *The development of sex differences* (pp. 82–173). Palo Alto, CA: Stanford University Press.

Krupinski, J., & Burrows, G. (1986). *The price of freedom: Young Indochinese refugees in Australia.* New York: Pergamom Press.

Kuoch, T., Miller, R. A., & Scully, M. F. (1992). Healing the wounds of the Mahantdori. In E. Cole, O. M. Espin, & E. D. Rothblum (Eds.), *Refugee women and their mental health: Shattered societies, shattered lives.* New York: Haworth Press.

Lee, E. (1988). Cultural factors in working with Southeast Asian refugee adolescents. *Journal of Adolescence, 11,* 167–179.

Lin, K. M., Masuda, M., & Tazuma, L. (1982). Adaptational problems of Vietnamese refugees: Part III. Case studies in clinic and field: Adaptive and maladaptive. *Psychiatric Journal of the University of Ottawa, 7,* 173–183.

Markstrom-Adams, C., & Spencer, M. B. (1994). A model for identity intervention with minority adolescents. In S. Archer (Ed.), *Interventions for adolescent identity development* (pp. 84–102). Beverly Hills, CA: Sage.

Marvit, R. A. (2000). *A phenomenological analysis of the experience of resilience in female, adolescent refugees.* Unpublished doctoral dissertation, Saybrook Graduate School, San Francisco, California.

McCandless, B. R., & Evans, F. D. (1973). *Children and youth: Psychosocial development.* Detroit: Drydon Press.

McLoyd, V. (1990). The declining fortunes of black children: Psychological distress, parenting, and socioemotional development in the context of economic hardship. *Child Development, 70,* 55–70.

Messer, M. M., & Rasmussen, N. H. (1986). Southeast Asian children in America: The impact of change. *Pediatrics, 78,* 323–329.

Nidorf, J. F. (1985). Mental health and refugee youths: A model for diagnostic training. In T. C. Owen (Ed.), *Southeast Asian mental health: Treatment, prevention, services, training, and research* (pp. 321–427). Washington, DC: National Institute of Mental Health.

Ogbu, J. U. (1986). The consequences of the American caste system. In U. Neisser (Ed.), *The school achievement of minority children: New perspectives* (pp. 19–56). Hillsdale, NJ: Erlbaum.

Ogbu, J. U. (1987a). Social stratification in the United States. In P. Hockings (Ed.), *Dimensions of social life: Essays in honor of David G. Mandelbaum* (pp. 585–597). New York: Mouton de Gruyter.

Ogbu, J. U. (1987b). Variability in minority school performance: A problem in search of an explanation. *Anthropology and Education Quarterly, 18,* 312–334.

Orley, J. (1994). Psychological disorders among refugees: Some clinical and epidemiological considerations. In A. J. Marsella, T. Bornemann, S. Ekblad, & J. Orley (Eds.), *Amidst peril and pain* (pp. 193–206). Washington, DC: American Psychological Association.

Pipher, M. (2002). *The middle of everywhere: The world's refugees come to our town.* New York: Harcourt.

Rumbaut, R. G. (1991). The agony of exile: A study of the migration and adaptation of Indochinese refugee adults and children. In J. L. Athey & F. L. Ahearn (Eds.), *Refugee children: theory, research, and services* (pp. 53–91). Baltimore: Johns Hopkins University Press.

Rumbaut, R. G., & Portes, A. (1997). *Reports of a five-year study of the educational progress of immigrants.* Unpublished manuscript, University of Michigan, Ann Arbor.

Rutter, M. (1985). Resilience in the face of adversity: Protective factors and resistance to psychiatric disorder. *British Journal of Psychiatry, 147,* 598–611.

Rutter, M., Yule, W., Berger, M., Yule, B., Morton, J., & Bagley, C. (1974). Children of West Indian Immigrants: I. Rates of behavioral deviance and psychiatric disorder. *Journal of Child Psychology and Psychiatry, 15,* 241–262.

Sack, W. H., Angell, R. H., Kinzie, J. D., & Rath, B. (1986). The psychiatric effects of massive trauma on Cambodian children: II. The family, the home, and the school. *American Academy of Child Psychiatry, 25,* 377–383.

Spencer, M. B. (1988). Afro-American adolescents: Adaptational processes and socioeconomic diversity in behavioral outcomes. *Journal of Adolescence, 11,* 351–370.

Spencer, M. B., Cunningham, M., & Swanson, D. P. (1995). Identity as coping: Adolescent African-American males' adaptive responses to high-risk environments. In H. C. Blue, H. W. Harris, & E. H. Griffith (Eds.), *Racial and ethnic identity* (pp. 31–52). New York: Routledge.

Spencer, M. B., & Dornbush, S. M. (1990). Challenges in studying minority youth. In S. S. Feldman & G. R. Elliott (Eds.), *At the threshold* (pp. 123–146). Cambridge, MA: Harvard University Press.

Stein, B. N. (1986). The experience of being a refugee: Insights from the research literature. In C. L. Williams & J. Westermeyer (Eds.), *Refugee mental health in resettlement countries* (pp. 1–3). Washington, DC: Hemisphere.

Stryck, L. (1968). *World of the Buddha.* New York: Grove Weidenfeld.

Westermeyer, J. (1986). Indochinese refugees in community and clinic: A report from Asia and the United States. In C. L. Williams & J. Westermeyer (Eds.), *Refugee mental health in resettlement countries* (pp. 113–130). Washington, DC: Hemisphere.

Westermeyer, J. (1987). Clinical considerations in cross-cultural diagnosis. *Hospital and Community Psychiatry, 38,* 160–165.

25

Why War? Fear Is the Mother of Violence

Sheldon Solomon, Jeff Greenberg, and Tom Pyszczynski

Dear Mr. Freud:

The proposal of the League of Nations and its International Institute of Intellectual Co-operation at Paris that I should invite a person, to be chosen by myself, to a frank exchange of views on any problem that I might select affords me a very welcome opportunity of conferring with you upon a question which, as things now are, seems the most insistent of all the problems civilization has to face. This is the problem: Is there any way of delivering mankind from the menace of war? It is common knowledge that, with the advance of modern science, this issue has come to mean a matter of life and death for Civilization as we know it; nevertheless, for all the zeal displayed, every attempt at its solution has ended in a lamentable breakdown.

I believe, moreover, that those whose duty it is to tackle the problem professionally and practically are growing only too aware of their impotence to deal with it, and have now a very lively desire to learn the views of men who, absorbed in the pursuit of science, can see world problems in the perspective distance lends.

Albert Einstein, July 30, 1932 (1960, p. 188)

Why war? This was the question posed by Einstein to Sigmund Freud as the most urgent human concern of the 20th century. In 1932, it was already quite obvious that World War I, the "war to end all wars," had been catastrophically unsuccessful in doing so—as the rest of the century proved. World War II was the centerpiece of human evil, featuring Adolf Hitler's annihilation of over 100 million people through a clever juxtaposition of genocide and commerce. But even that horrific war seemed to teach humankind very little. In the 1990s one-third of the Tutsi population of Rwanda was exterminated in less than 100 days by their Hutu neighbors; in the Serbian-Bosnian conflict, Serbian soldiers in the country formerly known as Yugoslavia gang-raped Muslim women while their colleagues played soccer with the recently decapitated heads of the women's children.

In his reply to Einstein, Freud acknowledged that humanity's fate depended on understanding the lust for violence, not so much to eradicate aggression (which Freud felt was impossible and in many instances undesirable) as to off-set it, by marshaling and directing humankind's instinctive proclivity to love.

WHY WAR?

Our understanding of humankind's inhumanity is informed by the late cultural anthropologist Ernest Becker. In books such as *The Birth and Death of Meaning* (1962/1971), *The Denial of Death* (1973), and *Escape from Evil* (1975), he attempted to integrate ideas from the sciences, social sciences, and humanities to develop a conception of human behavior that fosters constructive individual and social change. For Becker, an appreciation of the human condition requires considering how human beings are similar to, and different from, other forms of life. Following Darwin, Becker asserted that human beings share with all creatures a biological inclination toward self-preservation. The main difference lay in a special kind of intelligence: an ability to think abstractly and symbolically that, in turn, enables humans to imagine things that do not exist and to transform these dreams into reality. Other creatures must change to fit the world, while humans can change the world to fit themselves.

Becker, influenced by Søren Kierkegaard, asserted that one consequence of abstract and linguistic thinking is a highly evolved self-awareness. For Kierkegaard, self-awareness necessarily engenders awe and terror: awe because it's great to be alive and to know it (in Otto Rank's [1936/1978] words, to be "the temporary representative of the cosmic primal force" [p. 4]), and terror because the very same awareness brings knowledge of death—that we are essentially breathing pieces of defecating and copulating meat; momentary aggregations of blood, guts, and organs not fundamentally superior to or more enduring than ferrets. James Joyce (1914/1966) comes to very similar conclusions in his classic novel *Ulysses:*

Integral parts of the human whole: the necessity of destruction to procure alimentary sustenance: the painful character of the ultimate functions of separate existence, the agonies of birth and death: the monotonous menstruation of simian and (particularly) human females extending from the age of puberty to the menopause: inevitable accidents at sea, in mines and factories: certain very painful maladies and their resultant surgical operations, innate lunacy and congenital criminality, decimating epidemics: catastrophic cataclysms which make terror the basis of human mentality. (p. 697)

Following Rank, Becker (1973, 1975) contended that humans would be riddled with abject terror if not for culture, and particularly mass beliefs about reality that serve to ameliorate the anxiety of death. Cultures serve to reduce anxiety by providing their constituents with: (a) an account of the origin of the universe (e.g., God created the earth in 6 days [Judeo-Christian tradition]; God created the earth out of a giant drop of milk [Fulani in Mali]; the earth was originally inhabited by aliens from space [Scientology]) that suggests that we live in a meaningful and orderly world; (b) a blueprint for daily conduct through the creation of social roles with associated values and standards, the satisfaction of which provide self-esteem—the belief that one is a valuable member of a meaningful universe; and (c) a sense of immortality for those who meet culturally constructed standards of value, either symbolically, through performing great deeds, amassing huge fortunes, erecting enduring monuments, identifying with the group or nation, and/or having children to ensure biological succession; or literally, by entering the afterlife that is a common feature to almost every religion on the planet, past and present.

From this perspective, which we have labeled *terror management theory*, human beings purchase psychological equanimity by collectively deluding themselves about the fragility of existence and the inevitability of its termination. This analysis, though a bit unsettling, helps us understand humanity's appalling violence by providing insights into three propensities that contribute to war.

Three Human Propensities That Contribute to War

The ideological menace of those who are different engenders a negative reaction to different others. Terror management offers a simple explanation for this: People within a culture embrace a particular conception of reality as a means of death denial, faith in which is ultimately forged and sustained by social consensus. Therefore, the mere existence of differing beliefs threatens the confidence with which people subscribe to their own culture's conception. Shaken faith in security and death transcendence threatens to unleash the potentially overwhelming terror that cultural worldviews are designed to control. Thus, different others pose a deep existential threat that necessitates a host of defenses to bolster faith in the prevailing worldview.

The second propensity is to use others as scapegoats, directing fears and hostilities onto such groups as if they were primary sources of evil. Because death prevails despite our most earnest efforts to avoid it, Becker (1973, 1975) argued that there will always be some residual anxiety, in his words, "a panic rumbling beneath" that is repressed and projected onto a group either outside or inside the culture that becomes the all-encompassing repository of evil, the eradication of which would make life on earth like it is in heaven. Thus, the inconsolable fear of death is posited to be the fundamental basis of the psychological necessity of scapegoats.

The third proclivity is for people to cling tenaciously to identities of self and their other and the history of conflict between them. The vast majority of serious conflicts around the globe have a long, long history, replete with oft-told tales of bloodbaths and other atrocities perpetrated by each side against the other. We recently interviewed a bright, well-educated Greek Cypriot woman about Greek-Turkish relations. She acknowledged that she might meet a Turkish person some time and find that person likeable but asserted vehemently that she would not have the right to become friends with that person because that would be a fundamental betrayal of her Greek identity.

The only simple way for current members of such groups to transcend their deep-seated bitterness and hatred, and progress toward peace, is to let go of cultural identifications and see each other first as simply fellow humans. Terror management theory offers one explanation for why this is not likely to happen any time soon. Seeing others, and more importantly ourselves, as simply members of this species reduces everyone to the status of nameless animals destined only to death and decay. And so, barring new psychological developments, it is not likely that people will relinquish their cultural identifications and link to bloody cultural heritages. By seeing ourselves as Greeks, Germans, Iraqis, Americans, Swedes, or Hopi, we remain steeped in death-denying conceptions of ourselves and the world.

Core Reactions to Different Others

Terror management theory helps to make sense of history and ongoing events by viewing reactions to others in light of the three propensities toward war. From this perspective, groups respond to those who are different in ways that serve their own psychological equanimity. The following three modes of response seem to be prevalent in this regard.

Derogation

Our initial reaction to alternative conceptions of reality is to disparage those who hold them. The Fulani in Mali believe that God created the earth out of a giant drop of milk, which if true, does not bode well for the account proffered in Genesis. Yet the average Christian, by noting that the Fulanis are subhuman, tent-dwelling African savages who worship piles of sticks and mud and have no cell phones, remains unfazed by the challenge otherwise posed by an alternative to Genesis. There is no factual evidence for preferring either creation account: Both are equally credible, equally functional as death-denying illusions, and neither is likely to be literally true.

Assimilation

Groups often try to convince others to dispense with their misbegotten cultural worldviews and adopt the "right" one. Historically, this has been particularly true of more technologically advanced Western cultures, and Christian missionary activity is the most obvious example: For centuries missionaries were proselytizing around the world in an effort to eradicate indigenous cultures by forcing people to abandon functional cultural traditions and adopt Christian beliefs. Besides the obvious material advantages of such activities, there is the great psychological benefit of adding new believers. Because all cultural worldviews are fragile fictions (none of them is absolutely true), the most powerful means of sustaining faith is through social consensus: The more people who believe in a particular conception of reality, the more "true" it must be.

Annihilation

There will always be some recalcitrant peoples who stubbornly cling to their indigenous cultural beliefs despite all. From prehistoric times to the moment at hand, it seems that our species has engaged in an ongoing succession of wars, ethnic cleansings, and brutal subjugation of "inferiors" because humans are fundamentally unable to tolerate those who do not share a particular socially constructed death-denying illusion.

From this perspective, wars are the price we pay for maintaining psychological equanimity with a delusion. This is not to suggest that wars have no pragmatic basis or that political and/or (more likely) economic contentions are never responsible for generating armed conflict. However, following Becker, we do assert that wars would occur even in the absence of rational political and economic disputes, because they are currently a psychological necessity. More importantly, we argue that whatever the initial impetus for intergroup conflict, the psychological function of cultural identifications plays a substantial role in both the escalation and perpetuation of such conflicts. Thus far in human history then, wars have served as a primary means of proving the heroic dominance of one culture over another, fostering a sense of immortality and, in so doing, momentarily quelling the "panic rumbling beneath." Until very recently, when cultures were widely dispersed and technology was relatively primitive, wars did not impact the long-term well-being of the human race. Today however, given the large numbers of people and peoples, combined with increasingly lethal technologies, the human race is clearly at risk for self-induced extinction. Einstein's question to Freud in 1932 thus looms even larger today:

Is there any way of delivering mankind from the menace of war? It is common knowledge that, with the advance of modern science, this issue has come to mean a matter of life and death for Civilization as we know it.

TERROR MANAGEMENT THEORY: IS IT TRUE?

We have argued, in light of Becker, that human beings construct culture in large measure to deny death through the belief that one is a valuable member of a meaningful universe; and the existence of others with different cultural worldviews is simultaneously threatening (an alternative conception of reality undermines faith in one's own death-denying illusion) and necessary (residual repressed anxiety must be projected onto an "inferior"). This inevitably results in efforts to derogate, assimilate, and annihilate those who do not share our beliefs. But to what extent are these claims true?

Becker, Freud, Rank, and other existential psychodynamic thinkers have traditionally been dismissed by "serious" academics because their ideas have never been proven empirically. As experimental social psychologists, we were somewhat sympathetic to this stance (although not entirely convinced it is warranted; see, e.g., Greenberg, Solomon, Pyszczynski, & Steinberg, 1988). Consequently, we developed terror management theory (Greenberg, Pyszczynski, & Solomon, 1986; Solomon, Greenberg, & Pyszczynski, 1991) to frame Becker's ideas in the language of social psychological discourse to derive hypotheses that have now been rigorously tested in over 100 published experiments (most recently reviewed in Greenberg, Solomon, & Pyszczynksi, 1997; Pyszczynski, Greenberg, & Solomon, 1999).

Most of these studies have been based on what we refer to as the *mortality salience hypothesis:* If cultural worldviews serve to provide beliefs about the world that assuage death-anxiety, then asking people to ponder their own mortality (*mortality salience*) should increase the need for the protection provided by such beliefs and result in vigorous agreement with and affection for those who share similar beliefs, and equally vigorous hostility and disdain for those who are different. *Worldview defense* refers to the exaggerated evaluations of similar and different others following mortality salience generally observed in these studies.

In a typical study, participants entering the lab are told we are interested in personality traits and are asked to complete some personality assessments. Embedded in several personality scales (e.g., neuroticism scale, social desirability scale) are two open-ended questions to render mortality momentarily salient: *"Please briefly describe the emotions that the thought of your own death arouse in you,"* and *"Jot down, as specifically as you can, what you think will happen to you as you physically die."* Participants in control conditions complete parallel questions about other topics (e.g., eating a meal, watching television, dental pain, social rejection). Subsequently, in what is often portrayed as a completely different experiment, participants are given an opportunity to evaluate others who either share or differ in cultural worldviews and/or dominant cultural values: This constitutes the primary dependent measure (e.g., Arndt, Greenberg, Pyszczynski, & Solomon, 1997; Greenberg, Simon, Porteus, Pyszczynski, & Solomon, 1995; Greenberg, Simon, Pyszczynski, Solomon, & Chatel, 1992; Harmon-Jones, Simon, Greenberg, Pyszczynski, Solomon, & McGregor, 1997; Pyszczynski, Wicklund, Floresku, Gauch, Koch, Solomon, & Greenberg, 1996).

For example, Greenberg et al. (1990) asked Christian participants to rate Christian and Jewish targets (who were portrayed as quite similar except for religious background) after a mortality salience or control induction. Whereas there were no differences in participants' evaluations of the targets in the control condition, a subtle reminder of death in the experimental condition produced increased affection for the fellow Christian target and exaggerated hostility for the Jewish target. In an additional study, Greenberg et al. (1990) exposed American college students to essays supposedly written by an author who either praised or condemned the American way of life following a mortality salience or control induction. Although participants rated the author of the pro-U.S. essay more favorably than the author of the anti-U.S. essay in the control condition, in response to mortality salience this tendency was exaggerated in both directions (i.e., more positive and negative reactions to pro- and anti-U.S. authors, respectively).

Earlier we argued that even in the absence of genuinely different others to disparage and terminate, people will designate others as different to serve a terror-assuaging function. To examine this notion empirically, Harmon-Jones, Greenberg, Solomon, and Simon (1995) assigned previously unacquainted people to different groups on the basis of their preference for abstract art works by Paul Klee or Wasily Kandinsky (see Tajfel, Billig, Bundy, & Flament, 1971). Then, after a mortality salience or control induction, participants rated themselves and other members of their group and the other group. Despite the fact that the group had just been formed minutes ago, participants did not know anyone in their group directly, and membership in the group was based on a relatively unimportant preference for obscure abstract art, thinking about death resulted in exaggerated regard for one's own group and disparagement of those who preferred a different kind of art. Perhaps Jonathan Swift's portrayal in *Gulliver's Travels* of people going to war over the issue of which side an egg should be cracked is not so far-fetched after all!

One possible criticism of these findings is that they are based on attitudinal measures, that is, perhaps thinking about death changes attitudes toward others but does not actually change behavior. Additional research has consequently examined the effects of mortality salience on actual behavior. Ochsmann and Mathy (1994) had German university students complete a mortality salience or control induction and, having told them that the experiment was over, directed them to a reception area, presumably to be paid for participating in the study. In the center of a row of chairs was another student, a confederate of the experimenters. For half of the participants, the confederate appeared to be a German student; for the other half, the confederate appeared to be a Turkish student (currently a despised minority in Germany). The investigators were interested in how close to or far away from the student each participant would sit as a function of his appearance (German or Turkish). Results showed no difference in physical distance as a function of the confederate's appearance in the control condition; however, mortality salient participants sat closer to the fellow German and farther away from the Turkish "infidel." This is an important finding, because it established that mortality salience influences actual behavior above and beyond changes in attitudes.

In another study, McGregor and colleagues (1998) demonstrated that subtle reminders of death produce actual physical aggression toward those who threaten deeply cherished beliefs. Liberal or conservative college students read an essay they believed was written by another student in the study that condemned either liberals or conservatives. Then, after thinking about death or an aversive control topic in what they believed was a separate study, participants were given an opportunity to administer a quantity of their choosing of very hot salsa to the student who wrote the essay in the "first study," and who claimed to dislike spicy foods. Results indicated no differences in salsa allocation for similar and dissimilar others in the control condition; however, following mortality salience, participants administered twice the amount of salsa to different others than they did to similar others.

SO WHAT AND NOW WHAT?

Can a proper appreciation of the role of death denial in cultures in any way help to ameliorate violence, or does it merely lead to a cynical view of human life? We share Freud's rather somber but nevertheless cautiously optimistic position. We agree with him that it is very unlikely that human beings will cease violence, because aggression has been essential to procure basic resources and to defend ourselves against predators (inter- or intraspecies). What we can do, however, is try to minimize the wantonly destructive, and simultaneously engage other behaviors that are incompatible with warlike aggression. How can this be accomplished?

Worldviews That Value Tolerance

Recall that the first human propensity toward war was to be threatened by those who are different. Perhaps worldviews could be molded to counteract this proclivity. If people need cultural beliefs for psychological equanimity and are unlikely to transcend them, perhaps we can encourage the development of worldviews that emphasize commonalities and foster tolerance of differences. As Freud noted in his response to Einstein, human beings are not only aggressive but also loving creatures, especially toward those with whom they identify. Our research has repeatedly demonstrated that reminders of death engender more positive reactions to similar others. Consequently, a culture that emphasizes similarities between humans should be much less likely to facilitate death-denial at others' expense.

Facing Our Fear of Death: Making the Unconscious Conscious

Freud always insisted that the purpose of psychoanalysis was to make the unconscious conscious, in that psychological defenses are only effective when we are unaware of their existence. Accordingly, conversion hysteria, a physical symptom in the absence of organic pathology (e.g., hysterical paralysis or blindness) was quite common in Vienna in the late 1800s, but essentially disappeared when it became common knowledge that these symptoms were the result of psychological distress transformed into physical maladies. Perhaps then, if it became open and public knowledge that death denial is the psychological basis of our cultural identification and that hostility is the inevitable result, such behaviors would be less prevalent. We would thus like to see these ideas widely disseminated and openly discussed in educational (starting in grade school), governmental (local, national, and international), and religious settings.

Even more optimistically, we can also hope that with the help of spreading this news, it will soon come time for the human race to grow up, in the sense that culture, according to Roheim (1943) is essentially a "childish" construction: Culture

originates in delayed infancy and its function is security. It is a huge network of more or less successful attempts to protect mankind against the danger of object-loss, the colossal efforts made by a baby who is afraid of being left alone in the dark. (p. 100)

Roheim's point is based on the evolutionary assumption that all changes in species over time must utilize existing physical, behavioral, and/or psychological attributes—rather than anything being created in a novel fashion to solve a problem of adaptation. As human beings became increasingly aware of their own existence as a by-product of burgeoning intelligence, the problem of death became manifest for the first time in natural history. According to Roheim, human beings used (not consciously, of course) the prolonged dependence of the extremely immature human infant, basking in the apparently omnipresent and omnipotent presence and protection of his or her loving parents, as the symbolic prototype for the development of culture. Now it is time for the human race to enter "adulthood" by a mature acceptance of life on life's terms, outside the lens of culture, which will in turn require a greater acceptance of death, or what Rank (1932/1989) referred to as "the volitional affirmation of the obligatory" (p. 64), which in turn will foster greater acceptance of one another.

Human beings able to accept the reality of death could divest themselves of the "childish" illusion that they and their culture are uniquely special and afforded a precious death transcendence that must be protected at all costs. Following Erik Erikson (1950), we hold out the hope that "healthy children will not fear life if their elders have integrity enough not to fear death" (p. 269). Although these thoughts can easily be dismissed as airy idealism, they must be seriously considered. In the words of Ferdinand Schiller (1912/1970),

Whether of course there is any possibility of actually realizing any such ideal is quite another question, and no one could be more keenly conscious than myself of the bitter contrast between such dreams of metaphysics and the stern facts of our daily life. But once upon a time our fairest facts, our most uncontroverted truths, were but the visions of a dream, divined by a prescience that slowly hardened into science; and so perchance even dreams like these may come true, or rather be made to come true, if we try. It is, moreover, certain that if we dismiss such thoughts as idle dreams, dreams they will remain, and no end will ever come to the conflict and the friction that wear out our world; whereas, if we consent to look for possibilities of harmony, our willingness may be the first condition of success. (pp. 217, 226–227)

We would argue that surely nothing useful will happen unless we seriously entertain the prospect that we can succeed, as fantastic as it may seem at this time. When Leonardo da Vinci envisioned the helicopter in the 15th century he was deemed mad; but today many thousands of people are routinely transported by the physical realization of such madness. Similarly, while the thought of a world in which people peacefully coexist seems like a Walt Disney cartoon or a John Lennon song at present, who knows what might happen in the future if we are willing to seriously consider the prospect and actively strive to achieve it?

NOTE

The authors share equal responsibility for this work, which was generously supported by grants from the National Science Foundation and the Ernest Becker Foundation.

REFERENCES

Arndt, J., Greenberg, J., Pyszczynski, T., & Solomon, S. (1997). Subliminal presentation of death reminders leads to increased defense of the cultural worldview. *Psychological Science, 8*, 379–385.

Becker, E. (1971). *The birth and death of meaning.* New York: Free Press. (Original work published 1962)

Becker, E. (1973). *The denial of death.* New York: Free Press.

Becker, E. (1975). *Escape from evil.* New York: Free Press.

Einstein, A. (1960). Why war? In O. Nathan & H. Norden (Eds.), *Einstein on peace* (pp. 188–202). New York: Schocken Books.

Erikson, E. H. (1950). *Childhood and society.* New York: Norton.

Greenberg, J., Pyszczynski, T., & Solomon, S. (1986). The causes and consequences of a need for self-esteem: A terror management theory. In R. F. Baumeister (Ed.), *Public self and private self* (pp. 189–212). New York: Springer-Verlag.

Greenberg, J., Pyszczynski, T., Solomon S., Rosenblatt, A., Veeder, M., Kirkland, S., & Lyon, D. (1990). Evidence for terror management theory II: The effects of mortality salience on reactions to those who threaten or bolster the cultural worldview. *Journal of Personality and Social Psychology, 58*, 308–318.

Greenberg, J., Simon, L., Porteus, J., Pyszczynski, T., & Solomon, S. (1995). Evidence of a terror management function of cultural icons: The effects of mortality salience on reactions to the inappropriate use of culturally valued objects. *Personality and Social Psychology Bulletin, 21*, 1221–1228.

Greenberg, J., Simon, L., Pyszczynski, T., Solomon, S., & Chatel, D. (1992). Terror management and tolerance: Does mortality salience always intensify negative reactions to others who threaten one's worldview? *Journal of Personality and Social Psychology, 63*, 212–220.

Greenberg, J., Solomon, S., & Pyszczynski, T. (1997). Terror management theory of self-esteem and cultural worldviews: Empirical assessments and conceptual refinements. In M. Zanna (Ed.), *Advances in experimental social psychology* (Vol. 29, pp. 61–139). Orlando, FL: Academic Press.

Greenberg, J., Solomon, S., Pyszczynski, T., & Steinberg, L. (1988). A reaction to Greenwald, Pratkanis, Leippe, and Baumgardner (1986): Under what conditions does research obstruct theory progress? *Psychological Review, 95*, 566–571.

Harmon-Jones, E., Greenberg, J., Solomon, S., & Simon, L. (1995). The effects of mortality salience on intergroup bias between minimal groups. *European Journal of Social Psychology, 25,* 78–115.

Harmon-Jones, E., Simon, L., Greenberg, J., Pyszczynski, T., Solomon, S., & McGregor, H. (1997). Terror management theory and self-esteem: Evidence that increased self-esteem reduces mortality salience effects. *Journal of Personality and Social Psychology, 72,* 24–36.

Joyce, J. (1966). *Ulysses.* New York: Vintage Books. (Original work published 1914)

McGregor, H., Lieberman, J. D., Greenberg, J., Solomon, S., Arndt, J., Simon, L., & Pyszczynski, T. (1998). Terror management and aggression: Evidence that mortality salience promotes aggression toward worldview threatening individuals. *Journal of Personality and Social Psychology, 74,* 590–605.

Ochsmann, R., & Mathy, M. (1994). *Depreciating of and distancing from foreigners: Effects of mortality salience.* Unpublished manuscript, Universitat Mainz, Mainz, Germany.

Pyszczynski, T., Greenberg, J., & Solomon, S. (1999). A dual process model of defense against conscious and unconscious death-related thoughts: An extension of terror management theory. *Psychological Review, 106,* 835–845.

Pyszczynski, T., Wicklund, R., Floresku, S., Gauch, G., Koch, H., Solomon, S., & Greenberg, J. (1996). Whistling in the dark: Exaggerated consensus estimates in response to incidental reminders of mortality. *Psychological Science, 7,* 332–336.

Rank, O. (1989). *Art and artist: Creative urge and personality development.* New York: Norton. (Original work published 1932)

Rank, O. (1978). *Truth and reality.* New York: Norton. (Original work published 1936)

Roheim, G. (1943). *The origin and function of culture* (Nervous and Mental Disease Monograph no. 69.) New York: Nervous and Mental Disease Monographs.

Schiller, F. C. S. (1970). *Humanism: Philosophical essays* (2nd ed.). Westport, CT: Greenwood. (Original work published 1912)

Solomon, S., Greenberg, J., & Pyszczynski, T. (1991). A terror management theory of social behavior: The psychological functions of self-esteem and cultural worldviews. In M. Zanna (Ed.), *Advances in experimental social psychology* (Vol. 24, pp. 91–159). Orlando, FL: Academic Press.

Tajfel, H., Billig, M. G., Bundy, R. P., & Flament, C. (1971). Social categorization and intergroup behavior. *European Journal of Social Psychology, 1,* 149–178.

Afterword

Jeanne Achterberg

A few years ago, Stan Krippner and Teresa McIntyre asked if I would be willing to write an afterword to an edited collection of manuscripts on war. The subject took me by surprise. War? Why a scholarly book on war? Why now? So few care. At that time, aside from seeing images in magazines and on television of the bloated and miserable starving babies and sensationalized carnage in countries that few of us could locate on a map, war and its aftermath were a sad curiosity. War was an event on foreign shores; for Americans, probably none of our business. Terrorism was shocking, but, I daresay, none of us gave it much thought. The irony, of course, is that this book could not be more timely or relevant today than any other time in modern history. We are at war. Our own shores are not protected.

As I read the manuscripts, I was awed and humbled by the scholarship, the sensitivity, and the enormous amount of information conveyed in these pages. It is a treasure, confirming my own observations and intuitions and adding immensely to my education. Had it been available in the summer of 1999 when I went to Kosovo, it would have given me information that would have enlightened and aided my feeble understanding of the impact of mass murder on cultures, countries, and the future of generations to come. What I especially appreciated was the sensitivity expressed for the different cultures, their mores and their cosmology. We simply cannot continue wearing the cloak of arrogance that our tools, developed out of our own peculiar worldview, will always offer solace or even yield data of value in such dire circumstances.

Stan knew that after I had returned from the refugee camps on the Kosovo border, my heart had been ripped open and my life would never again be the same. He has asked that I write a little of that experience. I went with Dr. James Gordon (an old friend and chairman of the President's Commission on Alternative and Complementary Medicine), and his group from the Mind/Body Center in Washington, D.C., right after the ethnic Albanian/Serbian war began. Jim is absolutely fearless and has been to the Balkans many times. He has developed what appears to be a simple formula for what I suppose psychologists and others call "stress management"—imagery, meditation, group work, movement, massage, biofeedback.

However, what I absolutely know is that these are only the delicate vessels that hold the healing elixir of compassion. He and his group do that so very well. The most memorable experience, and the one that changed my own life, was the last day we spent in Stankovitz—the largest camp on the border, and during the day of the heaviest migration. Thousands had made a forced march across a mine-infested border. Others arrived on busses. Thousands more watched for friends, relatives, community—anyone they knew who might be alive. I ran into the middle of the migration, and felt for the first time the tangible, unquestionable bonds of humanity. I have no words for this feeling—words are too small. What I knew then, and now, is that we must never do this to one another again. No options. I have no political statements, no profound thoughts, no brilliant comments on the nature of evil. Just that we, as a species, cannot survive ourselves if we continue. Life is not about borders, egos, power, or games that will never be won, but rather, our relationship with all living and nonliving things. What else became so very clear is that suffering connects our hearts— as they are broken, wounded, even frozen, we find ways to learn of our humanity.

And yes, I remembered something more about war as I read this book. Most of my generation are victims of war, knowingly or not. Our fathers saw too many dead boys; suffered from fears and terrors that went unspoken and not addressed. My father was (by choice) on the front lines of both World War II and the Korean War, and I grew up as a noncommissioned soldier's daughter—in a caste system of the first order. I lived on military bases; married a young man in the army. The aftermath of the Vietnam war, of course, is still with us. But nothing, not a lifetime of viewing weapons, uniforms, parades, and maneuvers, prepares one for the visible shock of the modern war machine or the insidious and gruesome tactics of terrorism. The rules—and times—have changed.

My deepest gratitude to all of you who have contributed to this book. It is to be read and cherished by all of us who are concerned about and alarmed by life, as we know it.

"How Can This Be?"

John Cannon and W. Harrison Childers

Mothers moaning soft and low
Sad to see their children go
Off to fight the latest foe—
How can this be?

A father bows his head and cries
As he begins to realize
Sons will fight and sons will die—
How can this be?

We can talk about hatred
We can talk about war
We can talk about killing
While we all keep score.
We can count all the bodies,
And count them once more—
How can this be?

Madly plunging into war
Marching to the lies once more
Who knows what they're dying for?
How can this be?

It's the same old tragedy
What a hollow legacy
No one learns from history—
How can this be?

We can talk about hatred
We can talk about war
We can talk about killing
While we all keep score,
We count all the bodies
And count them once more—
How can this be?

Children have to pay the price
For debts they do not owe
Time and time again they pay
The children can't say no.

Grieve for every wounded child
Shrapnel, mines, and bombs gone wild
Innocence and love defiled—
How can this be?

Now this madness all must cease
The entire world cries out for peace
Sing along and share the dream,
When will this be?
It's up to you and me.

Index

About the Editors and Contributors

STANLEY KRIPPNER, Ph.D., Alan W. Watts Professor of Psychology at Saybrook Graduate School, San Francisco, is the former director of the Kent State University Child Study Center, Kent, OH, and the Maimonides Medical Center Dream Research Laboratory, Brooklyn, NY. He is coauthor of *Extraordinary Dreams* and coeditor of *Varieties of Anomalous Experience: Examining the Scientific Evidence.* Krippner is on the advisory board for the International School for Psychotherapy, Counseling, and Group Leadership (St. Petersburg). He holds faculty appointments at the Universidade Holistica Internacional (Brasilia), the Instituto de Gestalt do Brasil (São Paulo), and the Instituto de Medicina y Tecnología Avanzada de la Conducta (Ciudad Juárez). He has given invited addresses for the Chinese Academy of Sciences, the Russian Academy of Pedagogical Sciences, and the Artigas Foreign Service Institute, Montevideo, Uruguay. In 2002 he received the American Psychological Association's annual award for Distinguished Contributions to the International Advancement of Psychology.

TERESA M. McINTYRE, Ph.D., is Professor of Health Psychology at the University of Minho, Braga, Portugal, where she coordinates the graduate program in health psychology and directs the University of Minho Counseling Center. She has been elected president of the European Health Psychology Society and is book review editor for the European journal *Psychology and Health.* Among her edited books are *Health Psychology, Clinical Hypnosis: A Scientific Approach,* and *Pain and Suffering,* and she has published internationally in these fields. With the support of the Portuguese Science Foundation, she has embarked on research projects in patient satisfaction, gender and cardiac psychology, and post-traumatic stress disorders among Portuguese War Veterans. Dr. McIntyre has had a long-standing collaboration with the University of Lubango, Angola, where she has been a member of a team conducting research on trauma and health among women and children affected by war.

AUTHORS' AFFILIATIONS

Mary Bentley Abu-Saba, American University of Beirut, New York

Jeanne Achterberg, Saybrook Graduate School, San Francisco, California

Sandrine Arons, University of Pittsburgh, Pittsburgh, Pennsylvania

Marjorie Mandelstam Balzer, Georgetown University, Washington, D.C.

Árpád Baráth, Department of Sociology and Social Policy, University of Pécs, Rókus, Hungary

Deirdre Barrett, Harvard Medical School and the Cambridge Hospital, Cambridge, Massachusetts

Betty Bastien, University of Calgary, Alberta, Canada

Jaffar Behbehani, Kuwait Medical Faculty, Kuwait City, Kuwait

Paul Bolton, Center for International Emergency, Disaster, and Refugee Studies, Bloomberg School of Hygiene and Public Health, Johns Hopkins University, Baltimore, Maryland

Sally Broughton, International Relief Services, Washington, D.C.

John Cannon, Saybrook Graduate School, San Francisco, California

George M. Carter, Foundation for Integrative AIDS Research, New York, New York

W. Harrison Childers, Saybrook Graduate School, San Francisco, California

Leila F. Dane, Institute for Victims of Trauma, McLean, Virginia

Lucila Edelman, Argentine Team for Psychosocial Assistance and Research, Buenos Aires, Argentina

Adam Fish, The Alchemind Society, Davis, California

Ronald J. Fisher, School of International Service, American University, Washington, D.C.

Clay Foreman, Saybrook Graduate School, San Francisco, California

Benina B. Gould, Center for Slavic, East European, and Eurasian Studies, University of California, Berkeley, California

Glenn Graves, Saybrook Graduate School, San Francisco, California

Jeff Greenberg, University of Arizona, Tucson, Arizona

Stevan E. Hobfoll, Kent State University, Kent, Ohio

Daniel Kersner, Argentine Team for Psychosocial Assistance and Research, Buenos Aires, Argentina

Diana Kordon, Argentine Team for Psychosocial Assistance and Research, Buenos Aires, Argentina

Michael Korzinski, Amnesty International Medical Foundation, London, England

Jürgen W. Kremer, Saybrook Graduate School, San Francisco, California

Rauna Kuokkanen, University of British Columbia, Vancouver, British Columbia, Canada

Darío Lagos, Argentine Team for Psychosocial Assistance and Research, Buenos Aires, Argentina

Roben A. Marvit, private practice, Honolulu, Hawaii

Carlinda Monteiro, Christian Children's Fund, Angola

Vesna Ognjenovic, Croatian Social Services, Kulasi, Croatia

Steve S. Olweean, Common Bond Institute, Climax, Michigan

James D. Pappas, Saybrook Graduate School, San Francisco, California

Daryl S. Paulson, Science Laboratory, Boseman, Montana

Rona Popal, The Afghan Coalition, San Francisco, California

Tom Pyszczynski, University of Colorado, Colorado Springs, Colorado

Jovan Savic, Croatian Social Services, Kulasi, Croatia

Bojana Skorc, Croatian Social Services, Kulasi, Croatia

Sheldon Solomon, Brooklyn College, Brooklyn, New York

Margarida Ventura, Graduate Institute of Educational Science, Lubango, Angola

Patricia Vickers, University of Victoria, British Columbia, Canada

Michael Wessells, Department of Psychology, Randolph Macon College, Ashland, Virginia